# GEORGE ELIOT'S MIDLANDS: PASSION IN EXILE

# GEORGE ELIOT'S MIDLANDS: PASSION IN EXILE

by
Graham Handley

ALLISON & BUSBY

First published in Great Britain in 1991 by
Allison & Busby
an imprint of Virgin Publishing Ltd
338 Ladbroke Grove
London W10 5AH

Printed and bound in Great Britain by
Mackays of Chatham PLC, Chatham, Kent

ISBN 0 85031 997 8

The moral right of the author has been asserted

FOR BILL AND KATHLEEN ADAMS
in warm friendship and respect
and in recognition of their devoted work on
George Eliot

# Contents

# Illustrations

—

# Acknowledgments

I am grateful to Oxford University Press for allowing me to quote from those volumes of the Clarendon edition of the novels of George Eliot which have been published to date; to Yale University Press, The Beinecke Rare Book and Manuscript Library, Yale University, the Morrish L. Parrish Collection, Princeton University, The British Library and the National Library of Scotland, all of whom have granted me permission to quote from *The George Eliot Letters*, 9 vols (1954–78), ed. Gordon S. Haight. I am grateful to be allowed to reprint a map from F. B. Pinion's *A George Eliot Companion*, Macmillan, 1981, by courtesy of the author and publishers; to the Mistress and Fellows, Girton College, Cambridge, for permission to reproduce a photograph of Samuel Lawrence's portrait of George Eliot; to Andrew Mealey and Coventry City Libraries; to the Nuneaton Museum and Art Gallery and Gina Quant for permission to reproduce illustrations; and to John Burton in particular for photographing them and providing others himself. I should like to thank Mick Keates for designing the jacket.

I am grateful to Anne Dangerfield and Janet Hill for reading through this book and letting me have their comments; to Bill and Kathleen Adams of the George Eliot Fellowship for checking a number of facts for me; to Chelsey Fox for suggesting that I write it, and to Clive Allison for inviting me to do so. I thank Peter Day for his advice and help throughout, and Elfreda Powell for her dedicated work. I am obviously indebted to a number of written sources for some of the material in this book. But one personal debt stands out. Professor Barbara Hardy read my manuscript draft and made many invaluable comments and suggestions. I thank her most warmly for this, and hope that I have profited from her advice; any remaining shortcomings are my own.

Those long days measured by my little feet
Had chronicles which yield me many a text;
Where irony still finds an image meet
Of full-grown judgments in this world perplext.

One day my brother left me in high charge,
To mind the rod, while he went seeking bait,
And bade me, when I saw a nearing barge,
Snatch out the line, lest he should come too late.

Proud of the task, I watched with all my might
For one whole minute, till my eyes grew wide,
Till sky and earth took on a strange new light
And seemed a dream-world, floating on some tide −

A fair pavilioned boat for me alone
Bearing me onward through the vast unknown.

George Eliot − "Brother and Sister", sonnet vii

A human life, I think, should be well rooted in some spot of a native land, where it may get the love of tender kinship for the face of earth, for the labours men go forth to, for the sounds and accents that haunt it, for whatever will give that early home a familiar unmistakable difference amidst the future widening of knowledge: a spot where the definiteness of early memories may be inwrought with affection, and kindly acquaintance with all neighbours, even to the dogs and donkeys, may spread not by sentimental effort and reflection, but as a sweet habit of the blood. At five years old, mortals are not prepared to be citizens of the world, to be stimulated by abstract nouns, to soar above preference into impartiality; and that prejudice in favour of milk with which we blindly begin, is a type of the way body and soul must get nourished at least for a time. The best introduction to astronomy is to think of the nightly heavens as a little lot of stars belonging to one's own homestead.

George Eliot − *Daniel Deronda*, ch iii

# Introduction

On 22nd November 1819 Mary Anne Evans – usually Mary Ann, later Marian – was born at South Farm, Arbury, near Nuneaton in Warwickshire. Nearly thirty years afterwards, in May 1849, her father Robert Evans, farmer, surveyor, land agent to the Newdigate family at Arbury Hall, died. Mary Ann had nursed him faithfully for his last three and a half years, at Bird Grove, Foleshill, near Coventry, which had been their home since 1841. To her close friends, Charles and Cara Bray at nearby Rosehill, she wrote: "What shall I be without my Father? It will seem as if a part of my moral nature were gone."[1]* Her mother had died in 1836, and Mary Ann had been her father's housekeeper since her sister Chrissey's marriage in 1837. All her life had been spent in the Nuneaton–Coventry area, the first twenty-one years of it at Griff House on the Arbury estate.

Shortly after her father's death Mary Ann set off for the continent with the Brays, who spent some weeks with her before returning to Coventry where Charles Bray owned the *Coventry Herald*. Mary Ann remained in Geneva for six months, then returned to Foleshill, before, in November 1850, paying her first visit to John Chapman in London. Chapman, at 142 The Strand, had become the owner of the *Westminster Review*, a prestigious journal which had previously been edited by John Stuart Mill. Mary Ann had already established something of a learned reputation. She had translated Strauss's *Life of Jesus* from the German (1846) in the wake of her own rejection of Christianity. She had also written reviews for Charles Bray's *Coventry Herald*.

Mary Ann was to return to Coventry from time to time, but now she graduated to the demanding and stimulating world of London journalism, editing, writing, commissioning. She effectively ran the *Westminster Review* for Chapman. She made friends – and then fell in love – with the philosopher Herbert Spencer, and through him she came to know George Henry Lewes. She came to be in touch with many of the best minds of the day. It is virtually certain too that she fell in love with the Byronic Chapman, whose wife and mistress combined to oust her from 142 The Strand, where she had lodged with his family. But her friendship with Lewes deepened – "to know her was to love her",[2] he wrote much later in his Journal – and in July 1854 they left

*References begin on p. 239.

for the continent together. They could not marry, since Lewes had tacitly condoned his wife's adultery with Thornton Hunt, and was therefore debarred from getting a divorce. Significantly, it was to her friends in the Midlands that Mary Ann conveyed the news of her liaison with Lewes:

Dear Friends – all three
  I have only time to say good bye and God bless you. Poste Restante, Weimar for the next six weeks, and afterwards Berlin.
  Ever your loving and grateful

Marian[3]

The story of her life with Lewes is part of literary history and needs little retelling here: unfortunately it has attracted sensational, meretricious and fictional treatment. They lived together for the next twenty-four years. During that time she took on another identity, the masculine pseudonym by which she became known first to the literary and then to the wider world. After Lewes's death in 1878 George Eliot wrote nothing. She devoted herself to preparing Lewes's drafts of *Problems of Life and Mind* for publication, and founded the George Henry Lewes studentship at Cambridge.

However, eighteen months after his death, in May 1880, she married their friend John Walter Cross, who was twenty years her junior. Only a few months later, on 22nd December, she died, and was buried next to Lewes in Highgate cemetery.

This brief outline, of course, ignores her development as an artist who, in six of her eight major works, returned in imagination to the area of her childhood and young womanhood.

At the end of 1855 Marian, as she now called herself, went to stay with her sister Chrissey at Attleborough near Nuneaton. It was to be her last visit to her roots. For the whole of the time that she was writing fiction she lived in or near London: the only exceptions – important exceptions – were her trips to Europe. These were undertaken to help her recover from the strains of writing a novel or, in the case of *Romola* (1862–3), to gather material for one. In twenty-five years she never revisited the Midlands, but its conditioning and potent impressions were stamped on her character, on the intellect and emotions which produced her greatest fiction. Through that fiction, she *did* return, time and time again, with a fullness of recreative consciousness. When Lewes urged her to persevere with writing fiction, her first stories, *Scenes of Clerical Life* (1857), drew on the places and events which were her local inheritance. Twelve years later, in 1869, when she was a famous novelist, admired, respected, and even venerated, despite the supposedly irregular nature of her life, she wrote a sequence of eleven sonnets called "Brother and Sister". These are a loving, nostalgic, but ironically qualified recall of her childhood with her brother Isaac, who had renounced her because of her relationship with Lewes. (The poetry is generally undistinguished, though there

2

is a certain relaxed facility in her use of the sonnet form.) The last poem is unequivocal in its positive emphasis and its sympathetic self-recognition, both of which are concentrated in the closing couplet:

> But were another childhood-world my share,
> I would be born a little sister there.[4]

George Eliot's last work, published ten years after the sonnets were written, is the uncharacteristic *Impressions of Theophrastus Such*. It contains an important essay, "Looking Backward", which has much of the freshness and associations of genuine autobiographical recall, and is a thinly disguised acknowledgement of her Warwickshire roots.

The first thirty years of Marian Evans's life provided George Eliot with a rich yield of personal experience and sympathetic affiliation on which she was to draw imaginatively for the profound insights and truths of her novels. A line from one of her poems, "A Minor Prophet": "Our finest hope is finest memory"[5] and another from the sixth of the "Brother and Sister" sequence: "My present Past, my root of piety"[6] are sufficient indications of the enduring pull of her early ties. She wrote out of her past in a vibrantly productive present. Lewes helped to foster and release the springs of creativity within her. Her own account of how she came to write fiction, certainly informed with an idealized hindsight, shows how deeply planted were the roots of piety:

But one morning as I was lying in bed, thinking what should be the subject of my first story, my thoughts merged themselves into a dreamy doze, and I imagined myself writing a story of which the title was – "The Sad Fortunes of the Reverend Amos Barton". I was soon wide awake again, and told G. He said "O what a capital title!" and from that time I had settled in my mind that this should be my first story.[7]

The "dreamy doze" had taken her back to the village of her childhood and young womanhood: Chilvers Coton. There in the church she had heard the sermons of the curate John Gwyther, and in the first chapter of this story she introduced a remembered fact, for Amos's call for silence during the wedding psalm originated from Gwyther's own action on 12th February 1832. Robert Evans had noted in his Journal "Mr Gwyther preached and stopd the singers."[8] That Amos is based on Gwyther there is no doubt, and Gwyther himself wrote to the editor of *Blackwood's Magazine* in which the *Scenes of Clerical Life* first appeared. He was amazed when he read the first instalment of "Amos Barton". He showed it to his daughter, who felt that he himself might have written it because of the episode from his own life. As he read on, Gwyther found that the next two clerical "scenes" were "Historical reminiscences of the Former Vicar – where I was Curate and of a Clergyman and the persecutions to which he was subject, all in the immediate Neighbourhood where I resided, during the events recorded in the Story of Amos Barton."[9] Doubtless Gwyther resented his connection with Amos, who is described by Mr Pilgrim as "a confounded, methodistical, meddlesome chap, who must be putting his finger in every pie".[10] As Gordon Haight observes, "The whole parish was rendered with a clarity and vigour that distinguish the tale from most fiction of the time."[11]

In *Scenes of Clerical Life* George Eliot was translating local history, childhood experiences, associations and incidents of her past into fiction. In *Adam Bede* (1859) she took what she and Lewes called "My Aunt's Story" and gave it a local habitation and a name. At the same time she drew on the intimate memories of her father for her hero: one likes to think that in doing so she included the obstinacy as well as the pride in workmanship which characterized them both. She and Lewes were both quick to point out that there were no "portraits" in the novel. The time-span of *Adam Bede* is 1799–1807, well before her own birth, so that the concern with identifications, the natural reader-tendency to hunt for originals, concentrated on more than family connections. But what was certain was identification of localities: Hayslope, Broxton and the villages of Loamshire are Ellastone, Roston and villages in Staffordshire. Snowfield and Stoniton in Stonyshire are Wirksworth and Derby in Derbyshire. The Midland scene has been extended, the historical sense, so evident throughout her writing, is unobtrusive but insistent. Henry Auster points out the sophistication of this in another way: "In *Adam Bede* . . . George Eliot uses landscape to define, reinforce, and foreshadow the events of the plot and the moral situation."[12]

There is too the identification and dramatization of dialect: long after she wrote *Adam Bede*, she was to say that "the rendering of dialect, both in words and spelling, was constantly checked by the artistic duty of being generally intelligible. But for that check, I should have given a stronger colour to the dialogue . . . which is modelled on the talk of N. Staffordshire and the neighbouring part of Derbyshire."[13] The dialect, as in *Scenes of Clerical Life*, is given a proverbial authenticity heightened by art. In the early works, dialect is the distinguishing mark in her sure sense of place.

In *The Mill on the Floss* (1860), the geographical origin of St Ogg's is Gainsborough, but some identifications like the Red Deeps are obviously within the Nuneaton landscape of Marian Evans's childhood. The intensely remembered and recreated interiors – like the attic – are blended with known exteriors and purposefully visited new ones, like Ashcroft's Mill at Gainsborough. The autobiographical tone of the novel gives it an intimacy which centres on Maggie and the places most memorably associated with her. George Eliot drew on her relationship with her brother Isaac (one of her proposed titles for the novel was *Sister Maggie*) and the characters of her maternal aunts, the Pearsons, for the fictional Dodson sisters. She individualized with a careful particularity, through emotion and humour, creating a social, moral and psychological world. The associations with the familiar area and the inclusions of the unfamiliar one are cunningly worked into the action. The wish-fulfilment of the past is as strong as the river which sweeps Tom and Maggie to their deaths, though "In their death they were not divided", unlike Marian Evans and her brother Isaac at that time. Three years before the publication of *The Mill on the Floss*, she had written to tell Isaac that she had a husband to take care of her, and had signed herself "Marian Lewes". He had replied from his distant perspective, through the family solicitor. She had reached back into her childhood at Griff (Isaac still lived there), and she had been rejected.

After *The Mill on the Floss* she moved away from the felt past in her writings. *Silas Marner* (1861), that "millet-seed"[14] of thought sown across the arable (sometimes arid) researches for *Romola*, is different in emphasis and effect. As she put it:

The district imagined as the scene of "Silas Marner" is in N. Warwickshire. But here, and in all my other presentations of English life, except "Adam Bede", it has been my intention to give the general physiognomy rather than a close portraiture of the provincial speech as I have heard it in the Midland or Mercian region.[15]

The novel is set back in time, in the late 1780s and then the first decades of the nineteenth century. She has moved from her identifiable past to a locality with which she identifies sympathetically. At one stage she considered writing the story in verse and the epigraph or motto to *Silas Marner* is from Wordsworth's "Michael":

> A child, more than all other gifts,
> That earth can offer to declining man,
> Brings hope with it, and forward-looking thoughts.[16]

When we read this there is perhaps an association with the childless Marian Lewes: the story itself teems with realized life, blending realism and fable. The wordscape and landscape are integral and complementary, the memory of anonymous bowed-down weavers the starting point for a narrative of homely, humorous and tragic faith and superstition, as well as moral and material dishonesty. Dolly Winthrop is a slower and softer character than Mrs Poyser, while the morality of the narrative is even more tightly structured than in her previous works. Place is central and unchanging. George Eliot spoke of the pressing necessity she felt to write *Silas Marner*: the past had pushed aside the present even though *Romola*, which she was researching, was conceived in a contrived past.

George Eliot returned next to a known time and location. *Felix Holt* (1866) reflects her interest in political reform as well as in the complexity of legal machinery and plot contrivance. The Midland settings are those of her childhood. The region is North Loamshire, and within it is Treby Magna, identified by John Prest as Nuneaton,[17] the village of Little Treby and the towns of Duffield and Loamford, where Felix is imprisoned after the death of the policeman. Perhaps there is no finer description of the area than the historical, past-loving introduction to the narrative. George Eliot began *Felix Holt* on 29th March 1865 at The Priory, Regent's Park where she was living, and finished it there on 31st May 1866. Once more she was returning to the place she had known so well. Perhaps the political ferment of her present, just before the second Reform Bill of 1867, helped to recall the associations of the first Bill in 1832 and the riots in Nuneaton which preceded it.

Rarely does a novel have an Introduction, but here, like the Proem in *Romola* and the Prelude in *Middlemarch*, she establishes an historical base for the fictional events. In *Felix Holt* the setting is given a maturely considered stress. It is imbued with loving nostalgia, but has the cutting edge of moral and political appraisal: this extract describes a bird's eye view of the area, as if seen from a stage-coach.

Posterity may be shot, like a bullet through a tube, by atmospheric pressure from Winchester to Newcastle: that is a fine result to have among our hopes; but the slow old-fashioned way of getting from one end of our country to the other is the better thing to have in the memory. The tube-journey can never lend much to picture and narrative; it is as barren as an exclamatory O! Whereas the happy outside passenger seated on the box from the dawn to the gloaming gathered enough stories of English life, enough of English labours in town and country, enough aspects of earth and sky, to make episodes for a modern Odyssey. Suppose only that his journey took him through that central plain, watered at one extremity by the Avon, at the other by the Trent. As the morning silvered the meadows with their long lines of bushy willows marking the watercourses, or burnished the golden corn-ricks clustered near the long roofs of some midland homestead, he saw the full-uddered cows driven from their pasture to the early milking. Perhaps it was the shepherd, head-servant of the farm, who drove them, his sheep-dog following with a heedless unofficial air as of a beadle in undress. The shepherd with a slow and slouching walk, timed by the walk of grazing beasts, moved aside, as if unwillingly, throwing out a monosyllabic hint to his cattle; his glance, accustomed to rest on things very near the earth, seemed to lift itself with difficulty to the coachman. Mail or stage coach for him belonged to that mysterious distant system of things called "Gover'ment," which, whatever it might be, was no business of his, any more than the most out-lying nebula or the coal-sacks of the southern hemisphere: his solar system was the parish; the master's temper and the casualties of lambing-time were his region of storms. He cut his bread and bacon with his pocket-knife, and felt no bitterness except in the matter of pauper labourers and the bad-luck that sent contrarious seasons and the sheep-rot. He and his cows were soon left behind, and the homestead too, with its pond overhung by elder-trees, its untidy kitchen-garden and cone-shaped yew-tree arbour. But everywhere the bushy hedgerows wasted the land with their straggling beauty, shrouded the grassy borders of the pastures with catkined hazels, and tossed their long blackberry branches on the corn-fields. Perhaps they were white with May, or starred with pale pink dogroses; perhaps the urchins were already nutting amongst them, or gathering the plenteous crabs. It was worth the journey only to see those hedgerows, the liberal homes of unmarketable beauty – of the purple-blossomed ruby-berried nightshade, of the wild convolvulus climbing and spreading in tendrilled strength till it made a great curtain of pale-green hearts and white trumpets, of the many-tubed honeysuckle which, in its most delicate fragrance, hid a charm more subtle and penetrating than beauty. Even if it were winter the hedgerows showed their coral, the scarlet haws, the deep-crimson hips, with lingering brown leaves to make a resting-place for the jewels of the hoar-frost. Such hedgerows were often as tall as the labourers' cottages dotted along the lanes, or clustered into a small hamlet, their little dingy windows telling, like thick-filmed eyes, of nothing but the darkness within. The passenger on the coach-box, bowled along above such a hamlet, saw chiefly the roofs of it: probably it turned its back on the road, and seemed to lie away from everything but its own patch of earth and sky, away from the parish church by long fields and green lanes, away from all intercourse except that of tramps. If its face could be seen, it was most likely dirty; but the dirt was Protestant dirt, and the big, bold, gin-breathing tramps were Protestant tramps. There was no sign of superstition near, no crucifix or image to indicate a misguided reverence: the inhabitants were probably so free from superstition that they were in much less awe of the parson than of the overseer. Yet they were saved from the excesses of Protestantism by not knowing how to read, and by the absence of handlooms and mines to be the pioneers of Dissent: they were kept safely in the *via media* of indifference, and could have registered themselves in the census by a big black mark as members of the Church of England.[18]

This passage typifies George Eliot's art in many ways, and it also encapsulates her attitudes towards the past. It is nostalgic and critical, informed with hindsight and insight, inlaid with learning (sometimes ostentatious) and wisdom. It is descriptive and ironic, with touches of unsparing realism. It is a series of moods and movements, of political, social and moral comment. She inserted into the manuscript the sentence "Suppose only that his journey took him through that central plain, watered at one extremity by the Avon, at the other by the Trent", a clear indication of her own regional sympathy. The sights are initially recorded with a loving association, and a careful particularity brings the shepherd and his way of life into realistic close-up. This in turn is succeeded by the poetic descriptions of seasons, the hedgerows, and the poetry balanced by the details of dirt and tramps, as ignorance is seen with ironic compassion. We are made to feel the individuality of each village which "seemed to lie away from everything but its own patch of earth and sky". Love and tolerance are offset by realism. We sense identification and recognition without condescension: the moral and physical boundaries of the novel which is to follow are set. This is the epigraph to each volume of the first three-volume edition of *Felix Holt*.

Upon the midlands now the industrious muse doth fall,
The shires which we the heart of England well may call

. . . .

My native country thou, which so brave spirits hast bred,
If there be virtues yet remaining in thy earth,
Or any good of thine thou breds't into my birth,
Accept it as thine own, whilst now I sing of thee,
Of all thy later brood the unworthiest though I be.[19]

These lines of Michael Drayton's show clearly where her heart was. The background is foreground for the particularities and integration of character and relationships. Time and place were essential to her fullness of conception.

It is interesting to note that after *Felix Holt* – just as after *Silas Marner* – George Eliot took up again work which caused her extreme labour and frustration. She resumed her poem, *The Spanish Gypsy*, set in 1487 in Andalusia, whose subject is the conflict of social and personal values.

The "Brother and Sister" sequence was written a year after the publication of *The Spanish Gypsy* (1868) before she began to write the two narratives "Miss Brooke" and the Lydgates-Vincys-Bulstrodes story which were to become *Middlemarch* (1871–2). *Middlemarch* is based on Coventry, the time is 1829–32, and the sub-title "A Study of Provincial Life". The local habitation is clear, and the novel marks another return and an even more impressive use of detailed research into the treatment of medical practice and reform, which is set against the political reform already presented in *Felix Holt*. Although a contemporary reviewer praised George Eliot's "topographical power"[20] in *Middlemarch*, the actual location is reticently given, identifiable place being well subordinated to the consciousness of character relationships. There is an obvious movement on from the early works, and even from *Felix Holt*, for although the central urban identification is unquestionable, Lowick and Freshitt, for example, could be almost anywhere in the vicinity of Coventry and are perhaps a conflation of local villages. George Eliot was surprised to learn that "there was really a Lowick, in a Midland county too".[21]

*Middlemarch* is an analytical study of the provincial society George Eliot knew so well and which she recreated in its moral, religious and social entities. Particularly impressive is her awareness of the sense of change, the impact of outsiders like Lydgate, Bulstrode and Ladislaw, the mesh of social groupings, their structures, powers, morality, and aspirations. She was thinking back to the Coventry of her past and peopling it with her fictional characters. But she goes beyond such revision.

The characters are both individuals and symbols of what they represent within the provincial confines. Mr Brooke is landowning and leisured, indecisive and flirting with reform: when he tries reform he is humiliated by the thoroughly deserved mockery of his sherry-riddled speech. He is ineffectual and insensitive in social intercourse with his equals and with his tenant Dagley.

Mr Brooke is *not* Marian Evans's friend Charles Bray, but the derivations from that friend show the working of her imagination. Bray bought the *Coventry Herald* on 15th June 1846, and Marian Evans's fairly regular contributions include her important review of Froude's *The Nemesis of Faith*.[22] Mr Brooke bought *The Pioneer*, which was converted by Ladislaw into a reform newspaper. Bray skipped from one idea to another, from schools for poor children to working men's clubs, his only constant loyalty being to the pseudo-science of phrenology: Mr Brooke is always going into things – "it was my way to go about everywhere and take in everything"[23] – and never completing anything. Marian Evans had been close to Bray, perhaps standing, like Dorothea Brooke, in a niece-like relation to him. George Eliot, fond of Bray but removed in time, place and feeling, could pick out certain traits and transmute them into a fictional character.

In *Middlemarch* character symbolizes moral, social and spiritual place, within a habitat of physical place. Take the three clergymen, Casaubon, Cadwallader and Farebrother: their particular clerical scenes define their place, though that of the "fishing incumbent" Cadwallader is lightly brush-stroked in. Casaubon is the petrified scholar who holds a spiritual sinecure, Farebrother is the attractively fallible, scientific, loving, whist-playing humanist. Banking, light industry, estate management, the new fever hospital, medical practice and trade create the institutional life of a provincial town and its environs. Historical time is brought before us with invigorative, investigative particularity. We do *not* think of Coventry when we read *Middlemarch*, but George Eliot *did* think of Coventry when she wrote it. It is not simply because Casaubon, for example, derives in part from Dr Brabant and Marian Evans's experiences with that benevolent "archangel" in November 1843.[24] It is because she imprints her strong imagination on what she has experienced and on people who lend themselves to fictional adaptation and expansion. She works at, and certainly over, two levels – her own past as part of history, and her own present as exploration of that past with informed hindsight. In the early novels the materials were at hand: in *Middlemarch* the area is reworked with the intensely felt creations of imaginative life. If anything, their psychological reality and truth is greater, more convincing than those more factually derived. When she was asked on whom she had modelled Casaubon, George Eliot replied that he was within herself. What George Eliot does with her past in *Middlemarch* is to create the spirit of place through the lives of her fictitious characters: the physical identification of place is subordinate to the moral and spiritual concerns of character.

In her essay "Looking Backward" (already mentioned), an essay which has autobiographical elements, there is a mask, a masculinely clerical one at that, the narrator asserting "I am a bachelor". "George Eliot" began her writing with clerical scenes when Lewes sent "The Sad Fortunes of the Revd Amos Barton" to John Blackwood as from his "clerical friend", and ended with a clerical identity. In another essay in *Theophrastus* George Eliot wrote: "In all autobiography there is, nay, ought to be, an incompleteness which may have the effect of falsity. We are each of us bound to reticence by the piety we owe to those who have been nearest to us and have had a mingled influence over our lives."[25] Note the reticence and the use of the word "piety" to define the mask which the narrator adopts in "Looking Backward" where "he" says that he is the son of a country parson. He speaks of "that paternal time, the time of my father's youth" and recalls "his memories, which made a wondrous perspective to my little daily world of discovery".[26] The Midland identifications of the essay are specific in spirit if not in name, and there are echoes of the passage already quoted from *Felix Holt*. But the personal tone is more directly emphatic:

I cherish my childish loves – the memory of that warm little nest where my affections were fledged. Since then I have learned to care for foreign countries, for literatures foreign and ancient, for the life of Continental towns dozing round old cathedrals, for the life of London, half-sleepless with eager thought and strife, with indigestion or with hunger ... some of those who sallied forth went for the sake of a loved companionship, when they would willingly have kept sight of the familiar plains, and of the hills to which they had first lifted up their eyes.[27]

It is difficult not to see this autobiographically, or to read it as a comment on her own exile. She and Lewes lived at Holly Lodge, Blandford Square, The Priory, The Heights at Witley; they had country retreats as well as Continental tours, but they did not go to the Midlands. Perhaps they couldn't: certainly Cara Bray made it clear initially that she could not receive Lewes at Rosehill. When she did meet Marian and Lewes it was in London. The incidence of regret in the passage above is unmistakably personal. Cut off from the associations she loved, she spent the greatest part of her creative life exploring those areas where she could not go.

She did not always see the Midlands through this rosy glow of hindsight: after she had been to visit her sister Chrissey and her children she wrote that it would be "moral asphyxia" to her to live "in that hideous neighbourhood amongst ignorant bigots".[28] And much of her fiction of the past deals with the kind of people she would not have wished to have lived with, but they are presented with her characteristic tolerance and compassionate irony.

Her early work of course attracted local attention and identifications. While *Scenes of Clerical Life* was being published in *Blackwood's* in 1857, keys to the originals of the characters were circulating in Nuneaton. Shortly after *Adam Bede* was published in 1859 a book called *Seth Bede the Methody* was issued. And George Eliot suffered great annoyance on two other counts. The first was the emergence of a "local" author, Joseph Liggins, whose supporters claimed that he had written *Scenes* and *Adam Bede* but received no money from the publishers. He was variously supported by local people – he lived at Attleborough – and his claims achieved a national currency. The Liggins affair ran from April until October 1859, both John Blackwood and George Eliot writing to *The Times* to refute his claims. And after two fierce letters from Lewes, Charles Bracebridge, the leading Liggins adherent, renounced his man. Meanwhile an unscrupulous publisher, John Newby, had advertised a sequel to *Adam Bede* called *Adam Bede Jnr*. Lewes wrote to his sons: "There was a blackguard who wrote a book called 'Adam Bede Junior' – and advertized it as a 'Sequel to Adam Bede' – . . . This annoyed us at first because, we thought, the people in the provinces would believe the book was by George Eliot."[29] The touchiness on the point is worth noting. From the first she was a provincial novelist, proud to be judged for her regional knowledge and the authenticity her work derived as a result. As Henry Auster has rightly suggested, "Local attachments do not have to make a novelist's work parochial; on the contrary, they can, when exploited by a powerful, genuinely creative intelligence, direct it, nourish it, and enrich it."[30]

George Eliot kept up her correspondence with her Coventry friends, Charles and Cara Bray and the latter's sister Sara Hennell. They were, so we are told, genuinely surprised when she revealed to them that she had written *Adam Bede*.[31] But she never lost the feeling that moved her to confide in them the most important decision of her life. And she was moved again much later to reiterate her warm feelings:

. . . Dear Sara, you do not doubt that I love you? The circumstances of life – the changes that take place in ourselves – hem in the expression of affections and memories that live within us and enter almost into every day, and long separations often make intercourse difficult when the opportunity comes. But the delight I had in you, and in the hours we spent together and in all your acts of friendship to me, is really part of my life and can never die out of me.[32]

It is an emotional and loyal acknowledgement. Her past was the constant in her present.

While she was writing *The Mill on the Floss* George Eliot wrote to her close friend Barbara Bodichon, "at present my mind works with the most freedom and the keenest sense of poetry in my remotest past".[33] Her statements in that past and her use of it in her writing provide the frame for this book. The revival of interest in George Eliot which began about forty years ago led almost naturally to a revaluation of her status as a novelist: she is not only part of F. R. Leavis's great tradition, but of the greater tradition which followed him, that of an increasingly detailed critical analysis which has established the nature of her greatness. In one important sense that gain has made for a loss: she has come to be almost exclusively regarded as the subject of academic, scholarly, intellectual investigation.

Using substantial extracts and an evaluative commentary, I try to indicate the influences of Marian Evans's past on George Eliot's present, and to suggest how that present caused her to look at her past. Academics, responsive to her intellect, have tended to make her one of them. Biographers, sometimes looking for the sensational, have often veered to the other extreme in their determination to make her one of us. This book, I hope, does neither. I use the letters, the fiction, and some of the poetry, believing that much of George Eliot's art derives from the personal and intellectual affiliations of her Midland years.

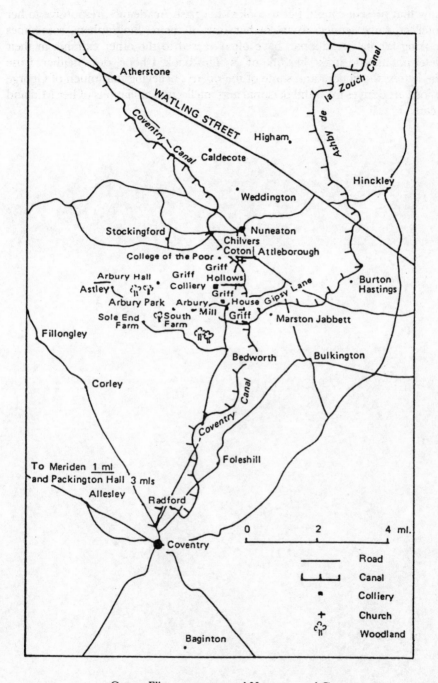

George Eliot country around Nuneaton and Coventry

# 1. Facts and Fictions:
# Life and Self

### SELF

Changeful comrade, Life of mine,
    Before we two must part,
I will tell thee, thou shalt say,
    What thou hast been and art.
Ere I lose my hold of thee
Justify thyself to me.

### LIFE

I was thy warmth upon thy mother's knee
    When light and love within her eyes were one;
We laughed together by the laurel-tree,
    Culling warm daisies 'neath the sloping sun;
    We heard the chickens' lazy croon,
      Where the trellised woodbines grew,
And all the summer afternoon
    Mystic gladness o'er thee threw.
    Was it person? Was it thing?
    Was it touch or whispering?
    It was bliss, and it was I:
    Bliss was what thou knew'st me by.

### SELF

Soon I knew thee more by Fear
    And sense of what was not,
Haunting all I held most dear;
    I had a double lot:
Ardour, cheated with alloy,
Wept the more for dreams of joy.[1]

In 1924 Isadore Mudge and M. E. Sears produced *A George Eliot Dictionary: The Characters and Scenes of the Novels Stories and Poems Alphabetically Arranged*. They

15

had already published *A Thackeray Dictionary*, but it was an optimistic venture to issue a book of this kind in the period of the most marked decline in George Eliot's reputation. Uncritically, it concentrates on originals, the particular index gratifying readers who want to "identify" characters "taken from life". The list here is generally derived from identifications of early biographers and from "keys" circularizing in Warwickshire at the time of the publication of *Scenes*, *Adam Bede*, and *The Mill*. It is wide-ranging and fanciful. It identifies George Eliot with three of her heroines, Maggie Tulliver, Esther Lyon and Dorothea Brooke. But although in *Scenes* George Eliot drew on local history and local people, she denied later that there were any "portraits" in her work. Yet one portrait is evident in her fiction, and it is perhaps unconsciously painted. Edward Dowden put it well when he wrote in 1872 that our centre of interest in reading her novels was in that " 'second self', who writes her books, and lives and speaks through them".[2]

We are, I suggest, aware of a primary self in many of her characters as well as the self who writes her books. Although we must be cautious when we speak of her originals, there seems to be little doubt that she put much of her past self – seen with an anguished but occasionally ecstatic nostalgia – into the character of Maggie Tulliver. "Book First" in *The Mill on the Floss* is called "Boy and Girl", and Chapter IV of "Book Sixth" "Brother and Sister". "Brother and Sister" encapsulates her feelings of love and frustration: in the chapter Maggie is accused by Tom of taking "pleasure in a sort of perverse self-denial, and at another you have not resolution to resist a thing that you know to be wrong".[3] There is a softening after this, Tom hoping for the best from Maggie, though still expressing doubt. There is a terrible irony in his words – and in the whole scene – in view of Maggie's later response to Stephen and "betrayal" of her cousin Lucy. The author's need to return to a personal past, however superbly fictionalized here, is seen nine years later. Just as Maggie depends on Tom's approval, hopeful of his love, catching at reconciliation and acceptance, so George Eliot, major novelist, moral lawgiver (despite her irregular union with George Henry Lewes), central figure in her own literary salon, returns suddenly to her childhood. In July 1869 she was beginning to write *Middlemarch*, which certainly involved an association with Coventry. Her Journal records that on the 3rd she had written five "Brother and Sister" sonnets, and by the 19th, when the Introduction to *Middlemarch* was begun, she had completed three more.[4] The last poems in the sequence were finished by the end of the month.

A combination of events perhaps moved her to write again about herself and Isaac. She had determined on the setting of her next novel; imagination and emotion, working on the familiar region, set up personal recollections which she wrote out less publicly than in *The Mill*. Thornton, Lewes's second son, had come home from Natal to die. Marian Lewes, as she called herself, nursed him until his death in October 1869. She wrote at the time in her

Journal, "This death seems to me the beginning of our own".[5] Oppressed by the presence of the son about to die, she may have found herself thinking yet again of the brother who was dead to her. When she had written to tell Isaac of her "husband", he instructed his solicitor to write to her with the question, "Permit me to ask when and where you were married".[6] Now, twelve years on from that time, she wrote the following:

## BROTHER AND SISTER

### I.

I cannot choose but think upon the time
When our two lives grew like two buds that kiss
At lightest thrill from the bee's swinging chime,
Because the one so near the other is.

He was the elder and a little man
Of forty inches, bound to show no dread,
And I the girl that puppy-like now ran,
Now lagged behind my brother's larger tread.

I held him wise, and when he talked to me
Of snakes and birds, and which God loved the best,
I thought his knowledge marked the boundary
Where men grew blind, though angels knew the rest.

If he said "Hush!" I tried to hold my breath
Wherever he said "Come!" I stepped in faith.[7]

The manuscript of this poem shows that "of that dear" in the first line was replaced by the less warmly nostalgic "upon the". But the first line shows clearly that she was unable to resist the strong pull of the intimate past. There the girl was supposedly the subordinate in every sense – in intelligence, age, knowledge, faith – and that word, the last word of the poem, carries an ironic overtone of ignorance, of a misguided faith perhaps complementary to the lost faith of the fifty-year-old woman writing the poem. As Cynthia Secor has wisely remarked of these poems, "It is this sense of loss that gives the sonnet sequence stature".[8] The sense of loss is rendered with some complexity.

Sonnet IX in that sequence carries a different emphasis:

We had the self-same world enlarged for each
By loving difference of girl and boy:
The fruit that hung on high beyond my reach
He plucked for me, and oft he must employ

A measuring glance to guide my tiny shoe
Where lay firm stepping-stones, or call to mind

> "This thing I like my sister may not do,
> For she is little, and I must be kind."
>
> Thus boyish will the nobler mastery learned
> Where inward vision over impulse reigns,
> Widening its life with separate life discerned,
> A Life unlike, a Self that self restrains.
>
> His years with others must the sweeter be
> For those brief days he spent in loving me.[9]

The irony of this is even more marked: the first eight lines of the sonnet show the brother acting for the sister, prescribing her actions, protectively but with a fixed sense of physical and moral authority. "The fruit" is temptation, "a measuring glance" and the "firm stepping-stones" the calculated anticipations of a narrow but respectable conformity. The inward and outward divisions of development are given in the next four lines, but the couplet, with its exquisite pathos and loving generosity of spirit, is yet tinged with an uncompromising realism – "brief days" is contrasted with "years", and the years are those of separation and rejection. Again the last line has been altered in the manuscript to emphasize the poignant fact. It was originally "For all the love he learned in loving me."

I shall return to "Brother and Sister" later, since the emphasis on self-identity and associations with a particular time and place are centrally relevant. The sonnets were not published until 1874 in *Jubal and Other Poems*, but the great nineteenth-century forger, T. J. Wise issued them (probably about 1885) as "Brother and Sister Sonnets by Marian Lewes", giving the correct date of 1869 for their composition. This unscrupulous publication marks the only instance in which the name she chose to be known by appears on her published work.

"Brother and Sister" is the dropping of the mask worn so insistently in *The Mill on the Floss*. The sonnets are clear and simple in form, though I believe they provide conflicting insights into George Eliot's feeling about her scarcely buried past. *The Mill* also dramatizes love, suffering, divisions, blame, and the mutability of the closest of relationships. Relationships are fraught for Maggie: she moves from worship to resentment without changing the fundamental basis of her feeling for Tom. In the fifth chapter of the novel Tom comes home from the academy and Maggie cannot contain her excitement: she is tremulous with love, and her guilt about Tom's rabbits is in abeyance. It surfaces when Tom, whose consciousness of his "little sister" is subordinated to the prospect of freedom, announces that he is going to see them:

Maggie's heart began to flutter with fear. She dared not tell the sad truth at once, but she walked after Tom in trembling silence as he went out, thinking how she could tell him the news so as to soften at once his sorrow and his anger; for Maggie dreaded Tom's anger of all things – it was quite a different anger from her own.

"Tom," she said, timidly, when they were out of doors, "how much money did you give for your rabbits?"

"Two half-crowns and a sixpence," said Tom, promptly.

"I think I've got a great deal more than that in my steel purse up-stairs. I'll ask mother to give it you."

"What for?" said Tom. "I don't want *your* money, you silly thing. I've got a great deal more money than you, because I'm a boy. I always have half-sovereigns and sovereigns for my Christmas boxes, because I shall be a man, and you only have five-shilling pieces, because you're only a girl."

"Well, but, Tom – if mother would let me give you two halfcrowns and a sixpence out of my purse to put into your pocket and spend, you know; and buy some more rabbits with it?"

"More rabbits? I don't want any more."

"O, but Tom, they're all dead."

Tom stopped immediately in his walk and turned round towards Maggie. "You forgot to feed 'em, then, and Harry forgot?" he said, his colour heightening for a moment, but soon subsiding. "I'll pitch into Harry – I'll have him turned away. And I don't love you, Maggie. You shan't go fishing with me to-morrow. I told you to go and see the rabbits every day." He walked on again.

"Yes, but I forgot – and I couldn't help it, indeed, Tom. I'm so very sorry," said Maggie, while the tears rushed fast.

"You're a naughty girl," said Tom severely, "and I'm sorry I brought you the fish-line. I don't love you."

"O, Tom, it's very cruel," sobbed Maggie. "I'd forgive you, if *you* forgot anything – I wouldn't mind what you did – I'd forgive you and love you."

"Yes, you're a silly – but I never *do* forget things – *I* don't."

"O, please forgive me, Tom; my heart will break," said Maggie, shaking with sobs, clinging to Tom's arm, and laying her wet cheek on his shoulder.

Tom shook her off, and stopped again, saying in a peremptory tone, "Now, Maggie, you just listen. Aren't I a good brother to you?"

"Ye-ye-es," sobbed Maggie, her chin rising and falling convulsedly.

"Didn't I think about your fish-line all this quarter, and mean to buy it, and saved my money o' purpose, and wouldn't go halves in the toffee, and Spouncer fought me because I wouldn't?"

"Ye-ye-es ... and I ... lo-lo-love you so, Tom."

"But you're a naughty girl. Last holidays you licked the paint off my lozenge box, and the holidays before that you let the boat drag my fish-line down when I'd set you to watch it, and you pushed your head through my kite, all for nothing."

"But I didn't mean," said Maggie; "I couldn't help it."

"Yes, you could," said Tom, "if you'd minded what you were doing. And you're a naughty girl, and you shan't go fishing with me to-morrow."

With this terrible conclusion, Tom ran away from Maggie towards the mill, meaning to greet Luke there, and complain to him of Harry.[10]

The significance of the passage in the psychological narrative is premonitory and poignant. The boy's world is to become the man's world, for she is "only a girl" and, later, a weak or supposedly sinful woman. Maggie (note the relegation of the endearment "Magsie") has to be put down when she is naughty, just as she has to be taught her duty when she secretly meets Philip Wakem, crippled son of her father's enemy, and more severely put down when she returns after drifting with Stephen Guest and losing her reputation. The phrase "it was quite a different anger from her own" indicates implacability: the gift of the fishing line is the simple symbol of conformity, but also of love. Tom loves fishing: Maggie loves Tom and if she is neglectful or forgetful it will show that she doesn't love him, that she is naughty or, later, irresponsible, uncaring, wicked. Here is the obverse side:

> But sudden came the barge's pitch-black prow,
> Nearer and angrier came my brother's cry,
> And all my soul was quivering fear, when lo!
> Upon the imperilled line, suspended high,
>
> A silver perch! My guilt that won the prey,
> Now turned to merit, had a guerdon rich
> Of hugs and praises, and made merry play,
> Until my triumph reached its highest pitch
>
> When all at home were told the wondrous feat,
> And how the little sister had fished well.[11]

Here is a complementary, extended passage from *The Mill*:

They were on their way to the Round Pool – that wonderful pool, which the floods had made a long while ago: no one knew how deep it was; and it was mysterious, too, that it should be almost a perfect round, framed in with willows and tall reeds, so that the water was only to be seen when you got close to the brink. The sight of the old favourite spot always heightened Tom's good-humour, and he spoke to Maggie in the most amicable whispers, as he opened the precious basket, and prepared their tackle. He threw her line for her, and put the rod into her hand. Maggie thought it probable that the small fish would come to her hook, and the large ones to Tom's. But she had forgotten all about the fish, and was looking dreamily at the glassy water, when Tom said, in a loud whisper, "Look, look, Maggie!" and came running to prevent her from snatching her line away.

Maggie was frightened lest she had been doing something wrong, as usual, but presently Tom drew out her line and brought a large tench bouncing on the grass.

Tom was excited.

"O Magsie! you little duck! Empty the basket."

Maggie was not conscious of unusual merit, but it was enough that Tom called her Magsie, and was pleased with her. There was nothing to mar her delight in the whispers and the dreamy silences, when she listened to the light dipping sounds of the rising fish, and the gentle rustling, as if the willows and the reeds and the water had their happy whisperings also. Maggie thought it would make a very nice heaven to sit by the pool in that way, and never be scolded. She never knew she had a bite till Tom told her; but she liked fishing very much.

It was one of their happy mornings. They trotted along and sat down together, with no thought that life would ever change much for them: they would only get bigger and not go to school, and it would always be like the holidays; they would always live together and be fond of each other. And the mill with its booming – the great chestnut-tree under which they played at houses – their own little river, the Ripple, where the banks seemed like home, and Tom was always seeing the water-rats, while Maggie gathered the purple plumy tops of the reeds, which she forgot and dropped afterwards – above all, the great Floss, along which they wandered with a sense of travel, to see the rushing spring-tide, the awful Eagre, come up like a hungry monster, or to see the Great Ash which had once wailed and groaned like a man – these things would always be just the same to them. Tom thought people were at a disadvantage who lived on any other spot of the globe; and Maggie, when she read about Christiana passing "the river over which there is no bridge," always saw the Floss between the green pastures by the Great Ash.

Life did change for Tom and Maggie; and yet they were not wrong in believing that the thoughts and loves of these first years would always make part of their lives. We could never have loved the earth so well if we had had no childhood in it, – if it were not the earth where the same flowers come up again every spring that we used to gather with our tiny fingers as we sat lisping to ourselves on the grass – the same hips and haws on the autumn hedgerows – the same redbreasts that we used to call "God's birds," because they did no harm to the precious crops. What novelty is worth that sweet monotony where everything is known, and *loved* because it is known?

The wood I walk in on this mild May day, with the younger yellow-brown foliage of the oaks between me and the blue sky, the white star-flowers and the blue-eyed speedwell and the ground ivy at my feet – what grove of tropic palms, what strange ferns or splendid broad-petalled blossoms, could ever thrill such deep and delicate fibres within me as this home-scene? These familiar flowers, these well-remembered bird-notes, this sky, with its fitful brightness, these furrowed and grassy fields, each with a sort of personality given to it by the capricious hedgerows – such things as these are the mother tongue of our imagination, the language that is laden with all the subtle inextricable associations the fleeting hours of our childhood left behind them. Our delight in the sunshine on the deep-bladed grass to-day, might be no more than the faint perception of wearied souls, if it were not for the sunshine and the grass in the far-off years which still live in us, and transform our perception into love.[12]

The experience, used twice by George Eliot, and here with moving insight, is autobiographical in the sense of being coloured with sympathetic identifications. The extract from the sonnet exemplifies luck – the moment of chance that makes us favoured. In the need to be loved the particular is subsumed in the general, here the family, but what is wonderfully simple about the verse is the sudden movement – unpremeditated, will-less, from "guilt" to "triumph". In a subtle sense it mirrors the situation of Marian Lewes, guilty or held to be guilty because she was living with a married man, and the triumph of George Eliot (by the time she wrote this poem – 1869 – her reputation was unquestioned) in part at least was fashioned by the partner to whom she privately dedicated each successive manuscript of her novels. Her "chance" meeting with him had made possible her literary triumphs.

The extract from *The Mill* is different in intensity of texture. The fictionalized narrative is held in the grip of tensely recalled relationship and place, both central to George Eliot's self-identification with her roots. Writing in 1888, S. Parkinson (*Scenes from the George Eliot Country*) says of Griff House, her childhood home, that "At the back of the house the flat fields stretch away towards Griff pits, and through some of these fields are footpaths leading to the 'round pool', the 'rookery elms', and probably to the 'Red Deeps', where Maggie Tulliver had her stolen interview with Philip Wakem."[13] The Red Deeps is a little valley between Nuneaton and Griff House called Griff Hollows.

In the extract we note the use of the intimate "Magsie", and in a wonderful evocation of the poetry of place, the humanized nature ("their happy whisperings"). The innocent responses of childhood are present in a medium of philosophical contemplation which blends nostalgia, regret and foreboding. The foreboding is factual within the fiction and symbolic too. The reiteration of water associations, the flood, the repetition of "the Great Ash" and the "great Floss" with the localized mythology of the power of fate, all lead to the climax of the plot where Tom and Maggie drown in the "awful Eagre". The drowning is a consummation, something arising from a deep wish. And the threats of change which punctuate the passage above are realized in the novel and in the lives of Isaac and Marian Evans. For George Eliot the return to the personal past is an experience of the living present. As she puts it here, "such things as these are the mother-tongue of our imagination, the language that is laden with all the subtle inextricable associations the fleeting hours of our childhood left behind them". And the transformation of these experiences into a kind of loving shows her humanism.

Since none of Marian's letters exist before 1836, when she was seventeen, her fictional account of the relationship with Isaac is the only one we have. It seems very likely that Isaac expected from his sister the same kind of conformity which Tom demanded and exacted from Maggie. The fear and defensiveness of life are surely seen in the letter already referred to (see p. 5) where she tells Isaac that she has someone to take care of her and refers boldly to "My Husband". There is a self-justifying tone throughout, as if she is explaining because she knows the exacting conventions and standards by which he lives – and expects her to live. The remembrances to "my tall nephews and nieces" show Marian paying lip-service to duty in life.[14] The timing of this letter in the brother–sister relationship is significant. The date is 26th May 1857, and she had finished "Mr Gilfil's Love Story", two instalments of which had appeared in *Blackwood's*. She was concerned about the continuing decline in the health of Chrissey (who died 15th March 1859) and in this letter reiterates "that you would pay £15 of my present half year's income to Chrissey".[15] But the tone of the letter is cool. The family solicitor responded that he (Isaac) "is so much hurt at your not having previously made some communication to him as to your intention and prospects that he cannot make up his mind to write, feeling that he could not do so in a Brotherly Spirit".[16] Marian (and George Eliot) received this in the other spirit in which it was written, replying "If his feelings towards me are unfriendly, there is no necessity for his paining himself by any direct intercourse with me. . . . Our marriage is not a legal one, though it is regarded by us both as a sacred bond. . . . I have been his wife and have borne his name for nearly three years; a fact which has been known to all my personal friends except the members of my own family, from whom I have withheld it because, knowing that their views of life differ in many respects from my own, I wished not to give them unnecessary pain."[17] This reply shows her hard fought for independence, resentment and guilt.

But there can be no third party between Maggie and Tom, now adult (like Marian and Isaac) where the words unsaid in life are said with passionate anger in fiction. Maggie has not committed adultery with Stephen Guest: she has done something much worse. She has been true to herself, she has resisted temptation, and she has returned innocent to be judged guilty:

Maggie had been kept on her bed at York for a day with that prostrating headache which was likely to follow on the terrible strain of the previous day and night. There was an expression of physical pain still about her brow and eyes, and her whole appearance, with her dress so long unchanged, was worn and distressed. She lifted the latch of the gate and walked in – slowly. Tom did not hear the gate; he was just then close upon the roaring dam; but he presently turned, and, lifting up his eyes, saw the figure whose worn look and loneliness seemed to him a confirmation of his worst conjectures. He paused, trembling and white with disgust and indignation.

Maggie paused too – three yards before him. She felt the hatred in his face: felt it rushing through her fibres; but she must speak.

"Tom," she began, faintly, "I am come back to you – I am come back home – for refuge – to tell you everything."

"You will find no home with me," he answered, with tremulous rage. "You have disgraced us all. You have disgraced my father's name. You have been a curse to your best friends. You have been base – deceitful; no motives are strong enough to restrain you. I wash my hands of you for ever. You don't belong to me."

Their mother had come to the door now. She stood paralysed by the double shock of seeing Maggie and hearing Tom's words.

"Tom," said Maggie, with more courage, "I am perhaps not so guilty as you believe me to be. I never meant to give way to my feelings. I struggled against them. I was carried too far in the boat to come back on Tuesday. I came back as soon as I could."

"I can't believe in you any more," said Tom, gradually passing from the tremulous excitement of the first moment to cold inflexibility. "You have been carrying on a clandestine relation with Stephen Guest – as you did before with another. He went to see you at my aunt Moss's; you walked alone with him in the lanes; you must have behaved as no modest girl would have done to her cousin's lover, else that could never have happened. The people at Luckreth saw you pass – you passed all the other places; you knew what you were doing. You have been using Philip Wakem as a screen to deceive Lucy – the kindest friend you ever had. Go and see the return you have made her: she's ill – unable to speak – my mother can't go near her, lest she should remind her of *you*."

Maggie was half stunned – too heavily pressed upon by her anguish even to discern any difference between her actual guilt and her brother's accusations, still less to vindicate herself.

"Tom," she said, crushing her hands together under her cloak, in the effort to speak again. "Whatever I have done, I repent it bitterly. I want to make amends. I will endure anything. I want to be kept from doing wrong again."

"What *will* keep you?" said Tom, with cruel bitterness. "Not religion; not your natural feelings of gratitude and honour. And he – he would deserve to be shot, if it were not – But you are ten times worse than he is. I loathe your character and your conduct. You struggled with your feelings, you say. Yes! *I* have had feelings to struggle with; but I conquered them. I have had a harder life than you have had: but I have found *my* comfort in doing my duty. But I will sanction no such character as yours: the world shall know that *I* feel the difference between right and wrong. If you are in want, I will provide for you – let my mother know. But you shall not come under my roof. It is enough that I have to bear the thought of your disgrace: the sight of you is hateful to me."[18]

Marian Evans returned from the continent to London, changed her name by her own wish, and was judged guilty. As she wrote to Cara Bray in September 1855: "if there be any one subject on which I feel no levity it is that of marriage and the relation of the sexes – if there is any one action or relation of my life which is and always has been profoundly serious, it is my relation to Mr Lewes. . . . Light and easily broken ties are what I neither desire theoretically nor could live for practically. Women who are satisfied with such ties do *not* act as I have done – they obtain what they desire and are still invited to dinner."[19] There is a wonderful contrast in the letter to Cara and the fictionalized version. The letter is intent on self-justification in the clear knowledge that love – responsible, committed, feeling love – is above man-made laws. But the obverse side, the might-have-been which is translated into fiction, is expressed with the anguish of rejection and humiliation. Three years after Isaac's rejection, his sister is living through her character, in her imagined world, where passions are more feverishly real than in the formal letter. Yet that letter, like Maggie's inner action, is an indictment of narrow, prescribed standards which pass for morality: in both texts she is holding up to the provincial world from which she came, and which held the deep memories of her life translated into her fiction, the mirror of hypocrisy. The letter to Cara is an attempt at explanation and reconciliation, for Cara had not yet written to her since she had announced that she was living with Lewes. The fictional extract is also an attempt at reconciliation – explanation which is so cruelly dismissed – and each is expressive of the writer's, and the author's, need. The reconciliation with Cara was achieved, though there was a longish cool period. The "reconciliation" with Isaac came twenty-three years after the letter.

Another passage in *The Mill*, Maggie's dream as she drifts with Stephen, shows how tenaciously George Eliot's feelings clung to reconciliation. It also reflects the deeply subconscious guilt being worked out in the fiction, where it fits character and narrative pattern alike:

## WAKING

When Maggie was gone to sleep, Stephen, weary too with his unaccustomed amount of rowing, and with the intense inward life of the last twelve hours, but too restless to sleep, walked and lounged about the deck with his cigar far on into midnight, not seeing the dark water – hardly conscious that there were stars – living only in the near and distant future. At last fatigue conquered restlessness, and he rolled himself up in a piece of tarpauling on the deck near Maggie's feet.

She had fallen asleep before nine, and had been sleeping for six hours before the faintest hint of a midsummer daybreak was discernible. She awoke from that vivid dreaming which makes the margin of our deeper rest: She was in a boat on the wide water with Stephen, and in the gathering darkness something like a star appeared, that grew and grew till they saw it was the Virgin seated in St Ogg's boat, and it came nearer and nearer, till they saw the Virgin was Lucy and the boatman was Philip – no, not Philip, but her brother, who rowed past without looking at her; and she rose to stretch out her arms and call to him, and their own boat turned over with the movement, and they began to sink, till with one spasm of dread she seemed to awake, and find she was a child again in the parlour at evening twilight, and Tom was not really angry. From the soothed sense of that false waking she passed to the real waking – to the splash of water against the vessel, and the sound of a footstep on the deck, and the awful starlit sky. There was a moment of utter bewilderment before her mind could get disentangled from the confused web of dreams; but soon the whole terrible truth urged itself upon her. Stephen was not by her now: she was alone with her own memory and her own dread. The irrevocable wrong that must blot her life had been committed: she had brought sorrow into the lives of others – into the lives that were knit up with hers by trust and love. The feeling of a few short weeks had hurried her into the sins her nature had most recoiled from – breach of faith and cruel selfishness; she had rent the ties that had given meaning to duty, and had made herself an outlawed soul, with no guide but the wayward choice of her own passion. And where would that lead her? – where had it led her now? She had said she would rather die than fall into that temptation. She felt it now – now that the consequences of such a fall had come before the outward act was completed. There was at least this fruit from all her years of striving after the highest and best – that her soul, though betrayed, beguiled, ensnared, could never deliberately consent to a choice of the lower. And a choice of what? O God – not a choice of joy, but of conscious cruelty and hardness; for could she ever cease to see before her Lucy and Philip, with their murdered trust and hopes? Her life with Stephen could have no sacredness: she must for ever sink and wander vaguely, driven by uncertain impulse;

25

for she had let go the clue of life – that clue which once in the far-off years her young need had clutched so strongly. She had renounced all delights then, before she knew them, before they had come within her reach. Philip had been right when he told her that she knew nothing of renunciation: she had thought it was quiet ecstasy; she saw it face to face now – that sad patient loving strength which holds the clue of life – and saw that the thorns were for ever pressing on its brow. The yesterday, which could never be revoked – if she could have changed it now for any length of inward silent endurance, she would have bowed beneath that cross with a sense of rest.[20]

The psychological tension is superb. Advised by her publisher John Blackwood to alter Caterina's murderous wish to kill Captain Wybrow in "Mr Gilfil's Love Story" by converting it to a dream, George Eliot refused and asserted the realism of the motive. In *Adam Bede* she had used the dream convincingly as Adam's wish-fulfilment in his love for Hetty; in *The Mill* the dream is part of the novel's mythology, and psychologically right for the real virgin of St Ogg's, whose reputation only is deflowered. The dream, with its changes of identity, forecasts the ending of the novel but with a difference. Tom does come to her: the deep-seated nature of Maggie's wishes (and the author's) take her back to that childhood where fear was passing and reconciliation and relief were part of the family cycle. Here there is no relief, no escape from the results of adult action – the chapter heading WAKING is indicative of commonplace happening and almost unbearable reality. And the river is the river of life – and death – while the words are the speaking life of Maggie's present and George Eliot's past. Images associated with faith, like a word, now broken, run throughout the chapter – "like a star", "sins", "breach of faith", "temptation", "fall", "sacredness", "renunciation", "thorns", "cross". These words represent Maggie's life as she sees it and feels it, and perhaps, in some measure, George Eliot's feelings about herself too. In fiction and in life the full reconciliation can never come about: the fictionalized one, powerful, dramatic and idealized, is imbued with the expression of self-identification which characterizes *The Mill*:

It was not till Tom has pushed off and they were on the wide water – he face to face with Maggie – that the full meaning of what had happened rushed upon his mind. It came with so overpowering a force – it was such a new revelation to his spirit, of the depths in life, that had lain beyond his vision which he had fancied so keen and clear – that he was unable to ask a question. They sat mutely gazing at each other: Maggie with eyes of intense life looking out from a weary, beaten face – Tom pale with a certain awe and humiliation. Thought was busy though the lips were silent: and though he could ask no question, he guessed a story of almost miraculous divinely-protected effort. But at last a mist gathered over the blue-grey eyes, and the lips found a word they could utter: the old childish – "Magsie!"

Maggie could make no answer but a long deep sob of that mysterious wondrous happiness that is one with pain.

As soon as she could speak, she said, "We will go to Lucy, Tom: we'll go and see if she is safe, and then we can help the rest."

Tom rowed with untired vigour, and with a different speed from poor Maggie's. The boat was soon in the current of the river again, and soon they would be at Tofton.

"Park House stands high up out of the flood," said Maggie. "Perhaps they have got Lucy there."

Nothing else was said; a new danger was being carried towards them by the river. Some wooden machinery had just given way on one of the wharves, and huge fragments were being floated along. The sun was rising now, and the wide area of watery desolation was spread out in dreadful clearness around them – in dreadful clearness floated onwards the hurrying, threatening masses. A large company in a boat that was working its way along under the Tofton houses, observed their danger, and shouted, "Get out of the current!"

But that could not be done at once, and Tom, looking before him, saw death rushing on them. Huge fragments, clinging together in fatal fellowship, made one wide mass across the stream.

"It is coming, Maggie!" Tom said, in a deep hoarse voice, loosing the oars, and clasping her.

The next instant the boat was no longer seen upon the water – and the huge mass was hurrying on in hideous triumph.

But soon the keel of the boat reappeared, a black speck on the golden water.

The boat reappeared – but brother and sister had gone down in an embrace never to be parted: living through again in one supreme moment the days when they had clasped their little hands in love, and roamed the daisied fields together.[21]

The strength of the association, like the strength of the river, or of feelings, or of the subconscious, is here .given a terrible immediacy. George Eliot's recreative imagination has been devoted to the feelings of Maggie, but in this last identification the wished-for illumination, transitory before death though it is, is her vision of Tom's: his narrow life is exposed to him in the moment of crisis, and Maggie's intuitive knowledge that this is so is presented in her "long deep sob of that mysterious wondrous happiness that is one with pain". And once again the exposition of passionate feeling makes for packed writing, so that when we read "Huge fragments, clinging together in fatal fellowship, made one wide mass across the stream" we feel that although, ironically, they have destroyed a human "fatal fellowship" their movement is as transitory as life. "Magsie", as we have seen, returned to the "daisied fields" in "Brother and Sister", and eleven years after she wrote that sonnet sequence she married John Walter Cross. Isaac wrote to her from the beloved Griff of her past:

My Dear Sister,

I have much pleasure in availing myself of the present opportunity to break the long silence which has existed between us, by offering our united and sincere congratulations to you and Mr Cross, upon the happy event of which Mr Holbeche has informed me. My wife joins me in sincerely hoping it will afford you much happiness and comfort. She and the younger branches unite with me in kind love and every good wish. Believe me

Your affectionate brother
Isaac P. Evans.[22]

In the life left to her, just over six months, his sister Marian saw to it that they were *not* divided any more in spirit; the conventional observance of being married according to the rites of the Church of England at St George's, Hanover Square, was in some ways more than national fame and moral integrity:

My dear Brother

Your letter was forwarded to me here, and it was a great joy to me to have your kind words of sympathy, for our long silence has never broken the affection for you which began when we were little ones. My Husband too was much pleased to read your letter. I have known his family for nine years, and they have received me amongst them very lovingly. He is of a most solid, well tried character and has had a great deal of experience.[23]

It is signed "Always your affectionate Sister, Mary Ann Cross". Even in Isaac's congratulations there is a studied formality, and there seems to be a degree of irony in both letters. The repetition of "long silence" emphasizes rather than diminishes the absoluteness of the division. But Marian, always the little sister as well as the great novelist, feels obliged to explain the eminent eligibility of her husband just as defensively as she had instanced, in the letter of twenty-three years earlier, the talents and achievements of Lewes. Always she looked back to her roots, to the Midlands where her brother still lived in the family home, for the provincial approval of her actions by standards she had treated ironically in her fiction.

*The Mill* and "Brother and Sister" draw on identifiable autobiographical experience. But the presence of George Eliot is found in individual characters in her works, often in moments of crisis, where an identification in life is sometimes possible, sometimes not. It is usually an intuitive and imaginative grasp of the essentials of self within the created character: it deals with revelation, discovery and self-discovery, guilt, repentance, renunciation and loyalty, to name a few examples. In the first works, *The Mill* apart, it is not pronounced, unless we except the possible identification with Nancy Cass – and even her egoistic husband Godfrey – which occurs in Chapter 18 of *Silas Marner*. Godfrey is moved to a confession of his past to his wife Nancy because his brother's body has been discovered in the Stone-pit, which has gone dry, after fifteen years. Godfrey and Nancy are childless: here is guilt, duty, retribution, hope and, above all, the changing temperature of marital intimacy. It is wise and honest: the two characters are exposed and personalised in crisis:

28

"That woman Marner found dead in the snow – Eppie's mother – that wretched woman – was my wife: Eppie is my child."

He paused, dreading the effect of his confession. But Nancy sat quite still, only that her eyes dropped and ceased to meet his. She was pale and quiet as a meditative statue, clasping her hands on her lap.

"You'll never think the same of me again," said Godfrey, after a little while, with some tremor in his voice.

She was silent.

"I oughtn't to have left the child unowned: I oughtn't to have kept it from you. But I couldn't bear to give you up, Nancy. I was led away into marrying her – I suffered for it."

Still Nancy was silent, looking down; and he almost expected that she would presently get up and say she would go to her father's. How could she have any mercy for faults that must seem so black to her, with her simple severe notions?

But at last she lifted up her eyes to his again and spoke. There was no indignation in her voice – only deep regret.

"Godfrey, if you had but told me this six years ago, we could have done some of our duty by the child. Do you think I'd have refused to take her in, if I'd known she was yours?"

At that moment Godfrey felt all the bitterness of an error that was not simply futile, but had defeated its own end. He had not measured this wife with whom he had lived so long. But she spoke again, with more agitation.

"And – O, Godfrey – if we'd had her from the first, if you'd taken to her as you ought, she'd have loved me for her mother – and you'd have been happier with me: I could better have bore my little baby dying, and our life might have been more like what we used to think it 'ud be."

The tears fell, and Nancy ceased to speak.

"But you wouldn't have married me then, Nancy, if I'd told you," said Godfrey, urged, in the bitterness of his self-reproach, to prove to himself that his conduct had not been utter folly. "You may think you would now, but you wouldn't then. With your pride and your father's, you'd have hated having anything to do with me after the talk there'd have been."

"I can't say what I should have done about that, Godfrey. I should never have married anybody else. But I wasn't worth doing wrong for – nothing is in this world. Nothing is so good as it seems beforehand – not even our marrying wasn't, you see." There was a faint sad smile on Nancy's face as she said the last words.

"I'm a worse man than you thought I was, Nancy," said Godfrey, rather tremulously. "Can you forgive me ever?"

"The wrong to me is but little, Godfrey: you've made it up to me – you've been good to me for fifteen years. It's another you did the wrong to; and I doubt it can never be all made up for."

"But we can take Eppie now," said Godfrey. "I won't mind the world knowing at last. I'll be plain and open for the rest o' my life."

"It'll be different coming to us, now she's grown up," said Nancy, shaking her head sadly. "But it's your duty to acknowledge her and provide for her; and I'll do my part by her, and pray to God Almighty to make her love me."

29

"Then we'll go together to Silas Marner's this very night, as soon as everything's quiet at the Stone-pits."[24]

The scenes of inner crisis seem to draw on Marian Evans's own experience of inner crisis either over religion in her Midland years or perhaps over her relationship with Lewes later. The choice of these Midland locations is a conscious emotional identification, allowing her to release into her fiction the moods and sympathies, the suffering and love of her own experience. Her love for Lewes involved her in a momentous decision: once she was living with him, she had his children to consider. Her writing, informed with recent and present experience, moved her naturally to the past time and region that she knew so well. These identifications occur in *Felix Holt* and *Middlemarch*. With the first-named the emotional association is implicit, and the feelings are those of renunciation and guilt. The first passage involves Esther who, in the unlikely plot of *Felix Holt*, is the rightful heiress to Transome Court and has the prospect of marrying Harold Transome, the defeated Radical candidate in the General Election preceding the first Reform Bill. The complication is that Esther loves Felix Holt, who is in prison, suspected of having caused the death of a constable during the election riot. Esther has testified in court on his behalf, and Harold has told her that "a very powerfully signed memorial to the Home Secretary" has been got up to help Felix. When Esther goes to her bedroom she knows that Harold would marry her if he could, that everything has been done to smooth her taking over of the Transome estates, and that Felix, a true radical and not a spurious one, would not marry an heiress:

Esther went up-stairs to her bedroom, thinking that she should not sleep that night. She set her light on a high stand, and did not touch her dress. What she desired to see with undisturbed clearness were things not present: the rest she needed was the rest of a final choice. It was difficult. On each side there was renunciation.

She drew up her blinds, liking to see the grey sky, where there were some veiled glimmerings of moonlight, and the lines of the for-ever running river, and the bending movement of the black trees. She wanted the largeness of the world to help her thought. This young creature, who trod lightly backward and forward, and leaned against the window-frame, and shook back her brown curls as she looked at something not visible, had lived hardly more than six months since she saw Felix Holt for the first time. But life is measured by the rapidity of change, the succession of influences that modify the being; and Esther had undergone something little short of an inward revolution. The revolutionary struggle, however, was not quite at an end.

There was something which she now felt profoundly to be the best thing that life could give her. But – if it was to be had at all – it was not to be had without paying a heavy price for it, such as we must pay for all that is greatly good. A supreme love, a motive that gives a sublime rhythm to a woman's life, and exalts habit into partnership with the soul's highest needs, is not to be had where and how she wills:

to know that high initiation, she must often tread where it is hard to tread, and feel the chill air, and watch through darkness. It is not true that love makes all things easy: it makes us choose what is difficult. Esther's previous life had brought her into close acquaintance with many negations, and with many positive ills too, not of the acutely painful, but of the distasteful sort. What if she chose the hardship, and had to bear it alone, with no strength to lean upon – no other better self to make a place for trust and joy? Her past experience saved her from illusions. She knew the dim life of the back street, the contact with sordid vulgarity, the lack of refinement for the senses, the summons to a daily task; and the gain that was to make that life of privation something on which she dreaded to turn her back, as if it were heaven – the presence and the love of Felix Holt – was only a quivering hope, not a certainty. It was not in her woman's nature that the hope should not spring within her and make a strong impulse. She knew that he loved her: had he not said how a woman might help a man if she were worthy? and if she proved herself worthy? But still there was the dread that after all she might find herself on the stony road alone, and faint and be weary. Even with the fulfilment of her hope, she knew that she pledged herself to meet high demands.

And on the other side there was a lot where everything seemed easy – but for the fatal absence of those feelings which, now she had once known them, it seemed nothing less than a fall and a degradation to do without. With a terrible prescience which a multitude of impressions during her stay at Transome Court had contributed to form, she saw herself in a silken bondage that arrested all motive, and was nothing better than a well-cushioned despair. To be restless amidst ease, to be languid among all appliances for pleasure, was a possibility that seemed to haunt the rooms of this house, and wander with her under the oaks and elms of the park. And Harold Transome's love, no longer a hovering fancy with which she played, but become a serious fact, seemed to threaten her with a stifling oppression. The homage of a man may be delightful until he asks straight for love, by which a woman renders homage. Since she and Felix had kissed each other in the prison, she felt as if she had vowed herself away, as if memory lay on her lips like a seal of possession. Yet what had happened that very evening had strengthened her liking for Harold, and her care for all that regarded him: it had increased her repugnance to turning him out of anything he had expected to be his, or to snatching anything from him on the ground of an arbitrary claim. It had even made her dread, as a coming pain, the task of saying anything to him that was not a promise of the utmost comfort under this newly-disclosed trouble of his.

It was already near midnight, but with these thoughts succeeding and returning in her mind like scenes through which she was living, Esther had a more intense wakefulness than any she had known by day. All had been stillness hitherto, except the fitful wind outside. But her ears now caught a sound within – slight, but sudden. She moved near her door, and heard the sweep of something on the matting outside. It came closer, and paused. Then it began again, and seemed to sweep away from her. Then it approached, and paused as it had done before. Esther listened, wondering. The same thing happened again and again, till she could bear it no longer. She opened her door, and in the dim light of the corridor, where the glass above seemed to make a glimmering sky, she saw Mrs Transome's tall figure pacing slowly, with her cheek upon her hand.[25]

The direct biographical connection with George Eliot is impossible, but the emotional connection, the whole rhythm of the writing, is one of complete inwardness in terms of mood, spirit, emotion, temper, dilemma. The sentence which begins 'A supreme love . . .' is instinct with personal identification. Deep feelings of self-decision are involved, and the fictional situation is perhaps drawn from one in real life. And once that reality has been captured it permeates the rest of the passage. By entering Esther's consciousness in reaction and vibrant identification with her own at some past time, George Eliot has succeeded in strongly dramatizing Harold Transome within that consciousness, and Esther's indecision is made convincing and immediate. We are in a country house in the Midlands at a particular crisis of historical and individual time: by the end of the passage, great as Esther's own needs are, she has been penetrated by another need greater than hers, that of Mrs Transome. The passage is typical of George Eliot, though elevated and many-sided even by her standards: it traces the movement in the individual from self-concerned thought to the beginnings of deep awareness outside self.

If George Eliot can encompass in Esther much of her own feeling, how much more remarkable is it that in Mrs Transome she can achieve the same depth of sympathetic identification, the same evidence of personal suffering laid bare but fictionally focused. Mrs Transome is a guilty woman: her son Harold was the result of her affair with the lawyer Jermyn, who has now revealed to Harold that he is his father. How will Harold respond to the mother who had disgraced him? Straight on from the identification with Esther comes this:

For two hours Mrs Transome's mind hung on what was hardly a hope – hardly more than the listening for a bare possibility. She began to create the sounds that her anguish craved to hear – began to imagine a footfall, and a hand upon the door. Then, checked by continual disappointment, she tried to rouse a truer consciousness by rising from her seat and walking to her window, where she saw streaks of light moving and disappearing on the grass, and heard the sound of bolts and closing doors. She hurried away and threw herself into her seat again, and buried her head in the deafening down of the cushions. There was no sound of comfort for her.

Then her heart cried out within her against the cruelty of this son. When he turned from her in the first moment, he had not had time to feel anything but the blow that had fallen on himself. But afterwards – was it possible that she should not be touched with a son's pity – was it possible that he should not have been visited by some thought of the long years through which she had suffered? The memory of those years came back to her now with a protest against the cruelty that had all fallen on *her*. She started up with a new restlessness from this spirit of resistance. She was not penitent. She had borne too hard a punishment. Always the edge of calamity had fallen on *her*. Who had felt for her? She was desolate. God had no pity, else her son would not have been so hard. What dreary future was there after this dreary past? She, too, looked out into the dim light; but the black boundary of trees and the long line of the river seemed only part of the loneliness and monotony of her life.

Suddenly she saw a light on the stone balustrades of the balcony that projected in front of Esther's window, and the flash of a moving candle falling on a shrub below. Esther was still awake and up. What had Harold told her – what had passed between them? Harold was fond of this young creature, who had been always sweet and reverential to her. There was mercy in her young heart; she might be a daughter who had no impulse to punish and to strike her whom fate had stricken. On the dim loneliness before her she seemed to see Esther's gentle look; it was possible still that the misery of this night might be broken by some comfort. The proud woman yearned for the caressing pity that must dwell in that young bosom. She opened her door gently, but when she had reached Esther's she hesitated. She had never yet in her life asked for compassion – had never thrown herself in faith on an unproffered love. And she might have gone on pacing the corridor like an uneasy spirit without a goal, if Esther's thought, leaping towards her, had not saved her from the need to ask admission.

Mrs Transome was walking towards the door when it opened. As Esther saw that image of restless misery, it blent itself by a rapid flash with all that Harold had said in the evening. She divined that the son's new trouble must be one with the mother's long sadness. But there was no waiting. In an instant Mrs Transome felt Esther's arm round her neck, and a voice saying softly,

"O why didn't you call me before?"

They turned hand in hand into the room, and sat down together on a sofa at the foot of the bed. The disordered grey hair – the haggard face – the reddened eyelids under which the tears seemed to be coming again with pain, pierced Esther to the heart. A passionate desire to soothe this suffering woman came over her. She clung round her again, and kissed her poor quivering lips and eyelids, and laid her young cheek against the pale and haggard one. Words could not be quick or strong enough to utter her yearning. As Mrs Transome felt that soft clinging, she said,

"God has some pity on me."[26]

The intensity of the second paragraph is almost unbearable. We are aware that the outside loneliness – "the black boundary of trees and the long line of the river" – complements the inner isolation of the character. George Eliot is here creating – or re-creating – the effects of desolation when *we* are rejected by someone whom we love.

Son rejects mother in this novel, brother rejects sister in the earlier novel – *The Mill* – and in life. But the next phase is remarkable in its family emphasis, and again we feel some kind of equivalent in George Eliot's own life. In an ironic twist of the platitude, Mrs Transome thinks she has lost a son – here she gains a daughter, albeit for a short period of time only. Esther's spontaneous love, her conscious adoption of the caring daughter's role, is finely realized. And it is not far-fetched to say that the childless Marian Lewes (as she wished to be called) consciously adopted the role of mother to Lewes's virtually motherless children. She was a mother to his boys, and nursed Thornie devotedly until his death. Just as Mrs Transome is desperate for her son's love, so George Eliot wanted family acceptance. When she married Cross it was one of her greatest delights to know that she was treated as a sister by his sisters. Her family was late in coming, but the need to feel and to receive family affection is seen in her letters to Cross's sister Eleanor.[27] Esther's giving to Mrs Transome has its equivalence in Marian Lewes's giving in surrogate motherhood.

In the fiction set in her country and urban past, and in recognizable if distanced places which evoke the associations of that past, George Eliot places some of her women characters (and of course the men) in particular situations of adversity. These sometimes show emotional and sympathetic connections with her past and her present. One reason for placing them in the Midland setting is, I suggest, to give herself a strong sense of empathy with them in their experiences. Another reason may be found in the weighted resonances of the line already quoted from "Brother and Sister", where she refers to her childhood as "My present Past, my root of piety." The pulses of early experiences beat in her blood: she could imagine, adapt, create in strong individuality the various characters of her novels. But she had to give them the additional intensity and authenticity of a spirit of place – her own known place – in order to achieve full emotional identity.

During the course of the works mentioned so far we come to know the leading characters – particularly the women – very well. But George Eliot, going back to Coventry in her mind and peopling it with her fictional characters, can also create another kind of selfhood – the character who is suddenly minted, takes on immediate life, is encapsulated by commentary and then comes to full identity – informed with her author's sympathy at one and the same time. Such a one is Harriet Bulstrode in *Middlemarch*. She learns from her brother that her husband is publicly disgraced, his guilty past exposed, his present guilt established at least in the minds of his provincial detractors:

She locked herself in her room. She needed time to get used to her maimed consciousness, her poor lopped life, before she could walk steadily to the place allotted her. A new searching light had fallen on her husband's character, and she could not judge him leniently: the twenty years in which she had believed in him and venerated him by virtue of his concealments came back with particulars that made them seem an odious deceit. He had married her with that bad past life hidden behind him and she had no faith left to protest his innocence of the worst that was imputed to him. Her honest ostentatious nature made the sharing of a merited dishonour as bitter as it could be to any mortal.

But this imperfectly-taught woman, whose phrases and habits were an odd patchwork, had a loyal spirit within her. The man whose prosperity she had shared through nearly half a life, and who had unvaryingly cherished her – now that punishment had befallen him it was not possible to her in any sense to forsake him. There is a forsaking which still sits at the same board and lies on the same couch with the forsaken soul, withering it the more by unloving proximity. She knew when she locked her door, that she should unlock it ready to go down to her unhappy husband

and espouse his sorrow, and say of his guilt, I will mourn and not reproach. But she needed time to gather up her strength; she needed to sob out her farewell to all the gladness and pride of her life. When she had resolved to go down, she prepared herself by some little acts which might seem mere folly to a hard onlooker; they were her way of expressing to all spectators visible or invisible that she had begun a new life in which she embraced humiliation. She took off all her ornaments and put on a plain black gown, and instead of wearing her much-adorned cap and large bows of hair, she brushed her hair down and put on a plain bonnet-cap, which made her look suddenly like an early Methodist.

Bulstrode, who knew that his wife had been out and had come in saying that she was not well, had spent the time in an agitation equal to hers. He had looked forward to her learning the truth from others, and had acquiesced in that probability, as something easier to him than any confession. But now that he imagined the moment of her knowledge come, he awaited the result in anguish. His daughters had been obliged to consent to leave him, and though he had allowed some food to be brought to him, he had not touched it. He felt himself perishing slowly in unpitied misery. Perhaps he should never see his wife's face with affection in it again. And if he turned to God there seemed to be no answer but the pressure of retribution.

It was eight o'clock in the evening before the door opened and his wife entered. He dared not look up at her. He sat with his eyes bent down, and as she went towards him she thought he looked smaller – he seemed so withered and shrunken. A movement of new compassion and old tenderness went through her like a great wave, and putting one hand on his which rested on the arm of the chair, and the other on his shoulder, she said, solemnly but kindly –

"Look up, Nicholas."

He raised his eyes with a little start and looked at her half amazed for a moment: her pale face, her changed, mourning dress, the trembling about her mouth, all said, "I know;" and her hands and eyes rested gently on him. He burst out crying and they cried together, she sitting at his side. They could not yet speak to each other of the shame which she was bearing with him, or of the acts which had brought it down on them. His confession was silent, and her promise of faithfulness was silent. Open-minded as she was, she nevertheless shrank from the words which would have expressed their mutual consciousness, as she would have shrunk from flakes of fire. She could not say, "How much is only slander and false suspicion?" and he did not say, "I am innocent."[28]

Certain words are central to the authorial intimacy, with "locked" in the first sentence having a striking association – Harriet is already locked in the prison of her husband's past and the prison of local condemnation in the present. The use of "espouse" is superb, since in a sense Harriet is marrying again – making her vows again – to this disgraced husband. Yet in that same sentence "mourn" reflects her sadness, grief at the loss of what she considered was their past pure marriage. How much of her old lost religion Marian Lewes is putting into Harriet is open to question: but what she is doing, with one empathic imaginative leap, is projecting the power of the consciousness and, equally, the power of silence in crisis. Only three words are spoken: any more would diminish the experience. And at the same time as she has injected the personal she has shown the suffering, the loyalty, the symbolic gesture of the changed life, the "movement of new compassion" and the sitting together as a universality; it is the type and trial of her crises – George Eliot's – and our own. At the back of her characters is the consensus of provincial condemnation, for by placing them in the setting that she knew so well George Eliot knows that the judgment of them will take its own unvarying course. There is a chapter in Book Seventh of *The Mill* called "St Ogg's Passes Judgment" in which Maggie stands condemned in all her innocence for what she is believed to have done. In chapter 74 of *Middlemarch*, from which the previous extract is taken, we find the following:

In Middlemarch a wife could not long remain ignorant that the town held a bad opinion of her husband. No feminine intimate might carry her friendship so far as to make a plain statement to the wife of the unpleasant fact known or believed about her husband; but when a woman with her thoughts much at leisure got them suddenly employed on something grievously disadvantageous to her neighbours, various moral impulses were called into play which tended to stimulate utterance. Candour was one. To be candid, in Middlemarch phraseology, meant, to use an early opportunity of letting your friends know that you did not take a cheerful view of their capacity, their conduct, or their position; and a robust candour never waited to be asked for its opinion. Then, again, there was the love of truth – a wide phrase, but meaning in this relation a lively objection to seeing a wife look happier than her husband's character warranted, or manifest too much satisfaction in her lot: the poor thing should have some hint given her that if she knew the truth she would have less complacency in her bonnet, and in light dishes for a supper-party. Stronger than all, there was the regard for a friend's moral improvement, sometimes called her soul, which was likely to be benefited by remarks tending to gloom, uttered with the accompaniment of pensive staring at the furniture and a manner implying that the speaker would not tell what was on her mind, from regard to the feelings of her hearer. On the whole, one might say that an ardent charity was at work setting the virtuous mind to make a neighbour unhappy for her good.

There were hardly any wives in Middlemarch whose matrimonial misfortunes would in different ways be likely to call forth more of this moral activity than Rosamond and her aunt Bulstrode.[29]

The delicious irony of this, with the author's voice in commentary on the provincial life she knew so well, is quite another use of self to those we have so far seen in the inwardness of character. It is a very deliberately employed perspective, an outward look back at the past which provides an ironic counterpoise to Harriet Bulstrode's present. Again, certain words are crucial to a full appreciation of the irony: words like "friendship", "plain statement", "moral impulses", "candour", "love of truth" to name a few, are themselves seen in contradistinction to the truth of the consciousness through which George Eliot reveals Harriet's suffering. We are aware here too of the universality referred to earlier, and also of a wise knowledge of human nature and motive which transcends the irony which is present. The linking of Harriet with Rosamond shows that once the provincial net closes there is no escape: noble motives in a confined area where everyone knows everyone else, or where everyone is pleased to know *about* everyone else, means that difference in quality of character is irrelevant. Both Rosamond and Harriet will be brought down: the moral stains of rumour mingled with fact ensure that they will leave Middlemarch. They do. That is the way of the provincial world, and perhaps why Marian Lewes never returned to it in person.

Dorothea is also caught up in the network of public opinions as well as the personal crisis of her love for Ladislaw, the constricting effect of her husband's will and her sudden recognition that – as she thinks – Ladislaw loves Rosamond. In an action which transcends provincial gossip she goes to Rosamond to explain the behaviour of Lydgate to his egoistic and complaining wife. Rosamond is conscious that Dorothea had seen her with Ladislaw on the previous day. Again, I suggest, we are aware throughout of the importance of place, but we are aware too of the author's selfhood, initially with Dorothea, then with her being taken over by both characters as the interaction deepens:

It was a newer crisis in Rosamond's experience than even Dorothea could imagine: she was under the first great shock that had shattered her dream-world in which she had been easily confident of herself and critical of others; and this strange unexpected manifestation of feeling in a woman whom she had approached with a shrinking aversion and dread, as one who must necessarily have a jealous hatred towards her, made her soul totter all the more with a sense that she had been walking in an unknown world which had just broken in upon her.

When Rosamond's convulsed throat was subsiding into calm, and she withdrew the handkerchief with which she had been hiding her face, her eyes met Dorothea's as helplessly as if they had been blue flowers. What was the use of thinking about behaviour after this crying? And Dorothea looked almost as childish, with the neglected trace of a silent tear. Pride was broken down between these two.

"We were talking about your husband," Dorothea said, with some timidity. "I thought his looks were sadly changed with suffering the other day. I had not seen him for many weeks before. He said he had been feeling very lonely in his trial; but I think he would have borne it all better if he had been able to be quite open with you."

"Tertius is so angry and impatient if I say anything," said Rosamond, imagining that he had been complaining of her to Dorothea. "He ought not to wonder that I object to speak to him on painful subjects."

"It was himself he blamed for not speaking," said Dorothea. "What he said of you was, that he could not be happy in doing anything which made you unhappy – that his marriage was of course a bond which must affect his choice about everything; and for that reason he refused my proposal that he should keep his position at the Hospital, because that would bind him to stay in Middlemarch, and he would not undertake to do anything which would be painful to you. He could say that to me, because he knows that I had much trial in my marriage, from my husband's illness, which hindered his plans and saddened him; and he knows that I have felt how hard it is to walk always in fear of hurting another who is tied to us."

Dorothea waited a little; she had discerned a faint pleasure stealing over Rosamond's face. But there was no answer, and she went on, with a gathering tremor, "Marriage is so unlike everything else. There is something even awful in the nearness it brings. Even if we loved some one else better than – than those we were married to, it would be no use" – poor Dorothea, in her palpitating anxiety, could only seize her language brokenly – "I mean, marriage drinks up all our power of giving or getting any blessedness in that sort of love. I know it may be very dear – but it murders our marriage – and then the marriage stays with us like a murder – and everything else is gone. And then our husband – if he loved and trusted us, and we have not helped him, but made a curse in his life . . ."

Her voice had sunk very low: there was a dread upon her of presuming too far, and of speaking as if she herself were perfection addressing error. She was too much preoccupied with her own anxiety, to be aware that Rosamond was trembling too; and filled with the need to express pitying fellowship rather than rebuke, she put her hands on Rosamond's, and said with more agitated rapidity, – "I know, I know that the feeling may be very dear – it has taken hold of us unawares – it is so hard, it may seem like death to part with it – and we are weak – I am weak –"

The waves of her own sorrow, from out of which she was struggling to save another, rushed over Dorothea with conquering force. She stopped in speechless agitation, not crying, but feeling as if she were being inwardly grappled. Her face had become of a deathlier paleness, her lips trembled, and she pressed her hands helplessly on the hands that lay under them.

Rosamond, taken hold of by an emotion stronger than her own – hurried along in a new movement which gave all things some new, awful, undefined aspect – could find no words, but involuntarily she put her lips to Dorothea's forehead which was very near her, and then for a minute the two women clasped each other as if they had been in a shipwreck.

"You are thinking what is not true," said Rosamond, in an eager half-whisper, while she was still feeling Dorothea's arms round her – urged by a mysterious necessity to free herself from something that oppressed her as if it were blood-guiltiness.

They moved apart, looking at each other.

"When you came in yesterday – it was not as you thought," said Rosamond in the same tone.

There was a movement of surprised attention in Dorothea. She expected a vindication of Rosamond herself.

"He was telling me how he loved another woman, that I might know he could never love me," said Rosamond, getting more and more hurried as she went on. "And now I think he hates me because – because you mistook him yesterday. He says it is through me that you will think ill of him – think that he is a false person. But it shall not be through me. He has never had any love for me – I know he has not – he has always thought slightly of me. He said yesterday that no other woman existed for him beside you. The blame of what happened is entirely mine. He said he could never explain to you – because of me. He said you would never think well of him again. But now I have told you, and he cannot reproach me any more."

Rosamond had delivered her soul under impulses which she had not known before.

She had begun her confession under the subduing influence of Dorothea's emotion; and as she went on she had gathered the sense that she was repelling Will's reproaches, which were still like a knife-wound within her.

The revulsion of feeling in Dorothea was too strong to be called joy. It was a tumult in which the terrible strain of the night and morning made a resistant pain: – she could only perceive that this would be joy when she had recovered her power of feeling it. Her immediate consciousness was one of immense sympathy without check; she cared for Rosamond without struggle now, and responded earnestly to her last words –

"No, he cannot reproach you any more."[30]

Dorothea's unselfish giving and her completely unrehearsed confession about marriage – with its application to her own past and even present suffering – is complemented by Rosamond's spontaneous, uncharacteristic generosity of response. These are the dominant emotional movements of the scene, enhanced by the expressively related imagery – "waves", "inwardly grappled", "shipwreck" – but although the impetus comes from Dorothea, Rosamond's own giving arises in part from the fact that she is pleased by what she has learned. This is that Lydgate will not commit himself to stay in Middlemarch: Rosamond, always intent on getting her own way and in any case wanting to leave her "trade" background and to set up elsewhere in an unprobed gentility, gives because she has been given to. Needless to say, both Rosamond and Dorothea leave Middlemarch. Lydgate dies at fifty, "leaving his wife and children provided for by a heavy insurance on his life. He had gained an excellent practice, alternating, according to the season, between London and a Continental bathing-place; having written a treatise on Gout . . ."[31] Dorothea marries Will, who was "at last returned to Parliament by a constituency who paid his expenses".[32] It is perhaps an ironic comment on George Eliot's use of past place that, in her final novel, the characters with whom she is most intimately concerned do what she herself did – leave the place behind them. The nostalgia of the early associations has gone, and this despite the fact that, as we have seen, she composed the "Brother and Sister" sequence as she began *Middlemarch*. Yet not completely. Much of the Finale is devoted to the lives of Fred and Mary Vincy and their children, living a happy and fulfilled existence in the place they hold dear. Fred publishes his " 'Cultivation of Green Crops and the Economy of Cattle-Feeding' which won him high congratulations at agricultural meetings." Mary meanwhile has written a book for her boys which she had "printed by Gripp & Co, Middlemarch".[33] The author's kindly irony has each work credited to the other writer by Middlemarch gossip. Fred and Mary are true to their past, and their roots, as their creator is true to hers.

# 2. Facts and Fictions: Family and Others

There are no straight portraits from life in George Eliot's work after *Scenes* (so she claimed), but there are interesting derivations. Lewes, writing to the persistently troublesome Charles Holte Bracebridge on her behalf, said "it is unequivocally false to say there is *a single portrait among the characters in Adam Bede*."[1] George Eliot herself is just as definite: "I could never have written *Adam Bede* if I had not learned something of my father's early experience: but no one who knew my father could call Adam a portrait of him – and the course of Adam's life is entirely different from my father's."[2]

On 30th September 1859 – eight months after the publication of *Adam Bede* – she wrote to Charles Bray (and she was still smarting from Bracebridge's identifications):

... there is one phrase which I am prompted to notice by my feeling towards my Father's memory. He speaks of my Father as a "farmer". Now my Father did not raise himself from being an artizan to be a farmer: he raised himself from being an artizan to be a man whose extensive knowledge in very varied practical departments made his services valued through several counties. He had large knowledge of building, of mines, of plantation, of various branches of valuation and measurement – of all that is essential to the management of large estates. He was held by those competent to judge as *unique* amongst land-agents for his manifold knowledge and experience, which enabled him to save the special fees usually paid by landowners for special opinions on the different questions incident to the proprietorship of land.[3]

Robert Evans's achievements are echoed in the novel of *Adam Bede*, where Adam's potential is seen early on. George Eliot's father was a man of great strength, considerable ability, and self-taught, thus corresponding to Adam in physical and mental outline. Adam gets his basic learning from Bartle Massey's night-school. There is a strong feeling throughout the novel that Adam is what we would now call upwardly mobile – he takes on the management of Arthur's estate and runs Burge's building business:

But Adam had no sooner caught his imagination leaping forward in this way – making arrangements for an uncertain future – than he checked himself. "A pretty

41

building I'm making, without either bricks or timber. I'm up i' the garret a'ready, and haven't so much as dug the foundation." Whenever Adam was strongly convinced of any proposition, it took the form of a principle in his mind: it was knowledge to be acted on, as much as the knowledge that damp will cause rust. Perhaps here lay the secret of the hardness he had accused himself of: he had too little fellow-feeling with the weakness that errs in spite of foreseen consequences. Without this fellow-feeling, how are we to get enough patience and charity towards our stumbling, falling companions in the long and changeful journey? And there is but one way in which a strong determined soul can learn it – by getting his heart-strings bound round the weak and erring, so that he must share not only the outward consequence of their error, but their inward suffering. That is a long and hard lesson, and Adam had at present only learned the alphabet of it in his father's sudden death, which, by annihilating in an instant all that had stimulated his indignation, had sent a sudden rush of thought and memory over what had claimed his pity and tenderness.

But it was Adam's strength, not its correlative hardness, that influenced his meditations this morning. He had long made up his mind that it would be wrong as well as foolish for him to marry a blooming young girl, so long as he had no other prospect than that of growing poverty with a growing family. And his savings had been so constantly drawn upon (besides the terrible sweep of paying for Seth's substitute in the militia), that he had not enough money beforehand to furnish even a small cottage, and keep something in reserve against a rainy day. He had good hope that he should be "firmer on his legs" by-and-by; but he could not be satisfied with a vague confidence in his arm and brain; he must have definite plans, and set about them at once. The partnership with Jonathan Burge was not to be thought of at present – there were things implicitly tacked to it that he could not accept; but Adam thought that he and Seth might carry on a little business for themselves in addition to their journeyman's work, by buying a small stock of superior wood and making articles of household furniture, for which Adam had no end of contrivances. Seth might gain more by working at separate jobs under Adam's direction than by his journeyman's work, and Adam, in his over-hours, could do all the "nice" work, that required peculiar skill. The money gained in this way, with the good wages he received as foreman, would soon enable them to get beforehand with the world, so sparingly as they would all live now. No sooner had this little plan shaped itself in his mind than he began to be busy with exact calculations about the wood to be bought, and the particular article of furniture that should be undertaken first – a kitchen cupboard of his own contrivance, with such an ingenious arrangement of sliding-doors and bolts, such convenient nooks . . .[4]

Admittedly, Adam is seen as a young man, but already the complexity of his character is clear in his growing self-awareness. He is only at the "alphabet" stage – the night-school echo is sufficiently obvious – but this carries the implication that he is learning all the time. With that learning he recognizes his intolerance of those morally weaker than himself, and ultimately this means he comes to genuine humility and acquires the capacity for forgiveness. One can't help feeling that the traits seen here in part at least derived from Robert Evans, and that his daughter experienced the severity of his moods during the three and a half years when she nursed him, and equally definite, much earlier, when she refused to go to church. But that aspect of her father's character which made the practicality of planning and work so dear to him is clearly brought out in Adam. He may not be much beyond the alphabet in the education of the feelings, but in ideas and details in his trade and beyond he is already a well-qualified man. The work-ethic, perhaps drawn from her father's example, is a constant in George Eliot's work. Ten years on from his death, here in *Adam Bede*, she is showing the warts as well as the smoothness of character. Twenty years on, distance from her father has lent a corresponding enchantment to the view. Here is Caleb Garth:

"Let them put the horse in the stable, and tell the surveyors they can come back for their traps," said Fred. "The ground is clear now."

"No, no," said Caleb, "here's a breakage. They'll have to give up for to-day, and it will be as well. Here, take the things before you on the horse, Tom. They'll see you coming, and they'll turn back."

"I'm glad I happened to be here at the right moment, Mr Garth," said Fred, as Tom rode away. "No knowing what might have happened if the cavalry had not come up in time."

"Ay, ay, it was lucky," said Caleb, speaking rather absently, and looking towards the spot where he had been at work at the moment of interruption. "But – deuce take it – this is what comes of men being fools – I'm hindered of my day's work. I can't get along without somebody to help me with the measuring-chain. However!" He was beginning to move towards the spot with a look of vexation, as if he had forgotten Fred's presence, but suddenly he turned round and said quickly, "What have you got to do to-day, young fellow?"

"Nothing, Mr Garth. I'll help you with pleasure – can I?" said Fred, with a sense that he should be courting Mary when he was helping her father.

"Well, you mustn't mind stooping and getting hot."

"I don't mind anything. Only I want to go first and have a round with that hulky fellow who turned to challenge me. It would be a good lesson for him. I shall not be five minutes."

"Nonsense!" said Caleb, with his most peremptory intonation. "I shall go and speak to the men myself. It's all ignorance. Somebody has been telling them lies. The poor fools don't know any better."

"I shall go with you, then," said Fred.

"No, no; stay where you are. I don't want your young blood. I can take care of myself."

Caleb was a powerful man and knew little of any fear except the fear of hurting others and the fear of having to speechify. But he felt it his duty at this moment to try and give a little harangue. There was a striking mixture in him – which came from his having always been a hard-working man himself – of rigorous notions about workmen and practical indulgence towards them. To do a good day's work and do it well, he held to be part of their welfare, as it was the chief part of his own happiness; but he had a strong sense of fellowship with them. When he advanced towards the labourers they had not gone to work again, but were standing in that form of rural grouping which consists in each turning a shoulder towards the other, at a distance of two or three yards. They looked rather sulkily at Caleb, who walked quickly with one hand in his pocket and the other thrust between the buttons of his waistcoat, and had his everyday mild air when he paused among them.

"Why, my lads, how's this?" he began, taking as usual to brief phrases, which seemed pregnant to himself, because he had many thoughts lying under them, like the abundant roots of a plant that just manages to peep above the water. "How came you to make such a mistake as this? Somebody has been telling you lies. You thought those men up there wanted to do mischief."

"Aw!" was the answer, dropped at intervals by each according to his degree of unreadiness.

"Nonsense! No such thing! They're looking out to see which way the railroad is to take. Now, my lads, you can't hinder the railroad: it will be made whether you like it or not. And if you go fighting against it, you'll get yourselves into trouble. The law gives those men leave to come on the land here. The owner has nothing to say against it, and if you meddle with them you'll have to do with the constable and Justice Blakesley, and with the handcuffs and Middlemarch jail. And you might be in for it now, if anybody informed against you."

Caleb paused here, and perhaps the greatest orator could not have chosen either his pause or his images better for the occasion.[5]

At the back of this incident is the local fear of the coming of the railways (Coventry was linked by direct line to London in 1838, a few years after the events described in *Middlemarch*, which run from 1829–32) and Caleb and Fred have just interrupted a confrontation between local labourers with pitchforks and the railway agents. Caleb in fact is there to value an outlying piece of land which belongs to Lowick farm, owned by Dorothea, in order to get the best possible price from the railway companies for it. Note the directness of the language, which reflects the straightness of the man, the natural imagery expressive of natural and uncalculated behaviour ("like the abundant roots of a plant . . ."), the interaction with Fred, who in helping her father is, as he thinks, closer to Mary his daughter, whom he loves; and consider the humanitarian and work-ethic combination which makes up the character and practical actions of Caleb Garth. Notice too the verisimilitude of the background: we are in a Midland field at a time of local crisis, we are seeing in ordinary and inarticulate men the fear of change – yet change is imminent – and, perhaps most important of all, this is a woman describing an all-male scene in a thoroughly convincing way. Just as she could step inside the Rainbow Inn in imagination in *Silas Marner*, recording that slow bovine humour and the temperature of rustic interaction, so here she can walk into a field with Caleb. The memory of her father in part informs the character she has created, but it is a memory which is informed with social awareness too, real speech (and non-speech), visual quality, the provincial actuality registered in the threats – a hard word to use of Caleb – which represent the hard fact of the law. An idealized Robert Evans may lend some of the outline to Caleb Garth: the fictional filling in and the realistic context demonstrate yet again George Eliot's artistic use of her past.

If the memories of her father gave the impetus for inspiration, there is little doubt that her aunts provided her with a rich store of association on which to draw. Marian was one of three children of her father's second marriage: his first wife had died in 1809, and in 1813 he married Christiana Pearson, youngest daughter of Isaac Pearson, eminently respectable yeoman, church-warden too, whose home was at Old Castle Farm, Astley. It is Christiana's three sisters who have been transformed and immortalized as the Dodson aunts in *The Mill*. Mary (Aunt Glegg) was the second wife of John Evarard of Attleborough; Ann (Aunt Deane) married George Garner of Astley, and Elizabeth (Aunt Pullet) married Richard Johnston of Marston Jabbett. Haight rightly stresses that "While the Pearson aunts are easily recognized in the Dodsons, there was nothing of Mr Tulliver in Robert Evans: he never failed at anything, never found the world too much for him."[6] The quality of the Dodson immortality may be seen in the following extract, with its superb sense of family interaction, conscious and unconscious humour, sound and sense authenticity of dialogue, and the tensions inherent in this kind of gathering:

"Why, you see, I've got a plan i' my head about Tom," said Mr Tulliver, pausing after that statement and lifting up his glass.

"Well, if I may be allowed to speak, and it's seldom as I am," said Mrs Glegg, with a tone of bitter meaning, "I should like to know what good is to come to the boy, by bringin' him up above his fortin."

"Why," said Mr Tulliver, not looking at Mrs Glegg, but at the male part of his audience, "you see, I've made up my mind not to bring Tom up to my own business. I've had my thoughts about it all along, and I made up my mind by what I saw with Garnett and *his* son. I mean to put him to some business, as he can go into without capital, and I want to give him an eddication as he'll be even wi' the lawyers and folks, and put me up to a notion now an' then."

Mrs Glegg emitted a long sort of guttural sound with closed lips, that smiled in mingled pity and scorn.

"It 'ud be a fine deal better for some people," she said, after that introductory note, "if they'd let the lawyers alone."

"Is he at the head of a grammar school, then, this clergyman – such as that at Market Bewley?" said Mr Deane.

"No – nothing o' that," said Mr Tulliver. "He won't take more than two or three pupils – and so he'll have the more time to attend to 'em, you know."

"Ah, and get his eddication done the sooner: they can't learn much at a time when there's so many of 'em," said uncle Pullet, feeling that he was getting quite an insight into this difficult matter.

"But he'll want the more pay, I doubt," said Mr Glegg.

"Ay, ay, a cool hundred a-year – that's all," said Mr Tulliver, with some pride at his own spirited course. "But then, you know, it's an investment; Tom's eddication 'ull be so much capital to him."

"Ay, there's something in that," said Mr Glegg. "Well, well, neighbour Tulliver, you may be right, you may be right:

> 'When land is gone and money's spent,
> Then learning is most excellent.'

I remember seeing those two lines wrote on a window at Buxton. But us that have got no learning had better keep our money, eh, neighbour Pullet?" Mr Glegg rubbed his knees and looked very pleasant.

"Mr Glegg, I wonder *at* you," said his wife. "It's very unbecoming in a man o' your age and belongings."

"What's unbecoming, Mrs G.?" said Mr Glegg, winking pleasantly at the company. "My new blue coat as I've got on?"

"I pity your weakness, Mr Glegg. I say it's unbecoming to be making a joke when you see your own kin going headlongs to ruin."

"If you mean me by that," said Mr Tulliver, considerably nettled, "you needn't trouble yourself to fret about me. I can manage my own affairs without troubling other folks."

"Bless me," said Mr Deane, judiciously introducing a new idea, "why, now I come to think of it, somebody said Wakem was going to send *his* son – the deformed lad – to a clergyman, didn't they, Susan?" (appealing to his wife).

"I can give no account of it, I'm sure," said Mrs Deane, closing her lips very tightly again. Mrs Deane was not a woman to take part in a scene where missiles were flying.

"Well," said Mr Tulliver, speaking all the more cheerfully, that Mrs Glegg might see he didn't mind her, "if Wakem thinks o' sending his son to a clergyman, depend on it I shall make no mistake i' sending Tom to one. Wakem's as big a scoundrel as Old Harry ever made, but he knows the length of every man's foot he's got to deal with. Ay, ay, tell me who's Wakem's butcher, and I'll tell you where to get your meat."

"But lawyer Wakem's son's got a hump-back," said Mrs Pullet, who felt as if the whole business had a funereal aspect; "it's more nat'ral to send *him* to a clergyman."

"Yes," said Mr Glegg, interpreting Mrs Pullet's observation with erroneous plausibility, "you must consider that, neighbour Tulliver; Wakem's son isn't likely to follow any business. Wakem 'ull make a gentleman of him, poor fellow."

"Mr Glegg," said Mrs G., in a tone which implied that her indignation would fizz and ooze a little, though she was determined to keep it corked up, "you'd far better hold your tongue. Mr Tulliver doesn't want to know your opinion nor mine neither. There's folks in the world as know better than everybody else."

"Why, I should think that's you, if we're to trust your own tale," said Mr Tulliver, beginning to boil up again.

"O, *I* say nothing," said Mrs Glegg, sarcastically. "My advice has never been asked, and I don't give it."

"It'll be the first time, then," said Mr Tulliver. "It's the only thing you're over-ready at giving."

"I've been over-ready at lending, then, if I haven't been over-ready at giving," said

Mrs Glegg. "There's folks I've lent money to, as perhaps I shall repent o'lending money to kin."

"Come, come, come," said Mr Glegg, soothingly. But Mr Tulliver was not to be hindered of his retort.

"You've got a bond for it, I reckon," he said; "and you've had your five per cent, kin or no kin."

"Sister," said Mrs Tulliver, pleadingly, "drink your wine and let me give you some almonds and raisins."

"Bessy, I'm sorry for you," said Mrs Glegg, very much with the feeling of a cur that seizes the opportunity of diverting his bark towards the man who carries no stick. "It's poor work, talking o'almonds and raisins."

"Lors, sister Glegg, don't be so quarrelsome," said Mrs Pullet, beginning to cry a little. "You may be struck with a fit, getting so red in the face after dinner, and we are but just out o' mourning, all of us – and all wi' gowns craped alike and just put by – it's very bad among sisters."

"I should think it *is* bad," said Mrs Glegg. "Things are come to a fine pass when one sister invites the other to her house o' purpose to quarrel with her and abuse her."

"Softly, softly, Jane – be reasonable – be reasonable," said Mr Glegg.

But while he was speaking, Mr Tulliver, who had by no means said enough to satisfy his anger, burst out again.

"Who wants to quarrel with you?" he said. "It's you as can't let people alone, but must be gnawing at 'em for ever. *I* should never want to quarrel with any woman, if she kept her place."

"My place, indeed!" said Mrs Glegg, getting rather more shrill. "There's your betters, Mr Tulliver, as are dead and in their grave, treated me with a different sort o' respect to what you do – *though* I've got a husband as'll sit by and see me abused by them as 'ud never ha' had the chance if there hadn't been them in our family as married worse than they might ha' done."

"If you talk o' that," said Mr Tulliver, "my family's as good as yours – and better, for it hasn't got a damned ill-tempered woman in it."

"Well!" said Mrs Glegg, rising from her chair, "I don't know whether you think it's a fine thing to sit by and hear me swore at, Mr Glegg; but I'm not going to stay a minute longer in this house. You can stay behind, and come home with the gig – and I'll walk home."

"Dear heart, dear heart!" said Mr Glegg in a melancholy tone, as he followed his wife out of the room.[7]

Mr Tulliver is assuredly not based on Robert Evans, though the latter, like Mr Tulliver, was thought to have married somewhat above himself when he married a Pearson, and the "my family's as good as yours" has the genuine ring of an observed family quarrel. It is the observation within the set confines of the family council and the background they relate to which makes this so convincing. The hindsight and the imaginative commentary in creation are those of the mature observer, but it is also *felt* as much as *reproduced*. It is perhaps hard to believe that the models – and their husbands – were as articulate or even as positively established as their fictional counterparts here. The whole interaction is a brilliant revivification of time and place past.

"My Aunt's Story", the familiar Lewes/Marian gloss on the idea for *Adam Bede*, springs from family in the person of Elizabeth Evans. George Eliot has dismissed physical derivation: Lewes, in the letter already quoted to Brace-bridge, says "for example, Mrs S. Evans did visit a poor girl in prison – but then, Mrs Evans is not Dinah, nor is that poor girl represented in Hetty."[8] Local tradition felt differently. The memorial tablet to Elizabeth Evans in Ebenezer Wesleyan Chapel, Wirksworth (the Snowfield of the novel), says that it was "ERECTED BY NUMEROUS FRIENDS / TO THE MEMORY OF / ELIZABETH EVANS, / KNOWN TO THE WORLD AS 'DINAH BEDE', / WHO DURING MANY YEARS PROCLAIMED ALIKE IN THE / OPEN-AIR, THE SANCTUARY, AND FROM HOUSE TO HOUSE, / THE LOVE OF CHRIST. . . ."[9] George Eliot said that "There is not a single portrait in the book, nor will there be in any future book of mine."[10] She admitted however that Dinah grew out of her memories of Elizabeth Evans. In her account there are two, as it seems to me, important emphases. The first is the lack of any physical derivations in the "portrait", for Elizabeth "was a very small, black-eyed woman, and (as I was told, for I never heard her preach) very vehement in her style of preaching." Later in the same note she tells how after Elizabeth had ceased to preach she became "much more gentle and subdued than she had been in the days of her active ministry" . . . "I was very fond of her, and enjoyed the few weeks of her stay with me greatly. She was loving and kind to me, and I could talk to her about my inward life, which was closely shut up from those usually round me."[11] These words have their application to the conception of Dinah, because in essence they capture something of the spirit of the fictional character, who is presented with a loving and intimate identification, so much so that she seems at times to be *too* good and *too* committed to make her renunciation of public preaching convincing. Yet George Eliot's words, written in her Journal on 30th November 1858 just two months *before* the publication of *Adam Bede*, convey emphases that are present in the development of the character of Dinah. Dinah too becomes "gentle and subdued" (and I think we might well choose these words to define her domestic mood) as she acknowledges that she loves Adam. The idea that "she could not rest without exhorting and remonstrating" is given a softer yet still an insistent emphasis in Dinah, who feels moved by her faith to return to Snowfield rather than stay at the Hall Farm, and whose "exhorting" is seen in her entering Hetty's bed-chamber from intuitive fear that she may be – or will be – in trouble. The major exhortation of course occurs in the prison scene where she converts Hetty.

But Dinah represents too the loving kindness that George Eliot obviously treasured so much over the years, and the "confession" here in the final sentence about her own closed "inward life" shows that the warmth of the recall influenced the conception of Dinah:

She held no book in her ungloved hands, but let them hang down lightly crossed before her, as she stood and turned her grey eyes on the people. There was no keenness in the eyes: they seemed rather to be shedding love than making observations. She stood with her left hand towards the descending sun, and leafy boughs screened her from its rays; but in this sober light the delicate colouring of her face seemed to gather a calm vividness, like flowers at evening. It was a small oval face, of a uniform transparent whiteness, with an egg-like line of cheek and chin, a full but firm mouth, a delicate nostril, and a low perpendicular brow, surmounted by a rising arch of parting between smooth locks of pale reddish hair. The hair was drawn straight back behind the ears, and covered, except for an inch or two, above the brow, by a net Quaker cap. The eyebrows, of the same colour as the hair, were perfectly horizontal and firmly pencilled; the eyelashes, though no darker, were long and abundant; nothing was left blurred or unfinished. It was one of those faces that make one think of white flowers with light touches of colour on their pure petals. The eyes had no peculiar beauty, beyond that of expression; they looked so simple, so candid, so gravely loving, that no accusing scowl, no light sneer could help melting away before their glance. Joshua Rann gave a long cough, as if he were clearing his throat in order to come to a new understanding with himself; Chad Cranage lifted up his leather skull-cap and scratched his head; and Wiry Ben wondered how Seth had the pluck to think of courting her.

"A sweet woman," the stranger said to himself, "but surely nature never meant her for a preacher."

Perhaps he was one of those who think that nature has theatrical properties, and, with the considerate view of facilitating art and psychology, "makes up" her characters, so that there may be no mistatke about them. But Dinah began to speak.

"Dear friends," she said, in a clear but not loud voice, "let us pray for a blessing."

She closed her eyes, and hanging her head down a little, continued in the same moderate tone, as if speaking to some one quite near her: –

"Saviour of sinners! when a poor woman, laden with sins, went out to the well to draw water, she found Thee sitting at the well. She knew Thee not; she had not sought Thee; her mind was dark; her life was unholy. But Thou didst speak to her, Thou didst teach her, Thou didst show her that her life lay open before Thee, and yet Thou wast ready to give her that blessing which she had never sought. Jesus, Thou art in the midst of us, and Thou knowest all men: if there is any here like that poor woman – if their minds are dark, their lives unholy – if they have come out not seeking Thee, not desiring to be taught; deal with them according to the free mercy which Thou didst show to her. Speak to them, Lord; open their ears to my message; bring their sins to their minds, and make them thirst for that salvation which Thou art ready to give."[12]

The description is clear, simple, direct, drawing on brief analogies with nature to emphasize both the purity of Dinah's character and her faith. The eyes "shedding love" and "so simple, so candid, so gravely loving" remind one of the *spirit* of George Eliot's description of her aunt, while the stranger's silent thought – "but surely nature never meant her for a preacher" – is a subtle index to Dinah's future development, that she must give herself to natural human love as distinct from her faith. The preaching on the green is given a specific time – the novel opens on 18th June 1799, and this is the evening of that day – and a specific place, the village of Hayslope, its church and the Donnithorne Arms (Ellastone in Staffordshire, its church and the Bromley Davenport Arms). The simplicity of Dinah's opening address reflects her sincerity. Women preachers were active in the beginnings of Methodism, though they were banned by the Wesleyan Methodists after 1803. Valentine Cunningham in his *Everywhere Spoken Against: Dissent in the Victorian Novel* (1975) indicates that in her preaching Dinah was observing the order laid down by Wesley, further evidence of George Eliot's scrupulous attention to truth. There is, however, a footnote to this scene, and it indicates the influence that Lewes had on George Eliot even when, as here, she was physically and spiritually on her home ground. In the same Journal entry quoted earlier she wrote: "Dinah's ultimate relation to Adam was suggested by George, when I had read to him the first part of the first volume: he was so delighted with the presentation of Dinah, and so convinced that the readers' interest would centre in her, that he wanted her to be the principal figure at the last. I accepted the idea at once, and from the end of the third chapter worked with it constantly in view."[13]

Other family identifications have been made – George Eliot's ill-starred sister Chrissey has been equated with Lucy Deane in *The Mill* and even with Celia in *Middlemarch* – but none seem to stand up to close scrutiny. The fact is that George Eliot looked back at family, friends, acquaintances or known local figures and, in the early works at least, subjected them to her transforming imagination. The first of the *Scenes*, 'The Sad Fortunes of the Reverend Amos Barton', is a good example of this transforming imagination at work. The suffering Milly Barton is superbly, pathetically drawn, the nature of her marriage to Amos and their attendant poverty traced with an immediacy of feeling and sympathetic identification which is, perhaps, occasionally under-mined by sentiment:

Mrs Barton was playfully undervaluing her skill in metamorphosing boots and shoes. She had at that moment on her feet a pair of slippers which had long ago lived through the prunella phase of their existence, and were now running a respectable career as black silk slippers, having been neatly covered with that material by Mrs Barton's own neat fingers. Wonderful fingers those! they were never empty; for if she went to spend a few hours with a friendly parishioner, out came her thimble and a piece of calico or muslin, which, before she left, had become a mysterious little garment with all sorts of hemmed ins and outs. She was even trying to persuade her husband to leave off tight pantaloons, because if he would wear the ordinary gun-cases, she knew she could make them so well that no one would suspect the sex of the tailor.

But by this time Mr Barton has finished his pipe, the candle begins to burn low, and Mrs Barton goes to see if Nanny has succeeded in lulling Walter to sleep. Nanny is that moment putting him in the little cot by his mother's bedside; the head, with its thin wavelets of brown hair, indents the little pillow; and a tiny, waxen, dimpled fist hides the rosy lips, for baby is given to the infantine peccadillo of thumb-sucking. So Nanny could now join in the short evening prayer, and all could go to bed.

Mrs Barton carried up-stairs the remainder of her heaps of stockings, and laid them on a table close to her bedside, where also she placed a warm shawl, removing her candle, before she put it out, to a tin socket fixed at the head of her bed. Her body was very weary, but her heart was not heavy, in spite of Mr Woods the butcher, and the transitory nature of shoe-leather; for her heart so overflowed with love, she felt sure she was near a fountain of love that would care for husband and babes better than she could foresee; so she was soon asleep. But about half-past five o'clock in the morning, if there were any angels watching round her bed – and angels might be glad of such an office – they saw Mrs Barton rise up quietly, careful not to disturb the slumbering Amos, who was snoring the snore of the just, light her candle, prop herself upright with the pillows, throw the warm shawl round her shoulders, and renew her attack on the heap of undarned stockings. She darned away until she heard Nanny stirring, and then drowsiness came with the dawn; the candle was put out, and she sank into a doze. But at nine o'clock she was at the breakfast-table, busy cutting bread-and-butter for five hungry mouths, while Nanny, baby on one arm, in rosy cheeks, fat neck and night-gown, brought in a jug of hot milk-and-water. Nearest her mother sits the nine-year-old Patty, the eldest child, whose sweet fair face is already rather grave sometimes, and who always wants to run up-stairs to save mamma's legs, which get so tired of an evening. Then there are four other blond heads – two boys and two girls, gradually decreasing in size down to Chubby, who is making a round O of her mouth to receive a bit of papa's "baton." Papa's attention was divided between petting Chubby, rebuking the noisy Fred, which he did with a somewhat excessive sharpness, and eating his own breakfast. He had not yet looked at Mamma, and did not know that her cheek was paler than usual. But Patty whispered, "Mamma, have you the headache?"

Happily, coal was cheap in the neighbourhood of Shepperton, and Mr Hackit would any time let his horses draw a load for "the parson" without charge; so there was a blazing fire in the sitting-room, and not without need, for the vicarage garden, as they looked out on it from the bow-window, was hard with black frost, and the sky had the white woolly look that portends snow.[14]

Milly's nature, her essential goodness, love, long-suffering but silent and uncomplaining care of her family, her early death foreshadowed and the economic realities that contribute to it: all these carry the author's compassionate commentary. There seems little doubt that George Eliot picked up the name from the Newdigate family at Arbury Hall, for whom her father worked, for in *The Cheverels of Cheverel Manor*, by Lady Newdigate-Newdegate (1898), Mrs Milly Barton is the real-life sister of Lady Newdigate, the second wife of Sir Roger Newdigate, the Cheverels in the second clerical scene, "Mr Gilfil's Love Story". But as factual basis for Milly George Eliot took Mrs Emma Gwyther, wife of the Rev. John Gwyther, curate of Chilvers Coton during Marian Evans's childhood, and the Amos of the story. They too had six children. Emma Gwyther died in 1836 at the age of thirty-four and is buried in the churchyard, her table tomb being damaged in an air raid in 1941. It was carefully restored. Mr Gwyther later became vicar of Fewston, Yorkshire, where he died in 1873. He wrote to Blackwood after he had identified himself as Amos (see p. 3) and George Eliot responded by excusing herself but underlining the distance from the original. She says that she was "under the impression that the clergyman whose long past trial suggested the groundwork of the story was no longer living, and that the incidents, not only through the licence and necessities of artistic writing, but in consequence of the writer's imperfect knowledge, must have been so varied from the actual facts, that anyone who discerned the core of truth must also recognize the large amount of arbitrary, imaginative addition."[15]

But in drawing on originals in this way she must have known that she was taking a calculated risk. For "Amos" she was going back some thirty odd years: for "Mr Gilfil" she went back even further, but again the location and many of the figures would be immediately recognizable. Mr Gilfil is the fictional name of the Rev. Bernard Gilpin Ebdell, vicar of Chilvers Coton who had baptized Mary Ann Evans a week after her birth in 1819 in Chilvers Coton Parish Church. In the story he marries Caterina Sarti, who had been left destitute in Milan by her father's death. She was brought up by Sir Christopher and Lady Cheverel (Sir Roger and Lady Newdigate of Arbury Hall). Caterina in her turn is transformed from Sally Shilton, the local girl who was trained to be a singer and who occupies so much of Lady Newdigate's time and attention as she brings her out in London, singing privately, but with the hope, it seems, of a career. Like Caterina, she suffers from ill-health and weakness. Lady Newdigate's note for Tuesday 6th March 1792 is typical: "I am sorry to say that Sally's numbness lasted all Sunday & yesterday & went off in ye night with an excruciating headach, which still continues tho' not so violent. She says she feels as if her Voice was quite gone, but I hope that is only fancy. . . . He [the doctor] says her nerves seem to be very delicate & that she has a Scorbutic irritability about her, that must be prevented fixing there by taking care to keep her in an even tranquil state of Mind."[16] It is tempting to think that Mary Ann knew all about this in view of her intimacy at Arbury Hall. Caterina is given Sally's subordinate position, and with love; and although the fictional differences are many, the similarities are many too. In fact, just as Sally came to dominate Lady Newdigate's society life, so Caterina comes to dominate the dramatic action of "Mr Gilfil". Here she is seen as protegée and dependant:

I think the first place in her childish heart was given to Sir Christopher, for little girls are apt to attach themselves to the finest-looking gentleman at hand, especially as he seldom has anything to do with discipline. Next to the Baronet came Dorcas, the merry rosy-cheeked damsel who was Mrs Sharp's lieutenant in the nursery, and thus played the part of the raisins in a dose of senna. It was a black day for Caterina when

Dorcas married the coachman, and went, with a great sense of elevation in the world, to preside over a "public" in the noisy town of Sloppeter. A little china box, bearing the motto "Though lost to sight, to memory dear," which Dorcas sent her as a remembrance, was among Caterina's treasures ten years after.

The one other exceptional talent, you already guess, was music. When the fact that Caterina had a remarkable ear for music, and a still more remarkable voice, attracted Lady Cheverel's notice, the discovery was very welcome both to her and Sir Christopher. Her musical education became at once an object of interest. Lady Cheverel devoted much time to it; and the rapidity of Tina's progress surpassing all hopes, an Italian singing-master was engaged, for several years, to spend some months together at Cheverel Manor. This unexpected gift made a great alteration in Caterina's position. After those first years in which little girls are petted like puppies and kittens, there comes a time when it seems less obvious what they can be good for, especially when, like Caterina, they give no particular promise of cleverness or beauty; and it is not surprising that in that uninteresting period there was no particular plan formed as to her future position. She could always help Mrs Sharp, supposing she were fit for nothing else, as she grew up; but now, this rare gift of song endeared her to Lady Cheverel, who loved music above all things, and it associated her at once with the pleasures of the drawing-room. Insensibly she came to be regarded as one of the family, and the servants began to understand that Miss Sarti was to be a lady after all.[17]

But Caterina is fated to suffer. She falls in love with Captain Wybrow, who brings the heiress he is destined to marry to Cheverel Manor (he is Sir Christopher's nephew) but continues to trifle with Tina. She is impassioned, angry, nervous, learns of his double treachery and determines to kill him. She takes a dagger, goes to meet him in the shrubbery, and finds him dead from a heart attack. She flees, overwhelmed with guilt, but, is eventually discovered by the man who loves her, Sir Christopher's chaplain, Maynard Gilfil. He later marries her but she is broken in spirit, in heart – and in nerves – until this:

At last – it was one of those bright days in the end of February, when the sun is shining with a promise of approaching spring. Maynard had been walking with her and Oswald round the garden to look at the snowdrops, and she was resting on the sofa after the walk. Ozzy, roaming about the room in quest of a forbidden pleasure, came to the harpsichord, and struck the handle of his whip on a deep bass note.

The vibration rushed through Caterina like an electric shock: it seemed as if at that instant a new soul were entering into her, and filling her with a deeper, more significant life. She looked round, rose from the sofa, and walked to the harpsichord. In a moment her fingers were wandering with their old sweet method among the keys, and her soul was floating in its true familiar element of delicious sound, as the water-plant that lies withered and shrunken on the ground expands into freedom and beauty when once more bathed in its native flood.

Maynard thanked God. An active power was reawakened, and must make a new epoch in Caterina's recovery.

Presently there were low liquid notes blending themselves with the harder tones of the instrument, and gradually the pure voices swelled into predominance. Little Ozzy stood in the middle of the room, with his mouth open and his legs very wide apart, struck with something like awe at this new power in "Tin-Tin," as he called her, whom he had been accustomed to think of as a playfellow not at all clever, and very much in need of his instruction on many subjects. A genie soaring with broad wings out of his milk-jug would not have been more astonishing.

Caterina was singing the very air from the *Orfeo* which we heard her singing so many months ago at the beginning of her sorrows. It was *Che faro*, Sir Christopher's favourite, and its notes seemed to carry on their wings all the tenderest memories of her life, when Cheverel Manor was still an untroubled home. The long happy days of childhood and girlhood recovered all their rightful predominance over the short interval of sin and sorrow.

She paused, and burst into tears – the first tears she had shed since she had been at Foxholm. Maynard could not help hurrying towards her, putting his arm round her, and leaning down to kiss her hair. She nestled to him, and put up her little mouth to be kissed.

The delicate-tendrilled plant must have something to cling to. The soul that was born anew to music was born anew to love.[18]

It does not last, for Caterina dies within the year. Fiction dramatizes and transforms: the real Sally Shilton indeed married Bernard Gilpin Ebdell, and lived on for twenty-two years, Ebdell himself remaining vicar until 1828. Captain Wybrow is thought to derive from Mr Charles Parker, presumptive heir of Sir Roger Newdigate, though this is tentative: Sally was eleven years old at the time of the story's action, so could hardly have been in love with him. But, as I have indicated, there seems to be a definite connection of talent and temperament between Sally and Caterina.

The third clerical scene has two startling originals and one heavily idealized one. "Janet's Repentance" is different in tone and temper from the previous scenes, and the marital viciousness of Lawyer Dempster against his suffering and unconvincingly alcoholic wife Janet certainly derives from the lawyer J. W. Buchanan of Nuneaton and his wife Nancy. But whatever the gossip – and George Eliot's early works lent themselves to identifications at once – the fictional temperature between husband and wife is brilliantly, even frighteningly sustained. The plot centres round the coming delivery of an evening lecture on a Sunday by the Reverend Edgar Tryan, fervently evangelical and new; individual in character, but his actions drawn from what George Eliot called "a real bit in the religious history of England that happened about eight and twenty years ago".[19] She also said that he was "not a portrait of any clergyman, living or dead".[20] Opposed to Tryan are Dempster and the Anglican Church supporters. The beginning of the story reveals the immediate, vitriolic personality of Dempster, his bloody-mindedness, prejudice, and bullying arrogance:

"No!" said lawyer Dempster, in a loud, rasping, oratorical tone, struggling against chronic huskiness, "as long as my Maker grants me power of voice and power of intellect, I will take every legal means to resist the introduction of demoralizing, methodistical doctrine into this parish; I will not supinely suffer an insult to be inflicted on our venerable pastor, who has given us sound instruction for half a century."

It was very warm everywhere that evening, but especially in the bar of the Red Lion at Milby, where Mr Dempster was seated mixing his third glass of brandy-and-water. He was a tall and rather massive man, and the front half of his large surface was so well dredged with snuff, that the cat, having inadvertently come near him, had been seized with a severe fit of sneezing – an accident which, being cruelly misunderstood, had caused her to be driven contumeliously from the bar. Mr Dempster habitually held his chin tucked in, and his head hanging forward, weighed down, perhaps, by a preponderant occiput and a bulging forehead, between which his closely-clipped coronal surface lay like a flat and new-mown table-land. The only other observable features were puffy cheeks and a protruding yet lipless mouth. Of his nose I can only say that it was snuffy, and as Mr Dempster was never caught in the act of looking at anything in particular, it would have been difficult to swear to the colour of his eyes.[21]

This "Mr" Dempster of the opening here soon becomes Dempster to us. Janet's pathetic attempts, and sometimes they are befuddled ones at that, fail to deflect him from the domestic brutality he regards as his right. He is a wife-beater, degraded, sadistic, heartless:

There was a large heavy knocker on the green door, and though Mr Dempster carried a latch-key, he sometimes chose to use the knocker. He chose to do so now. The thunder resounded through Orchard Street, and, after a single minute, there was a second clap louder than the first. Another minute, and still the door was not opened; whereupon Mr Dempster, muttering, took out his latch-key, and, with less difficulty than might have been expected, thrust it into the door. When he opened the door the passage was dark.

"Janet!" in the loudest rasping tone, was the next sound that rang through the house.

"Janet!" again – before a slow step was heard on the stairs, and a distant light began to flicker on the wall of the passage.

"Curse you! you creeping idiot! Come faster, can't you?"

Yet another few seconds, and the figure of a tall woman, holding aslant a heavy-plated drawing-room candlestick, appeared at the turning of the passage that led to the broader entrance.

See, she has on a light dress which sits loosely about her figure, but does not disguise its liberal, graceful outline. A heavy mass of straight jet-black hair has escaped from its fastening, and hangs over her shoulders. Her grandly-cut features, pale with the natural paleness of a brunette, have premature lines about them telling that the years have been lengthened by sorrow, and the delicately-curved nostril, which seems made to quiver with the proud consciousness of power and beauty, must have quivered to the heart-piercing griefs which have given that worn look to the corners of the mouth. Her wide open black eyes have a strangely fixed, sightless gaze, as she pauses at the turning, and stands silent before her husband.

"I'll teach you to keep me waiting in the dark, you pale staring fool!" advancing with his slow drunken step. "What, you've been drinking again, have you? I'll beat you into your senses."

He laid his hand with a firm grip on her shoulder, turned her round, and pushed her slowly before him along the passage and through the dining-room door which stood open on their left hand.

There was a portrait of Janet's mother, a grey-haired, dark-eyed old woman, in a neatly-fluted cap, hanging over the mantelpiece. Surely the aged eyes take on a look of anguish as they see Janet – not trembling, no! it would be better if she trembled – standing stupidly unmoved in her great beauty, while the heavy arm is lifted to strike her. The blow falls – another – and another. Surely the mother hears that cry – "O Robert! pity! pity!"[22]

The "Red Lion at Milby" is the Bull Hotel in Nuneaton (now the George Eliot Hotel), while Orchard Street is Church Street in the same town. The specific locations require an equally specific characterization, but the stress on Dempster's physical appearance in the first extract and on Janet's sad beauty in the second show George Eliot as yet young in experience. The "preponderant occiput" and the "coronal surface" are self-conscious, as if the provincial writer is displaying her knowledge for the benefit of a partly provincial audience: they make a poor contrast with the direct and emotive language of Dempster's opening remarks, which are as laced with clichés as he is with drink. The same self-consciousness is apparent not only in the very deliberate description of Janet but also in the sentimentalized focus on the picture of Janet's mother and the off-key invocation of her presence. Yet as the "scene" proceeds the quality of the realism deepens. Dempster dies later in *delirium tremens* and Janet, first turned out by him and befriended, indeed, saved, by the Reverend Edgar Tryan, returns to nurse her husband. As with the other scenes, the outlines of reality remain. Buchanan and his wife were married in Nuneaton Church in 1825. Their two daughters were baptized there (note that Janet is childless, a major psychological reason, perhaps, for her unhappy marriage). The family tomb is there (Buchanan died in 1846), and the mothers of Buchanan and his wife Nancy are also buried there. Both feature in "Janet's Repentance", Dempster's mother "Mamsey" being given a strikingly individualized character and a powerful influence on the marital situation.

Edgar Tryan, despite George Eliot's statement, at least derives if not in character then in outline from the Rev. J. E. Jones, the Evangelical curate of Stockingford Chapel of Ease. As Kathleen Adams puts it in her *George Eliot Country* (5th edition, 1988): "Although he was opposed by most of the townsfolk, the Rev. J. E. Jones obtained a licence from the Bishop to deliver lectures on Sunday evenings in Nuneaton Church. The story of the persecution of the Rev. Edgar Tryan by Lawyer Dempster and his friends is based to a certain extent on actual happenings in 1829, a year of much religious strife throughout the nation. Observant Mary Ann noticed Mr Jones's pallor at the confirmation service and other details which told of approaching illness. ..."[23] Tryan's courage, the support he received, and the anticipation in part of the end of the story, are brilliantly captured:

Mr Tryan showed no such symptoms of weakness on the critical Sunday. He unhesitatingly rejected the suggestion that he should be taken to church in Mr Landor's carriage – a proposition which that gentleman made as an amendment on the original plan, when the rumours of meditated insult became alarming. Mr Tryan declared he would have no precautions taken, but would simply trust in God and his good cause. Some of his more timid friends thought this conduct rather defiant than wise, and reflecting that a mob has great talents for impromptu, and that legal redress is imperfect satisfaction for having one's head broken with a brickbat, were beginning to question their consciences very closely as to whether it was not a duty they owed to their families to stay at home on Sunday evening. These timorous persons, however, were in a small minority, and the generality of Mr Tryan's friends and hearers rather exulted in an opportunity of braving insult for the sake of a preacher to whom they were attached on personal as well as doctrinal grounds. Miss Pratt spoke of Cranmer, Ridley, and Latimer, and observed that the present crisis afforded an occasion for emulating their heroism even in these degenerate times; while less highly instructed persons, whose memories were not well stored with precedents, simply expressed their determination, as Mr Jerome had done, to "stan' by" the preacher and his cause, believing it to be the "cause of God."

On Sunday evening, then, at a quarter past six, Mr Tryan, setting out from Mr Landor's with a party of his friends who had assembled there, was soon joined by two other groups from Mr Pratt's and Mr Dunn's; and stray persons on their way to church naturally falling into rank behind this leading file, by the time they reached the entrance of Orchard Street, Mr Tryan's friends formed a considerable procession, walking three or four abreast. It was in Orchard Street, and towards the church gates, that the chief crowd was collected; and at Mr Dempster's drawing-room window, on the upper floor, a more select assembly of Anti-Tryanites were gathered, to witness the entertaining spectacle of the Tryanites walking to church amidst the jeers and hootings of the crowd.

To prompt the popular wit with appropriate sobriquets, numerous copies of Mr Dempster's play-bill were posted on the walls, in suitably large and emphatic type. As it is possible that the most industrious collector of mural literature may not have been fortunate enough to possess himself of this production, which ought by all means to be preserved amongst the materials of our provincial religious history, I subjoin a faithful copy.

GRAND ENTERTAINMENT!!!
To be given at Milby on Sunday evening next, by the
FAMOUS COMEDIAN, TRY-IT-ON!
And his first-rate company, including not only an
UNPARALLELED CAST FOR COMEDY!

But a Large Collection of *reclaimed and converted Animals;*
Among the rest
*A Bear,* who used to *dance!*
*A Parrot,* once given to *swearing!!*
*A Polygamous Pig!!!*
and
A Monkey who used to *catch fleas on a Sunday!!!!*
Together with a
Pair of *regenerated* LINNETS!
With an entirely new song, and *plumage.*
MR TRY-IT-ON
Will first pass through the streets, in procession, with his unrivalled Company,
warranted to have their *eyes turned up higher,* and the *corners of their mouths
turned down lower,* than any other company of Mountebanks in this circuit!

AFTER WHICH
The Theatre will be opened, and the entertainment will
commence at HALF-PAST SIX,
When will be presented
A piece, never before performed on any stage, entitled,
THE WOLF IN SHEEP'S CLOTHING;
*or*
THE METHODIST IN A MASK.

| | | |
|---|---|---|
| Mr Boanerges Soft Sawder, | . . . | Mr TRY-IT-ON. |
| Old Ten-per-cent Godly, | . . . . | Mr GANDER. |
| Dr Feedemup, | . . . . . | Mr TONIC. |
| Mr Lime-Twig Lady-winner, | . . . | Mr TRY-IT-ON. |
| Miss Piety Bait-the-hook, | . . . | Miss TONIC. |
| Angelica, | . . . . . | Miss SERAPHINA TONIC. |

After which
A miscellaneous Musical Interlude, commencing with
The *Lamentations of Jerom-iah!*
In nasal recitative.
To be followed by
The favourite Cackling Quartette,
by
Two Hen-birds who are *no chickens!*
The well-known *counter*-tenor, Mr Done, and a *Gander,*
lineally descended from the *Goose* that laid golden eggs!

To conclude with a
GRAND CHORUS by the
*Entire Orchestra of converted Animals!!*
But owing to the unavoidable absence (from illness) of
the *Bull-dog, who has left off fighting,* Mr Tonic has kindly
undertaken, at a moment's notice, to supply the *"bark!"*
The whole to conclude with a

*Screaming Farce of*
## THE PULPIT SNATCHER

| | | |
|---|---|---|
| Mr Saintly Smooth-face, | . . . . . | Mr TRY-IT-ON! |
| Mr Worming Sneaker, | . . . . . | Mr TRY-IT-ON!! |
| Mr All-grace No-works, | . . . . . | Mr TRY-IT-ON!!! |
| Mr Elect-and-Chosen Apewell, | . . . . | Mr TRY-IT-ON!!!! |
| Mr Malevolent Prayerful, | . . . . . | Mr TRY-IT-ON!!!!! |
| Mr Foist-himself Everywhere, | . . . . | Mr TRY-IT-ON!!!!!! |
| Mr Flout-the-aged Upstart, | . . . . | Mr TRY-IT-ON!!!!!!! |

———

Admission Free. A *Collection* will be made at the Doors.
*Vivat Rex!*

   This satire, though it presents the keenest edge of Milby wit, does not strike you as lacerating, I imagine. But hatred is like fire – it makes even light rubbish deadly. And Mr Dempster's sarcasms were not merely visible on the walls; they were reflected in the derisive glances, and audible in the jeering voices of the crowd. Through this pelting shower of nicknames and bad puns, with an *ad libitum* accompaniment of groans, howls, hisses, and hee-haws, but of no heavier missiles, Mr Tryan walked pale and composed, giving his arm to old Mr Landor, whose step was feeble. On the other side of him was Mr Jerome, who still walked firmly, though his shoulders were slightly bowed.
   Outwardly Mr Tryan was composed, but inwardly he was suffering acutely from these tones of hatred and scorn. However strong his consciousness of right, he found it no stronger armour against such weapons as derisive glances and virulent words, than against stones and clubs: his conscience was in repose, but his sensibility was bruised.
   Once more only did the Evangelical curate pass up Orchard Street followed by a train of friends; once more only was there a crowd assembled to witness his entrance through the church gates. But that second time no voice was heard above a whisper, and the whispers were words of sorrow and blessing. That second time, Janet Dempster was not looking on in scorn and merriment; her eyes were worn with grief and watching, and she was following her beloved friend and pastor to the grave.[24]

   George Eliot is judged by her prose: here she is undertaking provincial parody. Her own humour is often, with the notable exceptions of the Dodson aunts, Mrs Poyser, and the Rainbow Inn sequence of *Silas Marner*, a little heavy-handed. So is this but, because it is, it is just right. In remembering her younger days and the omnipresence of the place – notice that Orchard Street, Dempster's home, is repeated three times – she recalled the local nature of the wit, the easy hits at people who would be recognized but would have no redress, the crudeness of analogy, the coarseness that appeals to the coarse mind, and mixed it with a Bunyanesque name-catalogue of her own devising. But this isn't all: there is the running irony that Janet, anxious to placate her vicious husband, wrote some of it: there is the carefully structured sequence

GRAHAM HANDLEY

(it constitutes one chapter of the story), beginning with Tryan courageous and alive and ending with the anticipation of great change for Janet and Tryan's death. Dempster's own death through the self-abuse of violence and alcohol – and the play-bills are verbal violence and drunken innuendo – is already embodied, so to speak, in his public crucifixion of Tryan. And beyond that there is George Eliot's own association with her fervent and bigoted past and the nature of the town she knew. Blackwood was rather shaken by the brutal nature of "Janet's Repentance", but George Eliot told him "The real town was more vicious than my Milby; the real Dempster was far more disgusting than mine; the real Janet alas! had a far sadder end than mine."[25] Fictional identity is more positive, more wide-flung, than factual identification. And in fact the Rev. John Edmund Jones, who was curate-in-charge of Stockingford Church from 1828–31, and who led the opposition to the Catholic Emancipation Bill in Nuneaton in 1829, died in December 1831.

It is tempting to make other cursory identifications: Charles S. Olcott in *George Eliot: Scenes and People in Her Novels* (1911) reproduces tables of *all* the characters in "Scenes of Clerical Life" and their originals. Does Casaubon in *Middlemarch* derive in some ways from Dr Brabant, with whom Marian conversed intimately but briefly in 1843 – his wife and her sister taking good care that she was sent back to Coventry some ten days or so after she had told Cara Bray "I am in a little heaven here, Dr Brabant being its archangel" . . .?[26] What is certain is that the Midland characters, and the ousiders who bulk so large in her fiction from the Countess Czerlaski onwards, are given a rich, convincing fullness of conception because their allotted context – social and physical place – is the major element in George Eliot's realism. Gordon Haight has referred to the fact that wherever she was, she was haunted by the sense of her physical past – "the slope of the land, the quality of the soil, the harvest"[27]. her imagination re-peopled what she had left.

It is in *Adam Bede*, I suggest, that the qualities of her realism are first seen in particular fullness as her imagination is released. Three characters of positive originality – or faint derivation – are seen against the locations as clearly, as faithfully, as the Dutch paintings which George Eliot admired and which provided her with some inspiration. Hetty in the dairy is given ironic and real focus:

It is of little use for me to tell you that Hetty's cheek was like a rose-petal, that dimples played about her pouting lips, that her large dark eyes hid a soft roguishness under their long lashes, and that her curly hair, though all pushed back under her round cap while she was at work, stole back in dark delicate rings on her forehead, and about her white shell-like ears; it is of little use for me to say how lovely was the contour of her pink-and-white neckerchief, tucked into her low plum-coloured stuff boddice, or how the linen butter-making apron, with its bib, seemed a thing to be imitated in silk by duchesses, since it fell in such charming lines, or how her brown stockings and thick-soled buckled shoes lost all that clumsiness which they must

60

certainly have had when empty of her foot and ankle; – of little use, unless you have seen a woman who affected you as Hetty affected her beholders, for otherwise, though you might conjure up the image of a lovely woman, she would not in the least resemble that distracting kitten-like maiden. I might mention all the divine charms of a bright spring day, but if you had never in your life utterly forgotten yourself in straining your eyes after the mounting lark, or in wandering through the still lanes when the fresh-opened blossoms fill them with a sacred silent beauty like that of fretted aisles, where would be the use of my descriptive catalogue? I could never make you know what I meant by a bright spring day. Hetty's was a spring-tide beauty; it was the beauty of young frisking things, round-limbed, gambolling, circumventing you by a false air of innocence – the innocence of a young star-browed calf, for example, that, being inclined for a promenade out of bounds, leads you a severe steeple-chase over hedge and ditch, and only comes to a stand in the middle of a bog.

And they are the prettiest attitudes and movements into which a pretty girl is thrown in making up butter – tossing movements that give a charming curve to the arm, and a sideward inclination of the round white neck; little patting and rolling movements with the palm of the hand, and nice adaptations and finishings which cannot at all be effected without a great play of the pouting mouth and the dark eyes. And then the butter itself seems to communicate a fresh charm – it is so pure, so sweet-scented; it is turned off the mould with such a beautiful firm surface, like marble in a pale yellow light! Moreover, Hetty was particularly clever at making up the butter; it was the one performance of hers that her aunt allowed to pass without severe criticism; so she handled it with all the grace that belongs to mastery.[28]

The duality of this description – the person and the place – establishes both the innocence and the dangers of it. The analogy with the calf, the "false air of innocence" applied to Hetty and the sensuous trap of the dairy where she is seen to full advantage, show subtle anticipations and sure atmospheric descriptions. All the more remarkable, and in complete contrast, is Hetty's journey, where the Derbyshire–Staffordshire spaces are given both a physical and a psychological currency, as in this extract:

Farther on there is a clump of trees on the low ground, and she is making her way towards it. No, it is not a clump of trees, but a dark shrouded pool, so full with the wintry rains that the under boughs of the elder-bushes lie low beneath the water. She sits down on the grassy bank, against the stooping stem of the great oak that hangs over the dark pool. She has thought of this pool often in the nights of the month that has just gone by, and now at last she is come to see it. She clasps her hands round her knees and leans forward, and looks earnestly at it, as if trying to guess what sort of bed it would make for her young round limbs.

No, she has not courage to jump into that cold watery bed, and if she had, they might find her – they might find out why she had drowned herself. There is but one thing left to her: she must go away, go where they can't find her.[29]

Hetty is in the Scantlands, a field on the outer edges of the Poyser farm, where she ponders whether to drown herself because she is pregnant. This first temptation is followed by a later greater one when her journey in despair shows her searching for a pool, finding it, collecting stones to weigh herself down, and then struggling on. The ironic gloss of the first "picture" has become a terrible reality. And George Eliot makes clear both here and elsewhere the attendant disgrace, the effect on those close to her, the changing of their lives as a result. The respectability of the Midland family like the Poysers is, so to speak, their life-blood.

Mrs Poyser is recognized as one of George Eliot's great creations. Here I give her in full interaction at a different kind of domestic crisis: Marian Evan's mother apparently suggested some of her traits, while the name Poyser belonged to a farmer's wife in Ellastone (Hayslope):

Mrs Poyser had had her eyes fixed on her husband with cold severity during his silence, but now she turned away her head with a toss, looked icily at the opposite roof of the cow-shed, and spearing her knitting together with the loose pin, held it firmly between her clasped hands.

"Say? Why, I say you may do as you like about giving up any o' your corn land afore your lease is up, which it won't be for a year come next Michaelmas, but I'll not consent to take more dairy work into my hands, either for love or money; and there's nayther love nor money here, as I can see, on'y other folks's love o' theirselves, and the money as is to go into other folks's pockets. I know there's them as is born t' own the land, and them as is born to sweat on't" – here Mrs Poyser paused to gasp a little – "and I know it's christened folks's duty to submit to their betters as fur as flesh and blood 'ull bear it; but I'll not make a martyr o' myself, and wear myself to skin and bone, and worret myself as if I was a churn wi' butter a-coming in't, for no landlord in England, not if he was King George himself."

"No, no, my dear Mrs Poyser, certainly not," said the Squire, still confident in his own powers of persuasion, "you must not overwork yourself; but don't you think your work will rather be lessened than increased in this way? There is so much milk required at the Abbey, that you will have little increase of cheese and butter making from the addition to your dairy; and I believe selling the milk is the most profitable way of disposing of dairy produce, is it not?"

"Ay, that's true," said Mr Poyser, unable to repress an opinion on a question of farming profits, and forgetting that it was not in this case a purely abstract question.

"I daresay," said Mrs Poyser bitterly, turning her head half-way towards her husband, and looking at the vacant arm-chair – "I daresay it's true for men as sit i' thi' chimney-corner and make believe as everything's cut wi'ins an' outs to fit int' everything else. If you could make a pudding wi' thinking o' the batter, it 'ud be easy getting dinner. How do I know whether the milk 'ull be wanted constant? What's to make me sure as the house won't be put o' board wage afore we're many months older, and then I may have to lie awake o' nights wi' twenty gallons o' milk on my mind – and Dingall 'ull take no more butter, let alone paying for it; and we must fat pigs till we're obliged to beg the butcher on our knees to buy 'em, and lose half of 'em wi' the measles. And there's the fetching and carrying, as 'ud be welly half a day's work for a man an' hoss – *that's* to be took out o' the profits, I reckon? But there's folks 'ud hold a sieve under the pump and expect to carry away the water."

"That difficulty – about the fetching and carrying – you will not have, Mrs Poyser," said the Squire, who thought that this entrance into particulars indicated a distant inclination to compromise on Mrs Poyser's part – "Bethell will do that regularly with the cart and pony."

"Oh, sir, begging your pardon, I've never been used t' having gentlefolk's servants coming about my back places, a-making love to both the gells at once, and keeping 'em with their hands on their hips listening to all manner o' gossip when they should be down on their knees a-scouring. If we're to go to ruin, it shanna be wi' having our back kitchen turned into a public."[30]

The squire has just proposed that the Poysers exchange their farm for another on the estate, and this is Mrs Poyser's reaction. It needs little comment – the racy language, the emotional temperature, the essential qualities of Mrs Poyser's character, all are superbly conveyed. In a fine phrase, George Eliot said that "the medium in which a character moves"[31] was as important to her conception as the character itself. Here, through the particularity of historical time, is the authentic medium.

Bartle Massey is strikingly individualized:

"Nonsense! It's the silliest lie a sensible man like you ever believed, to say a woman makes a house comfortable. It's a story got up, because the women are there, and something must be found for 'em to do. I tell you there isn't a thing under the sun that needs to be done at all, but what a man can do better than a woman, unless it's bearing children, and they do that in a poor make-shift way; it had better ha' been left to the men – it had better ha' been left to the men. I tell you, a woman 'ull bake you a pie every week of her life, and never come to see that the hotter th' oven the shorter the time. I tell you, a woman 'ull make your porridge every day for twenty years, and never think of measuring the proportion between the meal and the milk – a little more or less, she'll think, doesn't signify: the porridge *will* be awk'ard now and then: if it's wrong, it's summat in the meal, or it's summat in the milk, or it's summat in the water. Look at me! I make my own bread, and there's no difference between one batch and another from year's end to year's end."[32]

This is the bachelor schoolmaster, though there *is* a woman in his house in the shape of his "brown and tan-coloured" bitch Vixen with her brood. George Eliot took the name from that of her father's teacher, who ran a school at Roston Common. The woman-hating invective of Bartle is strongly felt. Although educated in a limited sense, the schoolmaster represents a particular bias, and this (though Bartle is a sympathetic character in many ways) is one of George Eliot's strengths in her representations of local characters.

In the first four works, from *Scenes* to *Silas Marner*, local individualities predominate. Mr Tulliver is recognizably of his area, and he too is in the grip of a provincial bias:

"What's been happening, then?" he said, sharply. "What are you meddling with my deeds for? Is Wakem laying hold of everything? . . . . Why don't you tell me what you've been a-doing?" he added, impatiently, as Mr Glegg advanced to the foot of the bed before speaking.

"No, no, friend Tulliver," said Mr Glegg, in a soothing tone. "Nobody's getting hold of anything as yet. We only came to look and see what was in the chest. You've been ill, you know, and we've had to look after things a bit. But let's hope you'll soon be well enough to attend to everything yourself."

Mr Tulliver looked round him meditatively – at Tom, at Mr Glegg, and at Maggie; then suddenly appearing aware that some one was seated by his side at the head of the bed, he turned sharply round and saw his sister.

"Eh, Gritty!" he said, in the half-sad, affectionate tone in which he had been wont to speak to her. "What! you're there, are you? How could you manage to leave the children?"

"O, brother!" said good Mrs Moss, too impulsive to be prudent, "I'm thankful I'm come now to see you yourself again – I thought you'd never know us any more."

"What! have I had a stroke?" said Mr Tulliver, anxiously, looking at Mr Glegg.

"A fall from your horse – shook you a bit – that's all, I think," said Mr Glegg. "But you'll soon get over it, let's hope."

Mr Tulliver fixed his eyes on the bed-clothes, and remained silent for two or three minutes. A new shadow came over his face. He looked up at Maggie first, and said in a lower tone, "You got the letter, then, my wench?"

"Yes, father," she said, kissing him with a full heart. She felt as if her father were come back to her from the dead, and her yearning to show him how she had always loved him could be fulfilled.

"Where's your mother?" he said, so preoccupied that he received the kiss as passively as some quiet animal might have received it.

"She's down-stairs with my aunts, father: shall I fetch her?"

"Ay, ay: poor Bessy!" and his eyes turned towards Tom as Maggie left the room.

"You'll have to take care of 'em both if I die, you know, Tom. You'll be badly off, I doubt. But you must see and pay everybody. And mind – there's fifty pound o' Luke's as I put into the business – he gave it me a bit at a time, and he's got nothing to show for it. You must pay him first thing."

Uncle Glegg involuntarily shook his head, and looked more concerned then ever, but Tom said firmly –

"Yes, father. And haven't you a note from my uncle Moss for three hundred pounds? We came to look for that. What do you wish to be done about it, father?"

"Ah! I'm glad you thought o' that my lad," said Mr Tulliver. "I allays meant to be easy about that money, because o' your aunt. You mustn't mind losing the money, if they can't pay it – and it's like enough they can't. The note's in that box, mind! I allays meant to be good to you, Gritty," said Mr Tulliver, turning to his sister; "but, you know, you aggravated me when you would have Moss."

At this moment Maggie re-entered with her mother, who came in much agitated by the news that her husband was quite himself again.

"Well, Bessy," he said, as she kissed him, "you must forgive me if you're worse off than you ever expected to be. But it's the fault o' the law – it's none o' mine," he added, angrily. "It's the fault o' raskills! Tom – you mind this: if ever you've got the chance, you make Wakem smart. If you don't, you're a good-for-nothing son. You might horse-whip him – but he'd set the law on you – the law's made to take care o' raskills."

Mr Tulliver was getting excited, and an alarming flush was on his face. Mr Glegg wanted to say something soothing, but he was prevented by Mr Tulliver's speaking again to his wife. "They'll make a shift to pay everything, Bessy," he said, "and yet leave you your furniture; and your sisters 'll do something for you ... and Tom 'll grow up ... though what he's to be I don't know. ... I've done what I could .... I've given him a eddication .... and there's the little wench, she'll get married .... but it's a poor tale. ..."[33]

This is Tulliver's partial recovery after his first stroke. His irritability and aggression are already in character, yet George Eliot crams in here so much of the family situation *and* of the man's character that the pressure on us as readers corresponds to the pressure on *him*. Note the intensity, the brokenly moving concern for his family, the money worries and the family love – the brother and sister love – that informs his saving of his sister Gritty, in much the same way as he hopes his son Tom will care for *his* sister Maggie. The economic pressures, the fear of being sold up (which is reality), the obsession with the law and his hatred of Wakem which have ruined him, above all, perhaps, the localized continuum – his poor dazed mind seeking some comfort in that – his son's revenge on Wakem, Tom's "eddication" which, unknown to his father, was useless, and his "little wench", with a terrible rider perhaps, if she is not disgraced by his fall: "it's a poor tale" and, in Mr Tulliver's case, "full of sound and fury, signifying nothing". Local opinion is to condemn Maggie: it has already done as much for Mr Tulliver, abetted by his own rooted obstinacy.

If Mr Tulliver finds life more than difficult, Dolly Winthrop in *Silas Marner* greets the miracle of the arrival of Eppie with simple faith and motherly practicality:

"Ah," said Dolly, with soothing gravity, "it's like the night and the morning, and the sleeping and the waking, and the rain and the harvest – one goes and the other comes, and we know nothing how nor where. We may strive and scrat and fend, but it's little we can do arter all – the big things come and go wi' no striving o' our'n – they do, that they do; and I think you're in the right on it to keep the little un, Master Marner, seeing as it's been sent to you, though there's folks as thinks different. You'll happen be a bit moithered with it while it's so little; but I'll come, and welcome, and see to it for you: I've a bit o' time to spare most days, for when one gets up betimes i' the morning, the clock seems to stan' still tow'rt ten, afore it's time to go about the victual. So, as I say, I'll come and see to the child for you, and welcome."

"Thank you ... kindly," said Silas, hesitating a little. "I'll be glad if you'll tell me things. But," he added, uneasily, leaning forward to look at Baby with some jealousy, as she was resting her head backward against Dolly's arm, and eyeing him contentedly from a distance – "But I want to do things for it myself, else it may get fond o' somebody else, and not fond o' me. I've been used to fending for myself in the house – I can learn, I can learn."

"Eh, to be sure," said Dolly, gently. "I've seen men as are wonderful handy wi' children. The men are awk'ard and contrairy mostly, God help 'em – but when the drink's out of 'em, they aren't unsensible, though they're bad for leeching and bandaging – so fiery and unpatient. You see this goes first, next the skin," proceeded Dolly, taking up the little shirt, and putting it on.[34]

This is a straight, simple, and uncloying presentation of love. Dolly is close to the earth – look at the tacit acceptance of the wonder and mystery of life which takes her to her own conception of God and her sensitive assertion of the woman's knowledge (what she says forms a natural contrast with Bartle Massey's remarks earlier). We are aware once again of a continuum, that Dolly represents in her generation the generations of Raveloe, a village which may lack a definite geographical identification but is certainly in the heart of Warwickshire.

George Eliot's rustic characters, some of whom are considered elsewhere, are the result of careful observation of local traits, actions, gossip, bias, but some are not just seen from the outside. By this I mean that there is more than a humorous or functional dimension to them. Consider Bob Jakin in interaction with Mrs Glegg – a battle of the profit-motive giants – in *The Mill on the Floss*:

"Let me look at the net again," said Mrs Glegg, yearning after the cheap spots and sprigs, now they were vanishing.

"Well, I can't deny *you*, mum," said Bob, handing it out. "Eh! see what a pattern now! Real Laceham goods. Now, this is the sort o' article I'm recommendin' Mr Tom to send out. Lors, it's a fine thing for anybody as has got a bit o' money – these Laceham goods 'ud make it breed like maggits. If *I* was a lady wi' a bit o' money! – why, I know one as put thirty pound into them goods – a lady wi' a cork leg; but as sharp – you wouldn't catch *her* runnin' her head into a sack; *she'd* see her way clear out o' anything afore she'd be in a hurry to start. Well, she let out thirty pound to a young man in the draperin' line, and he laid it out i' Laceham goods, an' a shupercargo o' my acquinetance (not Salt) took 'em out, an' she got her eight per zent fust go off – an' now you can't hold her but she must be sendin' out carguies wi' every ship, till she's gettin' as rich as a Jew. Bucks her name is – she doesn't live i' this town. Now then, mum, if you'll please to give me the net. . . ."

"Here's fifteen shilling, then, for the two," said Mrs Glegg. "But it's a shameful price."

"Nay, mum, you'll niver say that when you're upo' your knees i' church i' five years' time. I'm makin' you a present o' th' articles – I am, indeed. That eightpence shaves off my profit as clean as a razor. Now then, sir," continued Bob, shouldering his pack, "if you please, I'll be glad to go and see about makin' Mr Tom's fortin. Eh, I wish I'd got another twenty pound to lay out for *mysen*: I shouldn't stay to say my Catechism afore I knowed what to do wi't."

"Stop a bit, Mr Glegg," said the lady, as her husband took his hat, "you never *will* give me the chance o' speaking. You'll go away now, and finish everything about this business, and come back and tell me it's too late for me to speak. As if I wasn't my nephey's own aunt, and th' head o' the family on his mother's side! and laid by guineas, all full weight, for him – as he'll know who to respect when I'm laid in my coffin."

"Well, Mrs G., say what you mean," said Mr G., hastily.

"Well, then, I desire as nothing may be done without my knowing. I don't say as I shan't venture twenty pounds, if you make out as everything's right and safe. And if I do, Tom," concluded Mrs Glegg, turning impressively to her nephew, "I hope you'll allays bear it in mind and be grateful for such an aunt. I mean you to pay me interest, you know – I don't approve o' giving; we niver looked for that in *my* family."

"Thank you, aunt," said Tom, rather proudly. "I prefer having the money only lent to me."

"Very well: that's the Dodson sperrit," said Mrs Glegg, rising to get her knitting with the sense that any further remark after this would be bathos.[35]

The interaction is one of cunning, opportunism, bargaining, hypocrisy, pride and self-interest. There is also much natural humour. Here the context is St Ogg's (based on Gainsborough), the conversation about transporting goods in order to make money directly derived from the place. The characters are given through their conversation (and dialect) so that we know quickly the main features of each. There would be little point in combing through the Midland novels for any and every example of character tied to place and expressive of it. But in looking back George Eliot took great care to ensure that the "medium in which a character moves" was verified in part by the nature, personality and speech of the individual described.

This section has been mainly concerned with characters in the early works, where the local derivations are strongest. Character in fiction is pre-eminent, and will be considered throughout in relation to the chapter heading. In letting her imagination retrace its steps to her known areas, George Eliot often presents the particular impact of the outsider as well as the locals. By the time she wrote fiction she was an outsider too, but memory and imagination filled the regional particularity of her choice.

# 3. A Sense of Place

As I have mentioned, trying to trace the "originals" of fictional characters occupied the minds of a number of local people in Nuneaton and Coventry as George Eliot's early works appeared. Places were more readily identified. In *Scenes*, for example, place is concrete, solidly and even ostentatiously described, the "medium" having the bricks and mortar of detailed look and ironic commentary:

Shepperton Church was a very different-looking building five-and-twenty years ago. To be sure, its substantial stone tower looks at you through its intelligent eye, the clock, with the friendly expression of former days; but in everything else what changes! Now there is a wide span of slated roof flanking the old steeple; the windows are tall and symmetrical; the outer doors are resplendent with oak-graining, the inner doors reverentially noiseless with a garment of red baize; and the walls, you are convinced, no lichen will ever again effect a settlement on – they are smooth and innutrient as the summit of the Rev. Amos Barton's head, after ten years of baldness and supererogatory soap. Pass through the baize doors and you will see the nave filled with well-shaped benches, understood to be free seats; while in certain eligible corners, less directly under the fire of the clergyman's eye, there are pews reserved for the Shepperton gentility. Ample galleries are supported on iron pillars, and in one of them stands the crowning glory, the very clasp or aigrette of Shepperton church-adornment – namely, an organ, not very much out of repair, on which a collector of small rents, differentiated by the force of circumstances into an organist, will accompany the alacrity of your departure after the blessing, by a sacred minuet or an easy "Gloria."

Immense improvement! says the well-regulated mind, which unintermittingly rejoices in the New Police, the Tithe Commutation Act, the penny-post, and all guarantees of human advancement, and has no moments when conservative-reforming intellect takes a nap, while imagination does a little Toryism by the sly, revelling in regret that dear, old, brown, crumbling, picturesque inefficiency is everywhere giving place to spick-and-span new-painted, new-varnished efficiency, which will yield endless diagrams, plans, elevations, and sections, but alas! no picture. Mine, I fear, is not a well-regulated mind: it has an occasional tenderness for old abuses; it lingers with a certain fondness over the days of nasal clerks and top-booted parsons, and has a sigh for the departed shades of vulgar errors. So it is not surprising that I recall with a fond sadness Shepperton Church as it was in the old days, with its outer coat of rough stucco, its red-tiled roof, its heterogeneous windows patched with desultory bits of painted glass, and its little flight of steps with their wooden rail running up the outer wall, and leading to the school-children's gallery.

Then inside, what dear old quaintnesses! which I began to look at with delight, even when I was so crude a member of the congregation, that my nurse found it necessary to provide for the reinforcement of my devotional patience by smuggling bread-and-butter into the sacred edifice. There was the chancel, guarded by two little cherubim looking uncomfortably squeezed between arch and wall, and adorned with the escutcheons of the Oldinport family, which showed me inexhaustible possibilities of meaning in their blood-red hands, their death's-heads and cross-bones, their leopards' paws, and Maltese crosses. There were inscriptions on the panels of the singing-gallery, telling of benefactions to the poor of Shepperton, with an involuted elegance of capitals and final flourishes, which my alphabetic erudition traced with ever-new delight. No benches in those days; but huge roomy pews, round which devout church-goers sat during "lessons," trying to look anywhere else than into each other's eyes. No low partitions allowing you, with a dreary absence of contrast and mystery, to see everything at all moments; but tall dark panels, under whose shadow I sank with a sense of retirement through the Litany, only to feel with more intensity my burst into the conspicuousness of public life when I was made to stand up on the seat during the psalms or the singing.[1]

These are the opening paragraphs of George Eliot's first fiction and, although her style was to mature, this beginning exemplifies that intimate identification with place in time which is characteristic of her work. Shepperton Church is a portrait of the church at Chilvers Coton, about half a mile from the market place in Nuneaton, where Mary Ann Evans was baptized by the original of Mr Gilfil at the end of 1819. She attended the church regularly, and the narrator's childhood associations recalled here are an extension of historical and personal authenticity. She is writing of the period about 1832, when the Rev. J. Gwyther (the original of Amos Barton) lived in the vicarage, the real vicar (Mr Carpe in the story) being an absentee one during the period 1831-8. Of particular interest here is the attitude towards change, in the reference to the additions and alterations made in 1836-7. The running omniscient irony has a double reference, particularizing the narrator and author, conscious of the many changes she has passed through since this retrospect.

The habitat in the next story has an even more imposing physicality. Cheverel Manor in "Mr Gilfil's Love Story" is based on Arbury Hall. Persons and place are established in detail and perspective, in a consummate style which depicts and reflects:

And a charming picture Cheverel Manor would have made that evening, if some English Watteau had been there to paint it: the castellated house of grey-tinted stone, with the flickering sunbeams sending dashes of golden light across the many-shaped panes in the mullioned windows, and a great beech leaning athwart one of the flanking towers, and breaking, with its dark flattened boughs, the too formal symmetry of the front; the broad gravel-walk winding on the right, by a row of tall pines, alongside the pool – on the left branching out among swelling grassy mounds, surmounted by clumps of trees, where the red trunk of the Scotch fir glows in the descending sunlight against the bright green of limes and acacias; the great pool, where a pair of swans are swimming lazily with one leg tucked under a wing, and where the open water-lilies lie calmly accepting the kisses of the fluttering light-sparkles; the lawn, with its smooth emerald greenness, sloping down to the rougher and browner herbage of the park, from which it is invisibly fenced by a little stream that winds away from the pool, and disappears under a wooden bridge in the distant pleasure-ground; and on this lawn our two ladies, whose part in the landscape the painter, standing at a favourable point of view in the park, would represent with a few little dabs of red and white and blue.

Seen from the great Gothic windows of the dining-room, they had much more definiteness of outline, and were distinctly visible to the three gentlemen sipping their claret there, as two fair women, in whom all three had a personal interest. These gentlemen were a group worth considering attentively; but any one entering that dining-room for the first time, would perhaps have had his attention even more strongly arrested by the room itself, which was so bare of furniture that it impressed one with its architectural beauty like a cathedral. A piece of matting stretched from door to door, a bit of worn carpet under the dining-table, and a sideboard in a deep recess, did not detain the eye for a moment from the lofty groined ceiling, with its richly-carved pendants, all of creamy white, relieved here and there by touches of gold. On one side, this lofty ceiling was supported by pillars and arches, beyond which a lower ceiling, a miniature copy of the higher one, covered the square projection which, with its three large pointed windows, formed the central feature of the building. The room looked less like a place to dine in than a piece of space enclosed simply for the sake of beautiful outline; and the small dining-table, with the party round it, seemed an odd and insignificant accident, rather than anything connected with the original purpose of the apartment.

But, examined closely, that group was far from insignificant; for the eldest, who was reading in the newspaper the last portentous proceedings of the French parliaments, and turning with occasional comments to his young companions, was as fine a specimen of the old English gentleman as could well have been found in those venerable days of cocked-hats and pigtails. His dark eyes sparkled under projecting brows, made more prominent by bushy grizzled eyebrows; but any apprehension of severity excited by these penetrating eyes, and by a somewhat aquiline nose, was allayed by the good-natured lines about the mouth, which retained all its teeth and its vigour of expression in spite of sixty winters. The forehead sloped a little from the projecting brows, and its peaked outline was made conspicuous by the arrangement of the profusely-powdered hair, drawn backward and gathered into a pigtail. He sat in a small hard chair, which did not admit the slightest approach to a lounge, and which showed to advantage the flatness of his back and the breadth of his chest. In fact, Sir Christopher Cheverel was a splendid old gentleman, as any one may see who enters the saloon at Cheverel Manor, where his full-length portrait, taken when he was fifty, hangs side by side with that of his wife, the stately lady seated on the lawn.[2]

Again there is the historical authentication ("the last portentous proceedings of the French parliaments") but what is interesting is not only the appearance of precise recall but the authorial stance: the sheen of the painting is faintly scratched by irony. It is a past world: the figures are as set, as meticulous in bearing and effect, as the place. But the ripple of reality is what will change their lives. The sense of history is integral throughout George Eliot's works, and here it is centred in place which has seen changes. But just as the room is hardly for dining, more "a piece of space enclosed simply for the sake of beautiful outline", so the place is hardly for living, more an ornamented and ornamental shell in which to be seen to be living. Marian Evans was a frequent visitor to Arbury Hall with her father, having a free run of the library and unconsciously storing in her mind's eye the grandeur and grace. She heard the servants' gossip in the housekeeper's room by way of contrast, and looked back with ironic perspective at what she had once known. Grandeur and grace are subject to the author's revisionary memory.

As Gordon Haight points out, there is only one public building described in St Ogg's, the fictional name for Gainsborough. This is the old hall, where the bazaar is held at a crucial time in Maggie's relationship with Stephen. It witnesses Philip's awareness of that relationship:

All well-drest St Ogg's and its neighbourhood were there; and it would have been worth while to come, even from a distance, to see the fine old hall, with its open roof and carved oaken rafters, and great oaken folding-doors, and light shed down from a height on the many-coloured show beneath: a very quaint place, with broad faded stripes painted on the walls, and here and there a show of heraldic animals of a bristly, long-snouted character, the cherished emblems of a noble family once the seigniors of this now civic hall. A grand arch, cut in the upper wall at one end, surmounted an oaken orchestra, with an open room behind it, where hothouse plants and stalls for refreshments were disposed: an agreeable resort for gentlemen, disposed to loiter, and yet to exchange the occasional crush down below for a more commodious point of view. In fact, the perfect fitness of this ancient building for an admirable modern purpose, that made charity truly elegant, and led through vanity up to the supply of a deficit, was so striking that hardly a person entered the room without exchanging the remark more than once. Near the great arch over the orchestra was the stone oriel with painted glass, which was one of the venerable inconsistencies of the old hall; and it was close by this that Lucy had her stall, for the convenience of certain large plain articles which she had taken charge of for Mrs Kenn.[3]

Haight's comment is not accurate: "Gainsborough had no such hall, nor did George Eliot look there for one during her brief visit. Instead she described St Mary's Hall in Coventry, which she knew very well, the ancient Guildhall in Bayley Lane, opposite the Cathedral."[4] He then goes on to make specific identifications, but in fact there was Gainsborough's Old Hall, which George Eliot, despite the brevity of her visit, certainly knew about. As so often in *The Mill* there is conflation and deliberate mingling. Such was her fictional awareness and imaginative cunning that she adapted the known water-associated legends of the Gainsborough Hall, established in their antiquity, as a symbolic equivalence to her heroine's isolated state. Here is the old hall on its first appearance:

It was the Normans who began to build that fine old hall, which is like the town, telling of the thoughts and hands of widely-sundered generations; but it is all so old that we look with loving pardon at its inconsistencies, and are well content that they who built the stone oriel, and they who built the Gothic façade and towers of finest small brickwork with the trefoil ornament, and the windows and battlements defined with stone, did not sac- religiously pull down the ancient half-timbered body with its oak-roofed banqueting hall.

But older even than this old hall is perhaps the bit of wall now built into the belfry of the parish church, and said to be a remnant of the original chapel dedicated to St Ogg, the patron saint of this ancient town, of whose history I possess several manuscript versions. I incline to the briefest, since, if it should not be wholly true, it is at least likely to contain the least falsehood. "Ogg the son of Beorl," says my private hagiographer, "was a boatman who gained a scanty living by ferrying passengers across the river Floss. And it came to pass, one evening when the winds were high, that there sat moaning by the brink of the river a woman with a child in her arms; and she was clad in rags, and had a worn and withered look, and she craved to be rowed across the river. And the men thereabout questioned her, and said, 'Wherefore dost thou desire to cross the river? Tarry till the morning, and take shelter here for the night: so shalt thou be wise, and not foolish.' Still she went on to mourn and crave. But Ogg the son of Beorl came up and said, 'I will ferry thee across: it is enough that thy heart needs it.' And he ferried her across. And it came to pass, when she stepped ashore, that her rags were turned into robes of flowing white, and her face became bright with exceeding beauty, and there was a glory around it, so that she shed a light on the water like the moon in its brightness. And she said – 'Ogg the son of Beorl, thou art blessed in that thou didst not question and wrangle with the heart's need, but wast smitten with pity, and didst straightway relieve the same. And from henceforth whoso steps into thy boat shall be in no peril from the storm; and whenever it puts forth to the rescue, it shall save the lives both of men and beasts.' And when the floods came, many were saved by reason of that blessing on the boat. But when Ogg the son of Beorl died, behold, in the parting of his soul, the boat loosed itself from its moorings, and was floated with the ebbing tide in great swiftness to the ocean, and was seen no more. Yet it was witnessed in the floods of aftertime, that at the coming on of eventide, Ogg the son of Beorl was always seen with his boat upon the wide-spreading waters, and the Blessed Virgin sat in the prow, shedding a light around as of the moon in its brightness, so that the rowers in the gathering darkness took heart and pulled anew."

This legend, one sees, reflects from a far-off time the visitation of the floods, which, even when they left human life untouched, were widely fatal to the helpless cattle, and swept as sudden death over all smaller living things. But the town knew worse troubles even than the floods – troubles of the civil wars, when it was a continual fighting-place, where first Puritans thanked God for the blood of the Loyalists, and then Loyalists thanked God for the blood of the Puritans. Many honest citizens lost all their possessions for conscience' sake in those times, and went forth beggared from their native town. Doubtless there are many houses standing now on which those honest citizens turned their backs in sorrow: quaint-gabled houses looking on the river, jammed between newer warehouses, and penetrated by surprising passages, which turn and turn at sharp angles till they lead you out on a muddy strand . . .[5]

We have already seen the associations of Maggie with the Virgin, but the moral of the legend sounds the central theme of the novel, while the floods and wars which destroy lives, the deliberate anticipation of the novel's flood and the phrase "went forth beggared from their native town" stand for Maggie's fate. Here, as so often when she is presenting place, George Eliot embroiders the bare fact with the tapestry of fiction.

On 9th May 1874 George Eliot wrote to her brother's eldest daughter (she and Isaac were not yet reconciled). She said "Many thanks for the photographs which I am delighted to have. Dear old Griff still smiles at me with a face which is more like than unlike its former self, and I seem to feel the air through the window of the attic above the drawing room, from which when a little girl, I often looked towards the distant view of the Coton 'College' – thinking the view rather sublime."[6] This is loving recall, though there is a little self-irony, for the "College" is the workhouse visited by Amos Barton in the first clerical scene. Since Griff was her home for twenty-one years, her recall is hardly surprising. The attic is also transferred to the mill:

Before this remonstrance was finished, Maggie was already out of hearing, making her way towards the great attic that ran under the old high-pitched roof, shaking the water from her black locks as she ran, like a Skye terrier escaped from his bath. This attic was Maggie's favourite retreat on a wet day, when the weather was not too cold; here she fretted out all her ill-humours, and talked aloud to the worm-eaten floors and the worm-eaten shelves, and the dark rafters festooned with cobwebs; and here she kept a Fetish which she punished for all her misfortunes. This was the trunk of a large wooden doll, which once stared with the roundest of eyes above the reddest of cheeks; but was now entirely defaced by a long career of vicarious suffering. Three nails driven into the head commemorated as many crises in Maggie's nine years of earthly struggle; that luxury of vengeance having been suggested to her by the picture of Jael destroying Sisera in the old Bible. The last nail had been driven in with a fiercer stroke than usual, for the Fetish on that occasion represented aunt Glegg. But immediately afterwards Maggie had reflected that if she drove many nails in, she would not be so well able to fancy that the head was hurt when she knocked it against the wall, nor to comfort it, and make believe to poultice it, when her fury was abated; for even aunt Glegg would be pitiable when she had been hurt very much, and thoroughly humiliated, so as to beg her niece's pardon. Since then she had driven no more nails in, but had soothed herself by alternately grinding and beating the wooden head against the rough brick of the great chimneys that made two square pillars supporting the roof. That was what she did this morning on reaching the attic, sobbing all the while with a passion that expelled every other form of consciousness – even the memory of the grievance that had caused it. As at last the sobs were getting quieter, and the grinding less fierce, a sudden beam of sunshine, falling through the wire lattice across the worm-eaten shelves, made her throw away the Fetish and run to the window. The sun was really breaking out; the sound of the mill seemed cheerful again; the granary doors were open ...[7]

The autobiographical identification is a strong one, with the Fetish vivified into Aunt Glegg in a typical manifestation of childish creative passion. At the back of Griff was Griff House Pond, the Round Pool of *The Mill*, "that wonderful pool, which the floods had made a long while ago: no one knew how deep it was; and it was mysterious, too, that it should be almost a perfect round, framed in with willows and tall reeds, so that the water was only to be seen when you got close to the brink".[8] Place is indelibly associated in *The Mill* with Maggie's crises: when Tom tells her off for failing to feed the rabbits she retreats to the attic and vents her misery there. The Round Pool provides the sweet success of her accidental catch which wins Tom's praise. But it is in the Red Deeps that Maggie has her secret meetings with Philip Wakem, the one emotional relief and release from home:

It was far on in June now, and Maggie was inclined to lengthen the daily walk which was her one indulgence; but this day and the following she was so busy with work which must be finished that she never went beyond the gate, and satisfied her need of the open air by sitting out of doors. One of her frequent walks, when she was not obliged to go to St Ogg's, was to a spot that lay beyond what was called the "Hill" – an insignificant rise of ground crowned by trees, lying along the side of the road which ran by the gates of Dorlcote Mill. Insignificant I call it, because in height it was hardly more than a bank; but there may come moments when Nature makes a mere bank a means towards a fateful result, and that is why I ask you to imagine this high bank crowned with trees, making an uneven wall for some quarter of a mile along the left side of Dorlcote Mill and the pleasant fields behind it, bounded by the murmuring Ripple. Just where this line of bank sloped down again to the level, a by-road turned off and led to the other side of the rise, where it was broken into very capricious hollows and mounds by the working of an exhausted stone-quarry – so long exhausted that both mounds and hollows were now clothed with brambles and trees, and here and there by a stretch of grass which a few sheep kept close-nibbled. In her childish days Maggie held this place, called the Red Deeps, in very great awe, and needed all her confidence in Tom's bravery to reconcile her to an excursion thither – visions of robbers and fierce animals haunting every hollow. But now it had the charm for her which any broken ground, any mimic rock and ravine, have for the eyes that rest habitually on the level; especially in summer, when she could sit in a grassy hollow under the shadow of a branching ash, stooping aslant from the steep above her, and listen to the hum of insects, like tiniest bells on the garment of Silence, or see the sunlight piercing the distant boughs, as if to chase and drive home the truant heavenly blue of the wild hyacinths. In this June time too, the dog-roses were in their glory, and that was an additional reason why Maggie should direct her walk to the Red Deeps, rather than to any other spot, on the first day she was free to wander at her will – a pleasure she loved so well, that sometimes, in her ardours of renunciation, she thought she ought to deny herself the frequent indulgence in it.[9]

The original of this is that part of Griff Hollows which is on the Coventry road on the way to Nuneaton, between Griff House and Chilvers Coton. The loving association with the Griff area is seen too in the fourth sonnet of the "Brother and Sister" sequence, where there is a strong sense of known place:

IV.

Our meadow-path had memorable spots:
One where it bridged a tiny rivulet,
Deep hid by tangled blue Forget-me-nots;
And all along the waving grasses met

My little palm, or nodded to my cheek,
When flowers with upturned faces gazing drew
My wonder downward, seeming all to speak
With eyes of souls that dumbly heard and knew.

Then came the copse, where wild things rushed unseen,
And black-scathed grass betrayed the past abode
Of mystic gypsies, who still lurked between
Me and each hidden distance of the road.

A gypsy once had startled me at play,
Blotting with her dark smile my sunny day.[10]

The gypsies fascinated Mary Ann Evans and Maggie Tulliver, who runs away to them.

The greatest emphasis on place in *The Mill* comes in the final description of the flood. But the urban description present throughout her works characterizes a spirit of place. It is as evident in *Scenes* as in *Middlemarch*, which has both ironic perspective and historical verisimilitude.

Milby (Nuneaton) was surveyed with hindsight:

More than a quarter of a century has slipped by since then, and in the interval Milby has advanced at as rapid a pace as other market-towns in her Majesty's dominions. By this time it has a handsome railway station, where the drowsy London traveller may look out by the brilliant gas-light and see perfectly sober papas and husbands alighting with their leather-bags after transacting their day's business at the county town. There is a resident rector, who appeals to the consciences of his hearers with all the immense advantages of a divine who keeps his own carriage; the church is enlarged by at least five hundred sittings; and the grammar-school, conducted on reformed principles, has its upper forms crowded with the genteel youth of Milby. The gentlemen there fall into no other excess at dinner-parties than the perfectly well-bred and virtuous excess of stupidity; and though the ladies are still said sometimes to take too much upon themselves, they are never known to take too much in any other way. The conversation is sometimes quite literary, for there is a flourishing book-club, and many of the younger ladies have carried their studies so far as to have forgotten a little German. In short, Milby is now a refined, moral, and enlightened town; no more resembling the Milby of former days than the huge, long-skirted, drab greatcoat that embarrassed the ankles of our grandfathers resembled the light paletot in which we tread jauntily through the muddiest streets, or than the bottle-nosed Britons, rejoicing over a tankard, in the old sign of the Two Travellers at Milby, resembled the severe-looking gentlemen in straps and high collars whom a modern artist has represented as sipping the imaginary port of that well-known commercial house.

But pray, reader, dismiss from your mind all the refined and fashionable ideas associated with this advanced state of things, and transport your imagination to a time when Milby had no gas-lights; when the mail drove up dusty or bespattered to the door of the Red Lion; when old Mr Crewe, the curate, in a brown Brutus wig, delivered inaudible sermons on a Sunday, and on a week-day imparted the education of a gentleman – that is to say, an arduous inacquaintance with Latin through the medium of the Eton grammar – to three pupils in the upper grammar-school.

If you had passed through Milby on the coach at that time, you would have had no idea what important people lived there, and how very high a sense of rank was prevalent among them. It was a dingy-looking town, with a strong smell of tanning up one street, and a great shaking of handlooms up another; and even in that focus of aristocracy, Friar's Gate, the houses would not have seemed very imposing to the hasty and superficial glance of a passenger. You might still less have suspected that the figure in light fustian and large grey whiskers, leaning against the grocer's door-post in High Street, was no less a person than Mr Lowme, one of the most aristocratic men in Milby, said to have been "brought up a gentleman," and to have had the gay habits accordant with that station, keeping his harriers and other expensive animals. He was now quite an elderly Lothario, reduced to the most economical sins; the prominent form of his gaiety being this of lounging at Mr Gruby's door, embarrassing the servant-maids who came for grocery, and talking scandal with the rare passers-by. Still, it was generally understood that Mr Lowme belonged to the highest circle of Milby society; his sons and daughters held up their heads very high indeed; and in spite of his condescending way of chatting and drinking with inferior people, he would himself have scorned any closer identification with them. It must be admitted that he was of some service to the town in this station at Mr Gruby's door, for he and Mr Landor's Newfoundland dog, who stretched himself and gaped on the opposite causeway, took something from the lifeless air that belonged to the High Street on every day except Saturday.[11]

Change within place is registered through the double irony of the appraisal: one of the changes is of course the arrival of the railway. The main-line railway from London to Birmingham reached Coventry in 1838 but work on a branch line to Nuneaton, which passes in a cutting only 200 yards from Rosehill, where the Brays lived and George Eliot often stayed, was begun in 1847, and the line was opened in 1850. So here she is still writing about her own time in the region, and the updating is that of a mature woman looking back on the associations of two earlier periods. Despite the changes, there is a strong feeling of the continuity of the provincial spirit of place. There is a wonderful indication of the activities, the social surface, class and snobberies. What gives a sense of continuity is the ironic control: there is change and yet not change, since people's attitudes are a constant in the movement of time.

In *Silas Marner* the spirit of place is used as contrast in Silas's consciousness after his banishment from Lantern Yard. There is the sense of a different history, of a different small world, of an isolation that is not yet remedial:

> And Raveloe was a village where many of the old echoes lingered, undrowned by new voices. Not that it was one of those barren parishes lying on the outskirts of civilisation – inhabited by meagre sheep and thinly-scattered shepherds: on the contrary, it lay in the rich central plain of what we are pleased to call Merry England, and held farms which, speaking from a spiritual point of view, paid highly-desirable tithes. But it was nestled in a snug well-wooded hollow, quite an hour's journey on horseback from any turnpike, where it was never reached by the vibrations of the coach-horn, or of public opinion. It was an important-looking village, with a fine old church and large churchyard in the heart of it, and two or three large brick-and-stone homesteads, with well-walled orchards and ornamental weather-cocks, standing close upon the road, and lifting more imposing fronts than the rectory, which peeped from among the trees on the other side of the churchyard; – a village which showed at once the summits of its social life, and told the practised eye that there was no great park and manor-house in the vicinity, but that there were several chiefs in Raveloe who could farm badly quite at their ease, drawing enough money from their bad farming, in those war times, to live in a rollicking fashion, and keep a jolly Christmas, Whitsun, and Easter tide . . .
>
> And what could be more unlike that Lantern Yard world than the world in Raveloe? – orchards looking lazy with neglected plenty; the large church in the wide churchyard, which men gazed at lounging at their own doors in service-time; the purple-faced farmers jogging along the lanes or turning in at the Rainbow; homesteads, where men supped heavily and slept in the light of the evening hearth, and where women seemed to be laying up a stock of linen for the life to come. There were no lips in Raveloe from which a word could fall that would stir Silas Marner's benumbed faith to a sense of pain.[12]

Here the spirit of place has considerable substance, since the irony is not only playful but is critical too: "what we are pleased to call Merry England", "drawing enough money from their bad farming", "the purple-faced farmers", all these phrases have enough bite to underline the realism of the appraisal, despite the fact that it is set back in time – here between 1804–7 – into the period of the Napoleonic Wars. Yet just as *Silas Marner* is a combination of realism and fable, so this description of Raveloe, of the spirit of the place, is an indication of what appears and what actually is. It is snug, isolated, an "important-looking village" (probably Bulkington in Warwickshire, about three miles or so from Nuneaton) but its way of life is static, indolent, as numbed to change as Silas's faith is benumbed by his experience. Hitherto we have seen different emphases in the presentation of place: here the link between the state of place and the state of character – both individual and communal – is given an index of association.

And just as the exterior is symbolic as well as factual, so is the interior. The first description of the Red House in *Silas Marner* accounts for the respective states of the Squire, Dunstan and Godfrey Cass:

For the Squire's wife had died long ago, and the Red House was without that presence of the wife and mother which is the fountain of wholesome love and fear in parlour and kitchen. . . . The fading grey light fell dimly on the walls, decorated with guns, whips, and foxes' brushes, on coats and hats flung on the chairs, on tankards sending forth a scent of flat ale, and on a half-coked fire, with pipes propped up in the chimney corners; signs of a domestic life destitute of any hallowing charm.[13]

We see why the Squire is frustrated, Godfrey has secretly married, and Dunstan has gone to the bad. The spirit of this place is socially and morally dead, and in its decay nourishes new degradations.

The genius of provincial place is prominent in the provincial press. Charles Bray bought the *Coventry Herald* in June 1846. Marian Evans, her translation of Strauss's *Life of Jesus* just published in the same month, was free to contribute reviews to her friend's paper. She also wrote her earliest series of essays, "Poetry and Prose from the Notebook of an Eccentric", which began in the December issue. In February 1847 she submitted her first satirical piece, called "Vice and Sausages", about a police inspector in Coventry called John Vice. She neatly gauged public interest in local affairs, and turned her knowledge to good account in her two novels set at the time of the first Reform Bill, *Felix Holt* and *Middlemarch*. In the first Harold Transome, having returned from abroad, decides to stand as a Liberal, in total opposition to what might have been expected from his Tory inheritance, and this is fuel for the local newspapers:

How Harold Transome came to be a Liberal in opposition to all the traditions of his family, was a more subtle inquiry than he had ever cared to follow out. The newspapers undertook to explain it. The *North Loamshire Herald* witnessed with a grief and disgust certain to be shared by all persons who were actuated by wholesome British feeling, an example of defection in the inheritor of a family name which in times past had been associated with attachment to right principle, and with the maintenance of our constitution in Church and State; and pointed to it as an additional proof that men who had passed any large portion of their lives beyond the limits of our favoured country, usually contracted not only a laxity of feeling towards Protestantism, nay, towards religion itself – a latitudinarian spirit hardly distinguishable from atheism – but also a levity of disposition, inducing them to tamper with those institutions by which alone Great Britain had risen to her pre-eminence among the nations. Such men, infected with outlandish habits, intoxicated with vanity, grasping at momentary power by flattery of the multitude, fearless because godless, liberal because un-English, were ready to pull one stone from under another in the national edifice, till the great structure tottered to its fall. On the other hand, the *Duffield Watchman* saw in this signal instance of self-liberation from the trammels of prejudice, a decisive guarantee of intellectual pre-eminence, united with a generous sensibility to the claims of man as man, which had burst asunder, and cast off, by a spontaneous exertion of energy, the cramping out-worn shell of hereditary bias and class interest.

But these large-minded guides of public opinion argued from wider data than could be furnished by any knowledge of the particular case concerned. Harold Transome was neither the dissolute cosmopolitan so vigorously sketched by the Tory *Herald*, nor the intellectual giant and moral lobster suggested by the liberal imagination of the *Watchman*.[14]

Obviously the provincial press conveys the public opinion of the place, or at least purports to. The fine irony is present here: Treby Magna is Nuneaton – though specific identifications are difficult – and North Loamshire is where the Transome estate is situated. In *Middlemarch* George Eliot uses a clever running notation to indicate the power of place, but she also uses a cunning mix and balance of local commentary and national associations:

The doubt hinted by Mr Vincy whether it were only the general election or the end of the world that was coming on, now that George the Fourth was dead, Parliament dissolved, Wellington and Peel generally depreciated and the new King apologetic, was a feeble type of the uncertainties in provincial opinion at that time. With the glow-worm lights of country places, how could men see which were their own thoughts in the confusion of a Tory Ministry passing Liberal measures, of Tory nobles and electors being anxious to return Liberals rather than friends of the recreant Ministers, and of outcries for remedies which seemed to have a mysteriously remote bearing on private interest, and were made suspicious by the advocacy of disagreeable neighbours? Buyers of the Middlemarch newspapers found themselves in an anomalous position: during the agitation on the Catholic Question many had given up the "Pioneer" – which had a motto from Charles James Fox and was in the van of progress – because it had taken Peel's side about the Papists, and had thus blotted its Liberalism with a toleration of Jesuitry and Baal; but they were ill-satisfied with the "Trumpet," which – since its blasts against Rome, and in the general flaccidity of the public mind (nobody knowing who would support whom) – had become feeble in its blowing.

It was a time, according to a noticeable article in the "Pioneer," when the crying needs of the country might well counteract a reluctance to public action on the part of men whose minds had from long experience acquired breadth as well as concentration, decision of judgment as well as tolerance, dispassionateness as well as energy – in fact, all those qualities which in the melancholy experience of mankind have been the least disposed to share lodgings.

Mr Hackbutt, whose fluent speech was at that time floating more widely than usual, and leaving much uncertainty as to its ultimate channel, was heard to say in Mr Hawley's office that the article in question "emanated" from Brooke of Tipton, and that Brooke had secretly bought the "Pioneer" some months ago.

"That means mischief, eh?" said Mr Hawley. "He's got the freak of being a popular man now, after dangling about like a stray tortoise. So much the worse for him. I've had my eye on him for some time. He shall be prettily pumped upon. He's a damned bad landlord. What business has an old county man to come currying favour with a low set of dark-blue freemen? As to his paper, I only hope he may do the writing himself. It would be worth our paying for."

"I understand he has got a very brilliant young fellow to edit it, who can write the highest style of leading article, quite equal to anything in the London papers. And he means to take very high ground on Reform."

"Let Brooke reform his rent-roll. He's a cursed old screw, and the buildings all over his estate are going to rack. I suppose this young fellow is some loose fish from London."

"His name is Ladislaw. He is said to be of foreign extraction."

"I know the sort," said Mr Hawley; "some emissary. He'll begin with flourishing about the Rights of Man and end with murdering a wench. That's the style."[15]

We are looking back to the period and region of *Felix Holt*. Again there is an outsider, and here it is Ladislaw, attracted to Middlemarch because he will be near Dorothea. There is a parallel situation – Mr Brooke, a bad landlord, is disseminating reform ideas (he is to stand as a candidate) when we might have expected him to be reactionary. At the back of the locally based comments is the national scene, which has also experienced bewildering changes of attitude, so bewildering that the provincial mind cannot grasp them. The "glow-worm lights of country places" is ironic but containing a certain pathos too, since opinion and certainty are unlikely to result from reading *The Pioneer*, opportunistically bought and being edited by a foreigner. Again George Eliot is looking back across a span of years, seeing Middlemarch as a microcosm for the country.

The notation which sets the spirit of place within the confines of judgment, opinion, evaluation, lies in a series of references. Mrs Cadwallader says to Mr Brooke: "I shall tell everybody that you are going to put up for Middlemarch on the Whig side when old Pinkerton resigns, and that Casaubon is going to help you in an underhand manner: going to bribe the voters with pamphlets, and throw open the public houses to distribute them."[16] Mrs Cadwallader is joking in the hope of embarrassing Mr Brooke, but there is a fine edge of truth to her words. Mr Brooke would not like to be talked about in this place. He is Brooke of Tipton; he inhabits the Grange, he is Squire and magistrate, and he is known as a bad landlord. His position in this environment is both traditional and insecure.

But if Mr Brooke has insecurities, he still indulges his position at the Grange, and entertains there before Dorothea marries Casaubon. He invites a miscellaneous group from Middlemarch: "There was the newly elected mayor of Middlemarch, who happened to be a manufacturer; the philanthropic banker his brother-in-law, who predominated so much in the town that some called him a Methodist, others a hypocrite, according to the resources of their vocabulary; and there were various professional men . . ."[17]

Place is barred to those whose social position does not merit an invitation. The rigid but subtle lines of social demarcation are observed: "The Miss Vincy who had the honour of being Mr Chichely's ideal was of course not present; for Mr Brooke, always objecting to go too far, would not have chosen that his nieces should meet the daughter of a Middlemarch manufacturer, unless it were on a public occasion."[18]

Place has its medical as well as its political differences as we shall see, but the class gradations are complex. Rosamond may not dine with Mr Brooke's nieces, but for Lydgate, the new doctor, it is socially easy to meet "that agreeable vision": "For who of any consequence in Middlemarch was not connected or at least acquainted with the Vincys?"[19] And as for "the philanthropic banker": "who, however, as a man not born in the town and altogether of dimly-known origin, was considered to have done well in uniting himself with a real Middlemarch family . . ."[20]

Rosamond has her own ideas of what constitutes provincial limitation: "Rosamond felt that she might have been happier if she had not been the daughter of a Middlemarch manufacturer."[21] Gossip can ruin one's expectations, especially if you are at the mercy of other relations as you wait for the rich man to die: " 'My brother Solomon tells me it's the talk up and down in Middlemarch how unsteady young Vincy is, and has been for ever gambling at billiards since home he came.' "[22] Rosamond, intent on seeing what the new young doctor is like, has her dreams: "Ever since that important new arrival in Middlemarch she had woven a little future. . . . And a stranger was absolutely necessary to Rosamond's social romance, which had always turned on a lover and bridegroom who was not a Middlemarcher."[23]

Lydgate the outsider may be conscious (as a pleasant background at the moment) of the "vision" of Rosamond, but he tells Bulstrode bluntly " 'I have not yet been pained by finding any excessive talent in Middlemarch.' "[24] Though Lydgate is not over-conceited, he feels that he has brought his own talents with him: "There was a general impression, however, that Lydgate was not altogether a common country doctor, and in Middlemarch at that time such an impression was significant of great things being expected from him."[25] He has no doubt that he will achieve them: "He would be a good Middlemarch doctor, and by that very means keep himself in the track of far-reaching investigation. Such was Lydgate's plan of his future: to do good small work for Middlemarch, and great work for the world."[26]

Provincial life, whether it be Lydgate's or Marian Evans's, is seen at a particular time and place: "The man was still in the making, as much as the Middlemarch doctor and immortal discoverer . . ."[27] And no one knows of Lydgate's past (except the privileged reader) but "Middlemarch, in fact, counted on swallowing Lydgate and assimilating him very comfortably."[28]

The insistence of the tone makes place profoundly and powerfully relevant. The previous quotation came at the end of Chapter 15, and Chapter 16 puts into effect, without explicit indication, the "assimilation" of Lydgate. He is already trapped by the forces of place: "The question whether Tyke should be appointed chaplain to the hospital was an exciting topic to the Middle-marchers; and Lydgate heard it discussed in a way that threw much light on the power exercised in the town by Mr Bulstrode."[29] Throughout *Middlemarch* the communal identity is employed to underline one of George Eliot's main beliefs: there is no private life which is not influenced by the public life which surrounds it, "the medium in which a character moves".

The effect of provincial pressures is strikingly indicated in another paragraph which has the usual wider historical currency and chronological placing:

Certainly nothing at present could seem much less important to Lydgate than the turn of Miss Brooke's mind, or to Miss Brooke than the qualities of the woman who had attracted this young surgeon. But any one watching keenly the stealthy convergence of human lots, sees a slow preparation of effects from one life on another, which tells like a calculated irony on the indifference or the frozen stare with which we look at our unintroduced neighbour. Destiny stands by sarcastic with our *dramatis personae* folded in her hand.

Old provincial society had its share of this subtle movement: had not only its striking downfalls, its brilliant young professional dandies who ended by living up an entry with a drab and six children for their establishment, but also those less marked vicissitudes which are constantly shifting the boundaries of social intercourse, and begetting new consciousness of interdependence. Some slipped a little downward, some got higher footing: people denied aspirates, gained wealth, and fastidious gentlemen stood for boroughs; some were caught in political currents, some in ecclesiastical, and perhaps found themselves surprisingly grouped in consequence; while a few personages or families that stood with rocky firmness amid all this fluctuation, were slowly presenting new aspects in spite of solidity and altering with the double change of self and beholder. Municipal town and rural parish gradually made fresh threads of connexion – gradually, as the old stocking gave way to the savings-bank, and the worship of the solar guinea became extinct; while squires and baronets, and even lords who had once lived blamelessly afar from the civic mind, gathered the faultiness of closer acquaintanceship. Settlers, too, came from distant counties, some with an alarming novelty of skill, others with an offensive advantage in cunning. In fact, much the same sort of movement and mixture went on in old England as we find in older Herodotus, who also, in telling what had been, thought it well to take a woman's lot for his starting-point; though Io, as a maiden apparently beguiled by attractive merchandise, was the reverse of Miss Brooke, and in this respect perhaps bore more resemblance to Rosamond Vincy, who had excellent taste in costume, with that nymph-like figure and pure blondness which give the largest range to choice in the flow and colour of drapery. But these things made only part of her charm. She was admitted to be the flower of Mrs Lemon's school, the chief school in the county, where the teaching included all that was demanded in the accomplished female – even to extras, such as the getting in and out of a carriage. Mrs Lemon herself had always held up Miss Vincy as an example: no pupil, she said, exceeded that young lady for mental acquisition and propriety of speech, while her musical execution was quite exceptional. We cannot help the way in which people speak of us, and probably if Mrs Lemon had undertaken to describe Juliet or Imogen, these heroines would not have seemed poetical. The first vision of Rosamond would have been enough with most judges to dispel any prejudice excited by Mrs Lemon's praise.[30]

George Eliot "assimilated" Marian Evans, and in doing so was able to view that young woman's Coventry experiences from the advantage of having left them behind. But not quite: they tend to surface in metaphorically alert generalizations like "the stealthy convergence of human lots",[31] eloquent of the experience of provincial space where social intercourse is with the few rather than the many. She knew that at the time of political change marked by the first Reform Bill other changes were already beginning, as in the medical profession, and these are carefully documented in the novel. Stealthy convergence is precisely registered in the class changes and movements dramatized here. The focus on Rosamond, for instance, ironic though it is, shows the superficiality which passed for woman's education, the aping of upper class manners – "such as the getting in and out of a carriage"[32] – which is an accomplishment calculated to ensure upward mobility. It does not let Rosamond down. It is no accident that she is making "a very pretty show" in her carriage on her last appearance in the novel.

The "looking backward" in *Middlemarch* is ironic, but irony is balanced by that loving identification we have noticed elsewhere. Place has such strongly rooted attraction for George Eliot that nostalgia seems part of the recall. The mores of place are defined from an experienced sense of life, a critical perspective. The region, however, is often a source of delight:

The ride to Stone Court, which Fred and Rosamond took the next morning, lay through a pretty bit of midland landscape, almost all meadows and pastures, with hedgerows still allowed to grow in bushy beauty and to spread out coral fruit for the birds. Little details gave each field a particular physiognomy, dear to the eyes that have looked on them from childhood: the pool in the corner where the grasses were dank and trees leaned whisperingly; the great oak shadowing a bare place in mid-pasture; the high bank where the ash-trees grew; the sudden slope of the old marl-pit making a red background for the burdock; the huddled roofs and ricks of the homestead without a traceable way of approach; the grey gate and fences against the depths of the bordering wood; and the stray hovel, its old, old thatch full of mossy hills and valleys with wondrous modulations of light and shadow such as we travel far to see in later life, and see larger, but not more beautiful. These are the things that make the gamut of joy in landscape to midland-bred souls – the things they toddled among, or perhaps learned by heart standing between their father's knees while he drove leisurely.

But the road, even the byroad, was excellent; for Lowick, as we have seen, was not a parish of muddy lanes and poor tenants; and it was into Lowick parish that Fred and Rosamond entered after a couple of miles' riding. Another mile would bring them to Stone Court, and at the end of the first half, the house was already visible, looking as if it had been arrested in its growth toward a stone mansion by an unexpected budding of farm-buildings on its left flank, which had hindered it from becoming anything more than the substantial dwelling of a gentleman farmer. It was not the less agreeable an object in the distance for the cluster of pinnacled corn-ricks which balanced the fine row of walnuts on the right.[33]

We have seen earlier that the "Brother and Sister" sonnets were written at the time George Eliot was contemplating *Middlemarch*: the end of the first paragraph above is one of the strongest autobiographical identifications we have anywhere in her work, a narrator's "Looking Backwards" which certainly has the feel of identification as it imagines and recalls as adult and for child. It gives way to the description of Stone Court in the second paragraph with some class significance for the plot: Bulstrode is ultimately to own Stone Court, employ Caleb Garth, be rejected by him, condone the death of Raffles and be replaced by Fred and Mary. Here the description of the "corn-ricks" and the "fine row of walnuts" is warmly appreciative though less personal than the description of the field's physiognomy and the thatch.

In 1860 George Eliot wrote a short story called "Brother Jacob". Four years later she gave it to George Smith, publisher of the *Cornhill* magazine in which *Romola* had appeared. The gift was a small compensation for that novel's lack of financial success. "Brother Jacob" is a minor work. The plot concerns David Faux, who steals his mother's money but is seen by his idiot brother Jacob. David goes to Jamaica, works as a cook, returns to England and sets up as a shopkeeper in Grimworth, a small market town, not specifically identified as being in the Midlands, though that location is virtually certain. The story shows George Eliot looking back in a rare mood of exuberantly satirical lightness, a kind of bubbling humour playing over the place:

Grimworth, to a discerning eye, was a good place to set up shopkeeping in. There was no competition in it at present; the Church-people had their own grocer and draper; the Dissenters had theirs; and the two or three butchers found a ready market for their joints without strict reference to religious persuasion – except that the rector's wife had given a general order for the veal sweet-breads and the mutton kidneys, while Mr Rodd, the Baptist minister, had requested that, so far as was compatible with the fair accommodation of other customers, the sheep's trotters might be reserved for him. And it was likely to be a growing place, for the trustees of Mr Zephaniah Crypt's Charity, under the stimulus of a late visitation by commissioners, were beginning to apply long-accumulating funds to the rebuilding of the Yellow Coat School, which was henceforth to be carried forward on a greatly-extended scale, the testator having left no restrictions concerning the curriculum, but only concerning the coat.

The shopkeepers at Grimworth were by no means unanimous as to the advantages promised by this prospect of increased population and trading, being substantial men, who liked doing a quiet business in which they were sure of their customers, and could calculate their returns to a nicety. Hitherto, it had been held a point of honour by the families in Grimworth parish, to buy their sugar and their flannel at the shops where their fathers and mothers had bought before them; but, if new-comers were to bring in the system of neck-and-neck trading, and solicit feminine eyes by gown-pieces laid in fan-like folds, and surmounted by artificial flowers, giving them a factitious charm (for on what human figure would a gown sit like a fan, or what female head was like a bunch of China-asters?), or, if new grocers were to fill their windows with mountains of currants and sugar, made seductive by contrast and tickets, – what security was there for Grimworth, that a vagrant spirit in shopping, once introduced, would not in the end carry the most important families to the larger market town of Cattleton, where, business being done on a system of small profits and quick returns, the fashions were of the freshest, and goods of all kinds might be bought at an advantage?

With this view of the times predominant among the tradespeople at Grimworth, their uncertainty concerning the nature of the business which the sallow-complexioned stranger was about to set up in the vacant shop, naturally gave some additional strength to the fears of the less sanguine. If he was going to sell drapery, it was probable that a pale-faced fellow like that would deal in showy and inferior articles – printed cottons and muslins which would leave their dye in the wash-tub, jobbed linen full of knots, and flannel that would soon look like gauze. If grocery, then it was to be hoped that no mother of a family would trust the teas of an untried grocer. Such things had been known in some parishes as tradesmen going about canvassing for custom with cards in their pockets: when people came from nobody knew where, there was no knowing what they might do. It was a thousand pities that Mr Moffat, the auctioneer and broker, had died without leaving anybody to follow him in the business, and Mrs Cleve's trustee ought to have known better than to let a shop to a stranger. Even the discovery that ovens were being put up on the premises, and that the shop was, in fact, being fitted up for a confectioner and pastry-cook's business, hitherto unknown in Grimworth, did not quite suffice to turn the scale in the new-comer's favour, though the landlady at the Woolpack defended him warmly, said he seemed to be a very clever young man, and from what she could make out, came of a very good family; indeed, was most likely a good many people's betters.

It certainly made a blaze of light and colour, almost as if a rainbow had suddenly descended into the market-place, when, one fine morning, the shutters were taken down from the new shop, and the two windows displayed their decorations. On one side, there were the variegated tints of collared and marbled meats, set off by bright green leaves, the pale brown of glazed pies, the rich tones of sauces and bottled fruits enclosed in their veil of glass – altogether a sight to bring tears into the eyes of a Dutch painter; and on the other, there was a predominance of the more delicate hues of pink, and white, and yellow, and buff, in the abundant lozenges, candies, sweet biscuits and icings, which to the eyes of a bilious person might easily have been blended into a faëry landscape in Turner's latest style. What a sight to dawn upon the eyes of Grimworth children! They almost forgot to go to their dinner that day, their appetites being preoccupied with imaginary sugar-plums; and I think even Punch, setting up his tabernacle in the market-place, would not have succeeded in drawing them away from those shop-windows, where they stood according to gradations of size and strength, the biggest and strongest being nearest the window, and the little ones in the outermost rows lifting wide-open eyes and mouths towards the upper tier of jars, like small birds at meal-time.[34]

Again we have the advent of the stranger, coming to disturb the set attitudes of a set populace (or to be assimilated by them), again we have the cross-section of sects in a provincial town which is a recurring pattern in George Eliot's fiction. The story deals with trade, a subject generally avoided by nineteenth-century novelists, and here treated with comic indulgence. It shows the variety of which George Eliot was capable, and the story in itself is light in expression but has a dark emphasis. The breath of scandal is killing in a small town. It is very much a scene of provincial life.

I have indicated that historical perspective is conspicuous when George Eliot looks back to her roots or to familiar regions. Such perspective is very apparent in *Felix Holt*, where facts are extended by fiction to delineate the name and nature of change:

Treby Magna, on which the Reform Bill had thrust the new honour of being a polling-place, had been, at the beginning of the century, quite a typical old market-town, lying in pleasant sleepiness among green pastures, with a rush-fringed river meandering through them. Its principal street had various handsome and tall-windowed brick houses with walled gardens behind them; and at the end, where it widened into the marketplace, there was the cheerful rough-stuccoed front of that excellent inn, the Marquis of Granby, where the farmers put up their gigs, not only on fair and market days, but on exceptional Sundays when they came to church. And the church was one of those fine old English structures worth travelling to see, standing in a broad churchyard with a line of solemn yew-trees beside it, and lifting a majestic tower and spire far above the red-and-purple roofs of the town. It was not large enough to hold all the parishioners of a parish which stretched over distant villages and hamlets; but then they were never so unreasonable as to wish to be all in at once, and had never complained that the space of a large side-chapel was taken up by the tombs of the Debarrys, and shut in by a handsome iron screen. For when the black Benedictines ceased to pray and chant in this church, when the Blessed Virgin and St Gregory were expelled, the Debarrys, as lords of the manor, naturally came next to Providence and took the place of the saints. Long before that time, indeed, there had been a Sir Maximus Debarry who had been at the fortifying of the old castle, which now stood in ruins in the midst of the green pastures, and with its sheltering wall towards the north made an excellent strawyard for the pigs of Wace & Co., brewers of the celebrated Treby beer. Wace & Co. did not stand alone in the town as prosperous traders on a large scale, to say nothing of those who had retired from business; and in no country town of the same small size as Treby was there a larger proportion of families who had handsome sets of china without handles, hereditary punch-bowls, and large silver ladles with a Queen Anne's guinea in the centre. Such people naturally took tea and supped together frequently; and as there was no professional man or tradesman in Treby who was not connected by business, if not by blood, with the farmers of the district, the richer sort of these were much invited, and gave invitations in their turn. They played at whist, ate and drank generously, praised Mr Pitt and the war as keeping up prices and religion, and were very humorous about each other's property, having much the same coy pleasure in allusions to their secret ability to purchase, as blushing lasses sometimes have in jokes about their secret preferences. The Rector was always of the Debarry family, associated only with county people, and was much respected for his affability; a clergyman who would have taken tea with the townspeople would have given a dangerous shock to the mind of a Treby Churchman.

Such was the old-fashioned, grazing, brewing, wool-packing, cheese-loading life of Treby Magna, until there befell new conditions, complicating its relation with the rest of the world, and gradually awakening in it that higher consciousness which is known to bring higher pains. First came the canal; next, the working of the coal-mines at Sproxton, two miles off the town; and, thirdly, the discovery of a saline spring, which suggested to a too constructive brain the possibility of turning Treby Magna into a fashionable watering-place. So daring an idea was not originated by a native Trebian, but by a young lawyer who came from a distance, knew the dictionary by heart, and was probably an illegitimate son of somebody or other. The idea, although it promised an increase of wealth to the town, was not well received at first; ladies objected to seeing "objects" drawn about in hand-carriages, the doctor foresaw the advent of unsound practitioners, and most retail tradesmen concurred with him that new doings were usually for the advantage of new people. The more unanswerable reasoners urged that Treby had prospered without baths, and it was yet to be seen how it would prosper with them; while a report that the proposed name for them was Bethesda Spa, threatened to give the whole affair a blasphemous aspect. Even Sir Maximus Debarry, who was to have an unprecedented return for the thousands he would lay out on a pump-room and hotel, regarded the thing as a little too new, and held back for some time. But the persuasive powers of the young lawyer, Mr Matthew Jermyn, together with the opportune opening of a stone-quarry, triumphed at last; the handsome buildings were erected, an excellent guide-book and descriptive cards, surmounted by vignettes, were printed, and Treby Magna became conscious of certain facts in its own history, of which it had previously been in contented ignorance.

But it was all in vain. The Spa, for some mysterious reason, did not succeed. Some attributed the failure to the coal-mines and the canal, others to the peace, which had had ruinous effects on the country, and others, who disliked Jermyn, to the original folly of the plan. Among these last was Sir Maximus himself, who never forgave the too persuasive attorney: it was Jermyn's fault not only that a useless hotel had been built, but that he, Sir Maximus, being straitened for money, had at last let the building, with the adjacent land lying on the river, on a long lease, on the supposition that it was to be turned into a benevolent college, and had seen himself subsequently powerless to prevent its being turned into a tape manufactory – a bitter thing to any gentleman, and especially to the representative of one of the oldest families in England.

In this way it happened that Treby Magna gradually passed from being simply a respectable market-town – the heart of a great rural district, where the trade was only such as had close relations with the local landed interest – and took on the more complex life brought by mines and manufacturers, which belong more directly to the great circulating system of the nation than to the local system to which they have been superadded; and in this way it was that Trebian Dissent gradually altered its character. Formerly it had been of a quiescent, well-to-do kind, represented architecturally by a small, venerable, dark-pewed chapel, built by Presbyterians, but long occupied by a sparse congregation of Independents, who were as little moved by doctrinal zeal as their church-going neighbours, and did not feel themselves deficient in religious liberty, inasmuch as they were not hindered from occasionally slumbering in their pews, and were not obliged to go regularly to the weekly prayer-meeting. But when stone-pits and coal-pits made new hamlets that threatened to spread up to the very town, when the tape-weavers came with their newsreading inspectors and book-keepers, the Independent chapel began to be filled with eager men and women, to whom the exceptional possession of religious truth was the condition which reconciled them to a meagre existence and made them feel in secure alliance with the unseen but supreme rule of a world in which their own visible part was small. There were Dissenters in Treby now who could not be regarded by the Church people in the light of old neighbours to whom the habit of going to chapel was an innocent, unenviable inheritance along with a particular house and garden, a tan-yard, or a grocery business – Dissenters who, in their turn, without meaning to be in the least abusive, spoke of the high-bred Rector as a blind leader of the blind. And Dissent was not the only thing that the times had altered; prices had fallen, poor-rates had risen, rent and tithe were not elastic enough, and the farmer's fat sorrow had become lean; he began to speculate on causes, and to trace things back to that causeless mystery, the cessation of one-pound notes. Thus, when political agitation swept in a great current through the country, Treby Magna was prepared to vibrate. The Catholic Emancipation Bill opened the eyes of neighbours, and made them aware how very injurious they were to each other and to the welfare of mankind generally. Mr Tiliot, the Church spirit-merchant, knew now that Mr Nuttwood, the obliging grocer, was one of those Dissenters, Deists, Socinians, Papists, and Radicals, who were in league to destroy the Constitution. A retired old London tradesman, who was believed to understand politics, said that thinking people must wish George the Third alive again in all his early vigour of mind; and even the farmers became less materialistic in their view of causes, and referred much to the agency of the devil and the Irish Romans.[35]

I give this passage at length because it shows the density of George Eliot's embodied conception of place and the ever-present historical perspective. The narrative dynamically records change, the failure of the Spa being set against the increasing industrialization of the area. Political awareness and religious difference have their emphasis, and the "tape manufactory" has direct associations with Coventry – we remember that Charles Bray was a ribbon manufacturer, though a failed one. The range of reference, the full register of the nature of the population, the almost casual delineation of class interaction, the sense of space – all these are part of George Eliot's mature art. She is not only aware of a religious and political activity, but also of a capital and labour one. And we notice that this early, in Chapter III of the novel, the roles of Jermyn and Sir Maximus in their professional and economic respects, are spelled out, while the mention of Sproxton and the mining community prepares us for Felix's visit to talk to the men who are being got at by the professional corrupters of reform.

As we have seen, place is sometimes confined: after Janet is turned out into the cold by her brutal husband, she is taken care of by her good friend Mrs Pettifer:

She drew the poor sobbing thing gently up-stairs, and persuaded her to get into the warm bed. But it was long before Janet could lie down. She sat leaning her head on her knees, convulsed by sobs, while the motherly woman covered her with clothes and held her arms round her to comfort her with warmth. At last the hysterical passion had exhausted itself, and she fell back on the pillow; but her throat was still agitated by piteous after-sobs, such as shake a little child even when it has found a refuge from its alarms on its mother's lap.

Now Janet was getting quieter, Mrs Pettifer determined to go down and make a cup of tea, the first thing a kind old woman thinks of as a solace and restorative under all calamities. Happily there was no danger of awaking her servant, a heavy girl of sixteen, who was snoring blissfully in the attic, and might be kept ignorant of the way in which Mrs Dempster had come in. So Mrs Pettifer busied herself with rousing the kitchen fire, which was kept in under a huge "raker" – a possibility by which the coal of the midland counties atones for all its slowness and white ashes.

When she carried up the tea, Janet was lying quite still; the spasmodic agitation had ceased, and she seemed lost in thought; her eyes were fixed vacantly on the rushlight shade, and all the lines of sorrow were deepened in her face.

"Now, my dear," said Mrs Pettifer, "let me persuade you to drink a cup of tea; you'll find it warm you and soothe you very much. Why, dear heart, your feet are like ice still. Now, do drink this tea, and I'll wrap 'em up in flannel, and then they'll get warm."

Janet turned her dark eyes on her old friend and stretched out her arms. She was too much oppressed to say anything; her suffering lay like a heavy weight on her power of speech; but she wanted to kiss the good kind woman. Mrs Pettifer, setting down the cup, bent towards the sad beautiful face, and Janet kissed her with earnest sacramental kisses – such kisses as seal a new and closer bond between the helper and the helped.

She drank the tea obediently. "It *does* warm me," she said. "But now you will get into bed. I shall lie still now."

Mrs Pettifer felt it was the best thing she could do to lie down quietly, and say no more. She hoped Janet might go to sleep. As for herself, with that tendency to wakefulness common to advanced years, she found it impossible to compose herself to sleep again after this agitating surprise. She lay listening to the clock, wondering what had led to this new outrage of Dempster's, praying for the poor thing at her side, and pitying the mother who would have to hear it all to-morrow.[36]

This moving scene is enhanced by the confined nature of the place, which makes for warmth, intimacy, and love, all lacking in Janet's marriage. She is put to bed like a child, and the bed and the companionship are a refuge. The domestic space provides the closeness of love, protective and protected and secret, though there is the little detail of the servant's proximity in the attic of the small provincial house. And of course there is suspense generated by the imagined fear of Dempster's reactions. A phrase like "the helper and the helped" sums up this experience and expresses a central theme of the story. "The helper and the helped" are seen again in the way Janet and Tryan help and minister to each other. Mrs Pettifer's care for Janet is the type of that sympathy which Tryan possesses and which Janet acquires: it exemplifies the intimacy and warmth, not the divisions of place.

Other confined spaces have associations within the narrative, and occasionally they can be identified too. The Stoniton in *Adam Bede* is a town in Stonyshire, based on Derby and Derbyshire. It is here that Hetty Sorrel is tried for child murder. Her original, Mary Voce, was found guilty at Nottingham and executed there in March, 1802. Just as George Eliot transferred, at least in part, St Mary's Hall in Coventry to St Ogg's, so here she substantiates the scene by directly drawing on a building in Derby:

The place fitted up that day as a court of justice was a grand old hall, now destroyed by fire. The mid-day light that fell on the close pavement of human heads, was shed through a line of high pointed windows, variegated with the mellow tints of old painted glass. Grim dusty armour hung in high relief in front of the dark oaken gallery at the farther end; and under the broad arch of the great mullioned window opposite, was spread a curtain of old tapestry, covered with dim melancholy figures, like a dozing indistinct dream of the past. It was a place that through the rest of the year was haunted with the shadowy memories of old kings and queens, unhappy, discrowned, imprisoned; but today all those shadows had fled, and not a soul in the vast hall felt the presence of any but a living sorrow, which was quivering in warm hearts.[37]

This too is the Coventry hall. William Mottram in *The True Story of George Eliot* (1905), mentions that the town hall of Derby was burned down in 1841.[38] The hall represents the public restraint of Hetty: in a terrible sense it, more than the privacy of the prison, both confines her *and* displays her. The witnesses take their places: they say their say at length, perhaps at excessive length. There is a clever underlining of the hardness of justice and indeed of unconscious humanity in the use of the word "pavement" (we are in Stoniton, and perhaps by verbal design the first witness is called Sarah Stone). The history of the place has associations with its present usage – "unhappy, discrowned, imprisoned" – though Hetty only wanted to be a lady or even a lady's maid. The place is made sad by its past: it is made oppressively tragic by its present.

By the time George Eliot presents the trial in *Felix Holt*, she has learned much more about the creation of the social scene. There is certain establishment of place when Felix is tried. It is done not by a concentration on physical detail, but on the representation of the place as a whole. And we are always made aware of the effect on the leading characters:

If Esther had been less absorbed by supreme feelings, she would have been aware that she was an object of special notice. In the bare squareness of a public hall, where there was not one jutting angle to hang a guess or a thought upon, not an image or a bit of colour to stir the fancy, and where the only objects of speculation, of admiration, or of any interest whatever, were human beings, and especially the human beings that occupied positions indicating some importance, the notice bestowed on

Esther would not have been surprising, even if it had been merely a tribute to her youthful charm, which was well companioned by Mrs Transome's elderly majesty. But it was due also to whisperings that she was an hereditary claimant of the Transome estates, whom Harold Transome was about to marry. Harold himself had of late not cared to conceal either the fact or the probability: they both tended rather to his honour than his dishonour. And today, when there was a good proportion of Trebians present, the whisperings spread rapidly.[39]

The emphasis in this scene is striking: as I said in the introduction, people reflect place, they give it its character at moments of crisis or importance. As she wrote on, George Eliot learned how to use place with greater effect.

In *Adam Bede* and *Felix Holt*, just as there are two trial scenes, so there are two prison scenes. Again the difference is marked. Dinah sees Hetty after the verdict: Esther sees Felix before, and that meeting is what determines her to go to court. In the first scene the oppressive sense of prison is directly physical:

As Dinah crossed the prison court with the turnkey, the solemn evening light seemed to make the walls higher than they were by day, and the sweet pale face in the cap was more than ever like a white flower on this background of gloom. The turnkey looked askance at her all the while, but never spoke: he somehow felt that the sound of his own rude voice would be grating just then. He struck a light as they entered the dark corridor leading to the condemned cell, and then said in his most civil tone, "It'll be pretty nigh dark in the cell already; but I can stop with my light a bit, if you like."[40]

The effects are achieved by the generalized description – the walls seeming "higher" – and by the particular contrasts – "solemn", "sweet", "light", "dark", "white", "gloom". But place takes second place to persons because we are made to feel anxiety to see how Hetty (in the "condemned cell") will respond to Dinah. In *Felix Holt* Esther goes to her father's house and is conducted to the prison: "She had no consciousness of the road along which they passed; she could never remember anything but a dim sense of entering within high walls and going along passages, till they were ushered into a larger space than she expected. . . ."[41] The movement through place to *the* place is done with a functional vagueness which heightens the reader's expectancy and also acts as a tremulous index to Esther's anxiety and anticipation.

George Eliot frequently uses place to describe dramatic events. Perhaps the most dramatic sequence derived from fact is seen in *Felix Holt*. As Gordon Haight puts it:

. . . the vivid touches that illuminate the novel were drawn from her childhood memories of Nuneaton at the time of the Reform Bill, when she was a schoolgirl at Mrs Wallington's. She had clear recollection of the soup kitchens for unemployed weavers and miners and of the excitement during the election riots in December 1832. The sentiment of the majority of the townspeople was strongly Radical. Dempster

Heming, lately returned from successful practice of the law in India, had decided –
like Harold Transome – to stand for the Radicals. In a fair election he would have
won easily. But the Tories, seeing the tide going against them, suspended the poll,
and called in a detachment of Scots Greys, which had been kept in readiness at
Meriden; the Riot Act was read, and when the mob did not disperse, horse soldiers
with drawn swords rode through the town, charging the people, cutting and trampling
them down. One man died of his injuries. These were events not to be forgotton.
Though one seldom feels that she is sketching from originals, as in the earlier novels,
these memories gave a convincing density of background.[42]

From this account (taken from a note-book called *Occurrences at Nuneaton*)
George Eliot "placed" one of the major events in a "convincing density of
background":

Felix was perfectly conscious that he was in the midst of a tangled business. But he
had chiefly before his imagination the horrors that might come if the mass of wild
chaotic desires and impulses around him were not diverted from any further attack
on places where they would get in the midst of intoxicating and inflammable materials.
It was not a moment in which a spirit like his could calculate the effect of
misunderstanding as to himself: nature never makes men who are at once energetically
sympathetic and minutely calculating. He believed he had the power, and he was
resolved to try, to carry the dangerous mass out of mischief till the military came to
awe them – which he supposed, from Mr Crow's announcement long ago, must be
a near event.

He was followed the more willingly, because Tiliot's Lane was seen by the hindmost
to be now defended by constables, some of whom had fire-arms; and where there is
no strong counter-movement, any proposition to do something unspecified stimulates
stupid curiosity. To many of the Sproxton men who were within sight of him, Felix
was known personally, and vaguely believed to be a man who meant many queer
things, not at all of an everyday kind. Pressing along like a leader, with the sabre in
his hand, and inviting them to bring on Spratt, there seemed a better reason for
following him than for doing anything else. A man with a definite will and an energetic
personality acts as a sort of flag to draw and bind together the foolish units of a mob.
It was on this sort of influence over men whose mental state was a mere medley of
appetites and confused impressions, that Felix had dared to count. He hurried them
along with words of invitation, telling them to hold up Spratt and not drag him; and
those behind followed him, with a growing belief that he had some design worth
knowing, while those in front were urged along partly by the same notion, partly by
the sense that there was a motive in those behind them, not knowing what the motive
was. It was that mixture of pushing forward and being pushed forward, which is a
brief history of most human things.

What Felix really intended to do, was to get the crowd by the nearest way out of
the town, and induce them to skirt it on the north side with him, keeping up in them
the idea that he was leading them to execute some stratagem by which they would
surprise something worth attacking, and circumvent the constables who were
defending the lanes. In the mean time he trusted that the soldiers would have arrived,
and with this sort of mob, which was animated by no real political passion or fury

93

against social distinctions, it was in the highest degree unlikely that there would be any resistance to a military force. The presence of fifty soldiers would probably be enough to scatter the rioting hundreds. How numerous the mob was, no one ever knew: many inhabitants afterwards were ready to swear that there must have been at least two thousand rioters. Felix knew he was incurring great risks; but "his blood was up:" we hardly allow enough in common life for the results of that enkindled passionate enthusiam which, under other conditions, makes world-famous deeds.

He was making for a point where the street branched off on one side towards a speedy opening between hedgerows, on the other towards the shabby wideness of Pollard's End. At this forking of the street there was a large space, in the centre of which there was a small stone platform, mounting by three steps, with an old green finger-post upon it. Felix went straight to this platform and stepped upon it, crying "Halt!" in a loud voice to the men behind and before him, and calling to those who held Spratt to bring him there. All came to a stand with faces towards the finger-post, and perhaps for the first time the extremities of the crowd got a definite idea that a man with a sabre in his hand was taking the command.

"Now!" said Felix, when Spratt had been brought on to the stone platform, faint and trembling, "has anybody got cord? if not, handkerchiefs knotted fast; give them to me."

He drew out his own handkerchief, and two or three others were mustered and handed to him. He ordered them to be knotted together, while curious eyes were fixed on him. Was he going to have Spratt hanged? Felix kept fast hold of his weapon, and ordered others to act.

"Now, put it round his waist, wind his arms in, draw them a little backward – so! and tie it fast on the other side of the post."

When that was done, Felix said, imperatively,

"Leave him there – we shall come back to him; let us make haste; march along lads! Up Park Street and down Hobb's Lane."

It was the best chance he could think of for saving Spratt's life. And he succeeded. The pleasure of seeing the helpless man tied up sufficed for the moment, if there were any who had ferocity enough to count much on coming back to him. Nobody's imagination represented the certainty that some one out of the houses at hand would soon come and untie him when he was left alone.

And the rioters pushed up Park Street, a noisy stream, with Felix still in the midst of them, though he was labouring hard to get his way to the front. He wished to determine the course of the crowd along a by-road called Hobb's Lane, which would have taken them to the other – the Duffield end of the town. He urged several of the men round him, one of whom was no less a person than the big Dredge, our old Sproxton acquaintance, to get forward, and be sure that all the fellows would go down the lane, else they would spoil sport. Hitherto Felix had been successful, and he had gone along with an unbroken impulse. But soon something occurred which brought with a terrible shock the sense that his plan might turn out to be as mad as all bold projects are seen to be when they have failed.

Mingled with the more headlong and half-drunken crowd there were some sharp-visaged men who loved the irrationality of riots for something else than its own sake, and who at present were not so much the richer as they desired to be, for the pains they had taken in coming to the Treby election, induced by certain prognostics gathered at Duffield on the nomination-day that there might be the conditions favourable to that confusion which was always a harvest-time. It was known to some of these sharp men that Park Street led out towards the grand house of Treby Manor, which was as good – nay, better for their purpose than the bank. While Felix was entertaining his ardent purpose, these other sons of Adam were entertaining another ardent purpose of their peculiar sort, and the moment was come when they were to have their triumph.

From the front ranks backward towards Felix there ran a new summons – a new invitation.

"Let us go to Treby Manor!"

From that moment Felix was powerless; a new definite suggestion overrode his vaguer influence. There was a determined rush past Hobb's Lane, and not down it. Felix was carried along too. He did not know whether to wish the contrary. Once on the road, out of the town, with openings into fields and with the wide park at hand, it would have been easy for him to liberate himself from the crowd. At first it seemed to him the better part to do this, and to get back to the town as fast as he could, in the hope of finding the military and getting a detachment to come and save the Manor. But he reflected that the course of the mob had been sufficiently seen, and that there were plenty of people in Park Street to carry the information faster than he could. It seemed more necessary that he should secure the presence of some help for the family at the Manor by going there himself. The Debarrys were not of the class he was wont to be anxious about; but Felix Holt's conscience was alive to the accusation that any danger they might be in now was brought on by a deed of his. In these moments of bitter vexation and disappointment, it did occur to him that very unpleasant consequences might be hanging over him of a kind quite different from inward dissatisfaction; but it was useless now to think of averting such consequences. As he was pressed along with the multitude into Treby Park, his very movement seemed to him only an image of the day's fatalities, in which the multitudinous small wickednesses of small selfish ends, really undirected towards any larger result, had issued in widely-shared mischief that might yet be hideous.

The light was declining: already the candles shone through many windows of the Manor. Already the foremost part of the crowd had burst into the offices, and adroit men were busy in the right places to find plate, after setting others to force the butler into unlocking the cellars; and Felix had only just been able to force his way on to the front terrace, with the hope of getting to the rooms where he would find the ladies of the household and comfort them with the assurance that rescue must soon come, when the sound of horses' feet convinced him that the rescue was nearer than he had expected. Just as he heard the horses, he had approached the large window of a room, where a brilliant light suspended from the ceiling showed him a group of women clinging together in terror. Others of the crowd were pushing their way up the terrace-steps and gravel-slopes at various points. Hearing the horses, he kept his post in front of the window, and, motioning with his sabre, cried out to the on-comers, "Keep back! I hear the soldiers coming." Some scrambled back, some paused automatically.

The louder and louder sound of the hoofs changed its pace and distribution. "Halt! Fire!" Bang! bang! bang! – came deafening the ears of the men on the terrace.

Before they had time or nerve to move, there was a rushing sound closer to them

– again "Fire!" a bullet whizzed, and passed through Felix Holt's shoulder – the shoulder of the arm that held the naked weapon which shone in the light from the window.

Felix fell. The rioters ran confusedly, like terrified sheep. Some of the soldiers, turning, drove them along with the flat of their swords. The greater difficulty was to clear the invaded offices.

The Rector, who with another magistrate and several other gentlemen on horseback had accompanied the soldiers, now jumped on to the terrace, and hurried to the ladies of the family.

Presently there was a group round Felix, who had fainted, and, reviving, had fainted again. He had had little food during the day, and had been overwrought. Two of the group were civilians, but only one of them knew Felix, the other being a magistrate not resident in Treby. The one who knew Felix was Mr John Johnson, whose zeal for the public peace had brought him from Duffield when he heard that the soldiers were summoned.

"I know this man very well," said Mr Johnson. "He is a dangerous character – quite revolutionary."

It was a weary night; and the next day, Felix, whose wound was declared trivial, was lodged in Loamford Gaol.[43]

The density of the background, or rather foreground, is of vital importance to the excitement of the narrative. Felix leaves Tucker (the constable he is later accused of killing) on the ground though he has done nothing aggressive. Afterwards his aim is to save the life of Spratt, the much-hated manager of Sproxton Colliery, and to divert the rioters from looting and pillaging the town. He is unsuccessful, because the rioters make for Treby Manor. But what provides the realism is the route taken by Felix – we do not need to hunt each original place, for what is important is the author's convincing specification of a warren of streets, Tiliot's Lane, Hobb's Lane, Park Street, the "shabby wideness of Pollard's End". The whole sense of place has been mapped and integrated by the imagination. The sheer urban intensity creates an atmosphere of noise and violence, of the crowd and its actions. In complete contrast, George Eliot uses wide space, natural space, in order to establish a different kind of intensity. Here is the wood in *Adam Bede*:

. . . it was still scarcely four o'clock when he stood before the tall narrow gate leading into the delicious labyrinthine wood which skirted one side of the Chase, and which was called Fir Tree Grove, not because the firs were many, but because they were few. It was a wood of beeches and limes, with here and there a light, silver-stemmed birch – just the sort of wood most haunted by the nymphs: you see their white sunlit limbs gleaming athwart the boughs, or peeping from behind the smooth-sweeping outline of a tall lime; you hear their soft liquid laughter – but if you look with a too curious sacrilegious eye, they vanish behind the silvery beeches, they make you believe that their voice was only a running brooklet, perhaps they metamorphose themselves into a tawny squirrel that scampers away and mocks you from the topmost bough. It was not a grove with measured grass or rolled gravel for you to tread upon, but with narrow, hollow-shaped earthy paths, edged with faint dashes of delicate moss – paths which look as if they were made by the free-will of the trees and underwood, moving reverently aside to look at the tall queen of the white-footed nymphs.[44]

This is place endowed with imaginative symbolic association as well as physical particularity. It is also immediate and suggestive, for it is both fact and fancy which are comment on the illusions and delusions of Arthur and Hetty. Each is living in a separate world of the imagination which is unknown to the other. They come together here in the wood, the location each needs. This location is given an ominous aspect:

It was along the broadest of these paths that Arthur Donnithorne passed, under an avenue of limes and beeches. It was a still afternoon – the golden light was lingering languidly among the upper boughs, only glancing down here and there on the purple pathway and its edge of faintly-sprinkled moss: an afternoon in which destiny disguises her cold awful face behind a hazy radiant veil, encloses us in warm downy wings, and poisons us with violet-scented breath.[45]

The inevitable occurs: the power of the seen place – and the power of what neither of them fully understands – exerts itself later when they meet in the evening, Hetty fearing that Arthur would not come, Arthur fearing himself and failing to conquer his feelings. His need to see Hetty is great, but the delusion is working, and he thinks that he is going to see her "to set things right with her by a kindness which would have the air of friendly civility". This is what actually happens:

Hetty turned her head towards him, whispered, "I thought you wouldn't come," and slowly got courage to lift her eyes to him. That look was too much: he must have had eyes of Egyptian granite not to look too lovingly in return.

"You little frightened bird! little tearful rose! silly pet! You won't cry again, now I'm with you, will you?"

Ah, he doesn't know in the least what he is saying. This is not what he meant to say. His arm is stealing round the waist again, it is tightening its clasp; he is bending his face nearer and nearer to the round cheek, his lips are meeting those pouting child-lips, and for a long moment time has vanished. He may be a shepherd in Arcadia for aught he knows, he may be the first youth kissing the first maiden, he may be Eros himself, sipping the lips of Psyche – it is all one.

There was no speaking for minutes after. They walked along with beating hearts till they came within sight of the gate at the end of the wood. Then they looked at each other, not quite as they had looked before, for in their eyes there was the memory of a kiss.

But already something bitter had begun to mingle itself with the fountain of sweets: already Arthur was uncomfortable. He took his arm from Hetty's waist, and said –

"Here we are, almost at the end of the Grove. I wonder how late it is," he added, pulling out his watch. "Twenty minutes past eight – but my watch is too fast. However,

I'd better not go any further now. Trot along quickly with your little feet, and get home safely. Good-bye."

He took her hand, and looked at her half sadly, half with a constrained smile. Hetty's eyes seemed to beseech him not to go away yet; but he patted her cheek and said "Good-bye" again. She was obliged to turn away from him, and go on.

As for Arthur, he rushed back through the wood, as if he wanted to put a wide space between himself and Hetty. He would not go to the Hermitage again; he remembered how he had debated with himself there before dinner, and it had all come to nothing – worse than nothing. He walked right on into the Chase, glad to get out of the Grove, which surely was haunted by his evil genius. Those beeches and smooth limes – there was something enervating in the very sight of them; but the strong knotted old oaks had no bending languor in them – the sight of them would give a man some energy. Arthur lost himself among the narrow openings in the fern, winding about without seeking any issue, till the twilight deepened almost to night under the great boughs, and the hare looked black as it darted across his path.[46]

The Arcadian imagery is part of the ironic comment on the nature of delusion, while the various names – the Grove (where one may be secluded), the Chase (associated with hunting) and the Hermitage (the ascetically named, luxurious isolated cottage in the woods) – all create a theatre for the inevitable seduction. The place too in its particularity contributes to the illusion: the beeches and limes, with combined phallic and yielding suggestion, are an index to Arthur's desire while the "knotted old oaks" represent his delusory strength of will.

The space within Cheverel Manor in "Mr Gilfil's Love-Story" also witnesses love passages. Caterina loves Captain Wybrow, Sir Christopher's nephew, but he is soon to become engaged to Miss Assher, who has been invited to the Manor. Caterina goes to their usual meeting-place:

She had made her way along the cloistered passages, now lighted here and there by a small oil-lamp, to the grand-staircase, which led directly to a gallery running along the whole eastern side of the building, where it was her habit to walk when she wished to be alone. The bright moonlight was streaming through the windows, throwing into strange light and shadow the heterogeneous objects that lined the long walls. Greek statues, and busts of Roman emperors; low cabinets filled with curiosities, natural and antiquarian; tropical birds and huge horns of beasts; Hindoo gods and strange shells; swords and daggers, and bits of chain-armour; Roman lamps, and tiny models of Greek temples; and, above all these, queer old family portraits – of little boys and girls, once the hope of the Cheverels, with close-shaven heads imprisoned in stiff ruffs – of faded, pink-faced ladies, with rudimentary features and highly-developed head-dresses – of gallant gentlemen, with high hips, high shoulders, and red pointed beards.

Here, on rainy days, Sir Christopher and his lady took their promenade, and here billiards were played; but, in the evening, it was forsaken by all except Caterina – and, sometimes, one other person.

She paced up and down in the moonlight, her pale face and thin white-robed form making her look like the ghost of some former Lady Cheverel come to revisit the glimpses of the moon.

By-and-by she paused opposite the broad window above the portico, and looked out on the long vista of turf and trees now stretching chill and saddened in the moonlight.

Suddenly a breath of warmth and roses seemed to float towards her, and an arm stole gently round her waist, while a soft hand took up her tiny fingers. Caterina felt an electric thrill, and was motionless for one long moment; then she pushed away the arm and hand, and, turning round, lifted up to the face that hung over her, eyes full of tenderness and reproach. The fawn-like unconsciousness was gone, and in that one look were the ground tones of poor little Caterina's nature – intense love and fierce jealousy.

"Why do you push me away, Tina?" said Captain Wybrow in a half-whisper; "are you angry with me for what a hard fate puts upon me? Would you have me cross my uncle – who has done so much for us both – in his dearest wish? You know I have duties – we both have duties – before which feeling must be sacrificed."

"Yes, yes," said Caterina, stamping her foot, and turning away her head; "don't tell me what I know already."

There was a voice speaking in Caterina's mind, to which she had never yet given vent. That voice said continually, "Why did he make me love him – why did he let me know he loved me, if he knew all the while that he couldn't brave everything for my sake?" Then love answered, "He was led on by the feeling of the moment, as you have been, Caterina; and now you ought to help him to do what is right." Then the voice rejoined, "It was a slight matter to him. He doesn't much mind giving you up. He will soon love that beautiful woman, and forget a poor little pale thing like you."

Thus love, anger, and jealousy were struggling in that young soul.

"Besides, Tina," continued Captain Wybrow in still gentler tones, "I shall not succeed. Miss Assher very likely prefers some one else; and you know I have the best will in the world to fail. I shall come back a hapless bachelor – perhaps to find you already married to the good-looking chaplain, who is over head and ears in love with you. Poor Sir Christopher has made up his mind that you're to have Gilfil."

"Why will you speak so? You speak from your own want of feeling. Go away from me."[47]

Apart from the specificity of description, of part of the interior of Arbury Hall, the place is filled with ironic commentary. The gallery is space enough to contain Caterina's love and jealousy and Wybrow's opportunism. The objects, the collection and the portraits, represent the dead past life as distinct from the quivering present. The place with its silent collection is part of the inward and outward drama – Caterina's inward dialogue with herself which is registering the truth, Wybrow's outward words about Gilfil. And in a wonderful sense the place dominates them, for both have to do what Sir Christopher wishes, both are dependants. The place represents their social and institutional constraints, as well as representing the institution dependent on their conformity. The gallery, theatre of their secret intimacy, is also their prison, rather as the wood in *Adam Bede* is a trap for the feelings and illusions of Arthur and Hetty. Their dialogue is functionally interrupted by the bell which summons them to another place, the chapel:

It was a pretty sight, that family assembled to worship in the little chapel, where a couple of wax-candles threw a mild faint light on the figures kneeling there. In the desk was Mr Gilfil, with his face a shade graver than usual. On his right hand, kneeling on their red velvet cushions, were the master and mistress of the household, in their elderly dignified beauty. On his left, the youthful grace of Anthony and Caterina, in all the striking contrast of their colouring – he, with his exquisite outline and rounded fairness, like an Olympian god; she, dark and tiny, like a gypsy changeling. Then there were the domestics kneeling on red-covered forms, – the women headed by Mrs Bellamy, the natty little old housekeeper, in snowy cap and apron, and Mrs Sharp, my lady's maid, of somewhat vinegar aspect and flaunting attire; the men by Mr Bellamy the butler, and Mr Warren, Sir Christopher's venerable valet.[48]

It is a small, contained (and privileged) community, exclusive and excluding. The dramatic switch from the place of deception to the place of worship is telling indeed, particularly when we look at Mr Gilfil's face, which suggests that he knows what is going on. The contrast in the places is perhaps underlined by the overt contrast between Anthony and Caterina: and the emphasis on appearances, especially of people, implies that places, like people, are deceptive and deceiving.

Despite the recurrence to her early landscape and townscape George Eliot's range in the use of place – and space – is considerable. What is important is the movement of her intellect and imagination over the known locations. Many of these we can identify, while some are deliberately conflated, I suggest, so as to give us new places or new spirits of place rather than a recognizable geography. The heart of her fictional matter resides where she has chosen to place it, that is, in the heart of England where she grew up, and which she regards as her own fictional territory. She is a regional novelist in the fullest sense of the word, for she is faithful to the sights and sounds, the language of the landscape and the subtler linguistics of change. In her urban and rural scenes there is place for tradition and space for change. Her fine perspective enables her to convey both.

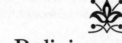

# 4. Religion and Clerics

The presentation of religion plays an important part in George Eliot's fiction, just as it was central to the young womanhood of Marian Evans. Her first three stories are clerical scenes, while her first novel has a Methodist preacher in Dinah Morris and an Anglican rector of Hayslope, Mr Irwine, both of whom have important roles in the plot. *The Mill on the Floss* has Maggie's discovery of Thomas à Kempis, while Dr Kenn, whose wife has recently died, befriends Maggie in her adversity and is condemned by his narrow-minded parishioners. It also has the Rev. Walter Stelling, perhaps the original "clerical tutor" of that other clerical "scene" which she contemplated writing earlier. *Silas Marner* opens with Silas's rejection by the sect in Lantern Yard, while the homespun christianity of Dolly Winthrop helps to restore Silas to a tremulous acceptance of goodness if not of faith. *Felix Holt* has the memorably eccentric Rufus Lyon, almost certainly based upon the Rev. Francis Franklin, the Baptist minister of the Cow Lane chapel in Coventry for fifty-four years until he died in 1852. Marian Evans attended the school run by his daughters the Misses Franklin from 1832 to December 1835. He is seen in contrast with the Rev. Augustus Debarry, rector of Treby Magna, an "old-fashioned aristocratic clergyman, preaching short sermons, understanding business, and acting liberally about his tithe."[1] Even more old-fashioned, in another sense of the word, is Mrs Transome's brother, the Rector of Little Treby, who swore when he was emphasizing a joke, was once known as "Cockfighting Jack" and wore "a coloured bandana tied loosely over his cravat".[2]

In *Middlemarch* we find that clergymen still occupy positions of central interest – Casaubon is rector of Lowick, though his projected *Key to All Mythologies* occupies him more than his Christian office, which is delegated to his curate, Tucker. Next to Casaubon is the man who will succeed him as rector, thanks to Dorothea, namely Camden Farebrother, for most of the action vicar of St Botolph's, Middlemarch. He is generous, interested in science, collects moths, gambles at whist and supports his mother, sister and aunt. Mr Tyke is the apostolic curate in Middlemarch who is made chaplain of the Infirmary on Lydgate's casting vote. In addition to this list and the other individuals not named here there is also that large body of men and women – like Dorothea, for instance – whose various religious feelings and practices contribute to the sense of period and place.

Marian Evans became a fervent believer, narrow, self-denying, enjoying renunciation for its own sake, bigoted, self-righteous and somewhat arrogant in her assertions:

I wonder if you have read Mr Williams's account of his missionary enterprises in the South Seas. It is deeply interesting; truly the "isles are submitting to the Lord" and literally "wailing for His law" for in many islands the parting request of the inhabitants was "Do send us a teacher." If you have not seen the book and have an opportunity of choosing one for your society I think I may venture to say that it could not fail to interest any person of taste to say nothing of religion. Mr W. is a dissenter but the B[isho]p of Chester highly commended his work in a speech at a meeting of the Bible Society and it has since been purchased by all denominations. If you have any bigots near you there could not be a better book for them.

I have just begun the Life of Wilberforce and I am expecting a rich treat from it. There is a similarity, if I may compare myself with such a man, between his temptations or rather besetments and my own that makes his experience very interesting to me. O that I might be made as useful in my lowly and obscure station as he was in the exalted one assigned to him. I feel myself to be a mere cumberer of the ground. May the Lord gi[ve] me such an insight into what is truly good and su[ch] realizing views of an approaching eternity, that I may not rest contented with making Christianity a mere addendum to my pursuits, or with tacking it as a fringe to my garments. May I seek to be sanctified wholly. My nineteenth birthday will soon be here (the 22d) an awakening signal! My mind has been much clogged lately by languor of body, to which I am prone to give way and for the removal of which I shall feel thankful.

If egotism be at any time excusable it is in writing to a friend, and to the charity of so kind a friend as yourself I dare trust for the pardon of all that is tedious and impertinent in this careless letter. After all it is an unspeakable mercy to have our souls at all occupied on our eternal interests, to have commenced in however small a degree to commune with our own hearts. A dear friend said to me the other day and the words made a deep impression on me "A little grace is an inestimable treasure; we should beware of rejecting or refusing to acknowledge what we have because it is so little."

My writing takes up so much room owing to its untidiness that I have no room to answer all your kind enquires. My dear Sister is quite well and so is her baby. I am not aware that there is any truth in the report you have heard of another member of our family. Dear Father is as well as usual.

We have had an oratorio at Coventry lately, Braham, Phillips, Mrs Knyvett and Mrs Shaw, the last I think I shall attend. I am not fitted to decide on the question of the propriety of lawfulness of such exhibitions of talent and so forth because I have no soul for music. "Happy is he that condemneth not himself in that thing which he alloweth" but for my part I humbly conceive it to be little less than blasphemy for such words as "Now then we are ambassadors for Christ" to be taken on the lips of such a man as Braham (a Jew too!). I am a tasteless person but it would not cost me any regrets if the only music heard in our land were that of strict worship, nor can I think a pleasure that involves the devotion of all the time and powers of an immortal being to the acquirement of an expertness in so useless (at least in ninety nine cases out of a hundred) an accomplishment can be quite pure or elevating in its tendency.

Thanks, you will say to the lack of room that prevents this everlasting prate-apace from annoying me farther.[3]

The attitudes embodied in this letter – and the pedantic tone of some of them undermines their force – belong to the devout phase of Mary Ann's Anglican evangelicalism within the Established Church. This is one of a number of letters to her old teacher and friend Maria Lewis, interesting because they may be set beside the fictional expressions put into the mouths of her characters and her recorded rejection of these sentiments which she was to express later. Ironically, this letter was written in November 1838, the year in which Charles Christian Hennell published his *An Inquiry into the Origins of Christianity* just a few weeks after Mary Ann's birthday. She did not read the book until three years later, in November 1841,[4] as a result of her introduction to the Brays at Rosehill, Coventry, where she soon became intimate. Meanwhile, her fervour continued. In 1839 she set to work on a chart of ecclesiastical history: it was never published, since a competitor got in before her.[5] She made it clear to Maria Lewis that she strongly disapproved of *The Tracts for the Times* (her brother Isaac was High Church in his views, the opposite to her). She sent Maria Lewis her poem, quoted below, which was later published in the *Christian Observer*. It gives a sufficient indication of the state of her mind and, particularly, the state of her faith:

"Knowing that shortly I must put off this tabernacle" – 2 Pet. 1. 16.

> As o'er the fields by evening's light I stray,
> I hear a still, small whisper – "Come away!
> Thou must to this bright, lovely world soon say
> > Farewell!"

> The mandate I'd obey, my lamp prepare,
> Gird up my garments, give my soul to pray'r
> And say to earth and all that breathe earth's air
> > Farewell!

> Thou sun, to whose parental beam I owe
> All that has gladden'd me while here below, –
> Moon, stars, and covenant confirming bow,
> > Farewell!

> Ye verdant meads, fair blossoms, stately trees,
> Sweet song of birds, and soothing hum of bees,
> Refreshing odours, wafted on the breeze,
> > Farewell!

> Ye patient servants of creation's lord
> Whose mighty strength is govern'd by his word,
> Who raiment, food and help in toil afford,
> > Farewell!

Ye feebler, freer tribes, that people air,
Fairy like insects, making buds your lair,
Ye that in water shine, and frolic there,
                    Farewell!

Books that have been to me as chests of gold,
Which, miser like, I secretly have told,
And for them love, health, friendship, peace have sold,
                    Farewell!

Blest volume! whose clear truth-writ page, once known,
Fades not before heaven's sunshine or hell's moan,
To thee I say not, of earth's gifts alone,
                    Farewell!

Dear kindred, whom the Lord to me has given,
Must the dear tie that binds us, now be riven?
No! say I *only* till we meet in heaven,
                    Farewell!

There shall my newborn senses find new joy,
New sounds, new sights my eyes and ears employ,
Nor fear that word that here brings sad alloy,
                    Farewell![6]

The combination of morbidity and assurance is typical of Mary Ann in her Griff period: sometimes it takes the form of a spiritual scourging (her word). The following letter to Maria Lewis in 1840 has a particular interest for the reader of her fiction:

My heart has lately been with you more than ever and had I any magic at command it would certainly be used in transporting me to Burton for one day. My last accounts of the poor sufferer at Nuneaton were favourable; but you will probably receive more regular and trustworthy information concerning him than I. I cherish hopes concerning the result of this scourging should God see fit in His immeasurable longsuffering, to uphold his life under such excruciating pain as he must endure. I long to know Mrs. B's spiritual state. It is an inexpressible mercy, enough to absorb our finite gratitude and leave none for other gifts, to feel that the "Lord God hath opened our ear" to His voice, which is to be heard in every note of the scale to which His dealings in the Kingdom of Grace and of Providence are set; from the still and gently drawing whispers of His Spirit in the soul to the deep-toned and almost stunning thunder of his power when whole nations, while falling a sacrifice on the shrine of His incensed justice, subserve at the same time the designs of His compassion by putting others in fear that they may know themselves to be but men. We may so far agree with the Quietists as to exercise that constant waiting on God for instruction and comfort which they make the sum total of religion but which we would unite with that active obedience that reasonable service, so prominently set forth in precept both figurative and literal and embodied in the conduct of God's saints, throughout the "lively oracles" that have been committed to us. Our poor bodies are in league with our spiritual enemies within and without to make us weary in well doing, we get troubled by reason of the way and we sit down weeping in the camp at the prospect of encountering the terrific giants that stand between us and our promised Canaan, after all the trials of the traversed wilderness. What is the remedy in this case? Surely more of the grace that has subdued kingdoms wrought righteousness stopped the mouths of lions, *out of weakness* has *produced strength*, waxed valiant in fight, turned to flight the armies of the aliens. How replete with meaning for doctrine, for reproof, for instruction in righteousness is the historical part of Scripture. Is it not clear that strong faith in the promises, real appropriation of them, must be a fountain ever sending forth streams of love and joy? The greater our assurance of pardon, the more lively and active our gratitude. While enjoying the light of God's countenance and feeding on the supplies that His Spirit imparts through the word and works of God we shall scarcely miss inferior comforts when withdrawn. Blessed state! O that I could attain it – and why not? Because I am straitened not in Christ but in my own bowels. We are like poor creatures of whom I have read, who, for some cause or other, having been thrust out of a ship by their companions, try to grasp first one part of the vessel then another for support, until by the successive lashes that are given to make them loose their hold, they have no fingers left by which to venture another hopeless experiment on pitiless hearts. So we, having *voluntarily* caused ourselves to be cast out as evil by the world, are continually indicating a vacillation in our choice by trying to lean on some part of it within reach, and it is mercy that orders the lashing of our disobedient fingers, even though for a time we be faint and bleeding from the correction.[7]

Apart from the excessively self-indulgent religiosity of this, there is the reference to "the poor sufferer at Nuneaton". This was J. W. Buchanan, who had suffered a severe accident: "While driving towards Coventry, one of the wheels of his carriage came off, near the second milestone, and in dismounting he fell, and the vehicle passed over his legs, one of which sustained a compound fracture, and the other was severely lacerated. Mr Ball, surgeon of Foleshill, set the broken limb, and he was removed home, where he lies in a very precarious state. The circumstance is rendered more distressing by the decease of Mrs Buchanan, who died after a short illness at Margate on Sunday last."[8] (*Coventry Standard* 24th July 1840.) As we can see from the letter, the religious Mary Ann Evans judged him severely: when she came to represent him fictionally, enough of her previous detestation was present for her to record the incident, transform it through her genius, and have Janet Dempster return to nurse her alcoholic husband. It is a terrible and terrifying sequence, and it is difficult to imagine the Mary Ann who wrote this letter from her fixation, breathing into her fictitious Janet, reclaimed to Divine Love by Mr Tryan, the compassion, love and tenderness seventeen years later.

But George Eliot looked back to other local happenings, and *Scenes* provides them in abundance. Though Lewes, always intent on promoting his partner, told Blackwood in the early correspondence he was acting for "my clerical friend"[9] (Blackwood replied, "I am glad to hear that your friend is as I supposed a Clergyman")[10] he soon changed this to "the writer of the clerical stories".[11] This is a sample of that writer's first story:

At Mr Ely's right hand you see a very small man with a sallow and somewhat puffy face, whose hair is brushed straight up, evidently with the intention of giving him a height somewhat less disproportionate to his sense of his own importance than the measure of five feet three accorded him by an oversight of nature. This is the Rev. Archibald Duke, a very dyspeptic and evangelical man, who takes the gloomiest view of mankind and their prospects, and thinks the immense sale of the "Pickwick Papers," recently completed, one of the strongest proofs of original sin. Unfortunately, though Mr Duke was not burdened with a family, his yearly expenditure was apt considerably to exceed his income; and the unpleasant circumstances resulting from this, together with heavy meat breakfasts, may probably have contributed to his desponding views of the world generally.

Next to him is seated Mr Furness, a tall young man, with blond hair and whiskers, who was plucked at Cambridge entirely owing to his genius; at least, I know that he soon afterwards published a volume of poems, which were considered remarkably beautiful by many young ladies of his acquaintance. Mr Furness preached his own sermons, as any one of tolerable critical acumen might have certified by comparing them with his poems: in both, there was an exuberance of metaphor and simile entirely original, and not in the least borrowed from any resemblance in the things compared.

On Mr Furness's left you see Mr Pugh, another young curate, of much less marked characteristics. He had not published any poems; he had not even been plucked; he had neat black whiskers and a pale complexion; read prayers and a sermon twice every Sunday, and might be seen any day sallying forth on his parochial duties in a white tie, a well-brushed hat, a perfect suit of black, and well-polished boots – an equipment which he probably supposed hieroglyphically to represent the spirit of Christianity to the parishioners of Whittlecombe.

Mr Pugh's *vis-à-vis* is the Rev. Martin Cleves, a man about forty – middle-sized, broad-shouldered, with a negligently-tied cravat, large irregular features, and a large head, thickly covered with lanky brown hair. To a superficial glance, Mr Cleves is the plainest and least clerical-looking of the party; yet, strange to say, *there* is the true parish priest, the pastor beloved, consulted, relied on by his flock; a clergyman who is not associated with the undertaker, but thought of as the surest helper under a difficulty, as a monitor who is encouraging rather than severe. Mr Cleves has the wonderful art of preaching sermons which the wheelwright and the blacksmith can understand; not because he talks condescending twaddle, but because he can call a spade a spade, and knows how to disencumber ideas of their wordy frippery. Look at him more attentively, and you will see that his face is a very interesting one – that there is a great deal of humour and feeling playing in his grey eyes, and about the corners of his roughly cut mouth: – a man, you observe, who has most likely sprung from the harder-working section of the middle class, and has hereditary sympathies with the chequered life of the people. He gets together the working men in his parish on a Monday evening, and gives them a sort of conversational lecture on useful practical matters, telling them stories, or reading some select passages from an agreeable book, and commenting on them; and if you were to ask the first labourer or artisan in Tripplegate what sort of man the parson was, he would say, – "a uncommon knowin', sensable, free-spoken gentleman; very kind an' good-natur'd too." Yet for all this, he is perhaps the best Grecian of the party, if we except Mr Baird, the young man on his left.

Mr Baird has since gained considerable celebrity as an original writer and metropolitan lecturer, but at that time he used to preach in a little church something like a barn, to a congregation consisting of three rich farmers and their servants, about fifteen labourers, and the due proportion of women and children. The rich farmers understood him to be "very high learnt;" but if you had interrogated them for a more precise description, they would have said that he was "a thinnish-faced man, with a sort o' cast in his eye, like."

Seven, altogether: a delightful number for a dinner-party, supposing the units to be delightful, but everything depends on that. During dinner Mr Fellowes took the lead in the conversation, which set strongly in the direction of mangel-wurzel and the rotation of crops; for Mr Fellowes and Mr Cleves cultivated their own glebes. Mr Ely, too, had some agricultural notions, and even the Rev. Archibald Duke was made alive to that class of mundane subjects by the possession of some potato-ground. The two young curates talked a little aside during these discussions, which had imperfect interest for their unbeneficed minds; and the transcendental and near-sighted Mr Baird seemed to listen somewhat abstractedly, knowing little more of potatoes and mangel-wurzel than that they were some form of the "Conditioned."

"What a hobby farming is with Lord Watling!" said Mr Fellowes, when the cloth was being drawn. "I went over his farm at Tetterley with him last summer. It is really a model farm; first-rate dairy, grazing and wheat land, and such splendid farm-buildings! An expensive hobby, though. He sinks a good deal of money there, I fancy. He has a great whim for black cattle, and he sends that drunken old Scotch bailiff of his to Scotland every year, with hundreds in his pocket, to buy these beasts."

"By the by," said Mr Ely, "do you know who is the man to whom Lord Watling has given the Bramhill living?"

"A man named Sargent. I knew him at Oxford. His brother is a lawyer, and was very useful to Lord Watling in that ugly Brounsell affair. That's why Sargent got the living."

"Sargent," said Mr Ely. "I know him. Isn't he a showy talkative fellow; has written travels in Mesopotamia, or something of that sort?"

"That's the man."

"He was at Witherington once, as Bagshawe's curate. He got into rather bad odour there, through some scandal about a flirtation, I think."

"Talking of scandal," returned Mr Fellowes, "have you heard the last story about Barton? Nisbett was telling me the other day that he dines alone with the Countess at six, while Mrs Barton is in the kitchen acting as cook."

"Rather an apocryphal authority, Nisbett," said Mr Ely.

"Ah," said Mr Cleves, with good-natured humour twinkling in his eyes, "depend upon it, that is a corrupt version. The original text is, that they all dined together *with* six – meaning six children – and that Mrs Barton is an excellent cook."

"I wish dining alone together may be the worst of that sad business," said the Rev. Archibald Duke, in a tone implying that his wish was a strong figure of speech.

"Well," said Mr Fellowes, filling his glass and looking jocose, "Barton is certainly either the greatest gull in existence, or he has some cunning secret, – some philtre or other to make himself charming in the eyes of a fair lady. It isn't all of us that can make conquests when our ugliness is past its bloom."

"The lady seemed to have made a conquest of him at the very outset," said Mr Ely. "I was immensely amused one night at Granby's, when he was telling us her story about her husband's adventures. He said, 'When she told me the tale, I felt I don't know how – I felt it from the crown of my head to the sole of my feet.' "

Mr Ely gave these words dramatically, imitating the Rev. Amos's fervour and symbolic action, and every one laughed except Mr Duke, whose after-dinner view of things was not apt to be jovial. He said, –

"I think some of us ought to remonstrate with Mr Barton on the scandal he is causing. He is not only imperilling his own soul, but the souls of his flock."

"Depend upon it," said Mr Cleves, "there is some simple explanation of the whole affair, if we only happened to know it. Barton has always impressed me as a right-minded man, who has the knack of doing himself injustice by his manner."

"Now *I* never liked Barton," said Mr Fellowes. "He's not a gentleman. Why, he used to be on terms of intimacy with that canting Prior, who died a little while ago; – a fellow who soaked himself with spirits, and talked of the Gospel through an inflamed nose."

"The Countess has given him more refined tastes, I dare say," said Mr Ely.

"Well," observed Mr Cleves, "the poor fellow must have a hard pull to get along, with his small income and large family. Let us hope the Countess does something towards making the pot boil."

"Not she," said Mr Duke; "there are greater signs of poverty about them than ever."

"Well, come," returned Mr Cleves, who could be caustic sometimes, and who was not at all fond of his reverend brother, Mr Duke, "that's something in Barton's favour at all events. He might be poor *without* showing signs of poverty."

Mr Duke turned rather yellow, which was his way of blushing, and Mr Ely came to his relief by observing, –

"They're making a very good piece of work of Shepperton Church. Dolby, the architect, who has it in hand, is a very clever fellow."

"It's he who has been doing Coppleton Church," said Mr Furness. "They've got it in excellent order for the visitation."

This mention of the visitation suggested the Bishop, and thus opened a wide duct, which entirely diverted the stream of animadversion from that small pipe – that capillary vessel, the Rev. Amos Barton.

The talk of the clergy about their Bishop belongs to the esoteric part of their profession; so we will at once quit the dining-room at Milby Vicarage, lest we should happen to overhear remarks unsuited to the lay understanding, and perhaps dangerous to our repose of mind.[12]

The delicious irony of this embraces not only the grades and status of the "religious" group, but also the gossip, the sitting in judgment, which George

Eliot must have seen when she looked back to the fervent Marian Evans. Mr Ely is based on the Rev. William King, curate of Nuneaton, while the dyspeptic Rev. Duke derives from a Rev. Hoke, though Marian herself suffered from Evangelical indigestion in her young womanhood. Rev. Cleves was drawn perhaps from the Rev. John Fisher, rector of Caldecot and Higham-on-the-Hill, near Nuneaton: obviously he is the ideal pastor, tolerant, unassuming, clerical in name and nature, without ostentation. We notice particularly his basic Christianity – his natural kinship with Amos Barton, his refusal to judge. This is a fair cross-section in terms of religious affiliation and practice: more, it is a representative cross-section of a community at a time when the parson was integrated into that community. It is a lay appraisal but wise and contemplative: a man is at once a clergyman and more than a clergyman. Fifteen years after her rejection of her faith George Eliot could look back with tolerance, compassion, understanding and irony to what she had left behind in the spiritual as well as the geographical sense.

If this is wise and kindly, consider the author's attitude towards pluralism and its effect on the life of the curate who is so gossiped about here:

You are not imagining, I hope, that Amos Barton was the incumbent of Shepperton. He was no such thing. Those were days when a man could hold three small livings, starve a curate a-piece on two of them, and live badly himself on the third. It was so with the Vicar of Shepperton; a vicar given to bricks and mortar, and thereby running into debt far away in a northern county – who executed his vicarial functions towards Shepperton by pocketing the sum of thirty-five pounds ten per annum, the net surplus remaining to him from the proceeds of that living, after the disbursement of eighty pounds as the annual stipend of his curate. And now, pray, can you solve me the following problem? Given a man with a wife and six children: let him be obliged always to exhibit himself when outside his own door in a suit of black broadcloth, such as will not undermine the foundations of the Establishment by a paltry plebeian glossiness or an unseemly whiteness at the edges; in a snowy cravat, which is a serious investment of labour in the hemming, starching, and ironing departments; and in a hat which shows no symptom of taking to the hideous doctrine of expediency, and shaping itself according to circumstances; let him have a parish large enough to create an external necessity for abundant shoe-leather, and an internal necessity for abundant beef and mutton, as well as poor enough to require frequent priestly consolation in the shape of shillings and sixpences; and, lastly, let him be compelled, by his own pride and other people's, to dress his wife and children with gentility from bonnet-strings to shoe-strings. By what process of division can the sum of eighty pounds per annum be made to yield a quotient which will cover that man's weekly expenses? This was the problem presented by the position of the Rev. Amos Barton, as curate of Shepperton, rather more then twenty years ago.[13]

The tone is unequivocal, a blunt condemnation of a practice she knew about at first hand: it moves from the spiritual to the economic. It establishes at once the realism within the fiction; and the economic problem precipitates the plot.

Here the retrospect has a controlled anger, but it is anger nevertheless. While the overall implication is that this was the way of a past world, its practice obviously continues in the world that she knows.

Mr Gilfil is another type of the many George Eliot portrays: his sad love and sad life partake of human suffering and survival without spiritual elevation. He is seen with loving kindness, his idiosyncrasies accepted with her familiar compassionate tolerance:

You already suspect that the Vicar did not shine in the more spiritual functions of his office; and indeed, the utmost I can say for him in this respect is, that he performed those functions with undeviating attention to brevity and dispatch. He had a large heap of short sermons, rather yellow and worn at the edges, from which he took two every Sunday, securing perfect impartiality in the selection by taking them as they came without reference to topics; and having preached one of these sermons at Shepperton in the morning, he mounted his horse and rode hastily with the other in his pocket to Knebley, where he officiated in a wonderful little church, with a chequered pavement which had once rung to the iron tread of military monks, with coats of arms in clusters on the lofty roof, marble warriors and their wives without noses occupying a large proportion of the area, and the twelve apostles, with their heads very much on one side, holding didactic ribbons, painted in fresco on the walls. Here, in an absence of mind to which he was prone, Mr Gilfil would sometimes forget to take off his spurs before putting on his surplice, and only become aware of the omission by feeling something mysteriously tugging at the skirts of that garment as he stepped into the reading-desk. But the Knebley farmers would as soon have thought of criticizing the moon as their pastor. He belonged to the course of nature, like markets and tollgates and dirty bank-notes; and being a vicar, his claim on their veneration had never been counteracted by an exasperating claim on their pockets. Some of them who did not indulge in the superfluity of a covered cart without springs, had dined half an hour earlier than usual – that is to say, at twelve o'clock – in order to have time for their long walk through miry lanes, and present themselves duly in their places at two o'clock, when Mr Oldinport and Lady Felicia, to whom Knebley Church was a sort of family temple, made their way among the bows and curtsies of their dependants to a carved and canopied pew in the chancel, diffusing as they went a delicate odour of Indian roses on the unsusceptible nostrils of the congregation. . . .

The same respect attended him in his strictly clerical functions. The benefits of baptism were supposed to be somehow bound up with Mr Gilfil's personality, so metaphysical a distinction as that between a man and his office being, as yet, quite foreign to the mind of a good Shepperton churchman, savouring, he would have thought, of Dissent on the very face of it. Miss Selina Parrot put off her marriage a whole month when Mr Gilfil had an attack of rheumatism, rather than be married in a makeshift manner by the Milby curate.

"We've had a very good sermon this morning," was the frequent remark, after hearing one of the old yellow series, heard with all the more satisfaction because it had been heard for the twentieth time; for to minds on the Shepperton level it is repetition, not novelty, that produces the strongest effect; and phrases, like tunes, are a long time making themselves at home in the brain.

Mr Gilfil's sermons, as you may imagine, were not of a highly doctrinal, still less of a polemical, cast. They perhaps did not search the conscience very powerfully; for you remember that to Mrs Patten, who had listened to them thirty years, the announcement that she was a sinner appeared an uncivil heresy; but, on the other hand, they made no unreasonable demand on the Shepperton intellect – amounting, indeed, to little more than an expansion of the concise thesis, that those who do wrong will find it the worse for them, and those who do well will find it the better for them; the nature of wrong-doing being exposed in special sermons against lying, backbiting, anger, slothfulness, and the like; and well-doing being interpreted as honesty, truthfulness, charity, industry, and other common virtues, lying quite on the surface of life, and having very little to do with deep spiritual doctrine. Mrs Patten understood that if she turned out ill-crushed cheeses, a just retribution awaited her; though, I fear, she made no particular application of the sermon on backbiting. Mrs Hackit expressed herself greatly edified by the sermon on honesty, the allusion to the unjust weight and deceitful balance having a peculiar lucidity for her, owing to a recent dispute with her grocer; but I am not aware that she ever appeared to be much struck by the sermon on anger.

As to any suspicion that Mr Gilfil did not dispense the pure Gospel, or any strictures on his doctrine and mode of delivery, such thoughts never visited the minds of the Shepperton parishioners – of those very parishioners who, ten or fifteen years later, showed themselves extremely critical of Mr Barton's discourses and demeanour. But in the interim they had tasted that dangerous fruit of the tree of knowledge – innovation, which is well known to open the eyes, often in an uncomfortable manner. At present, to find fault with the sermon was regarded as almost equivalent to finding fault with religion itself.[14]

The understanding here is generous and uncondescending. It shows a mind in touch with the reality of what "religion" means to the various kinds of common mind – and I do not use the term disparagingly. It is aware of the fluidity of attitude which comes with innovation or change, and aware also of the fixity of observance as it appears to those practising what they have always practised. And the lightness of the tone is a kind of moral latitudinarianism – an acceptance of ignorance or misinterpretation. If religion is rooted in common humanity, then this is profoundly religious writing.

In "Janet's Repentance" George Eliot presents a different kind of clergyman from any in the previous stories. We have already seen Edgar Tryan and his supporters subjected to the handbills which Janet and her husband produced. The calibre of the man is mixed, despite the unquestioned and obdurate assertion of his faith:

"He is evidently the brain and hand of the persecution," said Mr Tryan. "There may be a strong feeling against me in a large number of the inhabitants – it must be so, from the great ignorance of spiritual things in this place. But I fancy there would have been no formal opposition to the lecture, if Dempster had not planned it. I am not myself the least alarmed at anything he can do; he will find I am not to be cowed or driven away by insult or personal danger. God has sent me to this place, and, by

His blessing, I'll not shrink from anything I may have to encounter in doing His work among the people. But I feel it right to call on all those who know the value of the Gospel, to stand by me publicly. I think – and Mr Landor agrees with me – that it will be well for my friends to proceed with me in a body to the church on Sunday evening. Dempster, you know, has pretended that almost all the respectable inhabitants are opposed to the lecture. Now, I wish that falsehood to be visibly contradicted. What do you think of the plan? I have to-day been to see several of my friends, who will make a point of being there to accompany me, and will communicate with others on the subject."

. . . .

"Perhaps," said Mr Tryan, feeling slightly uncomfortable, "since you are not very strong, my dear sir, it will be well, as Mrs Jerome suggests, that you should not run the risk of any excitement."

"Say no more, Mr Tryan. I'll stan' by you, sir. It's my duty. It's the cause o' God, sir; it's the cause o' God."

Mr Tryan obeyed his impulse of admiration and gratitude, and put out his hand to the white-haired old man, saying, "Thank you, Mr Jerome, thank you."

Mr Jerome grasped the proffered hand in silence, and then threw himself back in his chair, casting a regretful look at his wife, which seemed to say, "Why don't you feel with me, Susan?"

The sympathy of this simple-minded old man was more precious to Mr Tryan than any mere onlooker could have imagined. To persons possessing a great deal of that facile psychology which prejudges individuals by means of formulæ, and casts them, without further trouble, into duly lettered pigeon-holes, the Evangelical curate might seem to be doing simply what all other men like to do – carrying out objects which were identified not only with his theory, which is but a kind of secondary egoism, but also with the primary egoism of his feelings. Opposition may become sweet to a man when he has christened it persecution: a self-obtrusive, over-hasty reformer complacently disclaiming all merit, while his friends call him a martyr, has not in reality a career the most arduous to the fleshly mind. But Mr Tryan was not cast in the mould of the gratuitous martyr. With a power of persistence which had been often blamed as obstinacy, he had an acute sensibility to the very hatred or ridicule he did not flinch from provoking. Every form of disapproval jarred him painfully; and, though he fronted his opponents manfully, and often with considerable warmth of temper, he had no pugnacious pleasure in the contest. It was one of the weaknesses of his nature to be too keenly alive to every harsh wind of opinion; to wince under the frowns of the foolish; to be irritated by the injustice of those who could not possibly have the elements indispensable for judging him rightly; and with all this acute sensibility to blame, this dependence on sympathy, he had for years been constrained into a position of antagonism. No wonder, then, that good old Mr Jerome's cordial words were balm to him. He had often been thankful to an old woman for saying "God bless you;" to a little child for smiling at him; to a dog for submitting to be patted by him.[15]

In her clergymen we are not merely being presented with scenes of clerical life: we are seeing scenes of human fallibility. We are seeing ourselves. And there is little doubt that the author is seeing at least part of herself, as she was at an impressionable time embracing a particular bias. Her rejection of faith did not involve a permanent rejection of the past which had made it. Rather it involved another look at that past, an evaluation of it, and acceptance of the various mixes of humanity seen in those who were the representatives in the formal sense of religion, and those who received it. There is irony and satire in *Scenes*, but the lasting impression is of a generosity not confined to Christianity.

The divine manifestation of Christianity, or rather the rejection of it, is seen in her two years' labour on the translation of Strauss's *Life of Jesus*. It was published anonymously in 1846. Rufa Brabant had married Charles Christian Hennell (author of *The Inquiry* which Mary Ann so admired), and was daughter of that Dr Brabant whom George Eliot may have partly drawn on for her portrait of Casaubon. Dorothea falls in love (as she supposes) with Casaubon; Mary Ann was certainly drawn to Dr Brabant, and had to leave his house at the instance of his wife and her sister. Rufa gave up the translation (from German) and, as Sarah Hennell wrote to her, "Your proposition to deliver up the Strauss to Mary Ann has been very cordially received, and I am sure will be a great benefit. I think she will do it admirably."[16]

By the time she had completed this labour of historical criticism which established that the gospel accounts of Jesus were un-historical, Mary Ann Evans was, according to Cara Bray, "Strauss-sick – it made her ill dissecting the beautiful story of the crucifixion, and only the sight of her Christ-image and picture made her endure it".[17] This was four years after her refusal to accompany her father to church. Coventry must have been indelibly associated with this part of her life, and Mrs Bray's remark surely shows the divisions within her. Those divisions probably made her sympathetic to the divisions within Christianity, and tolerant when she came to portray them. It is significant that when she departs from immediate local history, as in *Adam Bede*, for example, she goes further back in time, but chooses the firm Midland bases of Loamshire and Stonyshire for location, giving an appearance of authenticity to her settings and to their spiritual accompaniments.

We have already seen Dinah in action. Here is historical perspective and warm identification at the same time:

And this blessed gift of venerating love has been given to too many humble craftsmen since the world began, for us to feel any surprise that it should have existed in the soul of a Methodist carpenter half a century ago, while there was yet a lingering after-glow from the time when Wesley and his fellow-labourer fed on the hips and haws of the Cornwall hedges, after exhausting limbs and lungs in carrying a divine message to the poor.

That after-glow has long faded away; and the picture we are apt to make of Methodism in our imagination is not an amphitheatre of green hills, or the deep shade of broad-leaved sycamores, where a crowd of rough men and weary-hearted women drank in a faith which was a rudimentary culture, which linked their thoughts with the past, lifted their imagination above the sordid details of their own narrow lives, and suffused their souls with the sense of a pitying, loving, infinite Presence, sweet as summer to the houseless needy. It is too possible that to some of my readers Methodism may mean nothing more than low-pitched gables up dingy streets, sleek grocers, sponging preachers, and hypocritical jargon – elements which are regarded as an exhaustive analysis of Methodism in many fashionable quarters.

That would be a pity; for I cannot pretend that Seth and Dinah were anything else than Methodists – not indeed of that modern type which reads quarterly reviews and attends in chapels with pillared porticoes; but of a very old-fashioned kind. They believed in present miracles, in instantaneous conversions, in revelations by dreams and visions; they drew lots, and sought for Divine guidance by opening the Bible at hazard; having a literal way of interpreting the Scriptures, which is not at all sanctioned by approved commentators; and it is impossible for me to represent their diction as correct, or their instruction as liberal. Still – if I have read religious history aright – faith, hope, and charity have not always been found in a direct ratio with a sensibility to the three concords; and it is possible, thank Heaven! to have very erroneous theories and very sublime feelings. The raw bacon which clumsy Molly spares from her own scanty store, that she may carry it to her neighbour's child to "stop the fits," may be a piteously inefficacious remedy; but the generous stirring of neighbourly kindness that prompted the deed has a beneficent radiation that is not lost.

Considering these things, we can hardly think Dinah and Seth beneath our sympathy, accustomed as we may be to weep over the loftier sorrows of heroines in satin boots and crinoline, and of heroes riding fiery horses, themselves ridden by still more fiery passions.[18]

The emphasis is on Christian action as distinct from creed: the ironic comment on the fiction of her own period, much of which was artificial, reinforces her own realism in her treatment of people and their religion. Dinah and Seth are not types: their development of a spiritual affiliation is the mark of their individuality. The tolerance, the sympathetic overview, the deliberate invitation to the reader to eliminate his own prejudices and associate himself with fundamental Christian practice, all these are striking.

And when we come to meet Mr Irwine, socially and culturally so different from Dinah and Seth, we find that a like appreciation, kindliness and understanding are present too:

Nevertheless, to speak paradoxically, the existence of insignificant people has very important consequences in the world. It can be shown to affect the price of bread and the rate of wages, to call forth many evil tempers from the selfish, and many heroisms from the sympathetic, and, in other ways, to play no small part in the tragedy of life. And if that handome, generous-blooded clergyman, the Rev. Adolphus Irwine, had not had these two hopelessly-maiden sisters, his lot would have been shaped quite differently: he would very likely have taken a comely wife in his youth, and now, when his hair was getting grey under the powder, would have had tall sons and blooming daughters – such possessions, in short, as men commonly think will repay them for all the labour they take under the sun. As it was – having with all his three livings no

Robert Evans (1773–1849)
"What shall I be without my Father? It will seem as if a
part of my moral nature were gone."

Sara Hennell (1812–1899)

Caroline Bray née Hennell (1814–1905)

Charles Christian Hennell (1809–1850)

Sara, Caroline (Cara) and Charles Christian Hennell were the major influences on Marian Evans's Coventry years (1841–1849) and the sisters remained her lifelong friends.

Coventry by Sara Hennell: "Our first vision in 1833", she wrote.

Mᵣ. Jas. Buchanan.

Mʳˢ. J. W. Buchanan.

Mʳˢ. Robinson.

Mᵣ. John Towle.

Supposed prototypes for characters in "Janet's Repentance": the brutal Lawyer Dempster, his victimised wife Janet, her kind friend Mrs Pettifer, and Mr Lowme, "one of the most aristocratic men in Milby".

A nineteenth-century engraving of the parish church of St Nicolas, Nuneaton – the Milby Church of "Janet's Repentance".

Bernard Gilpin Ebdell (1786–1829), the prototype for
the hero of "Mr Gilfil's Love Story".

*Above:* Griff House, Marian Evans's home from March 1820 to March 1841.
*Below:* Arbury Mill at the back of Griff House, which provided the young Marian
Evans with her first experience of a working mill; later absorbed into
*The Mill on the Floss* as the Dorlcote Mill of St Ogg's.

Canal arm and Griff Bottoms or Hollows c. 1910: "Our brown canal"
of the "Brother and Sister" sonnets; and the Red Deeps, the meeting place of
Maggie Tulliver and Philip Wakem, in *The Mill on the Floss*.

more than seven hundred a-year, and seeing no way of keeping his splendid mother and his sickly sister, not to reckon a second sister, who was usually spoken of without any adjective, in such lady-like ease as became their birth and habits, and at the same time providing for a family of his own – he remained, you see, at the age of eight-and-forty, a bachelor, not making any merit of that renunciation, but saying laughingly, if any one alluded to it, that he made it an excuse for many indulgences which a wife would never have allowed him. And perhaps he was the only person in the world who did not think his sisters uninteresting and superfluous; for his was one of those large-hearted, sweet-blooded natures that never know a narrow or a grudging thought; epicurean, if you will, with no enthusiasm, no self-scourging sense of duty; but yet, as you have seen, of a sufficiently subtle moral fibre to have an unwearying tenderness for obscure and monotonous suffering. It was his large-hearted indulgence that made him ignore his mother's hardness towards her daughters, which was the more striking from its contrast with her doting fondness towards himself: he held it no virtue to frown at irremediable faults.

See the difference between the impression a man makes on you when you walk by his side in familiar talk, or look at him in his home, and the figure he makes when seen from a lofty historical level, or even in the eyes of a critical neighbour who thinks of him as an embodied system or opinion rather than as a man. Mr Roe, the "travelling preacher" stationed at Treudleston, had included Mr Irwine in a general statement concerning the Church clergy in the surrounding district, whom he described as men given up to the lusts of the flesh and the pride of life; hunting and shooting, and adorning their own houses; asking what shall we eat, and what shall we drink, and wherewithal shall we be clothed? – careless of dispensing the bread of life to their flocks, preaching at best but a carnal and soul-benumbing morality, and trafficking in the souls of men by receiving money for discharging the pastoral office in parishes where they did not so much as look on the faces of the people more than once a-year. The ecclesiastical historian, too, looking into parliamentary reports of that period, finds honourable members zealous for the Church, and untainted with any sympathy for the "tribe of canting Methodists," making statements scarcely less melancholy than that of Mr Roe. And it is impossible for me to say that Mr Irwine was altogether belied by the generic classification assigned him. He really had no very lofty aims, no theological enthusiasm: if I were closely questioned, I should be obliged to confess that he felt no serious alarms about the souls of his parishioners, and would have thought it a mere loss of time to talk in a doctrinal and awakening manner to old "Feyther Taft," or even to Chad Cranage the blacksmith. If he had been in the habit of speaking theoretically, he would perhaps have said that the only healthy form religion could take in such minds was that of certain dim but strong emotions, suffusing themselves as a hallowing influence over the family affections and neighbourly duties. He thought the custom of baptism more important than its doctrine, and that the religious benefits the peasant drew from the church where his fathers worshipped and the sacred piece of turf where they lay buried, were but slightly dependent on a clear understanding of the Liturgy or the sermon. Clearly the Rector was not what is called in these days an "earnest" man: he was fonder of church history than of divinity, and had much more insight into men's characters than interest in their opinions; he was neither laborious, nor obviously self-denying, nor very copious in alms-giving, and his theology, you perceive, was lax.[19]

115

All sacrifice is comparative, and such is Irwine's character that he would hardly understand the term. A phrase like "large-hearted, sweet-blooded natures" defines the man and, more than that, it establishes the author's loving respect. True Christianity, in those times and in that or indeed any location, did not rest on creed: as ever, it resides in individuals who transcend creed. It is again evidence of George Eliot's faith in human nature – the godhead in man which she had absorbed as a concept from Feuerbach – that when Dinah and Irwine meet there is respect and understanding – a kind of loving – on both sides. The pagan Loamshire rector of good family connection and the Stonyshire factory girl of fervent faith meet as the symbol of a wider reconciliation.

*The Mill on the Floss* has various religious emphases. The Rev. Walter Stelling, who pays scant attention to the needs of Tom Tulliver, comes in for more direct authorial commentary than his brethren in her previous fiction. The Christianity which we have seen in diverse forms hitherto has hardly touched Mr Stelling, though he would not regard the cloth as the means to an end:

Mr Stelling was a well-sized, broad-chested man, not yet thirty, with flaxen hair standing erect, and large lightish-grey eyes, which were always very wide open; he had a sonorous bass voice, and an air of defiant self-confidence inclining to brazenness. He had entered on his career with great vigour, and intended to make a considerable impression on his fellow-men. The Rev. Walter Stelling was not a man who would remain among the "inferior clergy" all his life. He had a true British determination to push his way in the world. As a schoolmaster, in the first place; for there were capital masterships of grammar-schools to be had, and Mr Stelling meant to have one of them. But as a preacher also, for he meant always to preach in a striking manner, so as to have his congregation swelled by admirers from neighbouring parishes, and to produce a great sensation whenever he took occasional duty for a brother clergyman of minor gifts. The style of preaching he had chosen was the extemporaneous, which was held little short of the miraculous in rural parishes like King's Lorton. Some passages of Massillon and Bourdaloue, which he knew by heart, were really very effective when rolled out in Mr Stelling's deepest tones; but as comparatively feeble appeals of his own were delivered in the same loud and impressive manner, they were often thought quite as striking by his hearers. Mr Stelling's doctrine was of no particular school; if anything, it had a tinge of evangelicalism, for that was "the telling thing" just then in the diocese to which King's Lorton belonged. In short, Mr Stelling was a man who meant to rise in his profession, and to rise by merit, clearly, since he had no interest beyond what might be promised by a problematic relationship to a great lawyer who had not yet become Lord Chancellor. A clergyman who has such vigorous intentions naturally gets a little into debt at starting; it is not to be expected that he will live in the meagre style of a man who means to be a poor curate all his life, and if the few hundreds Mr Timpson advanced towards his daughter's fortune did not suffice for the purchase of handsome furniture, together with a stock of wine, a grand piano, and the laying-out of a superior flower-garden, it followed in the most rigorous manner, either that these things must be procured by some other means, or else that the Rev. Mr Stelling must go without them – which last alternative would be an absurd procrastination of the fruits of success, where success was certain. Mr Stelling was so broad-chested and resolute that he felt equal to anything; he would become celebrated by shaking the consciences of his hearers, and he would by-and-by edit a Greek play, and invent several new readings. He had not yet selected the play, for having been married little more than two years, his leisure time had been much occupied with attentions to Mrs Stelling; but he had told that fine woman what he meant to do some day, and she felt great confidence in her husband, as a man who understood everything of that sort.[20]

The irony here is conclusive. This description of Stelling is placed historically just before the Tractarian Movement which began in 1833 with Keble's Assize sermon, but despite his "tinge of evangelicalism" there is little doubt that Stelling would go along opportunistically with any movement in which he could make a mark. The irony embraces the fact that religion, faith and everyday Christian practice, do not enter into his ideas. He is ambitious over a clerical/secular range, even to a headmastership, though knowing nothing of education.

Directly opposed to Stelling in faith and practice is the more elevated Anglican, Dr Kenn. He is a suffering and wise man, knowing the ways of the world. He is the practical Christian whose experience makes him a spiritual therapist, a mentor whose compassion draws him into dangerous personal involvement:

"Your inexperience of the world, Miss Tulliver, prevents you from anticipating the very unjust conceptions that will probably be formed concerning your conduct – conceptions which will have a baneful effect, even in spite of known evidence to disprove them."

"O, I do – I begin to see," said Maggie, unable to repress this utterance of her recent pain. "I know I shall be insulted: I shall be thought worse than I am."

"You perhaps do not yet know," said Dr Kenn, with a touch of more personal pity, "that a letter is come which ought to satisfy every one who has known anything of you, that you chose the steep and difficult path of a return to the right, at the moment when that return was most of all difficult."

"Oh – where is he?" said poor Maggie, with a flush and tremor that no presence could have hindered.

"He is gone abroad: he has written of all that passed to his father. He has vindicated you to the utmost; and I hope the communication of that letter to your cousin will have a beneficial effect on her."

Dr Kenn waited for her to get calm before he went on.

"That letter, as I said, ought to suffice to prevent false impressions concerning you. But I am bound to tell you, Miss Tulliver, that not only the experience of my whole life, but my observation within the last three days, makes me fear that there is hardly any evidence which will save you from the painful effect of false imputations. The persons who are the most incapable of a conscientious struggle such as yours, are precisely those who will be likely to shrink from you; because they will not believe in your struggle. I fear your life here will be attended not only with much pain, but with many obstructions. For this reason – and for this only – I ask you to consider whether it will not perhaps be better for you to take a situation at a distance, according to your former intention. I will exert myself at once to obtain one for you."

"O, if I could but stop here!" said Maggie. "I have no heart to begin a strange life again. I should have no stay. I should feel like a lonely wanderer – cut off from the past. I have written to the lady who offered me a situation to excuse myself. If I remained here, I could perhaps atone in some way to Lucy – to others: I could convince them that I'm sorry. And," she added, with some of the old proud fire flashing out, "I will not go away because people say false things of me. They shall learn to retract them. If I must go away at last, because – because others wish it, I will not go now."

"Well," said Dr Kenn, after some consideration, "if you determine on that, Miss Tulliver, you may rely on all the influence my position gives me. I am bound to aid and countenance you by the very duties of my office as a parish priest. I will add, that personally I have a deep interest in your peace of mind and welfare."

"The only thing I want is some occupation that will enable me to get my bread and be independent," said Maggie. "I shall not want much. I can go on lodging where I am."

"I must think over the subject maturely," said Dr Kenn, "and in a few days I shall be better able to ascertain the general feeling. I shall come to see you: I shall bear you constantly in mind."

When Maggie had left him, Dr Kenn stood ruminating with his hands behind him, and his eyes fixed on the carpet, under a painful sense of doubt and difficulty. The tone of Stephen's letter, which he had read, and the actual relations of all the persons concerned, forced upon him powerfully the idea of an ultimate marriage between Stephen and Maggie as the least evil; and the impossibility of their proximity in St Ogg's on any other supposition, until after years of separation, threw an insurmountable prospective difficulty over Maggie's stay there. On the other hand, he entered with all the comprehension of a man who had known spiritual conflict, and lived through years of devoted service to his fellow-men, into that state of Maggie's heart and conscience which made the consent to the marriage a desecration to her: her conscience must not be tampered with: the principle on which she had acted was a safer guide than any balancing of consequences. His experience told him that intervention was too dubious a reponsibility to be lightly incurred: the possible issue either of an endeavour to restore the former relations with Lucy and Philip, or of counselling submission to this irruption of a new feeling, was hidden in a darkness all the more impenetrable because each immediate step was clogged with evil.[21]

I used the term mentor deliberately, since in novels not considered here, like *Romola* and *Daniel Deronda*, the role is central. Kenn's attitude is a profoundly Christian one: it is based on reasonable argument but rests on the assurance of faith. He is defeated by public opinion – his Christian love and open charity, undertaken after his wife's death, are misconstrued as wilful indiscretion by his outwardly Christian parishioners. The provincial mind is unlikely to forgive adultery whether it is hypothetical or real. Maggie and Dr Kenn are Christian innocents in a place of destructive slander.

On 9th February 1849 Marian wrote to Sara Hennell, "I have at last the most delightful 'de imitatione Christi' with quaint woodcuts. One breathes a cool air as of the cloisters in the book – it makes one long to be a saint for a few months. Verily its piety has its foundations in the depth of the divine human-soul."[22] Ten years on from this Coventry experience she wrote in her Journal for 18th November 1859, "I am reading Thomas à Kempis."[23] Mary Ann Evans at thirty, George Eliot at forty, Maggie Tulliver at seventeen or so, all find themselves fascinated by his work. And since all three are close relations it is interesting to see how the experience is narrated:

At last Maggie's eyes glanced down on the books that lay on the window-shelf, and she half forsook her reverie to turn over listlessly the leaves of the "Portrait Gallery," but she soon pushed this aside to examine the little row of books tied together with string. "Beauties of the Spectator," "Rasselas," "Economy of Human Life," "Gregory's Letters" – she knew the sort of matter that was inside all these: the "Christian Year" – that seemed to be a hymn-book, and she laid it down again; but *Thomas à Kempis?* – the name had come across her in her reading, and she felt the satisfaction, which every one knows, of getting some ideas to attach to a name that strays solitary in the memory. She took up the little, old, clumsy book with some curiosity: it had the corners turned down in many places, and some hand, now for ever quiet, had made at certain passages strong pen-and-ink marks, long since browned by time. Maggie turned from leaf to leaf, and read where the quiet hand pointed . . .

"Know that the love of thyself doth hurt thee more than anything in the world. . . . . . If thou seekest this or that, and wouldst be here or there to enjoy thy own will and pleasure, thou shalt never be quiet nor free from care: for in everything somewhat will be wanting, and in every place there will be some that will cross thee. . . . . Both above and below, which way soever thou dost turn thee, everywhere thou shalt find the Cross: and everywhere of necessity thou must have patience, if thou wilt have inward peace, and enjoy an everlasting crown. . . . . If thou desire to mount unto this height, thou must set out courageously, and lay the axe to the root, that thou mayst pluck up and destroy that hidden inordinate inclination to thyself, and unto all private and earthly good. On this sin, that a man inordinately loveth himself, almost all dependeth, whatsoever is thoroughly to be overcome; which evil being once overcome and subdued, there will presently ensue great peace and tranquillity. . . . . It is but little thou sufferest in comparison of them that have suffered so much, were so strongly tempted, so grievously afflicted, so many ways tried and exercised. Thou oughtest therefore to call to mind the more heavy sufferings of others, that thou mayest the easier bear thy little adversities. And if they seem not little unto thee, beware lest thy impatience be the cause thereof. . . . . Blessed are those ears that receive the whispers of the divine voice, and listen not to the whisperings of the world. Blessed are those ears which hearken not unto the voice which soundeth outwardly, but unto the Truth, which teacheth inwardly . . .".

A strange thrill of awe passed through Maggie while she read, as if she had been wakened in the night by a strain of solemn music, telling of beings whose souls had been astir while hers was in stupor. She went on from one brown mark to another, where the quiet hand seemed to point, hardly conscious that she was reading – seeming rather to listen while a low voice said –

> "Why dost thou here gaze about, since this is not the place of thy rest? In heaven ought to be thy dwelling, and all earthly things are to be looked on as they forward thy journey thither. All things pass away, and thou together with them. Beware thou cleave not unto them, lest thou be entangled and perish. . . . . If a man should give all his substance, yet it is as nothing. And if he should do great penances, yet are they but little. And if he should attain to all knowledge, he is yet far off. And if he should be of great virtue, and very fervent devotion, yet is there much wanting; to wit, one thing, which is most necessary for him. What is that? That having left all, he leave himself, and go wholly out of himself, and retain nothing of self-love. . . . . I have often said unto thee, and now again I say the same, Forsake thyself, resign thyself, and thou shalt enjoy much inward peace. . . . . Then shall all vain imaginations, evil perturbations, and superfluous cares fly away; then shall immoderate fear leave thee, and inordinate love shall die."[24]

*The Imitation of Christ* is concerned with the progress of the Christian soul towards perfection, the resignation of the world and the approach to God. The style is simple and direct. It is above sect. But the link between George Eliot and Maggie is strong: at the stage in Marian Evans's life when she wrote to Sara Hennell her father was close to death. She had been nursing him for three years. Thomas à Kempis was obviously both her consolation and a sounding board for depression. Maggie's state is close to Marian Evans's – her father is physically, economically and emotionally stricken. The *Christian Year* became Maggie's favourite reading, and had been Marian Evans's. But Maggie has no interest in the evangelical movement so important to Marian Evans. Marian was reading Thomas à Kempis during the crisis of her relationship with John Chapman – self-denial is a major theme in her work. It is not simple renunciation for its own sake, it is rather self-abnegation in the interests of others, the altruism which is present in so many of her characters. Its roots were in her Coventry experience, or Maggie's St Ogg's one: in Maggie's case it gave her the strength to renounce Stephen.

The "Church Assembling" in Lantern Yard has a vague northern location, though George Eliot castigates its narrowness and primitive practice of the drawing of lots. But the theme of *Silas Marner* is a religious one – we have moved even farther into a religion of humanity (without reference to Comte), and George Eliot tells us that in the novel she "intended to set in a strong light the remedial influences of pure, natural human relations".[25] Indeed that is what she does. The discovery of Eppie gradually brings Silas into the community: no priest or pastor helps him – he would reject a formal presence anyway – but through Dolly Winthrop's direct Christian action he is eventually integrated somewhat mutedly into the community:

"Yes, I did; I heard 'em," said Silas, to whom Sunday bells were a mere accident of the day, and not part of its sacredness. There had been no bells in Lantern Yard.

"Dear heart!" said Dolly, pausing before she spoke again. "But what a pity it is you should work of a Sunday, and not clean yourself – if you *didn't* go to church; for if you'd a roasting bit, it might be as you couldn't leave it, being a lone man. But there's the bakehus, if you could make up your mind to spend a twopence on the oven now and then, – not every week, in course – I shouldn't like to do that myself, – you might carry your bit o' dinner there, for it's nothing but right to have a bit o' summat hot of a Sunday, and not to make it as you can't know your dinner from Saturday. But now, upo' Christmas-day, this blessed Christmas as is ever coming, if you was to take your dinner to the bakehus, and go to church, and see the holly and the yew, and hear the anthim, and then take the sacramen', you'd be a deal the better, and you'd know which end you stood on, and you could put your trust i' Them as knows better nor we do, seein' you'd ha' done what it lies on us all to do."

Dolly's exhortation, which was an unusually long effort of speech for her, was uttered in the soothing persuasive tone with which she would have tried to prevail on a sick man to take his medicine, or a basin of gruel for which he had no appetite. Silas had never before been closely urged on the point of his absence from church, which had only been thought of as a part of his general queerness; and he was too direct and simple to evade Dolly's appeal.

"Nay, nay," he said, "I know nothing o' church. I've never been to church."

"No!" said Dolly, in a low tone of wonderment. Then bethinking herself of Silas's advent from an unknown country, she said, "Could it ha' been as they'd no church where you was born?"

"O yes," said Silas, meditatively, sitting in his usual posture of leaning on his knees, and supporting his head. "There was churches – a many – it was a big town. But I knew nothing of 'em – I went to chapel."

Dolly was much puzzled at this new word, but she was rather afraid of inquiring further, lest "chapel" might mean some haunt of wickedness. After a little thought, she said –

"Well, Master Marner, it's niver too late to turn over a new leaf, and if you've niver had no church, there's no telling the good it'll do you. For I feel so set up and comfortable as niver was, when I've been and heard the prayers, and the singing to the praise and glory o' God, as Mr Macey gives out – and Mr Crackenthorp saying good words, and more partic'lar on Sacramen' Day; and if a bit o' trouble comes, I feel as I can put up wi' it, for I've looked for help i' the right quarter, and gev myself up to Them as we must all give ourselves up to at the last; and if we'n done our part, it isn't to be believed as Them as are above us 'ull be worse nor we are, and come short o' Theirn."

Poor Dolly's exposition of her simple Raveloe theology fell rather unmeaningly on Silas's ears, for there was no word in it that could rouse a memory of what he had known as religion, and his comprehension was quite baffled by the plural pronoun, which was no heresy of Dolly's, but only her way of avoiding a presumptuous familiarity. He remained silent, not feeling inclined to assent to the part of Dolly's speech which he fully understood – her recommendation that he should go to church. Indeed, Silas was so unaccustomed to talk beyond the brief questions and answers necessary for the transaction of his simple business, that words did not easily come to him without the urgency of a distinct purpose.[26]

This is "simple Raveloe theology" indeed, but from this moment of non-communication there comes a more positive movement with Eppie. The deep need for love and the giving of love – humanity without theology – means that Silas finds in himself a religion he didn't know existed. It is as important a self-discovery as Maggie's discovery of Thomas à Kempis, though Silas can't articulate it and merely follows the deep need which comes upon him. The story may have fabulous elements but it also has a subtle psychological realism. Given the isolation of place Silas becomes both father and mother. For him, the child is a miraculous birth. And Dolly's attentions, though resisted, gradually establish a community of faith. An outcast from religion and society, Silas is exalted by daily giving and loving. His spiritual needs have been provided for. By choosing ordinary, rustic lives in a set place and expressing their simple expressions of faith – or their practice of Christian love and charity – George Eliot is conveying her own humanist and secular affiliations.

*Felix Holt* has the religious mix we saw in *Adam Bede* but with a different emphasis. Rufus Lyon represents the dissenting Church. His origin is clear, the treatment distinctive: the line of descent is from the Cow Lane Chapel which, as we have mentioned, Mary Ann attended at the Misses Franklins, but although the portrait of Rufus Lyon has been traced to their father, the febrile individuality is remarkable:

Mr Lyon lived in a small house, not quite so good as the parish clerk's, adjoining the entry which led to the Chapel Yard. The new prosperity of Dissent at Treby had led to an enlargement of the chapel, which absorbed all extra funds and left none for the enlargement of the minister's income. He sat this morning, as usual, in a low upstairs room, called his study, which, by means of a closet capable of holding his bed, served also as a sleeping-room. The book-shelves did not suffice for his store of old books, which lay about him in piles so arranged as to leave narrow lanes between them; for the minister was much given to walking about during his hours of meditation, and very narrow passages would serve for his small legs, unencumbered by any other drapery than his black silk stockings and the flexible, though prominent, bows of black ribbon that tied his knee-breeches. He was walking about now, with his hands clasped behind him, an attitude in which his body seemed to bear about the same proportion to his head as the lower part of a stone Hermes bears to the carven image that crowns it. His face looked old and worn, yet the curtain of hair that fell from his bald crown and hung about his neck, retained much of its original auburn tint, and his large, brown, short-sighted eyes were still clear and bright. At the first glance, every one thought him a very odd-looking rusty old man; the free-school boys often hooted after him, and called him "Revelations"; and to many respectable Church people, old

Lyon's little legs and large head seemed to make Dissent additionally preposterous. But he was too short-sighted to notice those who tittered at him – too absent from the world of small facts and petty impulses in which titterers live. With Satan to argue against on matters of vital experience as well as of church government, with great texts to meditate on, which seemed to get deeper as he tried to fathom them, it had never occurred to him to reflect what sort of image his small person made on the retina of a light-minded beholder. The good Rufus had his ire and his egoism; but they existed only as the red heat which gave force to his belief and his teaching. He was susceptible concerning the true office of deacons in the primitive church, and his small nervous body was jarred from head to foot by the concussion of an argument to which he saw no answer. In fact, the only moments when he could be said to be really conscious of his body, were when he trembled under the pressure of some agitating thought.[27]

The sincerity, eccentricity, and the intensity of obsession to the point of neurosis, make this a full human portrait. We are dealing, as George Eliot puts it, with a bit of religious history. She herself had had evangelical views which were an aspect of the Anglicanism of the period before she gave up Christianity. Rufus is a brave man and requests a public debate with the Rector, Rev. Augustus Debarry, on the constitution of the true Church "*and, secondly, the bearing thereupon of the English Reformation*".[28] This is cunningly linked in the novel to the Tory-Radical public discussion before the election of 1832. Philip Debarry passes on the little minister's request, and the rector responds:

"Not at all. I should be making a figure which my brother clergy might well take as an affront to themselves. The character of the Establishment has suffered enough already through the Evangelicals, with their extempore incoherence and their pipe-smoking piety. Look at Wimple, the man who is vicar of Shuttleton – without his gown and bands, anybody would take him for a grocer in mourning."

"Well, I shall cut a still worse figure, and so will you, in the Dissenting magazines and newspapers. It will go the round of the kingdom. There will be a paragraph headed, 'Tory Falsehood and Clerical Cowardice,' or else 'The Meanness of the Aristocracy and the Incompetence of the Beneficed Clergy.' "

"There would be a worse paragraph if I were to consent to the debate. Of course it would be said that I was beaten hollow, and that now the question had been cleared up at Treby Magna, the Church had not a sound leg to stand on. Besides," the Rector went on, frowning and smiling, "it's all very well for you to talk, Phil, but this debating is not so easy when a man's close upon sixty. What one writes or says must be something good and scholarly; and after all had been done, this little Lyon would buzz about one like a wasp, and cross-question and rejoin. Let me tell you, a plain truth may be so worried and mauled by fallacies as to get the worst of it. There's no such thing as tiring a talking machine like Lyon."

"Then you absolutely refuse?"

"Yes, I do."

"You remember that when I wrote my letter of thanks to Lyon you approved my offer to serve him if possible."

"Certainly I remember it. But suppose he had asked you to vote for civil marriage, or to go and hear him preach every Sunday?"

"But he has not asked that."

"Something as unreasonable, though."

"Well," said Philip, taking up Mr Lyon's letter and looking graver – looking even vexed, "it is rather an unpleasant business for me. I really felt obliged to him. I think there's a sort of worth in the man beyond his class. Whatever may be the reason of the case, I shall disappoint him instead of doing him the service I offered."

"Well, that's a misfortune; we can't help it."

"The worst of it is, I should be insulting him to say, 'I will do anything else, but not just this that you want.' He evidently feels himself in company with Luther and Zwingle and Calvin, and considers our letters part of the history of Protestantism."

"Yes, yes. I know it's rather an unpleasant thing, Phil. You are aware that I would have done anything in reason to prevent you from becoming unpopular here. I consider your character a possession to all of us."

"I think I must call on him forthwith, and explain and apologize."

"No, sit still; I've thought of something," said the Rector, with a sudden revival of spirits. "I've just seen Sherlock coming in. He is to lunch with me to-day. It would do no harm for him to hold the debate – a curate and a young man – he'll gain by it; and it would release you from any awkwardness, Phil. Sherlock is not going to stay here long, you know; he'll soon have his title. I'll put the thing to him. He won't object if I wish it. It's a capital idea. It will do Sherlock good. He's a clever fellow, but he wants confidence."

Philip had not time to object before Mr Sherlock appeared – a young divine of good birth and figure, of sallow complexion and bashful address.

"Sherlock, you have come in most opportunely," said the Rector. "A case has turned up in the parish in which you can be of eminent use. I know that is what you have desired ever since you have been with me. But I'm about so much myself that there really has not been sphere enough for you. You are a studious man, I know; I dare say you have all the necessary matter prepared – at your finger-ends, if not on paper."

Mr Sherlock smiled with rather a trembling lip, willing to distinguish himself, but hoping that the Rector only alluded to a dialogue on Baptism by Aspersion, or some other pamphlet suited to the purposes of the Christian Knowledge Society. But as the Rector proceeded to unfold the circumstances under which his eminent service was to be rendered, he grew more and more nervous.

"You'll oblige me very much, Sherlock," the Rector ended, "by going into this thing zealously. Can you guess what time you will require? because it will rest with us to fix the day."

"I should be rejoiced to oblige you, Mr Debarry, but I really think I am not competent to –"

"That's your modesty, Sherlock. Don't let me hear any more of that. I know Filmore of Corpus said you might be a first-rate man if your diffidence didn't do you injustice. And you can refer anything to me, you know. Come, you will set about the thing at once. But, Phil, you must tell the preacher to send a scheme of the debate – all the different heads – and he must agree to keep rigidly within the scheme. There, sit down at my desk and write the letter now; Thomas shall carry it."

Philip sat down to write, and the Rector, with his firm ringing voice, went on at his ease, giving "indications" to his agitated curate.

"But you can begin at once preparing a good, cogent, clear statement, and considering the probable points of assault. You can look into Jewel, Hall, Hooker, Whitgift, and the rest: you'll find them all here. My library wants nothing in English divinity. Sketch the lower ground taken by Ussher and those men, but bring all your force to bear on marking out the true High-Church doctrine. Expose the wretched cavils of the Nonconformists, and the noisy futility that belongs to schismatics generally. I will give you a telling passage from Burke on the Dissenters, and some good quotations which I brought together in two sermons of my own on the Position of the English Church in Christendom. How long do you think it will take you to bring your thoughts together? You can throw them afterwards into the form of an essay; we'll have the thing printed; it will do you good with the Bishop."

With all Mr Sherlock's timidity, there was fascination for him in this distinction. He reflected that he could take coffee and sit up late, and perhaps produce something rather fine. It might be a first step towards that eminence which it was no more than his duty to aspire to. Even a polemical fame like that of a Phillpotts must have had a beginning. Mr Sherlock was not insensible to the pleasure of turning sentences successfully, and it was a pleasure not always unconnected with preferment. A diffident man likes the idea of doing something remarkable, which will create belief in him without any immediate display of brilliancy. Celebrity may blush and be silent, and win a grace the more. Thus Mr Sherlock was constrained, trembling all the while, and much wishing that his essay were already in print.

"I think I could hardly be ready under a fortnight."

"Very good. Just write that, Phil, and tell him to fix the precise day and place. And then we'll go to lunch."

The Rector was quite satisfied. He had talked himself into thinking that he should like to give Sherlock a few useful hints, look up his own earlier sermons, and benefit the Curate by his criticism, when the argument had been got into shape. He was a healthy-natured man, but that was not at all a reason why he should not have those sensibilities to the odour of authorship which belong to almost everybody who is not expected to be a writer − and especially to that form of authorship which is called suggestion, and consists in telling another man that he might do a great deal with a given subject, by bringing a sufficient amount of knowledge, reasoning, and wit to bear upon it.[29]

The Rector is honest enough to know that he is not up to the debate. He is the brother of Sir Maximus, while Philip, ultimately the successful Tory candidate for North Loamshire, realizes that he will lose face if the debate does not take place. The novel defines the conflict between Anglican Tory-landed gentry against the Dissenters − Radical, moneyed, middle and lower classes. Harold wants their support. But there are permutations. The rector is shown abnegating responsibility, transferring it to the diffident curate: once more George Eliot makes comedy out of a provincial situation involving the clergy. The exchanges smack of the set pattern of small town provincial life. A richer comedy is to come: while Rufus waits and waits for the debate, news of the curate Mr Sherlock is lacking. He does not arrive, for his "agitation had increased so much during his walk, that the passing coach had been a means of deliverance not to be resisted; and literally at the eleventh hour, he had hailed and mounted the cheerful Tally-ho! and carried away his portion of the debate in his pocket."[30] We can't help feeling sorry for Rufus, although his response takes on the mannered delivery which is at once pedantic and irritating:

"Speak not of it in the way of apology, sir," said Mr Lyon, in a tone of depression. "I doubt not that you yourself have acted in good faith. Nor will I open any door of egress to constructions such as anger often deems ingenious, but which the disclosure of the simple truth may expose as erroneous and uncharitable fabrications. I wish you good morning, sir."[31]

The divisions in *Middlemarch* are less keenly felt. The ironic criticism of the clergy put into the mouth of one of the clergymen – Cadwallader – carries authorial bite as well as self-deprecation:

"Casaubon is as good as most of us. He is a scholarly clergyman, and creditable to the cloth. Some Radical fellow speechifying at Middlemarch said that Casaubon was the learned straw-chopping incumbent, and Freke was the brick-and-mortar incumbent, and I was the angling incumbent. And upon my word, I don't see that one is worse or better than the other." The Rector ended with his silent laugh. He always saw the joke of any satire against himself. His conscience was large and easy, like the rest of him: it did only what it could do without any trouble.[32]

This broad tolerance on the part of George Eliot shows her identifying yet again the various types of clergy and their practice as they hover on the edge of reform, their own reform perhaps, just before the Tracts for the Times. Casaubon is arguably a "pagan" like Irwine in *Adam Bede*, and there is little evidence of any Christian concern. The clergy have a settled way of life, though Mrs Cadwallader has to practise cottage economies. The apostolic Tyke gets the chaplain's job as a result of Lydgate's casting vote, but we never meet him. Religion, in *Middlemarch* as in *Felix Holt*, is here bound in with local politics, and the images used speak nationally and provincially at one and the same time:

When the General Board of the Infirmary had met, however, and Lydgate had notice that the question of the chaplaincy was thrown on a council of the directors and medical men, to meet on the following Friday, he had a vexed sense that he must make up his mind on this trivial Middlemarch business. He could not help hearing within him the distinct declaration that Bulstrode was prime minister, and that the Tyke affair was a question of office or no office; and he could not help an equally pronounced dislike to giving up the prospect of office. For his observation was constantly confirming Mr Farebrother's assurance that the banker would not overlook opposition. "Confound their petty politics!" was one of his thoughts for three mornings in the meditative process of shaving, when he had begun to feel that he must really hold a court of conscience on this matter. Certainly there were valid things to be said against the election of Mr Farebrother: he had too much on his hands already, especially considering how much time he spent on non-clerical occupations. Then again it was a continually repeated shock, disturbing Lydgate's esteem, that the Vicar should obviously play for the sake of money, liking the play indeed, but evidently liking some end which it served. Mr Farebrother contended on theory for the desirability of all games, and said that Englishmen's wit was stagnant for want of them; but Lydgate felt certain that he would have played very much less but for the money. There was a billiard-room at the Green Dragon, which some anxious mothers and wives regarded as the chief temptation in Middlemarch. The Vicar was a first-rate billiard-player, and though he did not frequent the Green Dragon, there were reports that he had sometimes been there in the daytime and had won money. And as to the chaplaincy, he did not pretend that he cared for it, except for the sake of the forty pounds. Lydgate was no Puritan, but he did not care for play, and winning money at it had always seemed a meanness to him; besides, he had an ideal of life which made this subservience of conduct to the gaining of small sums thoroughly hateful to him. Hitherto in his own life his wants had been supplied without any trouble to himself, and his first impulse was always to be liberal with half-crowns as matters of no importance to a gentleman; it had never occurred to him to devise a plan for getting half-crowns. He had always known in a general way that he was not rich, but he had never felt poor, and he had no power of imagining the part which the want of money plays in determining the actions of men. Money had never been a motive to him. Hence he was not ready to frame excuses for this deliberate pursuit of small gains. It was altogether repulsive to him, and he never entered into any calculation of the ratio between the Vicar's income and his more or less necessary expenditure. It was possible that he would not have made such a calculation in his own case.

And now, when the question of voting had come, this repulsive fact told more strongly against Mr Farebrother than it had done before. One would know much better what to do if men's characters were more consistent, and especially if one's friends were invariably fit for any function they desired to undertake! Lydgate was convinced that if there had been no valid objection to Mr Farebrother, he would have voted for him, whatever Bulstrode might have felt on the subject: he did not intend to be a vassal of Bulstrode's. On the other hand, there was Tyke, a man entirely given to his clerical office, who was simply curate at a chapel of ease in St Peter's parish, and had time for extra duty. Nobody had anything to say against Mr Tyke, except that they could not bear him, and suspected him of cant. Really, from his point of view, Bulstrode was thoroughly justified.[33]

Here the question of the chaplaincy provides an opportunity for a pronouncement of tolerance: the narrator also emphasizes the strength of the provincial net or, to use George Eliot's analogy, this particular web. Just as Lydgate is trapped into marriage, so he is trapped by the local power game. George Eliot was only too aware of petty manoeuvring: the passage tells us more about Lydgate's character than anything else, but it also hints that Farebrother's small faults are nothing when weighed in the scale of good feeling. Once again a line is being drawn between office and practice. We have seen Maggie's and Esther's renunciations, but Farebrother's delicate prompting of Mary Garth is Christianity in practice:

He found Mary in the garden gathering roses and sprinkling the petals on a sheet. The sun was low, and tall trees sent their shadows across the grassy walks where Mary was moving without bonnet or parasol. She did not observe Mr Farebrother's approach along the grass, and had just stooped down to lecture a small black-and-tan terrier, which would persist in walking on the sheet and smelling at the rose-leaves as Mary sprinkled them. She took his fore-paws in one hand, and lifted up the forefinger of the other, while the dog wrinkled his brows and looked embarrassed. "Fly, Fly, I am ashamed of you," Mary was saying in a grave contralto. "This is not becoming in a sensible dog; anybody would think you were a silly young gentleman."

"You are unmerciful to young gentlemen, Miss Garth," said the Vicar, within two yards of her.

Mary started up and blushed. "It always answers to reason with Fly," she said, laughingly.

"But not with young gentlemen?"

"Oh, with some, I suppose; since some of them turn into excellent men."

"I am glad of that admission, because I want at this very moment to interest you in a young gentleman."

"Not a silly one, I hope," said Mary, beginning to pluck the roses again, and feeling her heart beat uncomfortably.

"No; though perhaps wisdom is not his strong point, but rather affection and sincerity. However, wisdom lies more in those two qualities than people are apt to imagine. I hope you know by those marks what young gentleman I mean."

"Yes, I think I do," said Mary, bravely, her face getting more serious, and her hands cold; "it must be Fred Vincy."

"He has asked me to consult you about his going into the Church. I hope you will not think that I consented to take a liberty in promising to do so."

"On the contrary, Mr Farebrother," said Mary, giving up the roses, and folding her arms, but unable to look up, "whenever you have anything to say to me I feel honoured."

"But before I enter on that question, let me just touch a point on which your father took me into confidence; by the way, it was that very evening on which I once before fulfilled a mission from Fred, just after he had gone to college. Mr Garth told me what happened on the night of Featherstone's death – how you refused to burn the will; and he said that you had some heart-prickings on that subject, because you had been the innocent means of hindering Fred from getting his ten thousand pounds. I have kept that in mind, and I have heard something that may relieve you on that score – may show you that no sin-offering is demanded from you there."

Mr Farebrother paused a moment and looked at Mary. He meant to give Fred his full advantage, but it would be well, he thought, to clear her mind of any superstitions, such as women sometimes follow when they do a man the wrong of marrying him as an act of atonement. Mary's cheeks had begun to burn a little, and she was mute.

"I mean, that your action made no real difference to Fred's lot. I find that the first will would not have been legally good after the burning of the last: it would not have stood if it had been disputed, and you may be sure it would have been disputed. So, on that score, you may feel your mind free."

"Thank you, Mr Farebrother," said Mary, earnestly. "I am grateful to you for remembering my feelings."

"Well, now I may go on. Fred, you know, has taken his degree. He has worked his way so far, and now the question is, what is he to do? That question is so difficult that he is inclined to follow his father's wishes and enter the Church, though you know better than I do that he was quite set against that formerly. I have questioned him on the subject, and I confess I see no insuperable objection to his being a clergyman, as things go. He says that he could turn his mind to doing his best in that vocation, on one condition. If that condition were fulfilled I would do my utmost in helping Fred on. After a time – not, of course, at first – he might be with me as my curate, and he would have so much to do that his stipend would be nearly what I used to get as vicar. But I repeat that there is a condition without which all this good cannot come to pass. He has opened his heart to me, Miss Garth, and asked me to plead for him. The condition lies entirely in your feeling."

Mary looked so much moved, that he said after a moment, "Let us walk a little;" and when they were walking he added, "To speak quite plainly, Fred will not take any course which would lessen the chance that you would consent to be his wife; but with that prospect, he will try his best at anything you approve."

"I cannot possibly say that I will ever be his wife, Mr Farebrother: but I certainly never will be his wife if he becomes a clergyman. What you say is most generous and kind; I don't mean for a moment to correct your judgment. It is only that I have my girlish, mocking way of looking at things," said Mary, with a returning sparkle of playfulness in her answer which only made its modesty more charming.

"He wishes me to report exactly what you think," said Mr Farebrother.

"I could not love a man who is ridiculous," said Mary, not choosing to go deeper. "Fred has sense and knowledge enough to make him respectable, if he likes, in some good worldly business, but I can never imagine him preaching and exhorting, and pronouncing blessings, and praying by the sick, without feeling as if I were looking at a caricature. His being a clergyman would be only for gentility's sake, and I think there is nothing more contemptible than such imbecile gentility. I used to think that of Mr Crowse, with his empty face and neat umbrella and mincing little speeches. What right have such men to represent Christianity – as if it were an institution for getting up idiots genteelly – as if –" Mary checked herself. She had been carried along as if she had been speaking to Fred instead of Mr Farebrother,

"Young women are severe; they don't feel the stress of action as men do, though perhaps I ought to make you an exception there. But you don't put Fred Vincy on so low a level as that?"

"No, indeed; he has plenty of sense, but I think he would not show it as a clergyman. He would be a piece of professional affectation."

"But if he braved all the difficulties of getting his bread in some other way – will you give him the support of hope? May he count on winning you?"

"I think Fred ought not to need telling again what I have already said to him," Mary answered, with a slight resentment in her manner. "I mean that he ought not to put such questions until he has done something worthy, instead of saying that he could do it."

Mr Farebrother was silent for a minute or more, and then, as they turned and paused under the shadow of a maple at the end of a grassy walk, said, "I understand that you resist any attempt to fetter you, but either your feeling for Fred Vincy excludes your entertaining another attachment, or it does not: either he may count on your remaining single until he shall have earned your hand, or he may in any case be disappointed. Pardon me, Mary – you know I used to catechize you under that name – but when the state of a woman's affections touches the happiness of another life – of more lives than one – I think it would be the nobler course for her to be perfectly direct and open."

Mary in her turn was silent, wondering not at Mr Farebrother's manner but at his tone, which had a grave restrained emotion in it. When the strange idea flashed across her that his words had reference to himself, she was incredulous, and ashamed of entertaining it. She had never thought that any man could love her except Fred, who had espoused her with the umbrella ring, when she wore socks and little strapped shoes; still less that she could be of any importance to Mr Farebrother, the cleverest man in her narrow circle. She had only time to feel that all this was hazy and perhaps illusory; but one thing was clear, and determined her answer.

"Since you think it my duty, Mr Farebrother, I will tell you that I have too strong a feeling for Fred to give him up for any one else. I should never be quite happy if I thought he was unhappy for the loss of me. It has taken such deep root in me – my gratitude to him for always loving me best, and minding so much if I hurt myself, from the time when we were very little. I cannot imagine any new feeling coming to make that weaker. I should like better than anything to see him worthy of every one's respect. But please tell him I will not promise to marry him till then: I should shame and grieve my father and mother. He is free to choose some one else."

"Then I have fulfilled my commission thoroughly," said Mr Farebrother, putting out his hand to Mary, "and I shall ride back to Middlemarch forthwith. With this prospect before him, we shall get Fred into the right niche somehow, and I hope I shall live to join your hands. God bless you!"

"Oh, please stay, and let me give you some tea," said Mary. Her eyes filled with tears, for something indefinable, something like the resolute suppression of a pain in Mr Farebrother's manner, made her feel suddenly miserable, as she had once felt when she saw her father's hands trembling in a moment of trouble.

"No, my dear, no. I must get back."

In three minutes the Vicar was on horseback again, having gone magnanimously through a duty much harder than the renunciation of whist, or even than the writing of penitential meditations.[34]

This exchange, which shows a clergyman catechizing a woman so that she reveals the quality of her love, is much more than Christian self-denial. Mary's replies show her integrity, the nature of her personal faith and duty in her rejection of a clerical vocation for Fred. The comment that men from Oxford and Cambridge frequently became clergymen without a deep commitment to their faith is a religious comment. Mary's indictment is an assertion of a profound truth, that you have to *believe*. Her own religion is found at least in her practical application to duty, to a clear knowledge of what is right and wrong, to moral responsibility.

But of course you don't have to wear the cloth to be religious; faith and its expression is found in many of George Eliot's lay characters as representative of their place and time. Valentine Cunningham has well observed (*Everywhere Spoken Against*, 1975) that of all the great English novelists George Eliot has got closest to what constitutes the essentials of Dissent. He underlines her compassion, her understanding and her sympathetic "insight into the Non-conformist spirit, the enthusiastic character of the Puritan temper", going on to instance her "authentic grasp of some aspects of Nonconformist history and historical process. And though her novels become progressively more distanced from the early tearful sympathy of her treatment of Dinah, until finally her Dissenter had become an out-and-out hypocrite in Bulstrode, George Eliot never lost her compassion and insight . . .".[35] She never forgot what she had known and lived through: her inward experiences and spiritual affiliations as a young woman are blended with her observation of those who were religious, those who affected religion, those who, like herself, passed through the crisis of faith only to find that the practice – not formal, but human and daily – of the Christian ethic remained as a major influence conditioning their standards and their behaviour. When we read *Theophrastus Such* we find that the need to return to the past identity, albeit fictionally, is still present, and in "Looking Backward" the narrator can confide in the reader, revealing those sympathetic affiliations which carry us back to the "clerical" base from which his creator began her fictional career: ". . . my father was a country parson, born much about the same time as Scott and Wordsworth . . . a father who was well-acquainted with all ranks of his neighbours. . . . 'A clergyman, lad,' he used to say to me, 'should feel in himself a bit of every class . . .' "[36]

# 5. Politics

George Eliot's political awareness, her researched sense of political history and her memory of Coventry/Nuneaton occurrences, feed into two novels, *Felix Holt* and *Middlemarch*. In both cases, working "Quarries"[1] are preserved which show her using the *Annual Register*, newspapers and reports in order to ensure authenticity of immediate background to her fictional creation. As she wrote to John Blackwood on 27th April 1866: "I took a great deal of pains to get a true idea of the period. My own recollections are childish, and of course disjointed, but they help to illuminate my reading. I went through *The Times* of 1832–3 at the British Museum to be sure of as many details as I could."[2] This is important, but even more important is the sense of place, the mixed agricultural-mining area which constituted her own inheritance in early years. Thus the ethos of reform which is felt in the provincial centres in both novels is given factual substance and fictional immediacy. For *Felix Holt*, for example, she studied such relevant documents as the *Agricultural Report for 1833* and the *Bribery Report on Elections* (1835),[3] the latter having particular reference to the machinations of the agent Johnson in the plot of her novel. But although she felt that her recollections were "childish", they had given a vividness which research alone cannot provide. Here Mr Lingon is describing the lawyer Jermyn, who is to act as agent for Harold Transome:

"A fat-handed, glib-tongued fellow, with a scented cambric handkerchief; one of your educated low-bred fellows; a foundling who got his Latin for nothing at Christ's Hospital; one of your middle-class upstarts who want to rank with gentlemen, and think they'll do it with kid gloves and new furniture."

But since Harold meant to stand for the county, Mr Lingon was equally emphatic as to the necessity of his not quarrelling with Jermyn till the election was over. Jermyn must be his agent; Harold must wink hard till he found himself safely returned; and even then it might be well to let Jermyn drop gently and raise no scandal. He himself had no quarrel with the fellow: a clergyman should have no quarrels, and he made it a point to be able to take wine with any man he met at table. And as to the estate, and his sister's going too much by Jermyn's advice, he never meddled with business: it was not his duty as a clergyman. That, he considered, was the meaning of Melchisedec and the tithe, a subject into which he had gone to some depth thirty years ago, when he preached the Visitation sermon.

The discovery that Harold meant to stand on the Liberal side – nay, that he boldly declared himself a Radical – was rather startling; but to his uncle's good-humour, beatified by the sipping of port-wine, nothing could seem highly objectionable, provided it did not disturb that operation. In the course of half an hour he had brought himself to see that anything really worthy to be called British Toryism had been entirely extinct since the Duke of Wellington and Sir Robert Peel had passed the Catholic Emancipation Bill; that Whiggery, with its rights of man stopping short at ten-pound householders, and its policy of pacifying a wild beast with a bite, was a ridiculous monstrosity; that therefore, since an honest man could not call himself a Tory, which it was, in fact, as impossible to be now as to fight for the old Pretender, and could still less become that execrable monstrosity a Whig, there remained but one course open to him. "Why, lad, if the world was turned into a swamp, I suppose we should leave off shoes and stockings, and walk about like cranes" – whence it followed plainly enough that, in these hopeless times, nothing was left to men of sense and good family but to retard the national ruin by declaring themselves Radicals, and take the inevitable process of changing everything out of the hands of beggarly demagogues and purse-proud tradesmen. It is true the Rector was helped to this chain of reasoning by Harold's remarks; but he soon became quite ardent in asserting the conclusion.

"If the mob can't be turned back, a man of family must try and head the mob, and save a few homes and hearths, and keep the country up on its last legs as long as he can. And you're a man of family, my lad – dash it! you're a Lingon, whatever else you may be, and I'll stand by you. I've no great interest; I'm a poor parson. I've been forced to give up hunting; my pointers and a glass of good wine are the only decencies becoming my station that I can allow myself. But I'll give you my countenance – I'll stick to you as my nephew. There's no need for me to change sides exactly. I was born a Tory, and I shall never be a bishop. But if anybody says you're in the wrong, I shall say, 'My nephew is in the right; he has turned Radical to save his country. If William Pitt had been living now, he'd have done the same; for what did he say when he was dying? Not "O save my party!" but "O save my country, heaven!" ' That was what they dinned in our ears about Peel and the Duke; and now I'll turn it round upon them. They shall be hoist with their own petard. Yes, yes, I'll stand by you."[4]

This brilliant combination of revealed prejudice and commentary is set in the class situation George Eliot knew so well: once again she is transposing knowledge gained from research, experience and hindsight into a fact of the past with verisimilitude. The hindsight perhaps gives it an additional cynicism which mere recollection could not provide. But when it comes to political activity there is little doubt that the critical sense is reinforced by vivid memory and local knowledge:

There was only evidence that the majority of the crowd were excited with drink, and that their action could hardly be calculated on more than those of oxen and pigs congregated amidst hootings and pushings. The confused deafening shouts, the incidental fighting, the knocking over, pulling and scuffling, seemed to increase every moment. Such of the constables as were mixed with the crowd were quite helpless;

and if an official staff was seen above the heads, it moved about fitfully, showing as little sign of a guiding hand as the summit of a buoy on the waves. Doubtless many hurts and bruises had been received but not one could know the amount of injuries that were widely scattered.

It was clear that no more voting could be done, and the poll had been adjourned. The probabilities of serious mischief had grown strong enough to prevail over the Rector's objection to getting military aid within reach; and when Felix re-entered the town, a galloping messenger had already been despatched to Duffield. The Rector wished to ride out again, and read the Riot Act from a point where he could be better heard than from the window of the Marquis; but Mr Crow, the high constable, who had returned from closer observation, insisted that the risk would be too great. New special constables had been sworn in, but Mr Crow said prophetically that if once mischief began, the mob was past caring for constables.

But the Rector's voice was ringing and penetrating, and when he appeared on the narrow balcony and read the formula commanding all men to go to their homes or about their lawful business there was a strong transient effect. Every one within hearing listened, and for a few moments after the final words, "God save the King!" the comparative silence continued. Then the people began to move, the buzz rose again, and grew, and grew, till it turned to shouts and roaring as before. The movement was that of a flood hemmed in; it carried nobody away. Whether the crowd would obey the order to disperse themselves within an hour, was a doubt that approached nearer and nearer to a negative certainty.

Presently Mr Crow, who held himself a tactician, took a well-intentioned step, which went far to fulfil his own prophecy. He had arrived with the magistrates by a back way at the Seven Stars, and here again the Riot Act was read from a window, with much the same result as before. The Rector had returned by the same way to the Marquis, as the headquarters most suited for administration, but Mr Crow remained at the other extremity of King Street, where some awe-striking presence was certainly needed. Seeing that the time was passing, and all effect from the voice of law had disappeared, he showed himself at an upper window, and addressed the crowd, telling them that the soldiers had been sent for, and that if they did not disperse they would have cavalry upon them instead of constables.

Mr Crow, like some other high constables more celebrated in history, "enjoyed a bad reputation;" that is to say, he enjoyed many things which caused his reputation to be bad, and he was anything but popular in Treby. It is probable that a pleasant message would have lost something from his lips, and what he actually said was so unpleasant, that, instead of persuading the crowd, it appeared to enrage them. Some one, snatching a raw potato from a sack in the greengrocer's shop behind him, threw it at the constable, and hit him on the mouth. Straightway raw potatoes and turnips were flying by twenties at the windows of the Seven Stars, and the panes were smashed. Felix, who was half-way up the street, heard the voices turning to a savage roar, and saw a rush towards the hardware shop, which furnished more effective weapons and missiles than turnips and potatoes. Then a cry ran along that the Tories had sent for the soldiers, and if those among the mob who called themselves Tories as willingly as anything else were disposed to take whatever called itself the Tory side, they only helped the main result of reckless disorder.

But there were proofs that the predominant will of the crowd was against "Debarry's men," and in favour of Transome. Several shops were invaded, and they were all of them "Tory shops." The tradesmen who could do so, now locked their doors and barricaded their windows within. There was a panic among the householders of this hitherto peaceful town, and a general anxiety for the military to arrive. The Rector was in painful anxiety on this head: he had sent out two messengers as secretly as he could towards Hathercote, to order the soldiers to ride straight to the town; but he feared that these messengers had been somehow intercepted.

It was three o'clock: more than an hour had elapsed since the reading of the Riot Act. The Rector of Treby Magna wrote an indignant message and sent it to the Ram, to Mr Lingon, the Rector of Little Treby, saying that there was evidently a Radical animus in the mob, and that Mr Transome's party should hold themselves peculiarly responsible. Where was Mr Jermyn?

Mr Lingon replied that he was going himself out towards Duffield to see after the soldiers. As for Jermyn, he was not that attorney's sponsor: he believed that Jermyn was gone away somewhere on business – to fetch voters.

A serious effort was now being made by all the civil force at command. The December day would soon be passing into evening, and all disorder would be aggravated by obscurity. The horrors of fire were as likely to happen as any minor evil. The constables, as many of them as could do so, armed themselves with carbines and sabres: . . .[5]

The origins of this are in Nuneaton, but there would seem here to be a strong Coventry connection as well. George Eliot is cleverly combining memories and associations and so deepening the sense of place. The treatment of Spratt (see p. 93–4) is strongly reminiscent of the *Coventry Lent Assizes Report* of 24th March 1832 on the "TRIAL of the PRISONERS charged with RIOTING, and DESTROYING THE HOUSE AND MACHINERY OF JOSIAH BECK IN COVENTRY, ON MONDAY, NOV 7, 1831."[6] In fact he was manhandled in the same way as Spratt – "They then threw pieces of coal and brickbats at him, they got him from the doorway into the yard, and severely beat him, and someone took hold of his jacket. . . . The mob then put him into a handcart, and in Ironmonger-row they threw him into some mud."[7]

The 10th December 1832 was known as "bloody tenth" or "Bloody Monday" in Coventry. On that day, according to Whitley's *Parliamentary Representation of the City of Coventry*, there was recruitment of some "noted pugilists from Birmingham" as well as about six hundred navvies. They were primed with gin. This is what happened:

The mob, having taken possession of the booth, placed its regiment of hirelings in such a manner as to prevent the approach of any persons to it except of their own side. Meanwhile, the dark Blues were collecting on Greyfriars Green. . . . Reaching between two and three thousand strong, and headed by "Bob Randall", his prizefighters and roughs, they proceeded to the booth to oust their opponents, when a dreadful scene of lawlessness and riot ensued.[8]

George Eliot's treatment of a similar scene is, of course, to give it particularity by using the situation as an event for her fiction. The provincial politics are important here, the local reputation of the high constable and the opposing rectors adding spice to what happens. There is evidence in the novel of the potent practices of the professional agitators, those paid to create as much trouble as possible. Another aspect of the election at Treby Magna deals with the bribery and corruption, very much present outside and inside the novel:

"Now, listen to me. Here's Garstin: he's one of the Company you work under. What's Garstin to you? who sees him? and when they do see him they see a thin miserly fellow who keeps his pockets buttoned. He calls himself a Whig, yet he'll split votes with a Tory – he'll drive with the Debarrys. Now, gentlemen, if I said I'd got a vote, and anybody asked me what I should do with it, I should say, 'I'll plump for Transome.' You've got no votes, and that's a shame. But you *will* have some day, if such men as Transome are returned; and then you'll be on a level with the first gentlemen in the land, and if he wants to sit in Parliament, he must take off his hat and ask your leave. But though you haven't got a vote you can give a cheer for the right man, and Transome's not a man like Garstin; if you lost a day's wages by giving a cheer for Transome, he'll make you amends. That's the way a man who has no vote can yet serve himself and his country: he can lift up his hand and shout 'Transome for ever' – 'hurray for Transome.' Let the working men – let colliers and navvies and stone-cutters, who between you and me have a good deal too much the worst of it, as things are now – let them join together and give their hands and voices for the right man, and they'll make the great people shake in their shoes a little, and when you shout for Transome, remember you shout for more wages, and more of your rights, and you shout to get rid of rats and *sprats* and such small animals, who are the tools the rich make use of to squeeze the blood out of the poor man."

"I wish there'd be a row – I'd pommel him," said Dredge, who was generally felt to be speaking to the question.

"No, no, my friend – there you're a little wrong. No pommelling – no striking first. There you have the law and the constable against you. A little rolling in the dust and knocking hats off, a little pelting with soft things that'll stick and not bruise – all that doesn't spoil the fun. If a man is to speak when you don't like to hear him, it is but fair you should give him something he doesn't like in return. And the same if he's got a vote and doesn't use it for the good of the country; I see no harm in splitting his coat in a quiet way. A man must be taught what's right if he doesn't know it. But no kicks, no knocking down, no pommelling."

"It 'ud be good fun, though, if so-*be*," said Old Sleck, allowing himself an imaginative pleasure.

"Well, well, if a Spratt wants you to say Garstin, it's some pleasure to think you can say Transome. Now, my notion is this. You are men who can put two and two together – I don't know a more solid lot of fellows than you are; and what I say is, let the honest men in this country who've got no vote show themselves in a body when they have the chance. Why, sirs, for every Tory sneak that's got a vote, there's fifty-five fellows who must stand by and be expected to hold their tongues. But I say, let 'em hiss the sneaks, let 'em groan at the sneaks, and the sneaks will be ashamed of themselves. The men who've got votes don't know how to use them. There's many a fool with a vote, who is not sure in his mind whether he shall poll, say for Debarry, or Garstin, or Transome – whether he'll plump or whether he'll split; a straw will turn him. Let him know your mind if he doesn't know his own. What's the reason Debarry gets returned? Because people are frightened at the Debarrys. What's that to you? You don't care for the Debarrys. If people are frightened at the Tories, we'll turn round and frighten *them*. You know what a Tory is – one who wants to drive the working men as he'd drive cattle. That's what a Tory is; and a Whig is no better, if he's like Garstin. A Whig wants to knock the Tory down and get the whip, that's all. But Transome's neither Whig nor Tory; he's the working man's friend, the collier's friend, the friend of the honest navvy. And if he gets into Parliament, let me tell you, it will be the better for you. I don't say it will be the better for overlookers and screws, and rats and *sprats*; but it will be the better for every good fellow who takes his pot at the Sugar Loaf."

Mr Johnson's exertions for the political education of the Sproxton men did not stop here, which was the more distinterested in him as he did not expect to see them again, and could only set on foot an organization by which their instruction could be continued with- out him. In this he was quite successful. A man known among the "butties" as Pack, who had already been mentioned by Mr Chubb, presently joined the party, and had a private audience of Mr Johnson, that he might be instituted as the "shepherd" of this new flock.

"That's a right down geneleman," said Pack, as he took the seat vacated by the orator, who had ridden away.

"What's his trade, think you?" said Gills, the wiry stone-cutter.

"Trade?" said Mr Chubb. "He's one of the top-sawyers of the country. He works with his head, you may see that."

"Let's have our pipes, then," said Old Sleck; "I'm pretty well tired o' jaw."[9]

To read this is to admire George Eliot's remarkable period awareness. The innuendo is ominous, a mockery of reform, the easy language of coercion used on the ignorant who are meant to remain ignorant so that they can continue to be used. The stirring of trouble which was fact in Coventry and Nuneaton is here given fictional equivalence; George Eliot has often been praised for the remarkable true-to-life humour of the Rainbow Inn scene in *Silas Marner*, but the responses of the locals here are just as convincing, just as close to reality, and more ironic and pathetic.

In *Middlemarch* the same period is explored, though the place is clearly Coventry. The tone however is different, mainly because Mr Brooke cannot be taken as seriously as Harold Transome, though his political motivation and alignment are as superficial and opportunistic as Harold's. He employs Ladislaw to edit *The Pioneer* for him but he cannot reform himself even down to the personal relationships he enjoys, or rather doesn't enjoy with his tenants. Again we remember the author's recollections of her early days, her riding around the estate with her father. They may have encountered something like this – or been told of a comparable incident:

"Your little lad Jacob has been caught killing a leveret, Dagley: I have told Johnson to lock him up in the empty stable an hour or two, just to frighten him, you know. But he will be brought home by-and-by, before night: and you'll just look after him, will you, and give him a reprimand, you know?"

"No, I woon't: I'll be dee'd if I'll leather my boy to please you or anybody else, not if you was twenty landlords istid o' one, and that a bad un."

Dagley's words were loud enough to summon his wife to the back-kitchen door – the only entrance ever used, and one always open except in bad weather – and Mr Brooke, saying soothingly, "Well, well, I'll speak to your wife – I didn't mean beating, you know," turned to walk to the house. But Dagley, only the more inclined to "have his say" with a gentleman who walked away from him, followed at once, with Fag slouching at his heels and sullenly evading some small and probably charitable advances on the part of Monk.

"How do you do, Mrs Dagley?" said Mr Brooke, making some haste. "I came to tell you about your boy: I don't want you to give him the stick, you know." He was careful to speak quite plainly this time.

Overworked Mrs Dagley – a thin, worn woman, from whose life pleasure had so entirely vanished that she had not even any Sunday clothes which could give her satisfaction in preparing for church – had already had a misunderstanding with her husband since he had come home, and was in low spirits, expecting the worst. But her husband was beforehand in answering.

"No, nor he woon't hev the stick, whether you want it or no," pursued Dagley, throwing out his voice, as if he wanted it to hit hard. "You've got no call to come an' talk about sticks o' these primises, as you woon't give a stick tow'rt mending. Go to Middlemarch to ax for *your* charrickter."

"You'd far better hold your tongue, Dagley," said the wife, "and not kick your own trough over. When a man as is father of a family has been an' spent money at market and made himself the worse for liquor, he's done enough mischief for one day. But I should like to know what my boy's done, sir."

"Niver do you mind what he's done," said Dagley, more fiercely, "it's my business to speak, an' not yourn. An' I wull speak, too. I'll hev my say – supper or no. An' what I say is, as I've lived upo' your ground from my father and grandfather afore me, an' hev dropped our money into't, an' me an' my children might lie an' rot on the ground for top-dressin' as we can't find the money to buy, if the King wasn't to put a stop."

"My good fellow, you're drunk, you know," said Mr Brooke, confidentially but not judiciously. "Another day, another day," he added, turning as if to go.

But Dagley immediately fronted him, and Fag at his heels growled low, as his master's voice grew louder and more insulting, while Monk also drew close in silent dignified watch. The labourers on the waggon were pausing to listen, and it seemed wiser to be quite passive than to attempt a ridiculous flight pursued by a bawling man.

"I'm no more drunk nor you are, nor so much," said Dagley. "I can carry my liquor, an' I know what I meean. An' I meean as the King 'ull put a stop to't, for them say it as knows it, as there's to be a Rinform, and them landlords as never done the right thing by their tenants 'ull be treated i' that way as they'll hev to scuttle off. An' there's them i' Middlemarch knows what the Rinform is – an' as knows who'll hev to scuttle. Says they, 'I know who *your* landlord is.' An' says I, 'I hope you're the better for knowin' him, I arn't.' Says they, 'He's a close-fisted un.' 'Ay, ay,' says I. 'He's a man for the Rinform,' says they. That's what they says. An' I made out what the Rinform were – an' it were to send you an' your likes a-scuttlin'; an' wi' pretty strong-smellin' things too. An' you may do as you like now, for I'm none afeard on you. An' you'd better let my boy aloan, an' look to yoursen, afore the Rinform has got upo' your back.[10]

Mr Brooke as unreforming landlord squares badly with Mr Brooke as overtly reforming politician, and his failure here in private condescension is mirrored by a wider public failure.

There is too the social and moral commentary which is worked into the scene by the author. As with *Felix Holt*, we get the impression that the ironic mode is here extended to embrace the morally grotesque nature of things as they were. Mr Brooke as magistrate fails to prevent a sheep-stealer from being hanged earlier in the novel; here he applies his own law to his tenant's son by locking him up. The division between the classes is social, moral and of course political. George Eliot is saying – as she returns to a period and place she knew well – that parliamentary legislation cannot at a stroke change the traditional patterns of society. Here Dagley is the worse for drink; when we next see Mr Brooke in action he, generally abstemious, helps to bring about his own political downfall by a rather more sudden indulgence. It is a neatly ironic turnabout:

However, Ladislaw's coaching was forthwith to be put to the test, for before the day of nomination Mr Brooke was to explain himself to the worthy electors of Middlemarch from the balcony of the White Hart, which looked out advantageously at an angle of the market-place, commanding a large area in front and two converging streets. It was a fine May morning, and everything seemed hopeful: there was some prospect of an understanding between Bagster's committee and Brooke's, to which Mr Bulstrode, Mr Standish as a Liberal lawyer, and such manufacturers as Mr Plymdale and Mr Vincy, gave a solidity which almost counterbalanced Mr Hawley and his associates who sat for Pinkerton at the Green Dragon. Mr Brooke, conscious of having weakened the blasts of the "Trumpet" against him, by his reforms as a landlord in the last half year, and hearing himself cheered a little as he drove into the town, felt his heart tolerably light under his buff-coloured waistcoat. But with regard to critical occasions, it often happens that all moments seem comfortably remote until the last.

"This looks well, eh?" said Mr Brooke as the crowd gathered. "I shall have a good audience, at any rate. I like this, now – this kind of public made up of one's own neighbours, you know."

The weavers and tanners of Middlemarch, unlike Mr Mawmsey, had never thought of Mr Brooke as a neighbour, and were not more attached to him than if he had been sent in a box from London. But they listened without much disturbance to the speakers who introduced the candidate, though one of them – a political personage from Brassing, who came to tell Middlemarch its duty – spoke so fully, that it was alarming to think what the candidate could find to say after him. Meanwhile the crowd became denser, and as the political personage neared the end of his speech, Mr Brooke felt a remarkable change in his sensations while he still handled his eye-glass, trifled with documents before him, and exchanged remarks with his committee, as a man to whom the moment of summons was indifferent.

"I'll take another glass of sherry, Ladislaw," he said, with an easy air, to Will, who was close behind him, and presently handed him the supposed fortifier. It was ill-chosen; for Mr Brooke was an abstemious man, and to drink a second glass of sherry quickly at no great interval from the first was a surprise to his system which tended to scatter his ener- gies instead of collecting them. Pray pity him: so many English gentlemen make them- selves miserable by speechifying on entirely private grounds! whereas Mr Brooke wished to serve his country by standing for Parliament – which, indeed, may also be done on private grounds, but being once undertaken does absolutely demand some speechifying.

It was not about the beginning of his speech that Mr Brooke was at all anxious; this, he felt sure, would be all right; he should have it quite pat, cut out as neatly as a set of couplets from Pope. Embarking would be easy, but the vision of open sea that might come after was alarming. "And questions, now," hinted the demon just waking up in his stomach, "somebody may put questions about the schedules. – Ladislaw," he continued, aloud, "just hand me the memorandum of the schedules."

When Mr Brooke presented himself on the balcony, the cheers were quite loud enough to counterbalance the yells, groans, braying, and other expressions of adverse theory, which were so moderate that Mr Standish (decidedly an old bird) observed in the ear next to him, "This looks dangerous, by God! Hawley has got some deeper plan than this." Still, the cheers were exhilarating, and no candidate could look more amiable than Mr Brooke, with the memorandum in his breast-pocket, his left hand on the rail of the balcony, and his right trifling with his eye-glass. The striking points in his appearance were his buff waistcoat, short-clipped blond hair, and neutral physiognomy. He began with some confidence.

"Gentlemen – Electors of Middlemarch!"

This was so much the right thing that a little pause after it seemed natural.

"I'm uncommonly glad to be here – I was never so proud and happy in my life – never so happy, you know."

This was a bold figure of speech, but not exactly the right thing; for, unhappily, the pat opening had slipped away – even couplets from Pope may be but "fallings from us, vanishings," when fear clutches us, and a glass of sherry is hurrying like smoke among our ideas. Ladislaw, who stood at the window behind the speaker, thought, "it's all up now. The only chance is that, since the best thing won't always do, floundering may answer for once." Mr Brooke, meanwhile, having lost other clues, fell back on himself and his qualifications – always an appropriate graceful subject for a candidate.

"I am a close neighbour of yours, my good friends – you've known me on the bench a good while – I've always gone a good deal into public questions – machinery, now, and machine-breaking – you're many of you concerned with machinery, and I've been going into that lately. It won't do, you know, breaking machines: everything must go on – trade, manufactures, commerce, interchange of staples – that kind of thing – since Adam Smith, that must go on. We must look all over the globe: –

'Observation with extensive view,' must look everywhere, 'from China to Peru,' as somebody says – Johnson, I think, 'The Rambler,' you know. That is what I have done up to a certain point – not as far as Peru; but I've not always stayed at home – I saw it wouldn't do. I've been in the Levant, where some of your Middlemarch goods go – and then, again, in the Baltic. The Baltic, now."

Plying among his recollections in this way, Mr Brooke might have got along, easily to himself, and would have come back from the remotest seas without trouble; but a diabolical procedure had been set up by the enemy. At one and the same moment there had risen above the shoulders of the crowd, nearly opposite Mr Brooke, and within ten yards of him, the effigy of himself: buff-coloured waistcoat, eye-glass, and neutral physiognomy, painted on rag; and there had arisen, apparently in the air, like the note of the cuckoo, a parrot-like, Punch-voiced echo of his words. Everybody looked up at the open windows in the houses at the opposite angles of the converging streets; but they were either blank, or filled by laughing listeners. The most innocent echo has an impish mockery in it when it follows a gravely persistent speaker, and this echo was not at all innocent; if it did not follow with the precision of a natural echo, it had a wicked choice of the words it overtook. By the time it said, "The Baltic, now," the laugh which had been running through the audience became a general shout, and but for the sobering effects of party and that great public cause which the entanglement of things had identified with "Brooke of Tipton," the laugh might have caught his committee. Mr Bulstrode asked, reprehensively, what the new police was doing; but a voice could not well be collared, and an attack on the effigy of the candidate would have been too equivocal, since Hawley probably meant it to be pelted.

Mr Brooke himself was not in a position to be quickly conscious of anything except a general slipping away of ideas within himself: he had even a little singing in the ears, and he was the only person who had not yet taken distinct account of the echo or discerned the image of himself. Few things hold the perceptions more thoroughly captive than anxiety about what we have got to say. Mr Brooke heard the laughter; but he had expected some Tory efforts at disturbance, and he was at this moment additionally excited by the tickling, stinging sense that his lost exordium was coming back to fetch him from the Baltic.

"That reminds me," he went on, thrusting a hand into his side-pocket, with an easy air, "if I wanted a precedent, you know – but we never want a precedent for the right thing – but there is Chatham, now; I can't say I should have supported Chatham, or Pitt, the younger Pitt – he was not a man of ideas, and we want ideas, you know."

"Blast your ideas! we want the Bill," said a loud rough voice from the crowd below. Immediately the invisible Punch, who had hitherto followed Mr Brooke, repeated, "Blast your ideas! we want the Bill." The laugh was louder than ever, and for the first time Mr Brooke being himself silent, heard distinctly the mocking echo. But it seemed to ridicule his interrupter, and in that light was encouraging; so he replied with amenity –

"There is something in what you say, my good friend, and what do we meet for but to speak our minds – freedom of opinion, freedom of the press, liberty – that kind of thing? The Bill, now – you shall have the Bill" – here Mr Brooke paused a moment to fix on his eye-glass and take the paper from his breast-pocket, with a sense of being practical and coming to particulars. The invisible Punch followed: –

"You shall have the Bill, Mr Brooke, per electioneering contest, and a seat outside Parliament as delivered, five thousand pounds, seven shillings, and fourpence."

Mr Brooke, amid the roars of laughter, turned red, let his eye-glass fall, and looking about him confusedly, saw the image of himself, which had come nearer. The next moment he saw it dolorously bespattered with eggs. His spirit rose a little, and his voice too.

"Buffoonery, tricks, ridicule the test of truth – all that is very well" – here an unpleasant egg broke on Mr Brooke's shoulder, as the echo said, "All that is very well;" then came a hail of eggs, chiefly aimed at the image, but occasionally hitting the original, as if by chance. There was a stream of new men pushing among the crowd; whistles, yells, bellowings, and fifes made all the greater hubbub because there was shouting and struggling to put them down. No voice would have had wing enough to rise above the uproar, and Mr Brooke, disagreeably anointed, stood his ground no longer. The frustration would have been less exasperating if it had been less gamesome and boyish: a serious assault of which the newspaper reporter "can aver that it endangered the learned gentleman's ribs," or can respectfully bear witness to "the soles of that gentleman's boots having been visible above the railing," has perhaps more consolations attached to it.

Mr Brooke re-entered the committee-room, saying, as carelessly as he could, "This is a little too bad, you know. I should have got the ear of the people by-and-by – but they didn't give me time. I should have gone into the Bill by-and-by, you know," he added, glancing at Ladislaw. "However, things will come all right at the nomination."

But it was not resolved unanimously that things would come right; on the contrary, the committee looked rather grim, and the political personage from Brassing was writing busily, as if he were brewing new devices.[11]

It is a serious blow to the amateur politician, and again it has more than research behind it. Brooke of Tipton exposes himself as a figure of fun, his credentials inadequate for the rough and tumble of political life. Yet although it is right within context – note Ladislaw's comment and the authorial commentary, as well as Brooke's own reference to *The Rambler* – we get a strong sense of political locality and a deliberate infiltration of it. The reiterated citing of "the Bill" is balanced by the local references – to the new police, for example, and to machine-breaking, both right in period. The innuendo is sceptical but light. In her "Quarry" for *Middlemarch* George Eliot refers specifically to machine-breaking. Indeed, the Josiah Beck case is a singular example of this: the weavers in this instance set out to destroy the power looms and other equipment, one of the men shouting at Beck, "I will make you destroy your own inventions!" Later in the report we are told: "The premises and machinery were destroyed by fire, and the engine damaged."[12] The new police were formed in Coventry in 1830. And the scene itself is wonderfully created, as memory and imagination coalesce.

Jerome Beaty's fine article, "History by Indirection: the Era of Reform in *Middlemarch*", which has stood the test of time, analyses "George Eliot's techniques for handling political history: she introduces it largely through references to historical personages; she mentions but never explains issues; she scatters references to the same person or issue through the novel rather than lumping them in a single paragraph or chapter; she separates the events from specific dates. In other words, she presents history dramatically, within the story, as part of the lives of the characters; she rarely offers it directly to the reader as history."[13] This statement, definitive in its general appraisal, perhaps needs a small but important addition: George Eliot presents convincingly (though fictionally) the spectrum, the moving medium of local history, so that her provincial scenes are as mirrors to the national background.

# 6. Education in Many Forms

All George Eliot's works are concerned with education in one form or another, the education of the feelings, the mind, and the spirit. Amos Barton is educated into an appreciation of his wife when it is almost too late; Caterina comes to a fuller knowledge of herself, and love, when she finds Anthony dead, though the knowledge eventually kills her; and Janet comes to a full appreciation of the moral and the spiritual life through the tutelage of Edgar Tryan.

This extract from *Adam Bede* speaks for itself (the factual time is 1800 or close to it):

"Nay, Bill, nay," Bartle was saying in a kind tone, as he nodded to Adam, "begin that again, and then perhaps, it'll come to you what d, r, y, spells. It's the same lesson you read last week, you know."

"Bill" was a sturdy fellow, aged four-and-twenty, an excellent stone-sawyer, who could get as good wages as any man in the trade of his years; but he found a reading lesson in words of one syllable a harder matter to deal with than the hardest stone he had ever had to saw. The letters, he complained, were so "uncommon alike, there was no tellin' 'em one from another," the sawyer's business not being concerned with minute differences such as exist between a letter with its tail turned up and a letter with its tail turned down. But Bill had a firm determination that he would learn to read, founded chiefly on two reasons: first, that Tom Hazelow, his cousin, could read anything "right off," whether it was print or writing, and Tom had sent him a letter from twenty miles off, saying how he was prospering in the world, and had got an overlooker's place; secondly, that Sam Phillips, who sawed with him, had learned to read when he was turned twenty; and what could be done by a little fellow like Sam Phillips, Bill considered, could be done by himself, seeing that he could pound Sam into wet clay if circumstances required it. So here he was, pointing his big finger towards three words at once, and turning his head on one side that he might keep better hold with his eye of the one word which was to be discriminated out of the group. The amount of knowledge Bartle Massey must possess was something so dim and vast that Bill's imagination recoiled before it: he would hardly have ventured to deny that the schoolmaster might have something to do in bringing about the regular return of daylight and the changes in the weather.

The man seated next to Bill was of a very different type: he was a Methodist brickmaker, who, after spending thirty years of his life in perfect satisfaction with his ignorance, had lately "got religion," and along with it the desire to read the Bible. But with him, too, learning was a heavy business, and on his way out to-night he had offered as usual a special prayer for help, seeing that he had undertaken this hard task with a single eye to the nourishment of his soul – that he might have a greater abundance of texts and hymns wherewith to banish evil memories and the temptations of old habit; or, in brief language, the devil.[1]

Here are instances of provincial ambition. Adam is obviously the outstanding pupil, but the whole scene of adult education is described with precision and pathos. It is typical of its time, but probably recreated from anecdote – perhaps from what her father told her. William Mottram, in *The True Story of George Eliot* (1905), observes, "I believe it is quite true that Bartle Massey did try to induce his pupils to carry on their studies by means of an evening school, and it is prob- able that his complainings that so few of his old scholars availed themselves of the advantages he offered them are genuine enough."[2] Adam's limited library, including the Bible, *The Pilgrim's Progress* and Taylor's *Holy Living and Dying*, is read over and over again, and these and some others were lent to him by Bartle Massey.

This is going back beyond George Eliot's own time. But in that time, we suspect, Maggie's self-education and her tastes are close to Marian Evans's too. There is her own moving account of *The Linnet's Life*, quoted by Cross: "This little book is the first present I ever remember having received from my father. Let any one who thinks of me with some tenderness after I am dead, take care of this book for my sake. It made me very happy when I held it in my little hands, and read it over and over again; and thought the pictures beautiful, especially the one where the linnet is feeding its young."[3] This present tenderness for precious memory, this rich humanitarian association with the past, is very much a part of the mature novelist:

Maggie's cheeks began to flush with triumphant excitement: she thought Mr Riley would have a respect for her now; it had been evident that he thought nothing of her before.

Mr Riley was turning over the leaves of the book, and she could make nothing of his face, with its high-arched eyebrows; but he presently looked at her and said,

"Come, come and tell me something about this book; here are some pictures – I want to know what they mean."

Maggie with deepening colour went without hesitation to Mr Riley's elbow and looked over the book, eagerly seizing one corner, and tossing back her mane, while she said,

"O, I'll tell you what that means, It's a dreadful picture, isn't it? But I can't help looking at it. That old woman in the water's a witch – they've put her in to find out whether she's a witch or no, and if she swims she's a witch, and if she's drowned – and killed, you know – she's innocent, and not a witch, but only a poor silly old woman. But what good would it do her then, you know, when she was drowned? Only, I suppose she'd go to heaven, and God would make it up to her. And this dreadful blacksmith with his arms akimbo, laughing – oh, isn't he ugly? – I'll tell you what he is. He's the devil *really*" (here Maggie's voice became louder and more emphatic), "and not a right blacksmith; for the devil takes the shape of wicked men, and walks about and sets people doing wicked things, and he's oftener in the shape of a bad man than any other, because, you know, if people saw he was the devil, and he roared at 'em, they'd run away, and he couldn't make 'em do what he pleased."

Mr Tulliver had listened to this exposition of Maggie's with petrifying wonder.

"Why, what book is it the wench has got hold on?" he burst out, at last.

" 'The History of the Devil,' by Daniel Defoe; not quite the right book for a little girl," said Mr Riley. "How came it among your books, Tulliver?"

Maggie looked hurt and discouraged, while her father said,

"Why, it's one o' the books I bought at Partridge's sale. They was all bound alike – it's a good binding, you see – and I thought they'd be all good books. There's Jeremy Taylor's 'Holy Living and Dying' among 'em; I read in it often of a Sunday" (Mr Tulliver felt somehow a familiarity with that great writer because his name was Jeremy); "and there's a lot more of 'em, sermons mostly, I think; but they've all got the same covers, and I thought they were all 'o one sample, as you may say. But it seems one mustn't judge by th' outside. This is a puzzlin' world."

"Well," said Mr Riley, in an admonitory patronizing tone, as he patted Maggie on the head, "I advise you to put by the 'History of the Devil,' and read some prettier book. Have you no prettier books?"

"O yes," said Maggie, reviving a little in the desire to vindicate the variety of her reading, "I know the reading in this book isn't pretty – but I like the pictures, and I make stories to the pictures out of my own head, you know. But I've got 'Æsop's Fables,' and a book about Kangaroos and things, and the 'Pilgrim's Progress.' " . . .

"Ah, a beautiful book," said Mr Riley; "you can't read a better."

"Well, but there's a great deal about the devil in that," said Maggie, triumphantly, "and I'll show you the picture of him in his true shape, as he fought with Christian."

Maggie ran in an instant to the corner of the room, jumped on a chair, and reached down from the small bookcase a shabby old copy of Bunyan, which opened at once, without the least trouble of search, at the picture she wanted.

"Here he is," she said, running back to Mr Riley, "and Tom coloured him for me with his paints when he was at home last holidays – the body all black, you know, and the eyes red, like fire, because he's all fire inside, and it shines out at his eyes."

"Go, go!" said Mr Tulliver, peremptorily, beginning to feel rather uncomfortable at these free remarks on the personal appearance of a being powerful enough to create lawyers; "shut up the book, and let's hear no more o' such talk. It is as I thought – the child 'ull learn more mischief nor good wi' the books. Go, go and see after your mother."

Maggie shut up the book at once, with a sense of disgrace, but not being inclined to see after her mother, she compromised the matter by going into a dark corner behind her father's chair, and nursing her doll, towards which she had an occasional fit of fondness in Tom's absence, neglecting its toilette, but lavishing so many warm kisses on it that the waxen cheeks had a wasted unhealthy appearance.

"Did you ever hear the like on't?" said Mr Tulliver, as Maggie retired. "It's a pity but what she'd been the lad – she'd ha' been a match for the lawyers, *she* would. It's the wonderful'st thing" – here he lowered his voice – "as I picked the mother because she wasn't o'er 'cute – bein' a good-looking woman too, an' come of a rare family for managing; but I picked her from her sisters o' purpose, 'cause she was a bit weak, like; for I wasn't agoin' to be told the rights o' things by my own fireside. But you see when a man's got brains himself, there's no knowing where they'll run to; an' a pleasant sort o' soft woman may go on breeding you stupid lads and 'cute wenches, till it's like as if the world was turned topsy-turvy. It's an uncommon puzzlin' thing."[4]

While this is finely in context – consider the irony of "she'd ha' been a match for the lawyers, *she* would" – it is probably strengthened by a personal identification with the clever child whose father is embarrassed by her unpredictable directions. And the remarkable self-education of a girl in a man's world (as Mr Tulliver makes clear) is achieved within the ambience of the emotional stability provided by that father. Maggie's education gives her the power to suffer, as Marian Evans must have suffered at times before her adulthood and the move to Bird Grove. But education, generally and in the fictional time of the novel and the factual time of Marian's early years, is for men. Not that Tom's education fulfils his father's wish for practical equipment, as is made clear by his being directed towards the norms of classical education and the particular case of Mr Stelling:

But the immediate step to future success was to bring on Tom Tulliver during this first half-year; for, by a singular coincidence, there had been some negotiation concerning another pupil from the same neighbourhood, and it might further a decision in Mr Stelling's favour, if it were understood that young Tulliver, who, Mr Stelling observed in conjugal privacy, was rather a rough cub, had made prodigious progress in a short time. It was on this ground that he was severe with Tom about his lessons: he was clearly a boy whose powers would never be developed through the medium of the Latin grammar, without the application of some sternness. Not that Mr Stelling was a harsh-tempered or unkind man – quite the contrary: he was jocose with Tom at table, and corrected his provincialisms and his deportment in the most playful manner; but Tom was only the more cowed and confused by this double novelty, for he had never been used to jokes at all like Mr Stelling's; and for the first time in his life he had a painful sense that he was all wrong somehow. When Mr Stelling said, as the roast-beef was being uncovered, "Now, Tulliver! which would you rather decline, roast-beef or the Latin for it?" – Tom, to whom in his coolest moments a pun would have been a hard nut, was thrown into a state of embarrassed alarm that made everything dim to him except the feeling that he would rather not have anything to do with Latin: of course he answered, "Roast-beef," whereupon there followed much laughter and some practical joking with the plates, from which Tom gathered that he had in some mysterious way refused beef, and, in fact, made himself appear "a silly."[5]

The method and the content prove irrelevant: that Tom succeeds in later life is because of his own doggedness and pride, in spite of the inhibiting and deadening nature of the instruction he receives:

Perhaps it was because teaching came naturally to Mr Stelling, that he set about it with that uniformity of method and independence of circumstances, which distinguish the actions of animals understood to be under the immediate teaching of nature. Mr Broderip's amiable beaver, as that charming naturalist tells us, busied himself as earnestly in constructing a dam, in a room up three pairs of stairs in London, as if he had been laying his foundation in a stream or lake in Upper Canada. It was "Binny's" function to build: the absence of water or of possible progeny was an accident for which he was not accountable. With the same unerring instinct Mr Stelling set to work at his natural method of instilling the Eton Grammar and Euclid into the mind of Tom Tulliver. This, he considered, was the only basis of solid instruction: all other means of education were mere charlatanism, and could produce nothing better than smatterers. Fixed on this firm basis, a man might observe the display of various or special knowledge made by irregularly educated people with a pitying smile: all that sort of thing was very well, but it was impossible these people could form sound opinions. In holding this conviction Mr Stelling was not biased, as some tutors have been, by the excessive accuracy or extent of his own scholarship; and as to his views about Euclid, no opinion could have been freer from personal partiality. Mr Stelling was very far from being led astray by enthusiasm, either religious or intellectual; on the other hand, he had no secret belief that everything was humbug.[6]

We can't help looking back at Bartle Massey, who concentrated on the essentials. But George Eliot looking back to Marian Evans was also deliberately contemplating a period before there was any kind of universal education. Poor man and middle-class woman were similarly deprived, and she knew that her own good fortune in schooling was uncommon. In her novels the past is seen from the vantage point of hindsight: *The Mill on the Floss* was written ten years before the Education Act of 1870.

Her awareness of the importance of education is always to the fore: although the three schools she attended contributed to the development of her abilities, they may have also contributed to the narrowness of outlook in her early religious affiliations. Maggie's education continues throughout her short life, but when she visits Tom at Mr Stelling's we see the deprivation of an intelligent girl:

"Now, then, come with me into the study, Maggie," said Tom, as their father drove away. "What do you shake and toss your head now for, you silly?" he continued; for though her hair was now under a new dispensation, and was brushed smoothly behind her ears, she seemed still in imagination to be tossing it out of her eyes. "It makes you look as if you were crazy."

"O, I can't help it," said Maggie, impatiently. "Don't tease me, Tom. O, what books!" she exclaimed, as she saw the bookcases in the study. "How I should like to have as many books as that!"

"Why, you couldn't read one of 'em," said Tom, triumphantly. "They're all Latin."

"No, they aren't," said Maggie. "I can read the back of this ... History of the Decline and Fall of the Roman Empire."

"Well, what does that mean? *You* don't know," said Tom, wagging his head.

"But I could soon find out," said Maggie, scornfully.

"Why, how?"

"I should look inside, and see what it was about."

"You'd better not, Miss Maggie," said Tom, seeing her hand on the volume. "Mr Stelling lets nobody touch his books without leave, and *I* shall catch it, if you take it out."

"O, very well! Let me see all *your* books, then," said Maggie, turning to throw her arms round Tom's neck, and rub his cheek with her small round nose.

Tom, in the gladness of his heart at having dear old Maggie to dispute with and crow over again, seized her round the waist, and began to jump with her round the large library table. Away they jumped with more and more vigour, till Maggie's hair flew from behind her ears, and twirled about like an animated mop. But the revolutions round the table became more and more irregular in their sweep, till at last reaching Mr Stelling's reading-stand, they sent it thundering down with its heavy lexicons to the floor. Happily it was the ground-floor, and the study was a one-storied wing to the house, so that the downfall made no alarming resonance, though Tom stood dizzy and aghast for a few minutes, dreading the appearance of Mr or Mrs Stelling.

"O, I say, Maggie," said Tom at last, lifting up the stand, "we must keep quiet here, you know. If we break anything, Mrs Stelling 'll make us cry peccavi."

"What's that?" said Maggie.

"O, it's the Latin for a good scolding," said Tom, not without some pride in his knowledge.

"Is she a cross woman?" said Maggie.

"I believe you!" said Tom, with an emphatic nod.

"I think all women are crosser than men," said Maggie. "Aunt Glegg's a great deal crosser than uncle Glegg, and mother scolds me more than father does."

"Well, *you'll* be a woman some day," said Tom, "so *you* needn't talk."

"But I shall be a *clever* woman," said Maggie, with a toss.

"O, I daresay, and a nasty conceited thing. Everybody 'll hate you."

"But you oughtn't to hate me, Tom: it'll be very wicked of you, for I shall be your sister."

"Yes, but if you're a nasty disagreeable thing, I *shall* hate you."

"O but, Tom, you won't! I shan't be disagreeable. I shall be very good to you – and I shall be good to everybody. You won't hate me really, will you, Tom?"

"O, bother! never mind! Come, it's time for me to learn my lessons. See here! what I've got to do," said Tom, drawing Maggie towards him and showing her his theorem, while she pushed her hair behind her ears, and prepared herself to prove her capability of helping him in Euclid. She began to read with full confidence in her own powers, but presently, becoming quite bewildered, her face flushed with irritation. It was unavoidable – she must confess her incompetency, and she was not fond of humiliation.

"It's nonsense!" she said, "and very ugly stuff – nobody need want to make it out."

"Ah, there now, Miss Maggie!" said Tom, drawing the book away, and wagging his head at her, "you see you're not so clever as you thought you were."

"O," said Maggie, pouting, "I daresay I could make it out, if I'd learned what goes before, as you have."

"But that's what you just couldn't, Miss Wisdom," said Tom. "For it's all the harder when you know what goes before: for then you've got to say what definition 3 is and what axiom V. is. But get along with you now: I must go on with this. Here's the Latin Grammar. See what you can make of that."

Maggie found the Latin Grammar quite soothing after her mathematical mortification; for she delighted in new words, and quickly found that there was an English Key at the end, which would make her very wise about Latin, at slight expense. She presently made up her mind to skip the rules in the Syntax – the examples became so absorbing. The mysterious sentences, snatched from an unknown context, – like strange horns of beasts, and leaves of unknown plants, brought from some far-off region – gave boundless scope to her imagination, and were all the more facinating because they were in a peculiar tongue of their own, which she could learn to interpret.[7]

George Eliot was sometimes accused of identifying too strongly with her heroine – F. R. Leavis and others saw this as a major weakness of the novel – but there is little doubt that the identification is a positive means of recalling her childhood and what it was like to be "a little sister". The situation is a classic one – the boy who doesn't understand why he is learning Euclid and wading through the Latin grammar (and not comprehending any of it) set beside the girl who is debarred by her sex from undertaking the intellectual nourishment which would bring her fulfilment. The failure of Tom's education is seen when he is interviewed by his uncle Deane for a junior post in his warehouse: he has no practical knowledge and must start at the bottom. There is an unvoiced commentary on this: not only was his education irrelevant, but the uneducated Bob Jakin, having the natural sharpness of the born survivor, helps Tom by putting trade in his way.

The kind of education that is useless for Tom would not only suit Maggie but would positively equip her for the governessing – or teaching – for which she seems destined before she meets Stephen. What education she gets is almost accidental, her taste coming from nature not nurture. George Eliot is both Maggie and not Maggie: she survives the provincial (and sexual) limitations. Her father provided her with an education, for she had private lessons in languages from Signor Brezzi and from the headmaster of the local grammar school in Coventry.[8] Maggie by contrast has to acquire what she can. Her conversations with Philip Wakem when she visits Tom, and her later discussions with him in the Red Deeps, show how much an inquiring mind can acquire. In this look back George Eliot is in part at least conveying her own constrictions and frustrations; there, but for the grace of a degree of provincial enlightenment, encouragement and the expansive effect of new friendships, went Marian Evans.

In *Felix Holt* education occupies an important rather than a prominent position. As Robert Liddell has rightly stressed, Felix Holt "is not the Warwickshire working-man, so well known to George Eliot, but a carefully excogitated urban working-man, whose voice she could never have heard except in fantasy . . ."[9] But Felix's area is unquestionably that of a Midland town loosely identified with Nuneaton, and his mission as an unenfranchized radical is to try to educate his fellow-workers, certainly in the political sense and in other ways too. Their voices, often ignorant and uninformed, are more real than his, and since he is the son of a quack doctor and an over-talkative mother, his education begins with himself, his experience of a brief debauchery bringing him quickly to moral and social responsibility. Felix is often outspoken and damns the accomplishments of education as exemplified by Esther in no uncertain terms. He knocks a book down, and then attempts to demolish her with words:

"Byron's Poems!" he said, in a tone of disgust, while Esther was recovering all the other articles. " 'The Dream' – he'd better have been asleep and snoring. What! do you stuff your memory with Byron, Miss Lyon?"

Felix, on his side, was led at last to look straight at Esther, but it was with a strong denunciatory and pedagogic intention. Of course he saw more clearly than ever that she was a fine lady.

She reddened, drew up her long neck, and said, as she retreated to her chair again, "I have a great admiration for Byron."

. . . .

"He is a worldly and vain writer, I fear," said Mr Lyon. He knew scarcely anything of the poet, whose books embodied the faith and ritual of many young ladies and gentlemen.

"A misanthropic debauchee," said Felix, lifting a chair with one hand, and holding the book open in the other, "whose notion of a hero was that he should disorder his stomach and despise mankind. His corsairs and renegades, his Alps and Manfreds, are the most paltry puppets that were ever pulled by the strings of lust and pride."[10]

George Eliot makes us feel that Felix is himself being pulled by the strings of priggish prudery and unconscious sexual fear. And I suggest that this is an association in George Eliot's own past: in 1840 and 1841 she was reading *Childe Harold*, and in a letter to Maria Lewis in May 1840 from Griff she observes, "Byron in his Childe Harold (which I have just begun the second time) checks reflections on individual and personal sorrows by reminding himself of the revolutions and woes beneath which the shores of the Mediterranean have groaned. We may with more effectual comparison think of the dangers of the Great Ark of the Church in these latter times of the deluge of sin."[11] It is typical of her early ascetic fervour, and her unconscious transference is back to the spirit of that earlier time. Felix in his reforming-educational Midland ethos is doubtless George Eliot's moral mouthpiece: he is also presented clearly, and with some awareness, as the prig that Marian Evans once was.

If *Felix Holt* begins with the poignant re-education of Mrs Transome, and expands to take in politics, dissent, social awareness – witness Esther and Harold – it ends with Felix marrying Esther after he has come out of prison.

On the momentous day of the riot Felix should have been engaged in teaching, an indication of how highly George Eliot valued the necessary education of the poor who were limited to what they could pick up.

Mrs Garth educates as she goes about her domestic business, for time and the saving of money are pressing. *Middlemarch* is George Eliot's fullest examination of the education of the feelings, seen centrally in Dorothea, passingly in Rosamond, poignantly in Mrs Bulstrode, tragically in Lydgate. Lydgate's education begins with his interest in the valves of the heart, but professional training is no help in his experiences of the heart, first with Laure and then with Rosamond. Dorothea's education at a Swiss finishing school hardly prepares her for Casaubon. Casaubon's education narrowed his interest and left him little energy for life, and little knowledge of it. In the one positive educational episode (see pp. 192–4) the work-ethic is paramount, and there is little doubt that Mrs Garth's practice has her creator's approval. In the *Finale* we are told that "Mary, in her matronly days, became as solid in figure as her mother; but, unlike her, gave the boys little formal teaching, so that Mrs Garth was alarmed lest they should never be well grounded in grammar and geography. Nevertheless they were found quite forward enough when they went to school; perhaps because they liked nothing so well as being with their mother."[12] The loving family is an education in itself, though Mary demonstrates in small measure her own absorption of her mother's theories by writing a book "for her boys, called 'Stories of Great Men', taken from Plutarch".[13] This is set against Rosamond's education for display at Mrs Lemon's; the ability to get in and out of a carriage gracefully is a lightweight acquirement in the moral scale. The span in the Midland novels is a social one, and it includes the educational spectrum, the bread-and-butter alphabet in *Adam Bede*, the remarkable self-education of Maggie Tulliver, Mrs Lemon's superficial refinements, and Dorothea's "toy-box history" as well as the teaching of Mrs Garth. Again we are conscious of the compassion and irony of the appraisal; the early experiences of Marian Evans helped to provide George Eliot with her mature perspective.

# 7. Class and Leisure

Of the pastimes and pleasures recorded in George Eliot's Midland novels, some have a traditional and class-based origin. Arthur's birthday celebrations and the harvest supper in *Adam Bede*, and the Squire's annual New Year's Eve dance in *Silas Marner* are examples. Like Hardy's, her view of relaxed and relaxing characters is not condescending. It is warm, immediate, and ironic appraisal which conveys, as we have seen, the atmosphere of place and the interaction of personality. Her rendering of the scene in the Rainbow Inn on the night when Silas loses his gold is superbly imagined:

The conversation, which was at a high pitch of animation when Silas approached the door of the Rainbow, had, as usual, been slow and intermittent when the company first assembled. The pipes began to be puffed in a silence which had an air of severity; the more important customers, who drank spirits and sat nearest the fire, staring at each other as if a bet were depending on the first man who winked; while the beer-drinkers, chiefly men in fustian jackets and smock-frocks, kept their eyelids down and rubbed their hands across their mouths, as if their draughts of beer were a funereal duty attended with embarrassing sadness. At last, Mr Snell, the landlord, a man of a neutral disposition, accustomed to stand aloof from human differences as those of beings who were all alike in need of liquor, broke silence, by saying in a doubtful tone to his cousin the butcher –
"Some folks 'ud say that was a fine beast you druv in yesterday, Bob?"
The butcher, a jolly, smiling, red-haired man, was not disposed to answer rashly. He gave a few puffs before he spat and replied, "And they wouldn't be fur wrong, John."
After this feeble delusive thaw, the silence set in as severely as before.
"Was it a red Durham?" said the farrier, taking up the thread of discourse after the lapse of a few minutes.
The farrier looked at the landlord, and the landlord looked at the butcher, as the person who must take the responsibility of answering.
"Red it was," said the butcher, in his good-humoured husky treble – "and a Durham it was."
"Then you needn't tell *me* who you bought it of," said the farrier, looking round with some triumph; "I know who it is has got the red Durhams o' this country-side. And she'd a white star on her brow, I'll bet a penny?" The farrier leaned forward with his hands on his knees as he put this question, and his eyes twinkled knowingly.
"Well; yes – she might," said the butcher, slowly, considering that he was giving a decided affirmative. "I don't say contrairy."

"I knew that very well," said the farrier, throwing himself backward again, and speaking defiantly; "if *I* don't know Mr Lammeter's cows, I should like to know who does – that's all. And as for the cow you've bought, bargain or no bargain, I've been at the drenching of her – contradick me who will."

The farrier looked fierce, and the mild butcher's conversational spirit was roused a little.

"I'm not for contradicking no man," he said; "I'm for peace and quietness. Some are for cutting long ribs – I'm for cutting 'em short myself; but *I* don't quarrel with 'em. All I say is, it's a lovely carkiss – and anybody as was reasonable, it 'ud bring tears into their eyes to look at it."

"Well, it's the cow as I drenched, whatever it is," pursued the farrier, angrily; "and it was Mr Lammeter's cow, else you told a lie when you said it was a red Durham."

"I tell no lies," said the butcher, with the same mild huskiness as before, "and I contradick none – not if a man was to swear himself black: he's no meat o' mine, nor none o' my bargains. All I say is it's a lovely carkiss. And what I say I'll stick to; but I'll quarrel wi' no man."

"No," said the farrier, with bitter sarcasm, looking at the company generally; "and p'rhaps you arn't pig-headed; and p'rhaps you didn't say the cow was a red Durham; and p'rhaps you didn't say she'd got a star on her brow – stick to that, now you're at it."

"Come, come," said the landlord; "let the cow alone. The truth lies atween you: you're both right and both wrong, as I allays say. And as for the cow's being Mr Lammeter's, I say nothing to that; but this I say, as the Rainbow's the Rainbow. And for the matter o' that, if the talk is to be o' the Lammeters, *you* know the most upo' that head, eh, Mr Macey? You remember when first Mr Lammeter's father come into these parts, and took the Warrens?"

Mr Macey, tailor and parish-clerk, the latter of which functions rheumatism had of late obliged him to share with a small-featured young man who sat opposite him, held his white head on one side, and twirled his thumbs with an air of complacency, slightly seasoned with criticism. He smiled pityingly, in answer to the landlord's appeal, and said –

"Ay, ay; I know, I know; but I let other folks talk. I've laid by now, and gev up to the young uns. Ask them as have been to school at Tarley: they've learnt pernouncing; that's come up since my day."

"If you're pointing at me, Mr Macey," said the deputy-clerk, with an air of anxious propriety, "I'm nowise a man to speak out of my place. As the psalm says –

'I know what's right, nor only so,
But also practise what I know.'"

"Well, then, I wish you'd keep hold o' the tune, when it's set for you; if you're for prac*tis*ing, I wish you'd prac*tise* that," said a large jocose-looking man, an excellent wheelwright in his week-day capacity, but on Sundays leader of the choir. He winked, as he spoke, at two of the company, who were known officially as the "bassoon" and the "key-bugle," in the confidence that he was expressing the sense of the musical profession in Raveloe.

156

Mr Tookey, the deputy-clerk, who shared the unpopularity common to deputies, turned very red, but replied, with careful moderation – "Mr Winthrop, if you'll bring me any proof as I'm in the wrong, I'm not the man to say I won't alter. But there's people set up their own ears for a standard, and expect the whole choir to follow 'em. There may be two opinions, I hope."

"Ay, ay," said Mr Macey, who felt very well satisfied with this attack on youthful presumption; "you're right there, Tookey: there's allays two 'pinions; there's the 'pinion a man has of himsen, and there's the 'pinion other folks have on him. There'd be two 'pinions about a cracked bell, if the bell could hear itself."

"Well, Mr Macey," said poor Tookey, serious amidst the general laughter, "I undertook to partially fill up the office of parish-clerk by Mr Crackenthorp's desire, whenever your infirmities should make you unfitting; and it's one of the rights thereof to sing in the choir – else why have you done the same yourself?"

"Ah! but the old gentleman and you are two folks," said Ben Winthrop. "The old gentleman's got a gift. Why, the Squire used to invite him to take a glass, only to hear him sing the 'Red Rovier'; didn't he, Mr Macey? It's a nat'ral gift. There's my little lad Aaron, he's got a gift – he can sing a tune off straight, like a throstle. But as for you, Master Tookey, you'd better stick to your 'Amens': your voice is well enough when you keep it up in your nose. It's your inside as isn't right made for music: it's no better nor a hollow stalk."

This kind of unflinching frankness was the most piquant form of joke to the company at the Rainbow, and Ben Winthrop's insult was felt by everybody to have capped Mr Macey's epigram.

"I see what it is plain enough," said Mr Tookey, unable to keep cool any longer. "There's a conspceracy to turn me out o' the choir, as I shouldn't share the Christmas money – that's where it is. But I shall speak to Mr Crackenthorp; I'll not be put upon by no man."

"Nay, nay, Tookey," said Ben Winthrop. "We'll pay you your share to keep out of it – that's what we'll do. There's things folks 'ud pay to be rid on, besides varmin."

"Come, come," said the landlord, who felt that paying people for their absence was a principle dangerous to society; "a joke's a joke. We're all good friends here, I hope. We must give and take. You're both right and you're both wrong, as I say. I agree wi' Mr Macey here, as there's two opinions; and if mine was asked, I should say they're both right. Tookey's right and Winthrop's right, and they've only got to split the difference and make themselves even."

The farrier was puffing his pipe rather fiercely, in some contempt at this trivial discussion. He had no ear for music himself, and never went to church, as being of the medical profession, and likely to be in requisition for delicate cows. But the butcher, having music in his soul, had listened with a divided desire for Tookey's defeat and for the preservation of the peace.

"To be sure," he said, following up the landlord's conciliatory view, "we're fond of our old clerk; it's nat'ral, and him used to be such a singer, and got a brother as is known for the first fiddler in this country-side. Eh, it's a pity but what Solomon lived in our village, and could give us a tune when we liked; eh, Mr Macey? I'd keep him in liver and lights for nothing – that I would."[1]

157

The agricultural and parish events and associations are strong: set well before her own time, the novel conveys the particularity of time past, the small community mirroring wider communities of hierarchy and corresponding power. The humour needs no comment: the dialogue is fresh with the leavening of dialect, the commentary rich in the contemplation and enjoyment of language, character, situation and interaction.

The Squire's New Year's Eve party, crucial to the plot because it coincides with Silas's discovery of Eppie – his gold come back to him – is invigorated with music and dancing. Again, there is the particularity of imaginative recreation – the scene is illuminated by movement and strong in tradition and ritual:

"Why, there's Solomon in the hall," said the Squire, "and playing my fav'rite tune, *I* believe – 'The flaxen-headed ploughboy' – he's for giving us a hint as we aren't enough in a hurry to hear him play. Bob," he called out to his third long-legged son, who was at the other end of the room, "open the door, and tell Solomon to come in. He shall give us a tune here."

Bob obeyed, and Solomon walked in, fiddling as he walked, for he would on no account break off in the middle of a tune.

"Here, Solomon," said the Squire, with loud patronage. "Round here, my man. Ah, I knew it was 'The flaxen-headed ploughboy:' there's no finer tune."

Solomon Macey, a small hale old man, with an abundant crop of long white hair reaching nearly to his shoulders, advanced to the indicated spot, bowing reverently while he fiddled, as much as to say that he respected the company though he respected the key-note more. As soon as he had repeated the tune and lowered his fiddle, he bowed again to the Squire and the Rector, and said, "I hope I see your honour and your reverence well, and wishing you health and long life and a happy New Year. And wishing the same to you, Mr Lammeter, sir; and to the other gentlemen, and the madams, and the young lasses."

As Solomon uttered the last words, he bowed in all directions solicitously, lest he should be wanting in due respect. But thereupon he immediately began to prelude, and fell into the tune which he knew would be taken as a special compliment by Mr Lammeter.

"Thank ye, Solomon, thank ye," said Mr Lammeter when the fiddle paused again. "That's 'Over the hills and far away,' that is. My father used to say to me, whenever we heard that tune, 'Ah, lad, *I* come from over the hills and far away.' There's a many tunes I don't make head or tail of; but that speaks to me like the blackbird's whistle. I suppose it's the name: there's a deal in the name of a tune."

But Solomon was already impatient to prelude again, and presently broke with much spirit into "Sir Roger de Coverley," at which there was a sound of chairs pushed back, and laughing voices.

"Ay, ay, Solomon, we know what that means," said the Squire, rising. "It's time to begin the dance, eh? Lead the way, then, and we'll all follow you."

So Solomon, holding his white head on one side, and playing vigorously, marched forward at the head of the gay procession into the White Parlour, where the mistletoe-bough was hung, and multitudinous tallow candles made rather a brilliant effect, gleaming from among the berried holly-boughs, and reflected in the old-fashioned oval mirrors fastened in the panels of the white wainscot. A quaint procession! Old Solomon, in his seedy clothes and long white locks, seemed to be luring that decent company by the magic scream of his fiddle – luring discreet matrons in turban-shaped caps, nay, Mrs Crackenthorp herself, the summit of whose perpendicular feather was on a level with the Squire's shoulder – luring fair lasses complacently conscious of very short waists and skirts blameless of front-folds – luring burly fathers in large variegated waistcoats, and ruddy sons, for the most part shy and sheepish, in short nether garments and very long coat-tails.

Already Mr Macey and a few other privileged villagers, who were allowed to be spectators on these great occasions, were seated on benches placed for them near the door; and great was the admiration and satisfaction in that quarter when the couples had formed themselves for the dance, and the Squire led off with Mrs Crackenthorp, joining hands with the Rector and Mrs Osgood. That was as it should be – that was what everybody had been used to – and the charter of Raveloe seemed to be renewed by the ceremony. It was not thought of as an unbecoming levity for the old and middle-aged people to dance a little before sitting down to cards, but rather as part of their social duties. For what were these if not to be merry at appropriate times, interchanging visits and poultry with due frequency, paying each other old-established compliments in sound traditional phrases, passing well-tried personal jokes, urging your guests to eat and drink too much out of hospitality, and eating and drinking too much in your neighbour's house to show that you liked your cheer? And the parson naturally set an example in these social duties. For it would not have been possible for the Raveloe mind, without a a peculiar revelation, to know that a clergyman should be a pale-faced memento of solemnities, instead of a reasonably faulty man whose exclusive authority to read prayers and preach, to christen, marry, and bury you, necessarily coexisted with the right to sell you the ground to be buried in and to take tithe in kind; on which last point, of course, there was a little grumbling, but not to the extent of irreligion – not of deeper significance than the grumbling at the rain, which was by no means accompanied with a spirit of impious defiance, but with a desire that the prayer for fine weather might be read forthwith.

There was no reason, then, why the rector's dancing should not be received as part of the fitness of things quite as much as the Squire's, or why, on the other hand, Mr Macey's official respect should restrain him from subjecting the parson's performance to that criticism with which minds of extraordinary acuteness must necessarily contemplate the doings of their fallible fellow-men.

"The Squire's pretty springe, considering his weight," said Mr Macey, "and he stamps uncommon well. But Mr Lammeter beats 'em all for shapes: you see he holds his head like a sodger, and he isn't so cushiony as most o' the oldish gentlefolks – they run fat in general; and he's got a fine leg. The parson's nimble enough, but he hasn't got much of a leg: it's a bit too thick down'ard, and his knees might be a bit nearer wi'out damage; but he might do worse, he might do worse. Though he hasn't that grand way o' waving his hand as the Squire has."

"Talk o' nimbleness, look at Mrs Osgood," said Ben Winthrop, who was holding his son Aaron between his knees. "She trips along with her little steps, so as nobody can see how she goes – it's like as if she had little wheels to her feet. She doesn't look a day older nor last year: she's the finest-made woman as is, let the next be where she will."

"I don't heed how the women are made," said Mr Macey, with some contempt. "They wear nayther coat nor breeches: you can't make much out o' their shapes."[2]

Song, for George Eliot, is an expression of tradition, and Solomon's elaborate ritual is close to her heart. There is a sense of class integration for the occasion, of the relationship between tenants and squire, of the organised leisure which is part of the annual experience of a small community. And, as in the previous extract, there is a lambent humour, an ironic contemplation, playing over the whole.

With *Adam Bede* we move nearer to her own youth. With her father's work as a manager of estates, she was socially aware of an occasion like the birthday celebrations, and in *Adam Bede* Arthur's birthday feast provides another ironic focal point of the action. First there is the scene of preparations:

The covered cart, without springs, was standing ready to carry the whole family except the men-servants: Mr Poyser and the grandfather sat on the seat in front, and within there was room for all the women and children; the fuller the cart the better, because then the jolting would not hurt so much, and Nancy's broad person and thick arms were an excellent cushion to be pitched on. But Mr Poyser drove at no more than a walking pace, that there might be as little risk of jolting as possible on this warm day; and there was time to exchange greetings and remarks with the foot-passengers who were going the same way, specking the paths between the green meadows and the golden cornfields with bits of movable bright colour – a scarlet waistcoat to match the poppies that nodded a little too thickly among the corn, or a dark-blue neckerchief with ends flaunting across a bran-new white smock-frock. All Broxton and all Hayslope were to be at the Chase, and make merry there in honour of "th' heir;" and the old men and women, who had never been so far down this side of the hill for the last twenty years, were being brought from Broxton and Hayslope in one of the farmer's waggons, at Mr Irwine's suggestion. The church-bells had struck up again now – a last tune, before the ringers came down the hill to have their share in the festival; and before the bells had finished, other music was heard approaching, so that even Old Brown, the sober horse that was drawing Mr Poyser's cart, began to prick up his ears. It was the band of the Benefit Club, which had mustered in all its glory; that is to say, in bright-blue scarfs and blue favours, and carrying its banner with the motto, "Let brotherly love continue," encircling a picture of a stone-pit.

The carts, of course, were not to enter the Chase. Every one must get down at the lodges, and the vehicles must be sent back.

"Why, the Chase is like a fair a'ready," said Mrs Poyser, as she got down from the cart, and saw the groups scattered under the great oaks, and the boys running about in the hot sunshine to survey the tall poles surmounted by the fluttering garments that were to be the prize of the successful climbers. "I should ha' thought there wasna so many people i' the two parishes. Mercy on us! how hot it is out o' the shade! Come here, Totty, else your little face 'ull be burnt to a scratchin'! They might ha' cooked the dinners i' that open space an' saved the fires. I shall go to Mrs Best's room an' sit down."

"Stop a bit, stop a bit," said Mr Poyser. "There's th' waggin coming wi'th' old folks in't; it'll be such a sight as wonna come o'er again, to see 'em get down an' walk along all together. You remember some on 'em i' their prime, eh, father?"

"Ay, ay," said old Martin, walking slowly under the shade of the lodge porch, from which he could see the aged party descend. "I remember Jacob Taft walking fifty mile after the Scotch raybels, when they turned back from Stoniton."

He felt himself quite a youngster, with a long life before him, as he saw the Hayslope patriarch, old Feyther Taft, descend from the waggon and walk towards him, in his brown nightcap, and leaning on his two sticks.

"Well, Mester Taft," shouted old Martin, at the utmost stretch of his voice, – for though he knew the old man was stone deaf, he could not omit the propriety of a greeting, – "you're hearty yet. You can enjoy yoursen to-day, for-all you're ninety an' better."

"Your sarvant, mesters, your sarvant," said Feyther Taft in a treble tone, perceiving that he was in company.

The aged group, under care of sons or daughters, themselves worn and grey, passed on along the least-winding carriage-road towards the house, where a special table was prepared for them; while the Poyser party wisely struck across the grass under the shade of the great trees, but not out of view of the house-front, with its sloping lawn and flower-beds, or of the pretty striped marquee at the edge of the lawn, standing at right angles with two larger marquees on each side of the open green space where the games were to be played. The house would have been nothing but a plain square mansion of Queen Anne's time, but for the remnant of an old abbey to which it was united at one end, in much the same way as one may sometimes see a new farmhouse rising high and prim at the end of older and lower farm-offices. The fine old remnant stood a little backward and under the shadow of tall beeches, but the sun was now on the taller and more advanced front, the blinds were all down, and the house seemed asleep in the hot mid-day: it made Hetty quite sad to look at it: Arthur must be somewhere in the back rooms, with the grand company, where he could not possibly know that she was come, and she should not see him for a long, long while – not till after dinner, when they said he was to come up and make a speech.

But Hetty was wrong in part of her conjecture. No grand company was come except the Irwines, for whom the carriage had been sent early, and Arthur was at that moment not in a back room, but walking with the Rector into the broad stone cloisters of the old abbey, where the long tables were laid for all the cottage tenants and the farm-servants. A very handsome young Briton he looked to-day, in high spirits and a bright-blue frock-coat, the highest mode.[3]

Now the purpose of this in part is to convey the stability of place and the rituals which attend it. The generations are linked, from Totty to old Martin Poyser and Feyther Taft, and the ironic counterplay takes in nature, with its seasonal cycles, the historic house, with its "remnant of an old abbey", and the immediate present celebration of Arthur Donnithorne's coming to maturity. There is heightened feeling about the significance of the day: all is geared to celebration, but the narrative irony creates apprehensions and reinterpretation. Hetty will not be singled out publicly by the young squire: but all the people we have encountered will remember this day and the resultant change. The birthday feast marks the beginning of the end of a family, and it signals change and suffering. This is a coming of age and an initiation of social responsibility with a difference.

But there is also ignorance, innocence, enjoyment and relaxation. As we would expect when the squirearchy play hosts to their tenants, there are games, and prizes to be won: rustic clumsiness and upper-class condescension are displayed:

"Here's a delicate bit of womanhood, or girlhood, coming to receive a prize, I suppose," said Mr Gawaine. "She must be one of the racers in the sacks, who had set off before we came."

The "bit of womanhood" was our old acquaintance Bessy Cranage, otherwise Chad's Bess, whose large red cheeks and blowsy person had undergone an exaggeration of colour, which, if she had happened to be a heavenly body, would have made her sublime. Bessy, I am sorry to say, had taken to her earrings again since Dinah's departure, and was otherwise decked out in such small finery as she could muster. Anyone who could have looked into poor Bessy's heart would have seen a striking resemblance between her little hopes and anxieties and Hetty's. The advantage, perhaps, would have been on Bessy's side in the matter of feeling. But then, you see, they were so very different outside! You would have been inclined to box Bessy's ears, and you would have longed to kiss Hetty.

Bessy had been tempted to run the arduous race, partly from mere hoidenish gaiety, partly because of the prize. Some one had said there were to be cloaks and other nice clothes for prizes, and she approached the marquee, fanning herself with her handkerchief, but with exultation sparkling in her round eyes.

"Here is the prize for the first sack-race," said Miss Lydia, taking a large parcel from the table where the prizes were laid, and giving it to Mrs Irwine before Bessy came up; "an excellent grogram gown and a piece of flannel."

"You didn't think the winner was to be so young, I suppose, aunt?" said Arthur. "Couldn't you find something else for this girl, and save that grim-looking gown for one of the older women?"

"I have bought nothing but what is useful and substantial," said Miss Lydia, adjusting her own lace; "I should not think of encouraging a love of finery in young women of that class. I have a scarlet cloak, but that is for the old woman who wins."

This speech of Miss Lydia's produced rather a mocking expression in Mrs Irwine's face as she looked at Arthur, while Bessy came up and dropped a series of curtsies.

"This is Bessy Cranage, mother," said Mr Irwine, kindly, "Chad Cranage's daughter. You remember Chad Cranage, the blacksmith?"

"Yes, to be sure," said Mrs Irwine. "Well, Bessy, here is your prize – excellent warm things for winter. I'm sure you have had hard work to win them this warm day."

Bessy's lip fell as she saw the ugly, heavy gown, – which felt so hot and disagreeable, too, on this July day, and was such a great ugly thing to carry. She dropped her curtsies again, without looking up, and with a growing tremulousness about the corners of her mouth, and then turned away.

"Poor girl," said Arthur; "I think she's disappointed. I wish it had been something more to her taste."

"She's a bold-looking young person," observed Miss Lydia. "Not at all one I should like to encourage."

Arthur silently resolved that he would make Bessy a present of money before the day was over, that she might buy something more to her mind; but she, not aware of the consolation in store for her, turned out of the open space, where she was visible from the marquee, and throwing down the odious bundle under a tree, began to cry – very much tittered at the while by the small boys. In this situation she was descried by her discreet matronly cousin, who lost no time in coming up, having just given the baby into her husband's charge.

"What's the matter wi' ye?" said Bess the matron, taking up the bundle and examining it. "Ye'n sweltered yoursen, I reckon, running that fool's race. An' here, they'n gi'en you lots o' good grogram and flannel, as should ha' been gi'en by good rights to them as had the sense to keep away from such foolery. Ye might spare me a bit o' this grogram to make clothes for the lad – ye war ne'er ill-natured, Bess; I ne'er said that on ye."

"Ye may take it all, for what I care," said Bess the maiden, with a pettish movement, beginning to wipe away her tears and recover herself.

"Well, I could do wi't, if so be ye want to get rid on't," said the disinterested cousin, walking quickly away with the bundle, lest Chad's Bess should change her mind.

But that bonny-cheeked lass was blessed with an elasticity of spirits that secured her from any rankling grief; and by the time the grand climax of the donkey-race came on, her disappointment was entirely lost in the delightful excitement of attempting to stimulate the last donkey by hisses, while the boys applied the argument of sticks.[4]

As always with George Eliot, the sense of psychology and class is evident. Situated as she was, she had grown up with the mixed social inheritance which provided her with experience of the various classes and their interactions. Of particular interest here are the attitudes of Miss Lydia, Mrs Irwine, and the (relative) kindliness of her son. At this social level Arthur's promise to himself typifies his character, that of the well-intentioned young man who always succumbs to his own needs. The exchange between the two Besses is sensitively perceived – the cadging of the matron accompanied by the resentment and quick resilience of the girl.

Before leaving this particular area I'd like to look briefly at another tenant gathering, the Poysers' harvest supper near the end of *Adam Bede*. The social surface is relaxed and easy, but here we are aware of another tension: by now Adam has discovered his real feelings for Dinah and she is on the edge of admitting her feelings for him, feelings which involve putting aside her vocation. At this stage Adam does not know how she feels but the Poysers' supper is a measure of their recovery after Hetty's trial, and it is inlaid with optimism on Adam's account:

He expected to see Dinah again this evening, and get leave to accompany her as far as Oakbourne; and then he would ask her to fix some time when he might go to Snowfield, and learn whether the last best hope that had been born to him must be resigned like the rest. The work he had to do at home, besides putting on his best clothes, made it seven before he was on his way again to the Hall Farm, and it was questionable whether, with his longest and quickest strides, he should be there in time even for the roast-beef, which came after the plum-pudding; for Mrs Poyser's supper would be punctual.

Great was the clatter of knives and pewter plates and tin cans when Adam entered the house, but there was no hum of voices to this accompaniment: the eating of excellent roast-beef, provided free of expense, was too serious a business to those good farm-labourers to be performed with a divided attention, even if they had had anything to say to each other, – which they had not; and Mr Poyser, at the head of the table, was too busy with his carving to listen to Bartle Massey's or Mr Craig's ready talk.

"Here, Adam," said Mrs Poyser, who was standing and looking on to see that Molly and Nancy did their duty as waiters, "here's a place kept for you between Mr Massey and the boys. It's a poor tale you couldn't come to see the pudding when it was whole."

Adam looked anxiously round for a fourth woman's figure; but Dinah was not there. He was almost afraid of asking about her; besides, his attention was claimed by greetings, and there remained the hope that Dinah was in the house, though perhaps disinclined to festivities on the eve of her departure.

It was a goodly sight – that table, with Martin Poyser's round good-humoured face and large person at the head of it, helping his servants to the fragrant roast-beef, and pleased when the empty plates came again. Martin, though usually blest with a good appetite, really forgot to finish his own beef to-night – it was so pleasant to him to look on in the intervals of carving, and see how the others enjoyed their supper; for were they not men who, on all the days of the year except Christmas Day and Sundays, ate their cold dinner, in a make-shift manner, under the hedgerows, and drank their beer out of wooden bottles – with relish certainly, but with their mouths towards the zenith, after a fashion more endurable to ducks than to human bipeds. Martin Poyser had some faint conception of the flavour such men must find in hot roast-beef and fresh-drawn ale. He held his head on one side, and screwed up his mouth, as he nudged Bartle Massey, and watched half-witted Tom Tholer, otherwise known as "Tom Saft," receiving his second plateful of beef. A grin of delight broke over Tom's face as the plate was set down before him, between his knife and fork, which he held erect, as if they had been sacred tapers; but the delight was too strong to continue smouldering in a grin – it burst out the next instant in a long-drawn "haw, haw!" followed by a sudden collapse into utter gravity, as the knife and fork darted down on the prey. Martin Poyser's large person shook with his silent unctuous laugh: he turned towards Mrs Poyser to see if she, too, had been observant of Tom, and the eyes of husband and wife met in a glance of good-natured amusement.

"Tom Saft" was a great favourite on the farm, where he played the part of the old jester, and made up for his practical deficiencies by his success in repartee. His hits, I imagine, were those of the flail, which falls quite at random, but nevertheless smashes an insect now and then. They were much quoted at sheep-shearing and haymaking times; but I refrain from recording them here, lest Tom's wit should prove to be like that of many other bygone jesters eminent in their day – rather of a temporary nature, not dealing with the deeper and more lasting relations of things.[5]

Traditional leisure extends to servants as well as their masters. In *Felix Holt* the valued time off on the Sunday is used for flirtation, the carrying of messages, opium to relieve "nervous pains", and a practical joke which furthers the plot:

The servants often walked in the park on a Sunday, and he wished to avoid any meeting. He would make a circuit, get into the house privately, and after delivering his packet to Mr Debarry, shut himself up till the ringing of the half-hour bell. But when he reached an elbowed seat under some sycamores, he felt so ill at ease that he yielded to the temptation of throwing himself on it to rest a little. He looked at his watch: it was but five; he had done his errand quickly hitherto, and Mr Debarry had not urged haste. But in less than ten minutes he was in a sound sleep. Certain conditions of his system had determined a stronger effect than usual from the opium.

As he had expected, there were servants strolling in the park, but they did not all choose the most frequented part. Mr Scales, in pursuit of a slight flirtation with the younger lady's-maid, had preferred a more sequestered walk in the company of that agreeable nymph. And it happened to be this pair, of all others, who alighted on the sleeping Christian – a sight which at the very first moment caused Mr Scales a vague pleasure as at an incident that must lead to something clever on his part. To play a trick, and make some one or other look foolish, was held the most pointed form of wit throughout the back regions of the Manor, and served as a constant substitute for theatrical entertainment: what the farce wanted in costume or "make up" it gained in the reality of the mortification which excited the general laughter. And lo! here was the offensive, the exasperatingly cool and superior, Christian caught comparatively helpless, with his head hanging on his shoulder, and one coat-tail hanging out heavily below the elbow of the rustic seat. It was this coat-tail which served as a suggestion to Mr Scales's genius. Putting his finger up in warning to Mrs Cherry, and saying, "Hush – be quiet – I see a fine bit of fun" – he took a knife from his pocket, stepped behind the unconscious Christian, and quickly cut off the pendent coat-tail. Scales knew nothing of the errand to the Rectory; and as he noticed that there was something in the pocket, thought it was probably a large cigar-case. So much the better – he had no time to pause. He threw the coat-tail as far as he could, and noticed that it fell among the elms under which they had been walking. Then, beckoning to Mrs Cherry, he hurried away with her towards the more open part of the park, not daring to explode in laughter until it was safe from the chance of waking the sleeper. And then the vision of the graceful well-appointed Mr Christian, who sneered at Scales about his "get up," having to walk back to the house with only one tail to his coat, was a source of so much enjoyment to the butler, that the fair Cherry began to be quite jealous of the joke. Still she admitted that it really was funny, tittered intermittently, and pledged herself to secrecy. Mr Scales explained to her that Christian would try to creep in unobserved, but that this must be made impossible; and he requested her to imagine the figure this interloping fellow would cut when everybody was asking what had happened. "Hallo, Christian! where's your coat-tail?" would become a proverb at the Manor, where jokes kept remarkably well without the aid of salt; and Mr Christian's comb would be cut so effectually that it would take a long time to grow again. Exit Scales, laughing, and presenting a fine example of dramatic irony to any one in the secret of Fate.

When Christian awoke, he was shocked to find himself in the twilight. He started up, shook himself, missed something, and soon became aware what it was he missed. He did not doubt that he had been robbed, and he at once foresaw that the consequences would be highly unpleasant. In no way could the cause of the accident be so represented to Mr Philip Debarry as to prevent him from viewing his hitherto unimpeachable factotum in a new and unfavourable light.[6]

Social groupings at leisure, culled from memory and extended by imagination and judgment, are always present in George Eliot's narrative. In *Middlemarch* Mr Brooke's evening party marks the beginning of fusion between the Dorothea and Lydgate stories. The niceness of social gradation perhaps owes something to Jane Austen:

It was time to dress. There was to be a dinner-party that day, the last of the parties which were held at the Grange as proper preliminaries to the wedding, and Dorothea was glad of a reason for moving away at once on the sound of the bell, as if she needed more than her usual amount of preparation. She was ashamed of being irritated from some cause she could not define even to herself; for though she had no intention to be untruthful, her reply had not touched the real hurt within her. Mr Casaubon's words had been quite reasonable, yet they had brought a vague instantaneous sense of aloofness on his part.

"Surely I am in a strangely selfish weak state of mind," she said to herself. "How can I have a husband who is so much above me without knowing that he needs me less than I need him?"

Having convinced herself that Mr Casaubon was altogether right, she recovered her equanimity, and was an agreeable image of serene dignity when she came into the drawing-room in her silver-grey dress – the simple lines of her dark-brown hair parted over her brow and coiled massively behind, in keeping with the entire absence from her manner and expression of all search after mere effect. Sometimes when Dorothea was in company, there seemed to be as complete an air of repose about her as if she had been a picture of Santa Barbara looking out from her tower into the clear air; but these intervals of quietude made the energy of her speech and emotion the more remarked when some outward appeal had touched her.

She was naturally the subject of many observations this evening, for the dinner-party was large and rather more miscellaneous as to the male portion than any which had been held at the Grange since Mr Brooke's nieces had resided with him, so that the talking was done in duos and trios more or less inharmonious. There was the newly-elected mayor of Middlemarch, who happened to be a manufacturer; the philanthropic banker his brother-in-law, who predominated so much in the town that some called him a Methodist, others a hypocrite, according to the resources of their vocabulary; and there were various professional men. In fact, Mrs Cadwallader said that Brooke was beginning to treat the Middlemarchers, and that she preferred the farmers at the tithe-dinner, who drank her health unpretentiously, and were not ashamed of their grandfathers' furniture. For in that part of the country, before Reform had done its notable part in developing the political consciousness, there was a clearer distinction of ranks and a dimmer distinction of parties; so that Mr Brooke's miscellaneous invitations seemed to belong to the general laxity which came from his inordinate travel and habit of taking too much in the form of ideas.

Already, as Miss Brooke passed out of the dining-room, opportunity was found for some interjectional "asides."

"A fine woman, Miss Brooke! an uncommonly fine woman, by God!" said Mr Standish, the old lawyer, who had been so long concerned with the landed gentry that he had become landed himself, and used that oath in a deep-mouthed manner as a sort of armorial bearings, stamping the speech of a man who held a good position.

Mr Bulstrode, the banker, seemed to be addressed, but that gentleman disliked coarseness and profanity, and merely bowed. The remark was taken up by Mr Chichely, a middle-aged bachelor and coursing celebrity, who had a complexion something like an Easter egg, a few hairs carefully arranged, and a carriage implying the consciousness of a distinguished appearance.

"Yes, but not my style of woman: I like a woman who lays herself out a little more to please us. There should be a little filigree about a woman – something of the coquette. A man likes a sort of challenge. The more of a dead set she makes at you the better."

"There's some truth in that," said Mr Standish, disposed to be genial. "And, by God, it's usually the way with them. I suppose it answers some wise ends: Providence made them so, eh, Bulstrode?"

"I should be disposed to refer coquetry to another source," said Mr Bulstrode. "I should rather refer it to the devil."

"Ay, to be sure, there should be a little devil in a woman," said Mr Chichely, whose study of the fair sex seemed to have been detrimental to his theology. "And I like them blond, with a certain gait, and a swan neck. Between ourselves, the mayor's daughter is more to my taste than Miss Brooke or Miss Celia either. If I were a marrying man I should choose Miss Vincy before either of them."

"Well, make up, make up," said Mr Standish, jocosely; "you see the middle-aged fellows carry the day."

Mr Chichely shook his head with much meaning: he was not going to incur the certainty of being accepted by the woman he would choose.

The Miss Vincy who had the honour of being Mr Chichely's ideal was of course not present; for Mr Brooke, always objecting to go too far, would not have chosen that his nieces should meet the daughter of a Middlemarch manufacturer, unless it were on a public occasion.[7]

Notice how the movement from Dorothea's consciousness to the social group is managed. Casaubon, her prematurely old fiancé, has unthinkingly suggested that her sister Celia might accompany them on their wedding journey. But the "proper preliminaries" have to be observed, and George Eliot captures through this mixed class dialogue much of the movement and concerns of the provincial society she knew so well.

The leisures of childhood are recalled in *The Mill on the Floss*. Tom's recreation is a boy's sport, rat-catchng, ferreting, birds' nesting and so on: the convenient medium with the message, preferable to the company of an irresponsible sister, is of course Bob Jakin:

It must be owned that Tom was fond of Bob's company. How could it be otherwise? Bob knew, directly he saw a bird's egg, whether it was a swallow's, or a tomtit's, or a yellow-hammer's; he found out all the wasps' nests, and could set all sorts of traps; he could climb the trees like a squirrel, and had quite a magical power of detecting hedgehogs and stoats; and he had courage to do things that were rather naughty, such as making gaps in the hedgerows, throwing stones after the sheep, and killing a cat that was wandering *incognito*. Such qualities in an inferior, who could always be treated with authority in spite of his superior knowingness, had necessarily a fatal fascination for Tom; and every holiday-time Maggie was sure to have days of grief because he had gone off with Bob.

Well! there was no hope for it: he was gone now, and Maggie could think of no comfort but to sit down by the holly, or wander by the hedgerow, and fancy it was all different, refashioning her little world into just what she should like it to be. Maggie's was a troublous life, and this was the form in which she took her opium.

Meanwhile Tom, forgetting all about Maggie and the sting of reproach which he had left in her heart, was hurrying along with Bob, whom he had met accidentally, to the scene of a great rat-catching in a neighbouring barn. Bob knew all about this particular affair, and spoke of the sport with an enthusiasm which no one who is not either divested of all manly feeling, or pitiably ignorant of rat-catching, can fail to imagine. For a person suspected of preternatural wickedness, Bob was really not so very villainous-looking; there was even something agreeable in his snub-nosed face, with its close-curled border of red hair. But then his trousers were always rolled up at the knee, for the convenience of wading on the slightest notice; and his virtue, supposing it to exist, was undeniably "virtue in rags," which, on the authority even of bilious philosophers, who think all well-dressed merit overpaid, is notoriously likely to remain unrecognized (perhaps because it is seen so seldom).

"I know the chap as owns the ferrets," said Bob, in a hoarse treble voice, as he shuffled along, keeping his blue eyes fixed on the river, like an amphibious animal who foresaw occasion for darting in. "He lives up the Kennel Yard at Sut Ogg's – he does. He's the biggest rot-catcher anywhere – he is. I'd sooner be a rot-catcher nor anything – I would. The moles is nothing to the rots. But Lors! you mun ha' ferrets. Dogs is no good. Why, there's that dog, now!" Bob continued, pointing with an air of disgust towards Yap, "he's no more good wi' a rot nor nothin'. I see it myself – I did – at the rot-catchin' i' your feyther's barn."

Yap, feeling the withering influence of this scorn, tucked his tail in and shrank close to Tom's leg, who felt a little hurt for him, but had not the superhuman courage to seem behindhand with Bob in contempt for a dog who made so poor a figure.

"No, no," he said, "Yap's no good at sport. I'll have regular good dogs for rats and everything, when I've done school."

"Hev ferrets, Measter Tom," said Bob, eagerly, – "them white ferrets wi' pink eyes; Lors, you might catch your own rots, an' you might put a rot in a cage wi' a ferret, an' see 'em fight – you might. That's what I'd do, I know, an' it 'ud be better fun a'most nor seein' two chaps fight – if it wasn't them chaps as sold cakes an' oranges at the Fair, as the things flew out o' their baskets, an' some o' the cakes was smashed ... But they tasted just as good," added Bob, by way of note or addendum, after a moment's pause.

"But, I say, Bob," said Tom, in a tone of deliberation, "ferrets are nasty biting things – they'll bite a fellow without being set on."

"Lors! why, that's the beauty on 'em. If a chap lays hold o' your ferret, he won't be long before he hollows out a good un – *he* won't."

At this moment a striking incident made the boys pause suddenly in their walk. It was the plunging of some small body in the water from among the neighbouring bulrushes: if it was not a water-rat, Bob intimated that he was ready to undergo the most unpleasant consequences.

"Hoigh! Yap – hoigh! there he is," said Tom, clapping his hands, as the little black snout made its arrowy course to the opposite bank. "Seize him, lad, seize him!"[8]

This is a good way from a girl's world, but only a few steps away from some men's idea of leisure – the buying and selling of horses.

In *Middlemarch* Fred Vincy's dealings with disreputable horse-traders lead to his being unable to discharge his debt to Caleb Garth, and make an important pivot in the plot. In *Silas Marner* the pivot is an even stronger one, for Dunsey's loss of his brother's horse Wildfire leads to the temptation of Silas's gold:

Godfrey would be ready enough to accept the suggestion: he would snatch eagerly at a plan that might save him from parting with Wildfire. But when Dunstan's meditation reached this point, the inclination to go on grew strong and prevailed. He didn't want to give Godfrey that pleasure: he preferred that Master Godfrey should be vexed. Moreover, Dunstan enjoyed the self-important consciousness of having a horse to sell, and the opportunity of driving a bargain, swaggering, and possibly taking somebody in. He might have all the satisfaction attendant on selling his brother's horse, and not the less have the further satisfaction of setting Godfrey to borrow Marner's money. So he rode on to cover.

Bryce and Keating were there, as Dunstan was quite sure they would be – he was such a lucky fellow.

"Heyday!" said Bryce, who had long had his eye on Wildfire, "you're on your brother's horse to-day: how's that?"

"Oh, I've swopped with him," said Dunstan, whose delight in lying, grandly independent of utility, was not to be diminished by the likelihood that his hearer would not believe him – "Wildfire's mine now."

"What! has he swopped with you for that big-boned hack of yours?" said Bryce, quite aware that he should get another lie in answer.

"Oh, there was a little account between us," said Dunsey, carelessly, "and Wildfire made it even. I accommodated him by taking the horse, though it was against my will, for I'd got an itch for a mare o' Jortin's – as rare a bit o' blood as ever you threw your leg across. But I shall keep Wildfire, now I've got him, though I'd a bid of a hundred and fifty for him the other day, from a man over at Flitton – he's buying for Lord Cromleck – a fellow with a cast in his eye, and a green waistcoat. But I mean to stick to Wildfire: I shan't get a better at a fence in a hurry. The mare's got more blood, but she's a bit too weak in the hind-quarters."

Bryce of course divined that Dunstan wanted to sell the horse, and Dunstan knew that he divined it (horse-dealing is only one of many human transactions carried on in this ingenious manner); and they both considered that the bargain was in its first stage, when Bryce replied, ironically –

"I wonder at that now; I wonder you mean to keep him; for I never heard of a man who didn't want to sell his horse getting a bid of half as much again as the horse was worth. You'll be lucky if you get a hundred."

Keating rode up now, and the transaction became more complicated. It ended with the purchase of the horse by Bryce for a hundred and twenty, to be paid on the delivery of Wildfire, safe and sound, at the Batherley stables. It did occur to Dunsey that it might be wise for him to give up the day's hunting, proceed at once to Batherley, and, having waited for Bryce's return, hire a horse to carry him home with the money in his pocket. But the inclination for a run, encouraged by confidence in his luck, and by a draught of brandy from his pocket-pistol at the conclusion of the bargain, was not easy to overcome, especially with a horse under him that would take the fences to the admiration of the field. Dunstan, however, took one fence too many, and got his horse pierced with a hedge-stake. His own ill-favoured person, which was quite unmarketable, escaped without injury; but poor Wildfire, unconscious of his price, turned on his flank and painfully panted his last. It happened that Dunstan, a short time before, having had to get down to arrange his stirrup, had muttered a good many curses at this interruption, which had thrown him in the rear of the hunt near the moment of glory, and under this exasperation had taken the fences more blindly. He would soon have been up with the hounds again, when the fatal accident happened; and hence he was between eager riders in advance, not troubling themselves about what happened behind them, and far-off stragglers, who were as likely as not to pass quite aloof from the line of road in which Wildfire had fallen. Dunstan, whose nature it was to care more for immediate annoyances than for remote consequences, no sooner recovered his legs, and saw that it was all over with Wildfire, than he felt a satisfaction at the absence of witnesses to a position which no swaggering could make enviable. Reinforcing himself, after his shake, with a little brandy and much swearing, he walked as fast as he could to a coppice on his right hand, through which it occurred to him that he could make his way to Batherley without danger of encountering any member of the hunt. His first intention was to hire a horse there and ride home forthwith, for to walk many miles without a gun in his hand and along an ordinary road, was as much out of the qeustion to him as to other spirited young men of his kind. He did not much mind about taking the bad news to Godfrey, for he had to offer him at the same time the resource of Marner's money; and if Godfrey kicked, as he always did, at the notion of making a fresh debt from which he himself got the smallest share of advantage, why, he wouldn't kick long: Dunstan felt sure he could worry Godfrey into anything. The idea of Marner's money kept growing in vividness, now the want of it had become immediate; the prospect of having to make his appearance with the muddy boots of a pedestrian at Batherley, and to encounter the grinning queries of stablemen, stood unpleasantly in the way of his impatience to be back at Raveloe and carry out his felicitous plan; and a casual visitation of his waistcoat-pocket, as he was ruminating, awakened his memory to the fact that the two or three small coins his fore-finger encountered there, were of too pale a colour to cover that small debt, without payment of which the stable-keeper had declared he would never do any more business with Dunsey Cass.[9]

The woman's world is one of domesticity, embroidery, pride in possessions, visiting the poor or even planning labourers' cottages. It embraces traditional occasions like feasts and parties. But for Maggie Tulliver the main relief is reading and, on rare occasions, the discussion of what she reads. Music too is important to her. Cultural deprivation leaves her emotionally and intellectually reduced.

"I have never had any doubt that you would be the same, whenever I might see you," said Philip. "I mean, the same in everything that made me like you better than any one else. I don't want to explain that: I don't think any of the strongest effects our natures are susceptible of can ever be explained. We can neither detect the process by which they are arrived at, nor the mode in which they act on us. The greatest of painters only once painted a mysteriously divine child; he couldn't have told how he did it, and we can't tell why we feel it to be divine. I think there are stories laid up in our human nature that our understandings can make no complete inventory of. Certain strains of music affect me so strangely – I can never hear them without their changing my whole attitude of mind for a time, and if the effect would last, I might be capable of heroisms."

"Ah! I know what you mean about music – *I* feel so," said Maggie, clasping her hands with her old impetuosity. "At least," she added, in a saddened tone, "I used to feel so when I had any music: I never have any now except the organ at church."

"And you long for it, Maggie?" said Philip, looking at her with affectionate pity. "Ah, you can have very little that is beautiful in your life. Have you many books? You were so fond of them when you were a little girl."

They were come back to the hollow, round which the dog-roses grew, and they both paused under the charm of the faëry evening light, reflected from the pale pink clusters.

"No, I have given up books," said Maggie, quietly, "except a very, very few."

Philip had already taken from his pocket a small volume, and was looking at the back, as he said –

"Ah, this is the second volume, I see, else you might have liked to take it home with you. I put it in my pocket because I am studying a scene for a picture."

Maggie had looked at the back too, and saw the title: it revived an old impression with overmastering force.

" 'The Pirate,' " she said, taking the book from Philip's hands. "O, I began that once; I read to where Minna is walking with Cleveland, and I could never get to read the rest. I went on with it in my own head, and I made several endings; but they were all unhappy. I could never make a happy ending out of that beginning. Poor Minna! I wonder what is the real end. For a long while I couldn't get my mind away from the Shetland Isles – I used to feel the wind blowing on me from the rough sea."

Maggie spoke rapidly, with glistening eyes.

"Take that volume home with you, Maggie," said Philip, watching her with delight. "I don't want it now. I shall make a picture of you instead – you, among the Scotch firs and the slanting shadows."

Maggie had not heard a word he had said: she was absorbed in a page at which she had opened. But suddenly she closed the book, and gave it back to Philip, shaking her head with a backward movement, as if to say "avaunt" to floating visions.

"Do keep it, Maggie," said Philip, entreatingly; "it will give you pleasure."

"No, thank you," said Maggie, putting it aside with her hand and walking on. "It would make me in love with this world again, as I used to be – it would make me long to see and know many things – it would make me long for a full life."

"But you will not always be shut up in your present lot: why should you starve your mind in that way? It is narrow asceticism – I don't like to see you persisting in it, Maggie. Poetry and art and knowledge are sacred and pure."

"But not for me – not for me," said Maggie, walking more hurriedly. "Because I should want too much. I must wait – this life will not last long."[10]

George Eliot, like Maggie, valued her books from an early age, as we have seen with "The Linnet's Life". Her letters as a young woman bear full testimony to this. Take, for instance, this response to a present or loan from her old teacher Maria Lewis: "I have received 'The Faerie Queen,' and am trebly pleased with it", though her earlier views on the pernicious influence of fiction show her at her most ascetic and bigoted.[11] Her inherent appreciation of literature is reflected throughout her fiction. Books are associated with warmth and affection, but in her life too she experienced the same kind of frustration as Maggie. According to Haight she borrowed a copy of *Waverley* (probably in 1827)[12], which had to be returned before she had finished it. This parallels the incident quoted above of Maggie, and it took such a hold on her mind that she went on with the story herself. Eleven years after the publication of *The Mill*, and nearly forty-five years after the incident, she commemorated it in the motto she wrote and prefixed to Chapter 57 of *Middlemarch*:

> They numbered scarce eight summers when a name
>   Rose on their souls and stirred such motions there
> As thrill the buds and shape their hidden frame
>   At penetration of the quickening air:
> His name who told of loyal Evan Dhu,
>   Of quaint Bradwardine, and Vich Ian Vor,
> Making the little world their childhood knew
>   Large with a land of mountain, lake, and scaur,
> And larger yet with wonder, love, belief
>   Toward Walter Scott, who living far away
> Sent them this wealth of joy and noble grief.
>   The book and they must part, but day by day,
> In lines that thwart like portly spiders ran,
>   They wrote the tale, from Tully Veolan.[13]

Maggie shares with Dorothea an emotional response to music: in her recently published study, *George Eliot and Music* (1989) Beryl Gray has brilliantly demonstrated the influence music had on Marian Evans ("Music arches over this existence, with another and a diviner")[14] and on George Eliot, who uses it for commentary, symbol and action. Maggie is sufficiently like her creator to respond as, we suspect, Marian Evans responded, to the power of music once she was made free of the Bray household:

When the strain passed into the minor, she half-started from her seat with the sudden thrill of that change. Poor Maggie! She looked very beautiful when her soul was being played on in this way by the inexorable power of sound. You might have seen the slightest perceptible quivering through the whole frame as she leaned a little forward, clasping her hands as if to steady herself; while her eyes dilated and brightened into that wide-open, childish expression of wondering delight, which always came back in her happiest moments. Lucy, who at other times had always been at the piano when Maggie was looking in this way, could not resist the impulse to steal up to her and kiss her. Philip, too, caught a glimpse of her now and then round the open book on the desk, and felt that he had never before seen her under so strong an influence.

"More, more!" said Lucy, when the duet had been encored. "Something spirited again. Maggie always says she likes a great rush of sound."

"It must be 'Let us take the road,' then," said Stephen – "so suitable for a wet morning. But are you prepared to abandon the most sacred duties of life, and come and sing with us?"

"O yes," said Lucy, laughing. "If you will look out the 'Beggar's Opera' from the large canterbury. It has a dingy cover."

"That is a great clue, considering there are about a score covers here of rival dinginess," said Stephen, drawing out the canterbury.

"O, play something the while, Philip," said Lucy, noticing that his fingers were wandering over the keys. "What is that you are falling into? – something delicious that I don't know."

"Don't you know that?" said Philip, bringing out the tune more definitely. "It's from the *Sonnambula* – 'Ah! perchè non posso odiarti.' I don't know the opera, but it appears the tenor is telling the heroine that he shall always love her though she may forsake him. You've heard me sing it to the English words, 'I love thee still.' "

It was not quite unintentionally that Philip had wandered into this song, which might be an indirect expression to Maggie of what he could not prevail on himself to say to her directly. Her ears had been open to what he was saying, and when he began to sing, she understood the plaintive passion of the music. That pleading tenor had no very fine qualities as a voice, but it was not quite new to her: it had sung to her by snatches, in a subdued way, among the grassy walks and hollows, and underneath the leaning ash-tree in the Red Deeps. There seemed to be some reproach in the words – did Philip mean that? She wished she had assured him more distinctly in their conversation that she desired not to renew the hope of love between them, *only* because it clashed with her inevitable circumstances. She was touched, not thrilled by the song: it suggested distinct memories and thoughts, and brought quiet regret in the place of excitement.

"That's the way with you tenors," said Stephen, who was waiting with music in his hand while Philip finished the song. "You demoralize the fair sex by warbling your sentimental love and constancy under all sorts of vile treatment. Nothing short of having your heads served up in a dish like that mediæval tenor or troubadour, would prevent you from expressing your entire resignation. I must administer an antidote, while Miss Deane prepares to tear herself away from her bobbins."

Stephen rolled out, with saucy energy –

"Shall I, wasting in despair,
Die because a woman's fair?"

and seemed to make all the air in the room alive with a new influence. Lucy, always proud of what Stephen did, went towards the piano with laughing, admiring looks at him; and Maggie, in spite of her resistance to the spirit of the song and to the singer, was taken hold of and shaken by the invisible influence – was borne along by a wave too strong for her.

But, angrily resolved not to betray herself, she seized her work, and went on making false stitches and pricking her fingers with much perseverance, not looking up or taking notice of what was going forward, until all the three voices united in "Let us take the road."

I am afraid there would have been a subtle, stealing gratification in her mind if she had known how entirely this saucy, defiant Stephen was occupied with her: how he was passing rapidly from a determination to treat her with ostentatious indifference to an irritating desire for some sign of inclination from her – some interchange of subdued word or look with her. It was not long before he found an opportunity, when they had passed to the music of "The Tempest." Maggie, feeling the need of a footstool, was walking across the room to get one, when Stephen, who was not singing just then, and was conscious of all her movements, guessed her want, and flew to anticipate her, lifting the footstool, with an entreating look at her, which made it impossible not to return a glance of gratitude.[15]

George Eliot's recording of leisure in her Midlands novels is both personal and traditional, and I have made no attempt here to do more than indicate a few of the directions she took.

# 8. Working Life

George Eliot covers many aspects of working life, some derived from her own father's wide experience as a land agent and some remembered from local folk, some brought fictionally into the identifiable area she is covering. Amos Barton's work included visits to the College to preach to the poor who are kept there: as a young lady Marian Evans had undertaken such work herself. Here is her brief account of such a visit: ". . . I relieved the turnpike of a little of its unimaginable, unfathomable mud on Monday by wending my way to the College alias the 'dustry, and there I found poor Mrs Kelley in her bedroom, as comfortable as in her afflicted state she can be made. She tells me she has been a great sufferer for some months, and does not anticipate recovery."[1]

And here is a fictional visit:

But now Amos Barton has made his way through the sleet as far as the College, has thrown off his hat, cape, and boa, and is reading, in the dreary stone-floored dining-room, a portion of the morning service to the inmates seated on the benches before him. Remember, the New Poor-law had not yet come into operation, and Mr Barton was not acting as paid chaplain of the Union, but as the pastor who had the cure of all souls in his parish, pauper as well as other. After the prayers he always addressed to them a short discourse on some subject suggested by the lesson for the day, striving if by this means some edifying matter might find its way into the pauper mind and conscience – perhaps a task as trying as you could well imagine to the faith and patience of any honest clergyman. For, on the very first bench, these were the faces on which his eye had to rest, watching whether there was any stirring under the stagnant surface.

Right in front of him – probably because he was stone-deaf, and it was deemed more edifying to hear nothing at a short distance than at a long one – sat "Old Maxum," as he was familiarly called, his real patronymic remaining a mystery to most persons. A fine philological sense discerns in this cognomen an indication that the pauper patriarch had once been considered pithy and sententious in his speech; but now the weight of ninety-five years lay heavy on his tongue as well as in his ears, and he sat before the clergyman with protruded chin, and munching mouth, and eyes that seemed to look at emptiness.

Next to him sat Poll Fodge – known to the magistracy of her country as Mary Higgins – a one-eyed woman, with a scarred and seamy face, the most notorious rebel in the workhouse, said to have once thrown her broth over the master's coat-tails, and who, in spite of nature's apparent safe-guards against that contingency, had contributed to the perpetuation of the Fodge characteristics in the person of a small boy, who was behaving naughtily on one of the back benches. Miss Fodge fixed her one sore eye on Mr Barton with a sort of hardy defiance.

Beyond this member of the softer sex, at the end of the bench, sat "Silly Jim," a young man afflicted with hydrocephalus, who rolled his head from side to side, and gazed at the point of his nose. These were the supporters of Old Maxum on his right.

On his left sat Mr Fitchett, a tall fellow, who had once been a footman in the Oldinport family, and in that giddy elevation had enunciated a contemptuous opinion of boiled beef, which had been traditionally handed down in Shepperton as the direct cause of his ultimate reduction to pauper commons. His calves were now shrunken, and his hair was grey without the aid of powder; but he still carried his chin as if he were conscious of a stiff cravat; he set his dilapidated hat on with a knowing inclination towards the left ear; and when he was on field-work, he carted and uncarted the manure with a sort of flunkey grace, the ghost of that jaunty demeanour with which he used to usher in my lady's morning visitors. The flunkey nature was nowhere completely subdued but in his stomach, and he still divided society into gentry, gentry's flunkeys, and the people who provided for them. A clergyman without a flunkey was an anomaly, belonging to neither of these classes. Mr Fitchett had an irrepressible tendency to drowsiness under spiritual instruction, and in the recurrent regularity with which he dozed off until he nodded and awaked himself, he looked not unlike a piece of mechanism, ingeniously contrived for measuring the length of Mr Barton's discourse.

Perfectly wide-awake, on the contrary, was his left-hand neighbour, Mrs Brick, one of those hard undying old women, to whom age seems to have given a network of wrinkles, as a coat of magic armour against the attacks of winters, warm or cold. The point on which Mrs Brick was still sensitive – the theme on which you might possibly excite her hope and fear – was snuff. It seemed to be an enbalming powder, helping her soul to do the office of salt.

And now, eke out an audience of which this front benchful was a sample, with a certain number of refractory children, over whom Mr Spratt, the master of the workhouse, exercised an irate surveillance, and I think you will admit that the university-taught clergyman, whose office it is to bring home the gospel to a handful of such souls, has a sufficiently hard task. For, to have any chance of success, short of miraculous intervention, he must bring his geographical, chronological, exegetical mind pretty nearly to the pauper point of view, or of no view; he must have some approximate conception of the mode in which the doctrines that have so much vitality in the plenum of his own brain will comport themselves *in vacuo* – that is to say, in a brain that is neither geographical, chronological, nor exegetical. It is a flexible imagination that can take such a leap as that, and an adroit tongue that can adapt its speech to so unfamiliar a position. The Rev. Amos Barton had neither that flexible imagination, nor that adroit tongue. He talked of Israel and its sins, of chosen vessels, of the Paschal lamb, of blood as a medium of reconciliation; and he strove in this way to convey religious truth within reach of the Fodge and Fitchett mind. This very morning, the first lesson was the twelfth chapter of Exodus, and Mr Barton's exposition turned on unleavened bread. Nothing in the world more suited to the simple understanding than instruction through familiar types and symbols! But there is always this danger attending it, that the interest or comprehension of your hearers may stop short precisely at the point where your spiritual interpretation begins. And Mr Barton this morning succeeded in carrying the pauper imagination to the dough-tub but unfortunately was not able to carry it upwards from that well-known object to the unknown truths which it was intended to shadow forth.

Alas! a natural incapacity for teaching, finished by keeping "terms" at Cambridge, where there are able mathematicians, and butter is sold by the yard, is not apparently the medium through which Christian doctrine will distil as welcome dew on withered souls.

And so, while the sleet outside was turning to unquestionable snow, and the stony dining-room looked darker and drearier, and Mr Fitchett was nodding his lowest, and Mr Spratt was boxing the boys' ears with a constant *rinforzando*, and he felt more keenly the approach of dinner-time, Mr Barton wound up his exhortation with something of the February chill at his heart as well as his feet. Mr Fitchett, thoroughly roused now the instruction was at an end, obsequiously and gracefully advanced to help Mr Barton in putting on his cape, while Mrs Brick rubbed her withered forefinger round and round her little shoe-shaped snuff-box, vainly seeking for the fraction of a pinch. I can't help thinking that if Mr Barton had shaken into that little box a small portion of Scotch high-dried, he might have produced something more like an amiable emotion in Mrs Brick's mind than anything she had felt under his morning's exposition of the unleavened bread. But our good Amos laboured under a deficiency of small tact as well as of small cash; and when he observed the action of the old woman's forefinger, he said, in his brusque way, "So your snuff is all gone, eh?"

Mrs Brick's eyes twinkled with the visionary hope that the parson might be intending to replenish her box, at least mediately, through the present of a small copper.[2]

The College is an almshouse at Bedworth, two miles from Griff: here the humour is inlaid with pathos, and moral and social comment. Irony permeates Amos Barton's address, its reception and its irrelevance to the pauper audience. This is work in the workhouse, a memory of Marian Evans's voluntary visiting given fictional expansion.

In *Adam Bede* the focus is on the carpentry and estate management which belong to Adam's situation. We have already considered (see pp. 41–3) his derivations from Robert Evans. Marian's father was the first-rate workman that Adam assuredly is. Haight tells us: "Bred to his father's trade of carpenter, he found good use for his experience in overseeing the buildings on the 7000 acres of the Arbury lands. He could estimate within a few feet the amount of timber a given tree would provide. He surveyed and built roads in many parts of the Chilvers Coton parish. He was a shrewd judge of land values. Beneath Arbury lay the richest coal deposits in Warwickshire, and part of his responsibility involved its mining on the Griff Arm of the Coventry Canal."[3]

For Adam Bede, pride in work carries with it the corollary of duty. It is no use being a good carpenter if you destroy your work and those you love. The following passage shows the quality of Adam's character and his pride in work. He is now finishing the coffins which his father neglected, just before the mysterious tap on the door which, according to local superstition, signifies death:

"So it will go on, worsening and worsening," thought Adam; "there's no slipping up-hill again, and no standing still when once you've begun to slip down." And then the day came back to him when he was a little fellow and used to run by his father's side, proud to be taken out to work, and prouder still to hear his father boasting to his fellow-workmen how "the little chap had an uncommon notion o' carpentering." What a fine active fellow his father was then! When people asked Adam whose little lad he was, he had a sense of distinction as he answered, "I'm Thias Bede's lad" – he was quite sure everybody knew Thias Bede: didn't he make the wonderful pigeon-house at Broxton parsonage? Those were happy days, especially when Seth, who was three years the younger, began to go out working too, and Adam began to be a teacher as well as a learner. But then came the days of sadness, when Adam was someway on in his teens, and Thias began to loiter at the public-houses, and Lisbeth began to cry at home, and to pour forth her plaints in the hearing of her sons. Adam remembered well the night of shame and anguish when he first saw his father quite wild and foolish, shouting a song out fitfully among his drunken companions at the "Waggon Overthrown." He had run away once when he was only eighteen, making his escape in the morning twilight with a little blue bundle over his shoulder, and his "mensuration book" in his pocket, and saying to himself very decidedly that he could bear the vexations of home no longer – he would go and seek his fortune, setting up his stick at the crossways and bending his steps the way it fell. But by the time he got to Stoniton, the thought of his mother and Seth, left behind to endure everything without him, became too importunate, and his resolution failed him. He came back the next day, but the misery and terror his mother had gone through in those two days had haunted her ever since.

"No!" Adam said to himself to-night, "that must never happen again. It 'ud make a poor balance when my doings are cast up at the last, if my poor old mother stood o' the wrong side. My back's broad enough and strong enough; I should be no better than a coward to go away and leave the troubles to be borne by them as aren't half so able. 'They that are strong ought to bear the infirmities of those that are weak, and not to please themselves.' There's a text wants no candle to show't; it shines by its own light. It's plain enough you get into the wrong road i' this life if you run after this and that only for the sake o' making things easy and pleasant to yourself. A pig may poke his nose into the trough and think o' nothing outside it; but if you've got a man's heart and soul in you, you can't be easy a-making your own bed an' leaving the rest to lie on the stones. Nay, nay, I'll never slip my neck out o' the yoke, and leave the load to be drawn by the weak uns. Father's a sore cross to me, an's likely to be for many a long year to come. What then? I've got th' health, and the limbs, and the sperrit to bear it."[4]

Adam is the craftsman, the rustic artisan bent on self-improvement, but George Eliot also takes a close look at the farming community.

Tom excepted, Martin Poyser had some pride in his servants and labourers, thinking with satisfaction that they were the best worth their pay of any set on the estate. There was Kester Bale, for example (Beale, probably, if the truth were known, but he was called Bale, and was not conscious of any claim to a fifth letter), – the old man with the close leather cap, and the network of wrinkles on his sun-browned face. Was there any man in Loamshire who knew better the "natur" of all farming work? He was one of those invaluable labourers who can not only turn their hand to everything, but excel in everything they turn their hand to. It is true Kester's knees were much bent outward by this time, and he walked with a perpetual curtsy, as if he were among the most reverent of men. And so he was; but I am obliged to admit that the object of his reverence was his own skill, towards which he performed some rather affecting acts of worship. He always thatched the ricks; for if anything were his forte more than another, it was thatching; and when the last touch had been put to the last beehive rick, Kester, whose home lay at some distance from the farm, would take a walk to the rickyard in his best clothes on a Sunday morning, and stand in the lane, at a due distance, to contemplate his own thatching, – walking about to get each rick from the proper point of view. As he curtsied along, with his eyes upturned to the straw knobs imitative of golden globes at the summits of the beehive ricks, which indeed were gold of the best sort, you might have imagined him to be engaged in some pagan act of adoration. Kester was an old bachelor, and reputed to have stockings full of coin, concerning which his master cracked a joke with him every pay-night: not a new, unseasoned joke, but a good old one, that had been tried many times before, and had worn well. "Th' young measter's a merry mon," Kester frequently remarked; for having begun his career by frightening away the crows under the last Martin Poyser but one, he could never cease to account the reigning Martin a young master. I am not ashamed of commemorating old Kester: you and I are indebted to the hard hands of such men – hands that have long ago mingled with the soil they tilled so faithfully, thriftily making the best they could of the earth's fruits, and receiving the smallest share as their own wages.[5]

The loving focus on farm-work is interior and exterior. George Eliot transforms a past way of life she knew well: the historical period is merged with her own early life:

Plenty of life there! though this is the drowsiest time of the year, just before hay-harvest; and it is the drowsiest time of the day too, for it is close upon three by the sun, and it is half-past three by Mrs Poyser's handsome eight-day clock. But there is always a stronger sense of life when the sun is brilliant after rain; and now he is pouring down his beams, and making sparkles among the wet straw, and lighting up every patch of vivid green moss on the red tiles of the cow-shed, and turning even the muddy water that is hurrying along the channel to the drain into a mirror for the yellow-billed ducks, who are seizing the opportunity of getting a drink with as much body in it as possible. There is quite a concert of noises; the great bull-dog, chained against the stables, is thrown into furious exasperation by the unwary approach of a cock too near the mouth of his kennel, and sends forth a thundering bark, which is answered by two fox-hounds shut up in the opposite cow-house; the old top-knotted hens, scratching with their chicks among the straw, set up a sympathetic croaking as the discomfited cock joins them; a sow with her brood, all very muddy as to the legs, and curled as to the tail, throws in some deep staccato notes; our friends the calves are bleating from the home croft; and, under all, a fine ear discerns the continuous hum of human voices.

For the great barn-doors are thrown wide open, and men are busy there mending the harness, under the superintendence of Mr Goby the "whittaw," otherwise saddler, who entertains them with the latest Treddleston gossip. It is certainly rather an unfortunate day that Alick, the shepherd, has chosen for having the whittaws, since the morning turned out so wet; and Mrs Poyser has spoken her mind pretty strongly as to the dirt which the extra number of men's shoes brought into the house at dinner-time. Indeed, she has not yet recovered her equanimity on the subject, though it is now nearly three hours since dinner, and the house-floor is perfectly clean again; as clean as everything else in that wonderful house-place, where the only chance of collecting a few grains of dust would be to climb on the salt-coffer, and put your finger on the high mantel-shelf on which the glittering brass candlesticks are enjoying their summer sinecure; for at this time of year, of course, every one goes to bed while it is yet light, or at least light enough to discern the outline of objects after you have bruised your shins against them. Surely nowhere else could an oak clock-case and an oak table have got to such a polish by the hand: genuine "elbow polish," as Mrs Poyser called it, for she thanked God she never had any of your varnished rubbish in her house. Hetty Sorrel often took the opportunity, when her aunt's back was turned, of looking at the pleasing reflection of herself in those polished surfaces, for the oak table was usually turned up like a screen, and was more for ornament than for use; and she could see herself sometimes in the great round pewter dishes that were ranged on the shelves above the long deal dinner-table, or in the hobs of the grate, which always shone like jasper.

Everything was looking at its brightest at this moment, for the sun shone right on the pewter dishes, and from their reflecting surfaces pleasant jets of light were thrown on mellow oak and bright brass; – and on a still pleasanter object than these; for some of the rays fell on Dinah's finely-moulded cheek, and lit up her pale red hair to auburn, as she bent over the heavy household linen which she was mending for her aunt. No scene could have been more peaceful, if Mrs Poyser, who was ironing a few things that still remained from the Monday's wash, had not been making a frequent clinking with her iron, and moving to and fro whenever she wanted it to cool; carrying the keen glance of her blue-grey eye from the kitchen to the dairy, where Hetty was making up the butter, and from the dairy to the back-kitchen, where Nancy was taking the pies out of the oven. Do not suppose, however, that Mrs Poyser was elderly or shrewish in her appearance; she was a good-looking woman, not more than eight-and-thirty, of fair complexion and sandy hair, well-shapen, light-footed: the most conspicuous article in her attire was an ample checkered linen apron, which almost covered her skirt; and nothing could be plainer or less noticeable than her cap and gown, for there was no weakness of which she was less tolerant than feminine vanity, and the preference of ornament to utility. The family likeness between her and her niece Dinah Morris, with the contrast between her keenness and Dinah's seraphic gentleness of expression, might have served a painter as an excellent suggestion for a Martha and Mary. Their eyes were just of the same colour, but a striking test of the difference in their operation was seen in the demeanour of Trip, the black-and-tan terrier, whenever that much-suspected dog unwarily exposed himself to the freezing arctic ray of Mrs Poyser's glance. Her tongue was not less keen than her eye, and, whenever a damsel came within earshot, seemed to take up an unfinished lecture, as a barrel-organ takes up a tune, precisely at the point where it had left off.

The fact that it was churning-day was another reason why it was inconvenient to have the whittaws, and why, consequently, Mrs Poyser should scold Molly the housemaid with unusual severity. To all appearance Molly had got through her after-dinner work in an exemplary manner, had "cleaned herself" with great despatch, and now came to ask, submissively, if she should sit down to her spinning till milking-time. But this blameless conduct, according to Mrs Poyser, shrouded a secret indulgence of unbecoming wishes, which she now dragged forth and held up to Molly's view with cutting eloquence.[6]

Here the range is expressive and impressive, the routines established through a natural familiarity. That familiarity is particularized and used with imaginative, atmospheric intensity as prelude to the affair of Arthur Donnithorne and Hetty Sorrel:

## THE DAIRY.

The dairy was certainly worth looking at: it was a scene to sicken for with a sort of calenture in hot and dusty streets – such coolness, such purity, such fresh fragrance of new-pressed cheese, of firm butter, of wooden vessels perpetually bathed in pure water; such soft colouring of red earthenware and creamy surfaces, brown wood and polished tin, grey lime-stone and rich orange-red rust on the iron weights and hooks and hinges. But one gets only a confused notion of these details when they surround a distractingly pretty girl of seventeen, standing on little pattens and rounding her dimpled arm to lift a pound of butter out of the scale.

Hetty blushed a deep rose-colour when Captain Donnithorne entered the dairy and spoke to her; but it was not at all a distressed blush, for it was inwreathed with smiles and dimples, and with sparkles from under long curled dark eyelashes; and while her aunt was discoursing to him about the limited amount of milk that was to be spared for butter and cheese so long as the calves were not all weaned, and a large quantity but inferior quality of milk yielded by the short-horn, which had been bought on experiment, together with other matters which must be interesting to a young gentleman who would one day be a landlord, Hetty tossed and patted her pound of butter with quite a self-possessed, coquettish air, slily conscious that no turn of her head was lost.

There are various orders of beauty, causing men to make fools of themselves in various styles, from the desperate to the sheepish; but there is one order of beauty which seems made to turn the heads not only of men, but of all intelligent mammals, even of women. It is a beauty like that of kittens, or very small downy ducks making gentle rippling noises with their soft bills, or babies just beginning to toddle and to engage in conscious mischief – a beauty with which you can never be angry, but that you feel ready to crush for inability to comprehend the state of mind into which it throws you. Hetty Sorrel's was that sort of beauty. Her aunt, Mrs Poyser, who professed to despise all personal attractions, and intended to be the severest of mentors, continually gazed at Hetty's charms by the sly, fascinated in spite of herself; and after administering such a scolding as naturally flowed from her anxiety to do well by her husband's niece – who had no mother of her own to scold her, poor thing! – she would often confess to her husband, when they were safe out of hearing, that she firmly believed, "the naughtier the little huzzy behaved, the prettier she looked."[7]

Admittedly, the focus is on Hetty, but the whole passage is informed also with the industry and indeed the sensuality of work. Captain Donnithorne is the coming squire as well, ironically and tragically, as the future seducer of Hetty. He will perpetuate, one feels, that tradition of working prosperity which his uncle's tenants now enjoy (although Mrs Poyser would perhaps question the advantages she is presumed to have). The scene is one of lushness and abundance, a kind of harvest of the senses, an accumulation of what is produced, made, gathered and sold. The author's irony is omnipresent, for Hetty's working life is seen as unappreciative of her state. Arthur, visiting this working area, is playing a role, taking his inheritance before it has arrived. Neither Arthur nor Hetty is conscious of work so much as self and the assertion of self, Arthur through his rank and hereditary position, Hetty through her sensuality. Mrs Poyser and Adam exemplify the work ethic: the moral commentary on Hetty considers her reduced commitment. She does what she has to do: work is a burden, not a delight.

In *The Mill on the Floss* work is closely associated with the area and its needs. To fail in your work is to face the exacting depredations of the law. Mr Tulliver, who has always gone to law to protect his rights, finds himself reduced to the status of employee. George Eliot gives us an insight into the precarious nature of provincial life at the economic level. It is an insight which, though particularized in her fiction, carries a wide application:

## WHAT HAD HAPPENED AT HOME.

When Mr Tulliver first knew the fact that the lawsuit was decided against him, and that Pivart and Wakem were triumphant, every one who happened to observe him at the time thought that, for so confident and hot-tempered a man, he bore the blow remarkably well. He thought so himself: he thought he was going to show that if Wakem or anybody else considered him crushed, they would find themselves mistaken. He could not refuse to see that the costs of this protracted suit would take more than he possessed to pay them; but he appeared to himself to be full of expedients by which he could ward off any results but such as were tolerable, and could avoid the appearance of breaking down in the world. All the obstinacy and defiance of his nature, driven out of their old channel, found a vent for themselves in the immediate formation of plans by which he would meet his difficulties, and remain Mr Tulliver of Dorlcote Mill in spite of them. There was such a rush of projects in his brain, that it was no wonder his face was flushed when he came away from his talk with his attorney, Mr Gore, and mounted his horse to ride home from Lindum. There was Furley, who held the mortgage on the land – a reasonable fellow, who would see his own interest, Mr Tulliver was convinced, and would be glad not only to purchase the whole estate, including the mill and homestead, but would accept Mr Tulliver as tenant, and be willing to advance money to be repaid with high interest out of the profits of the business, which would be made over to him, Mr Tulliver only taking enough barely to maintain himself and his family. Who would neglect such a profitable investment? Certainly not Furley, for Mr Tulliver had determined that Furley should meet his plans with the utmost alacrity; and there are men whose brains have not yet been dangerously heated by the loss of a lawsuit who are apt to see in their own interest or desires a motive for other men's actions. There was no doubt (in the miller's mind) that Furley would do just what was desirable; and if he did – why, things would not be so very much worse. Mr Tulliver and his family must live more meagrely and humbly, but it would only be till the profits of the business had paid off Furley's advances, and that might be while Mr Tulliver had still a good many years of life before him. It was clear that the costs of the suit could be paid without his being obliged to turn out of his old place, and look like a ruined man. It was certainly an awkward moment in his affairs. There was that suretyship for poor Riley, who had died suddenly last April, and left his friend saddled with a debt of two hundred and fifty pounds – a fact which had helped to make Mr Tulliver's banking book less pleasant reading than a man might desire towards Christmas. Well! he had never been one of those poor-spirited sneaks who would refuse to give a helping hand to a fellow-traveller in this puzzling world. The really vexatious business was the fact that some months ago the creditor who had lent him the five hundred pounds to repay Mrs Glegg, had become uneasy about his money (set on by Wakem, of course), and Mr Tulliver, still confident that he should gain his suit, and finding it eminently inconvenient to raise the said sum until that desirable issue had taken place, had rashly acceded to the demand that he should give a bill of sale on his household furniture, and some other effects, as security in lieu of the bond. It was all one, he had said to himself: he should soon pay off the money, and there was no harm in giving that security any more than another. But now the consequences of this bill of sale occurred to him in a new light, and he remembered that the time was close at hand, when it would be enforced unless the money were repaid. Two months ago he would have declared stoutly that he would never be beholden to his wife's friends; but now he told himself as stoutly that it was nothing but right and natural that Bessy should go to the Pullets and explain the thing to them: they would hardly let Bessy's furniture be sold, and it might be security to Pullet if he advanced the money – there would, after all, be no gift or favour in the matter. Mr Tulliver would never have asked for anything from so poor-spirited a fellow for himself, but Bessy might do so if she liked.

It is precisely the proudest and most obstinate men who are the most liable to shift their position and contradict themselves in this sudden manner: everything is easier to them than to face the simple fact that they have been thoroughly defeated, and must begin life anew. And Mr Tulliver, you perceive, though nothing more than a superior miller and maltster, was as proud and obstinate as if he had been a very lofty personage, in whom such dispositions might be a source of that conspicuous, far-echoing tragedy, which sweeps the stage in regal robes and makes the dullest chronicler sublime. The pride and obstinacy of millers, and other insignificant people, whom you pass unnoticingly on the road every day, have their tragedy too; but it is of that unwept, hidden sort, that goes on from generation to generation, and leaves no record – such tragedy, perhaps, as lies in the conflicts of young souls, hungry for joy, under a lot made suddenly hard to them, under the dreariness of a home where the morning brings no promise with it, and where the unexpectant discontent of worn and disappointed parents weighs on the children like a damp, thick air in which all the functions of life are depressed; or such tragedy as lies in the slow or sudden death that follows on a bruised passion, though it may be a death that finds only a parish funeral. There are certain animals to which tenacity of position is a law of life – they can never flourish again, after a single wrench: and there are certain human beings to whom predominance is a law of life – they can only sustain humiliation so long as they can refuse to believe in it, and, in their own conception, predominate still.

Mr Tulliver was still predominating in his own imagination as he approached St Ogg's, through which he had to pass on his way homeward. But what was it that suggested to him, as he saw the Laceham coach entering the town, to follow it to the coach-office, and get the clerk there to write a letter, requiring Maggie to come home the very next day? Mr Tulliver's own hand shook too much under his excitement for him to write himself, and he wanted the letter to be given to the coachman to deliver at Miss Firniss's school in the morning. There was a craving which he would not account for to himself, to have Maggie near him – without delay – she must come back by the coach to-morrow.

To Mrs Tulliver, when he got home, he would admit no difficulties, and scolded down her burst of grief on hearing that the lawsuit was lost, by angry assertions that there was nothing to grieve about. He said nothing to her that night about the bill of sale, and the application to Mrs Pullet, for he had kept her in ignorance of the nature of that transaction, and had explained the necessity for taking an inventory of the goods as a matter connected with his will. The possession of a wife conspicuously one's inferior in intellect, is, like other high privileges, attended with a few inconveniences, and, among the rest, with the occasional necessity for using a little deception.[8]

The irony is omnipresent: failure in one's work is attended by economic deprivation and loss of status. That irony is present too as Tom, ill-prepared by his education, has to go cap-in-hand to his Uncle Deane, where his confidence in his capabilities is quickly put down:

"Why, you know nothing about book-keeping, to begin with, and not so much of reckoning as a common shopman. You'll have to begin at a low round of the ladder, let me tell you, if you mean to get on in life. It's no use forgetting the education your father's been paying for, if you don't give yourself a new un."

Tom bit his lips hard; he felt as if the tears were rising, and he would rather die than let them.

"You want me to help you to a situation," Mr Deane went on; "well, I've no fault to find with that. I'm willing to do something for you. But you youngsters nowadays think you're to begin with living well and working easy: you've no notion of running afoot before you get on horseback. Now, you must remember what you are – you're a lad of sixteen, trained to nothing particular. There's heaps of your sort, like so many pebbles, made to fit in nowhere. Well, you might be apprenticed to some business – a chemist's and druggist's perhaps: your Latin might come in a bit there . . ."

Tom was going to speak, but Mr Deane put up his hand and said –

"Stop! hear what I've got to say. You don't want to be a 'prentice – I know, I know – you want to make more haste – and you don't want to stand behind a counter. But if you're a copying-clerk, you'll have to stand behind a desk, and stare at your ink and paper all day: there isn't much out-look there, and you won't be much wiser at the end of the year than at the beginning. The world isn't made of pen, ink, and paper, and if you're to get on in the world, young man, you must know what the world's made of. Now the best chance for you 'ud be to have a place on a wharf, or in a warehouse, where you'd learn the smell of things – but you wouldn't like that, I'll be bound; you'd have to stand cold and wet, and be shouldered about by rough fellows. You're too fine a gentleman for that."

Mr Deane paused and looked hard at Tom, who certainly felt some inward struggle before he could reply.

"I would rather do what will be best for me in the end, sir: I would put up with what was disagreeable."

"That's well, if you can carry it out. But you must remember it isn't only laying hold of a rope – you must go on pulling. It's the mistake you lads make that have got nothing either in your brains or your pocket, to think you've got a better start in the world if you stick yourself in a place where you can keep your coats clean, and have the shop-wenches take you for fine gentlemen. That wasn't the way *I* started, young man: when I was sixteen, my jacket smelt of tar, and I wasn't afraid of handling cheeses. That's the reason I can wear good broadcloth now, and have my legs under the same table with the heads of the best firms in St Ogg's."

Uncle Deane tapped his box, and seemed to expand a little under his waistcoat and gold chain, as he squared his shoulders in the chair.

"Is there any place at liberty that you know of now, uncle, that I should do for? I should like to set to work at once," said Tom, with a slight tremor in his voice.

"Stop a bit, stop a bit; we mustn't be in too great a hurry. You must bear in mind, if I put you in a place you're a bit young for, because you happen to be my nephew, I shall be responsible for you. And there's no better reason, you know, than your being my nephew; because it remains to be seen whether you're good for anything."

"I hope I should never do you any discredit, uncle," said Tom, hurt, as all boys are at the statement of the unpleasant truth that people feel no ground for trusting them. "I care about my own credit too much for that."

"Well done, Tom, well done! That's the right spirit, and I never refuse to help anybody if they've a mind to do themselves justice. There's a young man of two-and-twenty I've got my eye on now. I shall do what I can for that young man – he's got some pith in him. But then, you see, he's made good use of his time – a first-rate calculator – can tell you the cubic contents of anything in no time, and put me up the other day to a new market for Swedish bark; he's uncommonly knowing in manufactures, that young fellow."

"I'd better set about learning book-keeping, hadn't I, uncle?" said Tom, anxious to prove his readiness to exert himself.

"Yes, yes, you can't do amiss there. But ... ah, Spence, you're back again. Well, Tom, there's nothing more to be said just now, I think, and I must go to business again. Good-bye. Remember me to your mother."[9]

Tom learns quickly and enters the world of commerce. His old friend – and enemy – from his trouble-free youth is also in commerce, working in a way which is morally dubious but has the same motivation and requires a similar expertise. Bob Jakin is a packman, and his wares interest Aunt Glegg. The profit motive is often given an ironic colouring by George Eliot:

"Why, it nibbles off three shillin' o' the price i' no time, an' then a packman like me can carry't to the poor lasses as live under the dark thack, to make a bit of a blaze for 'em. Lors, it's as good as a fire, to look at such a hankicher!"

Bob held it at a distance for admiration, but Mrs Glegg said sharply –

"Yes, but nobody wants a fire this time o' year. Put these coloured things by – let me look at your nets, if you've got 'em."

"Eh, mum, I told you how it 'ud be," said Bob, flinging aside the coloured things with an air of desperation. "I knowed it 'ud turn again' you to look at such paltry articles as I carry. Here's a piece o' figured muslin now – what's the use o' you lookin' at it? You might as well look at poor folk's victual, mum – it 'ud only take away your appetite. There's a yard i' the middle on't as the pattern's all missed – lors, why it's a muslin as the Princess Victoree might ha' wore – but," added Bob, flinging it behind him on to the turf, as if to save Mrs Glegg's eyes, "it'll be bought up by the huckster's wife at Fibb's End – that's where it'll go – ten shillin' for the whole lot – ten yards, countin' the damaged un – five-an'-twenty shillin' 'ud ha' been the price – not a penny less. But I'll say no more, mum; it's nothing to you – a piece o' muslin like that; you can afford to pay three times the money for a thing as isn't half so good. It's nets *you* talked on; well, I've got a piece as 'ull serve you to make fun on. . . ."

"Bring me that muslin," said Mrs Glegg: "it's a buff – I'm partial to buff."

"Eh, but a *damaged* thing," said Bob, in a tone of deprecating disgust. "You'd do nothing with it, mum – you'd give it to the cook, I know you would – an' it 'ud be a pity – she'd look too much like a lady in it – it's unbecoming for servants."

"Fetch it, and let me see you measure it," said Mrs Glegg, authoritatively.

Bob obeyed with ostentatious reluctance.

"See what there is over measure!" he said, holding forth the extra half-yard, while Mrs Glegg was busy examining the damaged yard, and throwing her head back to see how far the fault would be lost on a distant view.

"I'll give you six shilling for it," she said, throwing it down with the air of a person who mentions an ultimatum.

"Didn't I tell you now, mum, as it 'ud turn your feelings to look at my pack? That damaged bit's turned your stomach now – I see it has," said Bob, wrapping the muslin up with the utmost quickness, and apparently about to fasten up his pack. "You're used to seein' a different sort o' article carried by packmen, when you lived at the stone house. Packs is come down i' the world; I told you that; *my* goods are for common folks. Mrs Pepper 'ull give me ten shillin' for that muslin, an' be sorry as I didn't ask her more. Such articles answer i' the wearin' – they keep their colour till the threads melt away i' the wash-tub, an' that won't be while *I*'m a young un."

"Well, seven shilling," said Mrs Glegg.

"Put it out o' your mind, mum, now do," said Bob. "Here's a bit o' net, then, for you to look at before I tie up my pack: just for you to see what my trade's come to: spotted and sprigged, you see, beautiful, but yellow – 's been lyin' by an' got the wrong colour. I could niver ha' bought such net, if it hadn't been yallow. Lors, it's took me a deal o' study to know the vally o' such articles; when I begun to carry a pack. I was as ignirant as a pig – net or calico was all the same to me. I thought them things the most vally as was the thickest. I was took in dreadful – for I'm a straightforrard chap – up to no tricks, mum. I can on'y say my nose is my own, for if I went beyond, I should lose myself pretty quick. An' I gev five-an'-eightpence for that piece o' net – if I was to tell y' anything else I should be tellin' you fibs: an' five-an-eightpence I shall ask for it – not a penny more – for it's a woman's article, an' I like to 'commodate the women. Five-an'-eightpence for six yards – as cheap as if it was only the dirt on it as was paid for."

"I don't mind having three yards of it," said Mrs Glegg.

"Why, there's but six altogether," said Bob. "No, mum, it isn't worth your while; you can go to the shop to-morrow an' get the same pattern ready whitened. It's on'y three times the money – what's that to a lady like you?" He gave an emphatic tie to his bundle.

"Come, lay me out that muslin," said Mrs Glegg. "Here's eight shilling for it."

"You *will* be jokin', mum," said Bob, looking up with a laughing face; "I see'd you was a pleasant lady when I fust come to the winder."

"Well, put it me out," said Mrs Glegg, peremptorily.

"But if I let you have it for ten shillin', mum, you'll be so good as not tell nobody. I should be a laughin'-stock – the trade 'ud hoot me, if they knowed it. I'm obliged to make believe as I ask more nor I do for my goods, else they'd find out I was a flat. I'm glad you don't insist upo' buyin' the net, for then I should ha' lost my two best bargains for Mrs Pepper o' Fibbs' End – an' she's a rare customer."

"Let me look at the net again," said Mrs Glegg, yearning after the cheap spots and sprigs, now they were vanishing.

"Well, I can't deny *you*, mum," said Bob, handing it out. "Eh! see what a pattern now! Real Laceham goods. Now, this is the sort o' article I'm recommendin' Mr Tom to send out. Lors, it's a fine thing for anybody as has got a bit o' money – these Laceham goods 'ud make it breed like maggits. If *I* was a lady wi' a bit o' money! – why, I know one as put thirty pound into them goods – a lady wi' a cork leg; but as sharp – you wouldn't catch *her* runnin' her head into a sack; *she*'d see her way clear out o' anything afore she'd be in a hurry to start. Well, she let out thirty pound to a young man in the drapering line, and he laid it out i' Laceham goods, an' a shupercargo o' my acquinetance (not Salt) took 'em out, an' she got her eight per zent fust go off – an' now you can't hold her but she must be sendin' out carguies wi' every ship, till she's gettin' as rich as a Jew. Bucks her name is – she doesn't live i' this town. Now then, mum, if you'll please to give me the net. . . ."

"Here's fifteen shilling, then, for the two," said Mrs Glegg. "But it's a shameful price."

"Nay, mum, you'll niver say that when you're upo' your knees i' church i' five years' time. I'm makin' you a present o' th' articles – I am, indeed. That eightpence shaves off my profit as clean as a razor. Now then, sir," continued Bob, shouldering his pack, "if you please, I'll be glad to go and see about makin' Mr Tom's fortin. Eh, I wish I'd got another twenty pound to lay out for *my*sen: I shouldn't stay to say my Catechism afore I knowed what to do wi't."

"Stop a bit, Mr Glegg," said the lady, as her husband took his hat, "you never *will* give me the chance o' speaking. You'll go away now, and finish everything about this business, and come back and tell me it's too late for me to speak. As if I wasn't my nephey's own aunt, and th' head o' the family on his mother's side! and laid by guineas, all full weight, for him – as he'll know who to respect when I'm laid in my coffin."

"Well, Mrs G., say what you mean," said Mr G., hastily.

"Well, then, I desire as nothing may be done without my knowing. I don't say as I shan't venture twenty pounds, if you make out as everything's right and safe. And if I do, Tom," concluded Mrs Glegg, turning impressively to her nephew, "I hope you'll allays bear it in mind and be grateful for such an aunt. I mean you to pay me interest, you know – I don't approve o' giving; we niver looked for that in *my* family."

"Thank you, aunt," said Tom, rather proudly. "I prefer having the money only lent to me."

"Very well: that's the Dodson sperrit," said Mrs Glegg, rising to get her knitting with the sense that any further remark after this would be bathos.

Salt – that eminently "briny chap" – having been discovered in a cloud of tobacco-smoke at the Anchor Tavern, Mr Glegg commenced inquiries which turned out satisfactorily enough to warrant the advance of the "nest-egg," to which aunt Glegg contributed twenty pounds; and in this modest beginning you see the ground of a fact which might otherwise surprise you – namely, Tom's accumulation of a fund unknown to his father, that promised in no very long time to meet the more tardy process of saving, and quite cover the deficit. When once his attention had been turned to this source of gain, Tom determined to make the most of it, and lost no opportunity of obtaining information and extending his small enterprises. In not telling his father, he was influenced by that strange mixture of opposite feelings which often gives equal truth to those who blame an action and those who admire it: partly, it was that disinclination to confidence which is seen between near kindred – that family repulsion which spoils the most sacred relations of our lives; partly, it was the desire to surprise his father with a great joy. He did not see that it would have been better to soothe the interval with a new hope, and prevent the delirium of a too sudden elation.

At the time of Maggie's first meeting with Philip, Tom had already nearly a hundred and fifty pounds of his own capital; and while they were walking by the evening light in the Red Deeps, he, by the same evening light was riding into Laceham; proud of being on his first journey on behalf of Guest & Co., and revolving in his mind all the chances that by the end of another year he should have doubled his gains, lifted off the obloquy of debt from his father's name, and perhaps – for he should be twenty-one – have got a new start for himself, on a higher platform of employment. Did he not deserve it? He was quite sure that he did.[10]

Part of this occurs on pp. 66–7 but merits repetition. Bob's sharp eye for profit is instrumental in bringing Tom up in the world: it is a reversal of their childhood, relationship. Among other things, George Eliot is reflecting the mobility but also the class determination of provincial existence. Tom, despite his father's fall, moves steadily upward through his work and his personal enterprise, helped by family contacts. Bob operates within his station with reasonable success. In his case there is an interesting sympathetic gloss. He buys back Maggie's precious books for her when the Tullivers are sold up:

her aunts and their husbands, who have worked and invested, are not moved
to such generous action, though Aunt Gritty, whose husband scrapes a bare
living from the land, offers to try to repay the loan which had kept her husband
going.

Urban and rural occupations are rendered with scrupulous reference to
place: Silas Marner, translated from an industrial northern town to the
Midland village of Raveloe, resumes the only occupation he knows in the new
region of isolation. Weaving is at the factual and the metaphorical heart of
*Silas Marner.*

## CHAPTER I.

In the days when the spinning wheels hummed busily in the farmhouses – and even
great ladies, clothed in silk and thread-lace, had their toy spinning-wheels of polished
oak – there might be seen in districts far away among the lanes, or deep in the bosom
of the hills, certain pallid undersized men, who, by the side of the brawny country-folk,
looked like the remnants of a disinherited race. The shepherd's dog barked fiercely
when one of these alien-looking men appeared on the upland, dark against the early
winter sunset; for what dog likes a figure bent under a heavy bag? – and these pale
men rarely stirred abroad without that mysterious burden. The shepherd himself,
though he had good reason to believe that the bag held nothing but flaxen thread,
or else the long rolls of strong linen spun from that thread, was not quite sure that
this trade of weaving, indispensable though it was, could be carried on entirely without
the help of the Evil One. In that far-off time superstition clung easily round every
person or thing that was at all unwonted, or even intermittent and occasional
merely, like the visits of the pedlar or the knife-grinder. No one knew where
wandering men had their homes or their origin; and how was a man to be
explained unless you at least knew somebody who knew his father and mother? To
the peasants of old times, the world outside their own direct experience was a region
of vagueness and mystery: to their untravelled thought a state of wandering was a
conception as dim as the winter life of the swallows that came back with the spring;
and even a settler, if he came from distant parts, hardly ever ceased to be viewed with
a remnant of distrust, which would have prevented any surprise if a long course of
inoffensive conduct on his part had ended in the commission of a crime; especially if
he had any reputation for knowledge, or showed any skill in handicraft. All cleverness,
whether in the rapid use of that difficult instrument the tongue, or in some other art
unfamiliar to villagers, was in itself suspicious: honest folk, born and bred in a visible
manner, were mostly not overwise or clever – at least, not beyond such a matter as
knowing the signs of the weather; and the process by which rapidity and dexterity of
any kind were acquired was so wholly hidden, that they partook of the nature of
conjuring. In this way it came to pass that those scattered linen-weavers – emigrants
from the town into the country – were to the last regarded as aliens by their rustic
neighbours, and usually contracted the eccentric habits which belong to a state of
loneliness.

In the early years of this century, such a linen-weaver, named Silas Marner, worked
at his vocation in a stone cottage that stood among the nutty hedgerows near the

189

village of Raveloe, and not far from the edge of a deserted stone-pit. The questionable sound of Silas's loom, so unlike the natural cheerful trotting of the winnowing-machine, or the simpler rhythm of the flail, had a half-fearful fascination for the Raveloe boys, who would often leave off their nutting or birds'-nesting to peep in at the window of the stone cottage, counterbalancing a certain awe at the mysterious action of the loom, by a pleasant sense of scornful superiority, drawn from the mockery of its alternating noises, along with the bent, tread-mill attitude of the weaver. But sometimes it happened that Marner, pausing to adjust an irregularity in his thread, became aware of the small scoundrels, and, though chary of his time, he liked their intrusion so ill that he would descend from his loom, and, opening the door, would fix on them a gaze that was always enough to make them take to their legs in terror.[11]

In crisis Silas does mechanically what he has done in subdued isolation over the years: work is the index to sanity:

Again he put his trembling hands to his head, and gave a wild ringing scream, the cry of desolation. For a few moments after, he stood motionless; but the cry had relieved him from the first maddening pressure of the truth. He turned, and tottered towards his loom, and got into the seat where he worked, instinctively seeking this as the strongest assurance of reality.

And now that all the false hopes had vanished, and the first shock of certainty was past, the idea of a thief began to present itself, and he entertained it eagerly, because a thief might be caught and made to restore the gold. The thought brought some new strength with it, and he started from his loom to the door.[12]

In *Middlemarch* George Eliot stresses the work ethic and it colours the fabrics of provincial life. It is so much a part of the plot and the moral resonance of the novel that it becomes identified with decision, dilemma, and consequence. Mary Garth is a housekeeper-companion to old Peter Featherstone, being treated by him as a poor relation. But she doesn't only care for his body: she cares also for his soul, as we see when he tries to persuade her to let him make a last-minute alteration to his will:

"Not do it? I tell you, you must," said the old man, his voice beginning to shake under the shock of this resistance.

"I cannot touch your iron chest or your will. I must refuse to do anything that might lay me open to suspicion."

"I tell you, I'm in my right mind. Shan't I do as I like at the last? I made two wills on purpose. Take the key, I say."

"No, sir, I will not," said Mary, more resolutely still. Her repulsion was getting stronger.

"I tell you, there's no time to lose."

"I cannot help that, sir. I will not let the close of your life soil the beginning of mine. I will not touch your iron chest or your will." She moved to a little distance from the bedside.

The old man paused with a blank stare for a little while, holding the one key erect on the ring; then with an agitated jerk he began to work with his bony left hand at emptying the tin box before him.

"Missy," he began to say, hurriedly, "look here! take the money – the notes and gold – look here – take it – you shall have it all – do as I tell you."

He made an effort to stretch out the key towards her as far as possible, and Mary again retreated.

"I will not touch your key or your money, sir. Pray don't ask me to do it again. If you do, I must go and call your brother."

He let his hand fall, and for the first time in her life Mary saw old Peter Featherstone begin to cry childishly. She said, in as gentle a tone as she could command, "Pray put up your money, sir;" and then went away to her seat by the fire, hoping this would help to convince him that it was useless to say more. Presently he rallied and said eagerly –

"Look here, then. Call the young chap. Call Fred Vincy."

Mary's heart began to beat more quickly. Various ideas rushed through her mind as to what the burning of a second will might imply. She had to make a difficult decision in a hurry.

"I will call him, if you will let me call Mr Jonah and others with him."

"Nobody else, I say. The young chap. I shall do as I like."

"Wait till broad daylight, sir, when every one is stirring. Or let me call Simmons now, to go and fetch the lawyer? He can be here in less than two hours."

"Lawyer? What do I want with the lawyer? Nobody shall know – I say, nobody shall know. I shall do as I like."

"Let me call some one else, sir," said Mary, persuasively. She did not like her position – alone with the old man, who seemed to show a strange flaring of nervous energy which enabled him to speak again and again without falling into his usual cough; yet she desired not to push unnecessarily the contradiction which agitated him. "Let me, pray, call some one else."

"You let me alone, I say. Look here, missy. Take the money. You'll never have the chance again. It's pretty nigh two hundred – there's more in the box, and nobody knows how much there was. Take it and do as I tell you."

Mary, standing by the fire, saw its red light falling on the old man, propped up on his pillows and bed-rest, with his bony hand holding out the key, and the money lying on the quilt before him. She never forgot that vision of a man wanting to do as he liked at the last. But the way in which he had put the offer of the money urged her to speak with harder resolution than ever.

"It is of no use, sir. I will not do it. Put up your money. I will not touch your money. I will do anything else I can to comfort you; but I will not touch your keys or your money."

"Anything else – anything else!" said old Featherstone, with hoarse rage, which, as if in a nightmare, tried to be loud, and yet was only just audible. "I want nothing else. You come here – you come here."

Mary approached him cautiously, knowing him too well. She saw him dropping his keys and trying to grasp his stick, while he looked at her like an aged hyena, the muscles of his face getting distorted with the effort of his hand. She paused at a safe distance.

"Let me give you some cordial," she said, quietly, "and try to compose yourself. You will perhaps go to sleep. And to-morrow by daylight you can do as you like."

He lifted the stick, in spite of her being beyond his reach, and threw it with a hard effort which was but impotence. It fell, slipping over the foot of the bed. Mary let it lie, and retreated to her chair by the fire. By-and-by she would go to him with the cordial. Fatigue would make him passive. It was getting towards the chillest moment of the morning, the fire had got low, and she could see through the chink between the moreen window-curtains the light whitened by the blind. Having put some wood on the fire and thrown a shawl over her, she sat down, hoping that Mr Featherstone might now fall asleep. If she went near him the irritation might be kept up. He had said nothing after throwing the stick, but she had seen him taking his keys again and laying his right hand on the money. He did not put it up, however, and she thought that he was dropping off to sleep.

But Mary herself began to be more agitated by the remembrance of what she had gone through, than she had been by the reality – questioning those acts of hers which had come imperatively and excluded all question in the critical moment.

Presently the dry wood sent out a flame which illuminated every crevice, and Mary saw that the old man was lying quietly with his head turned a little on one side. She went towards him with inaudible steps, and thought that his face looked strangely motionless; but the next moment the movement of the flame communicating itself to all objects made her uncertain. The violent beating of her heart rendered her perceptions so doubtful that even when she touched him and listened for his breathing, she could not trust her conclusions. She went to the window and gently propped aside the curtain and blind, so that the still light of the sky fell on the bed.

The next moment she ran to the bell and rang it energetically. In a very little while there was no longer any doubt that Peter Featherstone was dead, with his right hand clasping the keys, and his left hand lying on the heap of notes and gold.[13]

The Garth family are always working, frequently doing two things at the same time. Mrs Garth is a competent housekeeper in the Mrs Poyser tradition, but a practical teacher as well:

Mrs Garth, with her sleeves turned above her elbows, deftly handling her pastry – applying her rolling-pin and giving ornamental pinches, while she expounded with grammatical fervour what were the right views about the concord of verbs and pronouns with "nouns of multitude or signifying many," was a sight agreeably amusing. She was of the same curly-haired, square-faced type as Mary, but handsomer, with more delicacy of feature, a pale skin, a solid matronly figure, and a remarkable firmness of glance. In her snowy-frilled cap she reminded one of that delightful Frenchwoman whom we have all seen marketing, basket on arm. Looking at the mother, you might hope that the daughter would become like her, which is a prospective advantage equal to a dowry – the mother too often standing behind the daughter like a malignant prophecy – "Such as I am, she will shortly be."

"Now let us go through that once more," said Mrs Garth, pinching an apple-puff which seemed to distract Ben, an energetic young male with a heavy brow, from due attention to the lesson. " 'Not without regard to the import of the word as conveying unity or plurality of idea' – tell me again what that means, Ben."

(Mrs Garth, like more celebrated educators, had her favourite ancient paths, and in a general wreck of society would have tried to hold her 'Lindley Murray' above the waves.)

"Oh – it means – you must think what you mean," said Ben, rather peevishly. "I hate grammar. What's the use of it?"

"To teach you to speak and write correctly, so that you can be understood," said Mrs Garth, with severe precision. "Should you like to speak as old Job does?"

"Yes," said Ben, stoutly; "it's funnier. He says, 'Yo goo' – that's just as good as 'You go.'"

"But he says, 'A ship's in the garden,' instead of 'a sheep,' " said Letty, with an air of superiority. "You might think he meant a ship off the sea."

"No, you mightn't, if you weren't silly," said Ben. "How could a ship off the sea come there?"

"These things belong only to pronunciation, which is the least part of grammar," said Mrs Garth. "That apple-peel is to be eaten by the pigs, Ben; if you eat it, I must give them your piece of pasty. Job has only to speak about very plain things. How do you think you would write or speak about anything more difficult, if you knew no more of grammar than he does? You would use wrong words, and put words in the wrong places, and instead of making people understand you, they would turn away from you as a tiresome person. What would you do then?"

"I shouldn't care, I should leave off," said Ben, with a sense that this was an agreeable issue where grammar was concerned.

"I see you are getting tired and stupid, Ben," said Mrs Garth, accustomed to these obstructive arguments from her male offspring. Having finished her pies, she moved towards the clothes-horse, and said, "Come here and tell me the story I told you on Wednesday, about Cincinnatus."

"I know! he was a farmer," said Ben.

"Now, Ben, he was a Roman – let *me* tell," said Letty, using her elbow contentiously.

"You silly thing, he was a Roman farmer, and he was ploughing."

"Yes, but before that – that didn't come first – people wanted him," said Letty.

"Well, but you must say what sort of a man he was first," insisted Ben. "He was a wise man, like my father, and that made the people want his advice. And he was a brave man, and could fight. And so could my father – couldn't he, mother?"

"Now, Ben, let me tell the story straight on, as mother told it us," said Letty, frowning. "Please, mother, tell Ben not to speak."

"Letty, I am ashamed of you," said her mother, wringing out the caps from the tub. "When your brother began, you ought to have waited to see if he could not tell the story. How rude you look, pushing and frowning, as if you wanted to conquer with your elbows! Cincinnatus, I am sure, would have been sorry to see his daughter behave so." (Mrs Garth delivered this awful sentence with much majesty of enunciation, and Letty felt that between repressed volubility and general disesteem, that of the Romans inclusive, life was already a painful affair.) "Now, Ben."

"Well – oh – well – why, there was a great deal of fighting, and they were all blockheads, and – I can't tell it just how you told it – but they wanted a man to be captain and king and everything –"

"Dictator, now," said Letty, with injured looks, and not without a wish to make her mother repent.

"Very well, dictator!" said Ben, contemptuously. "But that isn't a good word: he didn't tell them to write on slates."

"Come, come, Ben, you are not so ignorant as that," said Mrs Garth, carefully serious. "Hark, there is a knock at the door! Run, Letty, and open it."[14]

Sometimes, a dedication to work brings its own rewards, even keeping a close-knit family together. Caleb and his daughter share an intense love of home: his work achieves local recognition and enables her to give up the school-teaching she dislikes:

"Have you made up your mind, my dear?" said Mrs Garth, laying the letters down.

"I shall go to the school at York," said Mary. "I am less unfit to teach in a school than in a family. I like to teach classes best. And, you see, I must teach: there is nothing else to be done."

"Teaching seems to me the most delightful work in the world," said Mrs Garth, with a touch of rebuke in her tone. "I could understand your objection to it if you had not knowledge enough, Mary, or if you disliked children."

"I suppose we never quite understand why another dislikes what we like, mother," said Mary, rather curtly. "I am not fond of a schoolroom: I like the outside world better. It is a very inconvenient fault of mine."

"It must be very stupid to be always in a girls' school," said Alfred. "Such a set of nincompoops, like Mrs Ballard's pupils walking two and two."

"And they have no games worth playing at," said Jim. "They can neither throw nor leap. I don't wonder at Mary's not liking it."

"What is that Mary doesn't like, eh?" said the father, looking over his spectacles and pausing before he opened his next letter.

"Being among a lot of nincompoop girls," said Alfred.

"Is it the situation you had heard of, Mary?" said Caleb, gently looking at his daughter.

"Yes, father: the school at York. I have determined to take it. It is quite the best. Thirty-five pounds a-year, and extra pay for teaching the smallest strummers at the piano."

"Poor child! I wish she could stay at home with us, Susan," said Caleb, looking plaintively at his wife.

"Mary would not be happy without doing her duty," said Mrs Garth, magisterially, conscious of having done her own.

"It wouldn't make me happy to do such a nasty duty as that," said Alfred – at which Mary and her father laughed silently, but Mrs Garth said, gravely –

"Do find a fitter word than nasty, my dear Alfred, for everything that you think disagreeable. And suppose that Mary could help you to go to Mr Hanmer's with the money she gets?"

"That seems to me a great shame. But she's an old brick," said Alfred, rising from his chair, and pulling Mary's head backward to kiss her.

Mary coloured and laughed, but could not conceal that the tears were coming. Caleb, looking on over his spectacles, with the angles of his eyebrows falling, had an expression of mingled delight and sorrow as he returned to the opening of his letter; and even Mrs Garth, her lips curling with a calm contentment, allowed that inappropriate language to pass without correction, although Ben immediately took it up, and sang, "She's an old brick, old brick, old brick!" to a cantering measure, which he beat out with his first on Mary's arm.

But Mrs Garth's eyes were now drawn towards her husband, who was already deep in the letter he was reading. His face had an expression of grave surprise, which alarmed her a little, but he did not like to be questioned while he was reading, and she remained anxiously watching till she saw him suddenly shaken by a little joyous laugh as he turned back to the beginning of the letter, and looking at her above his spectacles, said, in a low tone, "What do you think, Susan?"

She went and stood behind him, putting her hand on his shoulder, while they read the letter together. It was from Sir James Chettam, offering to Mr Garth the management of the family estates at Freshitt and elsewhere, and adding that Sir James had been requested by Mr Brooke of Tipton to ascertain whether Mr Garth would be disposed at the same time to resume the agency of the Tipton property. The Baronet added in very obliging words that he himself was particularly desirous of seeing the Freshitt and Tipton estates under the same management, and he hoped to be able to show that the double agency might be held on terms agreeable to Mr Garth, whom he would be glad to see at the Hall at twelve o'clock on the following day.

"He writes handsomely, doesn't he, Susan?" said Caleb, turning his eyes upward to his wife, who raised her hand from his shoulder to his ear, while she rested her chin on his head. "Brooke didn't like to ask me himself, I can see," he continued, laughing silently.

"Here is an honour to your father, children," said Mrs Garth, looking round at the five pair of eyes, all fixed on the parents. "He is asked to take a post again by those who dismissed him long ago. That shows that he did his work well, so that they feel the want of him."

"Like Cincinnatus – hooray!" said Ben, riding on his chair, with a pleasant confidence that discipline was relaxed.

"Will they come to fetch him, mother?" said Letty, thinking of the Mayor and Corporation in their robes.

Mrs Garth patted Letty's head and smiled, but seeing that her husband was gathering up his letters and likely soon to be out of reach in that sanctuary "business," she pressed his shoulder and said emphatically –

"Now, mind you ask fair pay, Caleb."

"Oh yes," said Caleb, in a deep voice of assent, as if it would be unreasonable to suppose anything else of him. "It'll come to between four and five hundred, the two together." Then with a little start of remembrance he said, "Mary, write and give up that school. Stay and help your mother. I'm as pleased as Punch, now I've thought of that."[15]

As she looks back to the Midlands George Eliot frequently introduces the outsider whose work influences, or changes, the community he enters. We know from her *Quarry for Middlemarch* (ed. Anna T. Kitchel, 1950) how carefully she researched the medical profession in order to authenticate Lydgate. He works hard, gets into financial difficulties, grows away from his wife and, after a successful career in a spa attending the rich, dies of diphtheria. His first public entrance is at Mr Brooke's party, where he meets Dorothea, who is intent upon good works. In their different ways they are to provide the major contributions to the new fever hospital:

"Certainly; she is fonder of geraniums, and seems more docile, though not so fine a figure. But we were talking of physic: tell me about this new young surgeon, Mr Lydgate. I am told he is wonderfully clever: he certainly looks it – a fine brow indeed."

"He is a gentleman. I heard him talking to Humphrey. He talks well."

"Yes. Mr Brooke says he is one of the Lydgates of Northumberland, really well connected. One does not expect it in a practitioner of that kind. For my own part, I like a medical man more on a footing with the servants; they are often all the cleverer. I assure you I found poor Hicks's judgment unfailing; I never knew him wrong. He was coarse and butcher-like, but he knew my constitution. It was a loss to me his going off so suddenly. Dear me, what a very animated conversation Miss Brooke seems to be having with this Mr Lydgate!"

"She is talking cottages and hospitals with him," said Mrs Cadwallader, whose ears and power of interpretation were quick. "I believe he is a sort of philanthropist, so Brooke is sure to take him up."

"James," said Lady Chettam when her son came near, "bring Mr Lydgate and introduce him to me. I want to test him."

The affable dowager declared herself delighted with this opportunity of making Mr Lydgate's acquaintance, having heard of his success in treating fever on a new plan.

Mr Lydgate had the medical accomplishment of looking perfectly grave whatever nonsense was talked to him, and his dark steady eyes gave him impressiveness as a listener. He was as little as possible like the lamented Hicks, especially in a certain careless refinement about his toilette and utterance. Yet Lady Chettam gathered much confidence in him. He confirmed her view of her own constitution as being peculiar, by admitting that all constitutions might be called peculiar, and he did not deny that hers might be more peculiar than others. He did not approve of a too lowering system, including reckless cupping, nor, on the other hand, of incessant port-wine and bark. He said "I think so" with an air of so much deference accompanying the insight of agreement, that she formed the most cordial opinion of his talents.

"I am quite pleased with your *protégé*," she said to Mr Brooke before going away.

"My *protégé*? – dear me! – who is that?" said Mr Brooke.

"This young Lydgate, the new doctor. He seems to me to understand his profession admirably."

"Oh, Lydgate! he is not my *protégé*, you know; only I knew an uncle of his who sent me a letter about him. However, I think he is likely to be first-rate – has studied in Paris, knew Broussais; has ideas, you know – wants to raise the profession."

"Lydgate has lots of ideas, quite new, about ventilation and diet, that sort of thing," resumed Mr Brooke, after he had handed out Lady Chettam, and had returned to be civil to a group of Middlemarchers.

"Hang it, do you think that is quite sound? – upsetting the old treatment, which has made Englishmen what they are?" said Mr Standish.

"Medical knowledge is at a low ebb among us," said Mr Bulstrode, who spoke in a subdued tone, and had rather a sickly air. "I, for my part, hail the advent of Mr Lydgate. I hope to find good reason for confiding the new hospital to his management."

"That is all very fine," replied Mr Standish, who was not fond of Mr Bulstrode; "if you like him to try experiments on your hospital patients, and kill a few people for charity, I have no objection. But I am not going to hand money out of my purse to have experiments tried on me. I like treatment that has been tested a little."

"Well, you know, Standish, every dose you take is an experiment – an experiment, you know," said Mr Brooke, nodding towards the lawyer.

"Oh, if you talk in that sense!" said Mr Standish, with as much disgust at such non-legal quibbling as a man can well betray towards a valuable client.

"I should be glad of any treatment that would cure me without reducing me to a skeleton, like poor Grainger," said Mr Vincy, the mayor, a florid man, who would have served for a study of flesh in striking contrast with the Franciscan tints of Mr Bulstrode. "It's an uncommonly dangerous thing to be left without any padding against the shafts of disease, as somebody said, – and I think it a very good expression myself."[16]

But the medical practitioner in the provinces cannot escape the confining pressures of local politics. He cannot separate himself from his patron or from his own capacity to offend by innovation or the flouting of tradition:

Here was plenty of preparation for the outburst of professional disgust at the announcement of the laws Mr Bulstrode was laying down for the direction of the New Hospital, which were the more exasperating because there was no present possibility of interfering with his will and pleasure, everybody except Lord Medlicote having refused help towards the building, on the ground that they preferred giving to the Old Infirmary. Mr Bulstrode met all the expenses, and had ceased to be sorry that he was purchasing the right to carry out his notions of improvement without hindrance from prejudiced coadjutors; but he had had to spend large sums, and the building had lingered. Caleb Garth had undertaken it, had failed during its progress, and before the interior fittings were begun had retired from the management of the business; and when referring to the Hospital he often said that however Bulstrode might ring if you tried him, he liked good solid carpentry and masonry, and had a notion both of drains and chimneys. In fact, the Hospital had become an object of intense interest to Bulstrode, and he would willingly have continued to spare a large yearly sum that he might rule it dictatorially without any Board; but he had another favourite object which also required money for its accomplishment: he wished to buy some land in the neighbourhood of Middlemarch, and therefore he wished to get considerable contributions towards maintaining the Hospital. Meanwhile he framed his plan of management. The Hospital was to be reserved for fever in all its forms; Lydgate was to be chief medical superintendent, that he might have free authority to pursue all comparative investigations which his studies, particularly in Paris, had shown him the importance of, the other medical visitors having a consultative influence, but no power to contravene Lydgate's ultimate decisions; and the general management was to be lodged exclusively in the hands of five directors associated with Mr Bulstrode, who were to have votes in the ratio of their contributions, the Board itself filling up any vacancy in its numbers, and no mob of small contributors being admitted to a share of government.

There was an immediate refusal on the part of every medical man in the town to become a visitor at the Fever Hospital.

"Very well," said Lydgate to Mr Bulstode, "we have a capital house-surgeon and dispenser, a clear-headed, neat-handed fellow; we'll get Webbe from Crabsley, as good a country practitioner as any of them, to come over twice a-week, and in case of any exceptional operation, Protheroe will come from Brassing. I must work the harder, that's all, and I have given up my post at the Infirmary. The plan will flourish in spite of them, and then they'll be glad to come in. Things can't last as they are: there must be all sorts of reform soon, and then young fellows may be glad to come and study here." Lydgate was in high spirits.

"I shall not flinch, you may depend upon it, Mr Lydgate," said Mr Bulstrode. "While I see you carrying out high intentions with vigour, you shall have my unfailing support. And I have humble confidence that the blessing which has hitherto attended my efforts against the spirit of evil in this town will not be withdrawn. Suitable directors to assist me I have no doubt of securing. Mr Brooke of Tipton has already given me his concurrence, and a pledge to contribute yearly: he has not specified the sum – probably not a great one. But he will be a useful member of the board."

A useful member was perhaps to be defined as one who would originate nothing, and always vote with Mr Bulstrode.

The medical aversion to Lydgate was hardly disguised now. Neither Dr Sprague nor Dr Minchin said that he disliked Lydgate's knowledge, or his disposition to improve treatment: what they disliked was his arrogance, which nobody felt to be altogether deniable. They implied that he was insolent, pretentious, and given to that reckless innovation for the sake of noise and show which was the essence of the charlatan.

The word charlatan once thrown on the air could not be let drop. In those days the world was agitated about the wondrous doings of Mr St John Long, "noblemen and gentlemen" attesting his extraction of a fluid like mercury from the temples of a patient.

Mr Toller remarked one day, smilingly, to Mrs Taft, that "Bulstrode had found a man to suit him in Lydgate; a charlatan in religion is sure to like other sorts of charlatans."

"Yes, indeed, I can imagine," said Mrs Taft, keeping the number of thirty stitches carefully in her mind all the while; "there are so many of that sort. I remember Mr Cheshire, with his irons, trying to make people straight when the Almighty had made them crooked."

"No, no," said Mr Toller, "Cheshire was all right – all fair and above board. But there's St John Long – that's the kind of fellow we call a charlatan, advertising cures in ways nobody knows anything about: a fellow who wants to make a noise by pretending to go deeper than other people. The other day he was pretending to tap a man's brain and get quicksilver out of it."

"Good gracious! what dreadful trifling with people's constitutions!" said Mrs Taft.

After this, it came to be held in various quarters that Lydgate played even with respectable constitutions for his own purposes, and how much more likely that in his flighty experimenting he should make sixes and sevens of hospital patients. Especially it was to be expected, as the landlady of the Tankard had said, that he would recklessly cut up their dead bodies. For Lydgate having attended Mrs Goby, who died apparently of a heart-disease not very clearly expressed in the symptoms, too daringly asked leave of her relatives to open the body, and thus gave an offence quickly spreading beyond Parley Street, where that lady had long resided on an income such as made this association of her body with the victims of Burke and Hare a flagrant insult to her memory.[17]

This is a long way from Felix Holt, the idealist who has to work, but who has very strong ideas of the kinds of work he does *not* want to do. Here the speaker's tone is moral and reflects his class loyalty:

"I'm not speaking lightly," said Felix. "If I had not seen that I was making a hog of myself very fast, and that pig-wash, even if I could have got plenty of it, was a poor sort of thing, I should never have looked life fairly in the face to see what was to be done with it. I laughed out loud at last to think of a poor devil like me, in a Scotch garret, with my stockings out at heel and a shilling or two to be dissipated upon, with a smell of raw haggis mounting from below, and old women breathing gin as they passed me on the stairs – wanting to turn my life into easy pleasure. Then I began to see what else it could be turned into. Not much, perhaps. This world is not a very fine place for a good many of the people in it. But I've made up my mind it shan't be the worse for me, if I can help it. They may tell me I can't alter the world – that there must be a certain number of sneaks and robbers in it, and if I don't lie and filch somebody else will. Well, then, somebody else shall, for I won't. That's the upshot of my conversion, Mr Lyon, if you want to know it."

Mr Lyon removed his hand from Felix's shoulder and walked about again. "Did you sit under any preacher at Glasgow, young man?"

"No: I heard most of the preachers once, but I never wanted to hear them twice."

The good Rufus was not without a slight rising of resentment at this young man's want of reverence. It was not yet plain whether he wanted to hear twice the preacher in Malthouse Yard. But the resentful feeling was carefully repressed: a soul in so peculiar a condition must be dealt with delicately.

"And now, may I ask," he said, "what course you mean to take, after hindering your mother from making and selling these drugs? I speak no more in their favour after what you have said. God forbid that I should strive to hinder you from seeking whatsoever things are honest and honourable. But your mother is advanced in years; she needs comfortable sustenance; you have doubtless considered how you may make her amends? 'He that provideth not for his own –' I trust you respect the authority that so speaks. And I will not suppose that, after beng tender of conscience towards strangers, you will be careless towards your mother. There be indeed some who, taking a mighty charge on their shoulders, must perforce leave their households to Providence, and to the care of humbler brethren, but in such a case the call must be clear."

"I shall keep my mother as well – nay, better – than she has kept herself. She has always been frugal. With my watch and clock cleaning, and teaching one or two little chaps that I've got to come to me, I can earn enough. As for me, I can live on bran porridge. I have the stomach of a rhinoceros."

"But for a young man so well furnished as you, who can questionless write a good hand and keep books, were it not well to seek some higher situation as clerk or assistant? I could speak to Brother Muscat, who is well acquainted with all such openings. Any place in Pendrell's Bank, I fear, is now closed against such as are not Churchmen. It used not to be so, but a year ago he discharged Brother Bodkin, although he was a valuable servant. Still, something might be found. There are ranks and degrees – and those who can serve in the higher must not unadvisedly change what seems to be a providential appointment. Your poor mother is not altogether –"

"Excuse me, Mr Lyon; I've had all that out with my mother, and I may as well save you any trouble by telling you that my mind has been made up about that a long while ago. I'll take no employment that obliges me to prop up my chin with a high cravat, and wear straps, and pass the livelong day with a set of fellows who spend their spare money on shirt-pins. That sort of work is really lower than many handicrafts; it only happens to be paid out of proportion. That's why I set myself to learn the watchmaking trade. My father was a weaver first of all. It would have been better for him if he had remained a weaver. I came home through Lancashire and saw an uncle of mine who is a weaver still. I mean to stick to the class I belong to – people who don't follow the fashions."

Mr Lyon was silent a few moments. This dialogue was far from plain sailing; he was not certain of his latitude and longitude. If the despiser of Glasgow preachers had been arguing in favour of gin and Sabbath-breaking, Mr Lyon's course would have been clearer. "Well, well," he said, deliberately, "it is true that St Paul exercised the trade of tent-making, though he was learned in all the wisdom of the Rabbis."

"St Paul was a wise man," said Felix. "Why should I want to get into the middle class because I have some learning? The most of the middle class are as ignorant as the working people about everything that doesn't belong to their own Brummagem life. That's how the working men are left to foolish devices and keep worsening themselves: the best heads among them forsake their born comrades, and go in for a house with a high door-step and a brass knocker."

Mr Lyon stroked his mouth and chin, perhaps because he felt some disposition to smile; and it would not be well to smile too readily at what seemed but a weedy resemblance of Christian unworldliness. On the contrary, there might be a dangerous snare in an unsanctified outstepping of average Christian practice.[18]

Felix is not conventionally motivated, but one doubts whether there were any like him for George Eliot to draw from life. His chosen occupation and his determinedly working-class affiliations show that his work lies in his words. He is an invented not an experienced character.

George Eliot's range covers rural, urban, professional and domestic occupations. Her fictional characters in their regions are people at work.

# 9. Nature and Nurture

Some of the extracts quoted from George Eliot's works in the preceding chapters show her mixed affiliations to country and town. Her return to the Midland landscape – and townscape – is frequent: sometimes it is loving, sometimes ironic. For her, landscape is the register of tradition and change. The past is her past seen with the eye of the exile still attached in the memory.

As early as 1936 Blanche Colton Williams asserted that some of the notes which George Eliot left on the back of a postcard "show that she would have met the challenge that she never reverted to memories of days other than of earlier childhood."[1] These postcard notes for what was apparently to be a new novel are more than offset by the ten pages identified in her hand by William Baker (now in the Hugh Walpole collection); these are the opening of a novel which appears to have been started in 1877–8 and set her "more familiar provincial scene". The tone may be unfamiliar, but the region is not:

[1]

This story will take you if you please into Central England and into what have been often called the Good old times. It is a telescope you may look through a telephone you may put your ear to: but there is no compulsion. If you only care about the present fashions in dress & talk in politics and religion pass on without offence as you would pass the man with the telescope in the Place de la Concorde, not mounting to look through his lenses and then abusing him because he does not show you something less distant and more to your taste than the aspects of the heavenly bodies. Allow those who like it to interest themselves in the sad or joyous fortunes of people who saw the beginning of the Times newspaper, trembled or felt defiant at the name of Buonoparte, defended bull baiting, were excited by the writing of Cobbett and submitted to some invisible power which ordained that their back waist buttons should be nine inches higher than those of their Fathers. These people did not manage the land well; they knew little about subsoils and top dressings, allowed trees and hedgerows to take title of their acres & in all ways helped the weather to make bad harvests. But their farming was picturesque & it suited the preservation of game. A large population of hares partridges & pheasants had short but let us hope merry lives between the times when they were made war on by the superior race who intervened between them & the unscrupulous foxes that would have killed & eaten them without ulterior views. And as many foxes were allowed to remain & enjoy their known pleasure in being hunted

[2]

were handsomely provided with covers. It was a bosky beautiful landscape that was
to be seen almost everywhere in our rich Central plain, when a little rise of ground
gave the horseman a possibility of seeing over a stretch of tree-studded hedgerows
enclosing here & there the long roofs of a homestead & merging in woods which gave
a wide-spread hint of the landowner's mansion hidden with its park & pools &
resounding rookery far away from the vulgar gaze.

One such mansion, whose parapet & curling smoke were to be seen by the traveller
in riding down the slope from Upper Lawtrey, was called Longwater & so far as the
parishioners generally cared to know had always been the property of the Pollexfens,
though it was understood that the family had waxed in importance & that some time
or other their Estate had been enlarged. For there was another house in the parish,
called Gatlands, which was believed always to have belonged to the Forrests until the
Pollexfens bought it & the former owners sank into tenants, at the same time entering
into a further relation with their landlord which had lasted ever since.[2]

There is a strong reminiscence of the Introduction to *Felix Holt*. The sense of
period is firm, and the method of generalizing a historical context before
introducing the narrative particularity is evident. The period corresponds to
that of *Adam Bede*; the subsoil is being worked again. The irony about men,
game and foxes, though unpolished, is familiar.

For George Eliot, nature and nurture are interactive. Sometimes she reflects
social conditions, sometimes she uses nature as a symbol, sometimes she uses
contrast, and at times she creates an unsparing realism. Her first discussion
of realism comes in her essay on Riehl's "The Natural History of German
Life". The title is significant, since her future fictions were a natural history
of English provincial life. Here is the quotation which looks closely at Riehl
but also at rural Warwickshire:

Probably, if we could ascertain the images called up by the terms "the people,"
"the masses," "the proletariat," "the peasantry," by many who theorize on those
bodies with eloquence, or who legislate for them without eloquence, we should find
that they indicate almost as small an amount of concrete knowledge – that they are
as far from completely representing the complex facts summed up in the collective
term, as the railway images of our non-locomotive gentleman. How little the real
characteristics of the working-classes are known to those who are outside them, how
little their natural history has been studied, is sufficiently disclosed by our Art as well
as by our political and social theories. Where, in our picture exhibitions, shall we find
a group of true peasantry? What English artist even attempts to rival in truthfulness
such studies of popular life as the pictures of Teniers or the ragged boys of Murillo?
Even one of the greatest painters of the pre-eminently realistic school, while, in his
picture of "The Hireling Shepherd," he gave us a landscape of marvellous truthfulness,
placed a pair of peasants in the foreground who were not much more real than the
idyllic swains and damsels of our chimney ornaments. Only a total absence of
acquaintance and sympathy with our peasantry, could give a moment's popularity to

such a picture as "Cross Purposes," where we have a peasant girl who looks as if she knew L.E.L.'s poems by heart, and English rustics, whose costume seems to indicate that they are meant for ploughmen, with exotic features that remind us of a handsome *primo tenore*. Rather than such cockney sentimentality as this, as an education for the taste and sympathies, we prefer the most crapulous group of boors that Teniers ever painted. But even those among our painters who aim at giving the rustic type of features, who are far above the effeminate feebleness of the "Keepsake" style, treat their subjects under the influence of traditions and prepossessions rather than of direct observation. The notion that peasants are joyous, that the typical moment to represent a man in a smock-frock is when he is cracking a joke and showing a row of sound teeth, that cottage matrons are usually buxom, and village children necessarily rosy and merry, are prejudices difficult to dislodge from the artistic mind, which looks for its subjects into literature instead of life. The painter is still under the influence of idyllic literature, which has always expressed the imagination of the cultivated and town-bred, rather than the truth of rustic life. Idyllic ploughmen are jocund when they drive their team afield; idyllic shepherds make bashful love under hawthorn bushes; idyllic villagers dance in the chequered shade and refresh themselves, not immoderately, with spicy nut-brown ale. But no one who has seen much of actual ploughmen thinks them jocund; no one who is well acquainted with the English peasantry can pronounce them merry. The slow gaze, in which no sense of beauty beams, no humour twinkles, – the slow utterance, and the heavy slouching walk, remind one rather of that melancholy animal the camel, than of the sturdy countryman, with striped stockings, red waistcoat, and hat aside, who represents the traditional English peasant. Observe a company of haymakers. When you see them at a distance, tossing up the forkfuls of hay in the golden light, while the wagon creeps slowly with its increasing burthen over the meadow, and the bright green space which tells of work done gets larger and larger, you pronounce the scene "smiling," and you think these companions in labour must be as bright and cheerful as the picture to which they give animation. Approach nearer, and you will certainly find that haymaking time is a time for joking, especially if there are women among the labourers; but the coarse laugh that bursts out every now and then, and expresses the triumphant taunt, is as far as possible from your conception of idyllic merriment. That delicious effervescence of the mind which we call fun, has no equivalent for the northern peasant, except tipsy revelry; the only realm of fancy and imagination for the English clown exists at the bottom of the third quart pot.[3]

Here is the beginning of the line which runs from Wiry Ben in *Adam Bede* to Dagley in *Middlemarch*. The essay allows for irony while the fictions embody the Dutch realism which George Eliot so praised and used as the basis for much of her own art.

Nature can provide an aesthetically pleasing background to the fiction of human nature and certain scenes, like those in the Chase in *Adam Bede*, provide a symbolic commentary, an ironic register of situation and event. Marian Evans's descriptions of nature in her letters generally lack the warmth and identification apparent in her fiction. Sometimes there is even the suggestion of self-indulgence or of routine description being undertaken:

I am in the country, without the trouble of packing up: I see the autumn berries, I snuff the peculiar freshness of the autumn air between the hedgerows in the green lane, and the new soil the plough is turning over in the next field; or I wrap my cloak round me and enjoy the December hoar frost that defines every lingering brown leaf on the brambles or the young oaks; or I please myself in detecting the very earliest spring buds, and the delicate hints of colour on the bough tips; or I hear the swirl of the scythe as I watch the delicate grasses trembling under the eager flight and restless alighting of the humming insects; or I stand entranced before the glory of form and colour in the ripe full-eared corn field.[4]

Or this:

Is not this a true autumn day? Just the still melancholy that I love – that makes life and nature harmonize. The birds are all consulting about their migrations, the trees are putting on the hectic or the pallid hues of decay, and begin to strew the ground that one's very footsteps may not disturb the repose of earth and air, while they give us a scent that is a perfect anodyne to the restless spirit. Delicious Autumn! my very soul is wedded to it, and if I were a bird I would fly about the earth seeking the successive autumns.[5]

These are a long way from the appraisal of nature in her stories and novels. In "Mr Gilfil's Love Story", for example, the development of Caterina is given a natural analogy:

While Cheverel Manor was growing from ugliness into beauty, Caterina too was growing from a little yellow bantling into a whiter maiden, with no positive beauty indeed, but with a certain light airy grace, which, with her large appealing dark eyes and a voice that, in its low-toned tenderness, recalled the love-notes of the stock-dove, gave her a more than usual charm.[6]

Even here there is a certain straining after effect, the phrase from "voice" to "stock-dove" being added presumably in proof, since it is not in the manuscript. The opening of the next chapter has a characteristic symbolic elevation as she returns to her childhood with artistic awareness. The fateful summer of 1788 has international, local and personal crises in the fictional sequence. The personal crisis is Caterina's, seen against natural process. The device, to be used again in *Adam Bede*, contrasts outward beauty with inward, undefined apprehension:

The inexorable ticking of the clock is like the throb of pain to sensations made keen by a sickening fear. And so it is with the great clock-work of nature. Daisies and buttercups give way to the brown waving grasses, tinged with the warm red sorrel; the waving grasses are swept away, and the meadows lie like emeralds set in the bushy hedgerows; the tawny-tipped corn begins to bow with the weight of the full ear; the reapers are bending amongst it, and it soon stands in sheaves; then, presently, the patches of yellow stubble lie side by side with streaks of dark red earth, which the plough is turning up in preparation for the new-thrashed seed. And this passage from beauty to beauty, which to the happy is like the flow of a melody, measures for many a human heart the approach of foreseen anguish – seems hurrying on the moment when the shadow of dread will be followed up by the reality of despair. How cruelly hasty that summer of 1788 seemed to Caterina! Surely the roses vanished earlier, and the berries on the mountain-ash were more impatient to redden, and bring on the autumn, when she would be face to face with her misery, and witness Antony giving all his gentle tones, tender words, and soft looks to another.[7]

This is movingly, if somewhat crudely, effective. Fictional fate is made as irrevocable as the seasons, and correspondences in nature are made to reflect mental and emotional states. In *Adam Bede* there is a similar kind of usage, but George Eliot also probes and reveals the enclosed rustic environment to suggest that, in the mind of a simple man, nature and fate are interconnected on a level of inherited superstition. Here Adam is interrupted as he works on the coffin in the small hours:

Adam, very much startled, went at once to the door and opened it. Nothing was there; all was still, as when he opened it an hour before; the leaves were motionless, and the light of the stars showed the placid fields on both sides of the brook quite empty of visible life. Adam walked round the house, and still saw nothing except a rat which darted into the woodshed as he passed. He went in again, wondering; the sound was so peculiar, that the moment he heard it, it called up the image of the willow wand striking the door. He could not help a little shudder, as he remembered how often his mother had told him of just such a sound coming as a sign when some one was dying. Adam was not a man to be gratuitously superstitious; but he had the blood of the peasant in him as well as of the artisan, and a peasant can no more help believing in a traditional superstition than a horse can help trembling when he sees a camel. Besides, he had that mental combination which is at once humble in the region of mystery, and keen in the region of knowledge: it was the depth of his reverence quite as much as his hard common-sense, which gave him his disinclination to doctrinal religion, and he often checked Seth's argumentative spiritualism by saying, "Eh, it's a big mystery; thee know'st but little about it." And so it happened that Adam was at once penetrating and credulous. If a new building had fallen down and he had been told that this was a divine judgment, he would have said, "May be; but the bearing o' the roof and walls wasn't right, else it wouldn't ha' come down;" yet he believed in dreams and prognostics, and to his dying day he bated his breath a little when he told the story of the stroke with the willow wand. I tell it as he told it, not attempting to reduce it to its natural elements: in our eagerness to explain impressions, we often lose our hold of the sympathy that comprehends them.
But he had the best antidote against imaginative dread in the necessity for getting on with the coffin, and for the next ten minutes his hammer was ringing so uninterruptedly, that other sounds, if there were any, might well be overpowered. A pause came, however, when he had to take up his ruler, and now again came the strange rap, and again Gyp howled. Adam was at the door without the loss of a moment; but again all was still, and the starlight showed there was nothing but the dew-laden grass in front of the cottage.[8]

205

Here the interaction is between nature and human nature – the isolation, the night, the peculiar circumstances, the imagery of Adam's thought all contribute to the artistic coherence, the simulated reality, and the immediate dramatic effect. As so often in George Eliot there is an element of prophecy, convincingly in character there. Writing to John Blackwood about this incident she observed, "Some readers seem not to have understood what I meant, namely that it is in Adam's peasant blood and nurture to believe in this, and that he narrated it with awed belief to his dying day. That is not a fancy of my own brain, but a matter of observation, and is in my mind an important feature in Adam's character."[9] We notice her use of the word "nurture", her insistence on Adam's consciousness and the natural setting Adam is placed against, a background-foreground of nature: it is, as we see from his thoughts, the best part of his nurture, and it expresses George Eliot's sense of interconnectedness.

The experience arises from Adam's rooted acceptance of things in the natural and supernatural world. In *The Mill* nature witnesses a different experience. Book Fifth is "Wheat and Tares", the first chapter "In the Red Deeps", and the fifth is given the ominous natural image of "The Cloven Tree". In that first chapter nature provides an index to Maggie's feelings – past, present, and to come. The passage below is pregnant with intimate identification: Maggie's emotional nurture is expressed through the physical actuality of nature – her "present Past, her root of piety" – which is to be the witness of her longing, muted need focused in the prospect of seeing Philip Wakem. In all the intense inwardness of *The Mill* the outwardness provides its own commentary:

You may see her now, as she walks down the favourite turning, and enters the Deeps by a narrow path through a group of Scotch firs – her tall figure and old lavender gown visible through an hereditary black silk shawl of some wide-meshed net-like material; and now she is sure of being unseen, she takes off her bonnet and ties it over her arm. One would certainly suppose her to be farther on in life than her seventeenth year – perhaps because of the slow resigned sadness of the glance, from which all search and unrest seem to have departed, perhaps because her broad-chested figure has the mould of early womanhood. Youth and health have withstood well the involuntary and voluntary hardships of her lot, and the nights in which she has lain on the hard floor for a penance have left no obvious trace; the eyes are liquid, the brown cheek is firm and rounded, the full lips are red. With her dark colouring and jet crown surmounting her tall figure, she seems to have a sort of kinship with the grand Scotch firs, at which she is looking up as if she loved them well. Yet one has a sense of uneasiness in looking at her – a sense of opposing elements, of which a fierce collision is imminent: surely there is a hushed expression, such as one often sees in older faces under borderless caps, out of keeping with the resistant youth, which one expects to flash out in a sudden, passionate glance, that will dissipate all the quietude, like a damp fire leaping out again when all seemed safe.

But Maggie herself was not uneasy at this moment. She was calmly enjoying the free air, while she looked up at the old fir-trees, and thought that those broken ends of branches were the records of past storms, which had only made the red stems soar higher. But while her eyes were still turned upward, she became conscious of a moving shadow cast by the evening sun on the grassy path before her, and looked down with a startled gesture to see Philip Wakem, who first raised his hat, and then, blushing deeply, came forward to her and put out his hand. Maggie, too, coloured with surprise, which soon gave way to pleasure. She put out her hand and looked down at the deformed figure before her with frank eyes, filled for the moment with nothing but the memory of her child's feelings – a memory that was always strong in her. She was the first to speak.[10]

The Red Deeps is central to the novel: it is Maggie's retreat, consolation, and a muted fulfilment. It provides nurture. There is a considered recall of Maggie's past and present, and the warm omniscient tone gives us Maggie's state of mind, a mood of renunciation contradicted by the "indulgence" of her walk. She becomes a living part of the scene, and the placing is important; the meeting with Philip, which leads to other meetings, is a prelude to the conflict with Tom which so undermines her. Her "sort of kinship with the grand Scotch firs" underlines her affinity and her "opposing elements".

Nature as the provider of nurture, and the background against which change is registered, appears at the end of the first three stories: the visit to the tomb in "Amos", the Epilogue in "Gilfil", and the final paragraph in "Janet's Repentance", but in *The Mill* it is animated and expanded:

## CONCLUSION.

Nature repairs her ravages – repairs them with her sunshine, and with human labour. The desolation wrought by that flood, had left little visible trace on the face of the earth, five years after. The fifth autumn was rich in golden corn-stacks, rising in thick clusters among the distant hedgerows; the wharves and warehouses on the Floss were busy again, with echoes of eager voices, with hopeful lading and unlading.

And every man and woman mentioned in this history was still living – except those whose end we know.

Nature repairs her ravages – but not all. The uptorn trees are not rooted again; the parted hills are left scarred: if there is a new growth, the trees are not the same as the old, and the hills underneath their green vesture bear the marks of the past rending. To the eyes that have dwelt on the past, there is no thorough repair.

Dorlcote Mill was rebuilt. And Dorlcote churchyard, – where the brick grave that held a father whom we know, was found with the stone laid prostrate upon it after the flood, – had recovered all its grassy order and decent quiet.

Near that brick grave there was a tomb erected, very soon after the flood, for two bodies that were found in close embrace; and it was visited at different moments by two men who both felt that their keenest joy and keenest sorrow were for ever buried there.

One of them visited the tomb again with a sweet face beside him – but that was years after.

The other was always solitary. His great companionship was among the trees of the Red Deeps, where the buried joy seemed still to hover – like a revisiting spirit.[11]

The rhetoric is insistent and moving: and if the natural cycle from "repairs her ravages" to "grassy order and decent quiet" outlines the flux of existence, there is also the presence of Philip and the "great companionship" of the Red Deeps. His fleeting happiness in the past and his solace (we feel) in the present and future are set in the childhood regions of Marian Evans and the prose of George Eliot.

Raveloe, in its North Warwickshire location, is as rural as any area in George Eliot's work. Here nature is seasonally lush or bleak, as it is in *Adam Bede*. We are aware of the winter hardness of labouring lives; we remember the misty lanes through which Dunstan Cass walks after the horse Wildfire is killed in a fall, and how he enters Silas's cottage, steals the gold, and disappears into the mist. The mists eventually dissolve to disclose his crime fifteen years later when his body is found in the Stone Pits. There is a crueller journey when Godfrey's wife Molly toils through the snow on New Year's Eve. She struggles with her child and collapses, drugged, to die beneath the snow-laden bush where Silas discovers her, having first discovered his lost "gold" in the shape of Eppie asleep on his hearth. The two deaths, Dunstan's and Molly's, occur at the dead times of nature.

But nature is also seen as celebration, as benign, idyllic, and related to work, good feelings and altruism. Some figures in George Eliot's fable have passed through wintry suffering and come out into the sunshine of happiness:

The gold had asked that he should sit weaving longer and longer, deafened and blinded more and more to all things except the monotony of his loom and the repetition of his web; but Eppie called him away from his weaving, and made him think all its pauses a holiday, re-awakening his senses with her fresh life, even to the old winter-flies that came crawling forth in the early spring sunshine, and warming him into joy because *she* had joy.

And when the sunshine grew strong and lasting, so that the buttercups were thick in the meadows, Silas might be seen in the sunny mid-day, or in the late afternoon when the shadows were lengthening under the hedgerows, strolling out with uncovered head to carry Eppie beyond the Stone-pits to where the flowers grew, till they reached some favourite bank where he could sit down, while Eppie toddled to pluck the flowers, and make remarks to the winged things that murmured happily above the bright petals, calling "Dad-dad's" attention continually by bringing him the flowers. Then she would turn her ear to some sudden bird-note, and Silas learned to please her by making signs of hushed stillness, that they might listen for the note to come again: so that when it came, she set up her small back and laughed with gurgling triumph. Sitting on the banks in this way, Silas began to look for the once familiar herbs again; and as the leaves, with their unchanged outline and markings, lay on his palm, there was a sense of crowding remembrances from which he turned away timidly, taking refuge in Eppie's little world, that lay lightly on his enfeebled spirit.

As the child's mind was growing into knowledge, his mind was growing into memory: as her life unfolded, his soul, long stupefied in a cold narrow prison, was unfolding too, and trembling gradually into full consciousness.[12]

This is very different from the pathetic nature in "Mr Gilfil": the simple language invokes a direct correspondence between spring sunshine and the love of Silas and Eppie. In it the author comes to a kind of motherhood. Silas discovers fatherhood and the rediscovery of the herbs revives his creativity. In representing the nature she knew so well George Eliot releases a human nature long trapped "in a cold narrow prison". We recall the epigraph to the novel and the author's assertion that since Wordsworth was dead no one else would be interested in her story. The seasons reflect their own innocent growths, and Silas and Eppie, each pure in nature, personalize that innocence. In a fine variation George Eliot shows Eppie running away. The natural background is used to convey Silas's apprehension – the tall grass is an obstacle, the pond is a threat, but the ease and absorption of the child is evident:

The cold drops stood on his brow. How long had she been out? There was one hope – that she had crept through the stile and got into the fields where he habitually took her to stroll. But the grass was high in the meadow, and there was no descrying her, if she were there, except by a close search that would be a trespass on Mr Osgood's crop. Still, that misdemeanour must be committed; and poor Silas, after peering all round the hedgerows, traversed the grass, beginning with perturbed vision to see Eppie behind every group of red sorrel, and to see her moving always farther off as he approached. The meadow was searched in vain; and he got over the stile into the next field, looking with dying hope towards a small pond which was now reduced to its summer shallowness, so as to leave a wide margin of good adhesive mud. Here, however, sat Eppie, discoursing cheerfully to her own small boot, which she was using as a bucket to convey the water into a deep hoof-mark, while her little naked foot was planted comfortably on a cushion of olive-green mud. A red-headed calf was observing her with alarmed doubt through the opposite hedge.
Here was clearly a case of aberration in a christened child which demanded severe treatment; but Silas, overcome with convulsive joy at finding his treasure again, could do nothing but snatch her up, and cover her with half-sobbing kisses.[13]

In the same chapter she defines the awakening, fulfilment and love:

There was love between him and the child that blent them into one, and there was love between the child and the world – from men and women with parental looks and tones, to the red lady-birds and the round pebbles.
Silas began now to think of the Raveloe life entirely in relation to Eppie: she must have everything that was good in Raveloe; and he listened docilely, that he might come to understand better what this life was, from which, for fifteen years, he had

stood aloof as from a strange thing, with which he could have no communion: as some man who has a precious plant to which he would give a nurturing home in a new soil, thinks of the rain and sunshine, and all influences, in relation to his nursling, and asks industriously for all knowledge that will help him to satisfy the wants of the searching roots, or to guard leaf and bud from invading harm.[14]

In other passages too the natural analogy is developed and strengthened: Aaron Winthrop for instance is the gardener cultivating a domestic paradise for Eppie: they will marry and share their home with her foster-father.

The Conclusion follows the pattern of the early works:

There was one time of the year which was held in Raveloe to be especially suitable for a wedding. It was when the great lilacs and laburnums in the old-fashioned gardens showed their golden and purple wealth above the lichen-tinted walls, and when there were calves still young enough to want bucketfuls of fragrant milk. People were not so busy then as they must become when the full cheese-making and mowing had set in; and besides, it was a time when a light bridal dress could be worn with comfort and seen to advantage.

Happily the sunshine fell more warmly than usual on the lilac tufts the morning that Eppie was married, for her dress was a very light one.[15]

The wedding is celebrated at a time of harmony in nature. The fable is over but George Eliot, reaching back to her roots, has shown that seasonal cold and sunshine, the outdoors of rural working lives, are central to the experiences of her characters. The Wordsworthian spirit infuses her known locality, and is indeed "emotion recollected in tranquillity". The short novel is a wise, tender and optimistic study of the relationship between nature and nurture, of what is natural and what is acquired as the result of experience. The development and the acquisition of goodness in individuals expresses the capacity for growth which is recorded in nature.

We have already noted the panoramic effects in the Introduction to *Felix Holt*, their emphatic chronology inlaid with childhood memories and a finely discriminatory perspective. The first chapter of the novel contains the first printed use of the motto. (Some were written for *Romola* but discarded.) From *Felix Holt* onwards George Eliot's use of the motto becomes a kind of index or signposting to the narrative itself. In the first chapter here motto and the opening paragraphs coalesce. The motto marks the consciousness of Mrs Transome, hopeful, apprehensive and guilt-ridden. There follows a natural scene and setting: the two sides of nature, the weary and the unaware, correspond to the two sides of human nature here, the hope and the fear, or even the two perspectives of the house, the decayed and the busy. The central figure of motto and scene is the waiting Mrs Transome, recording change in herself and fearful of change in the returning son of the motto who is so soon to arrive as fact in the narrative:

# CHAPTER I.

He left me when the down upon his lip
Lay like the shadow of a hovering kiss.
"Beautiful mother, do not grieve," he said;
"I will be great, and build our fortunes high,
And you shall wear the longest train at court,
And look so queenly, all the lords shall say,
'She is a royal changeling: there's some crown
Lacks the right head, since hers wears nought but braids,'"
O, he is coming now – but I am grey:
And he –

On the 1st of September, in the memorable year 1832, some one was expected at Transome Court. As early as two o'clock in the afternoon the aged lodge-keeper had opened the heavy gate, green as the tree trunks were green with nature's powdery paint, deposited year after year. Already in the village of Little Treby, which lay on the side of the steep hill not far off the lodge gates, the elder matrons sat in their best gowns at the few cottage doors bordering the road, that they might be ready to get up and make their curtsy when a travelling carriage should come in sight; and beyond the village several small boys were stationed on the look-out, intending to run a race to the barn-like old church, where the sexton waited in the belfry ready to set one bell in joyful agitation just at the right moment.

The old lodge-keeper had opened the gate and left it in the charge of his lame wife, because he was wanted at the Court to sweep away the leaves, and perhaps to help in the stables. For though Transome Court was a large mansion, built in the fashion of Queen Anne's time, with a park and grounds as fine as any to be seen in Loamshire, there were very few servants about it. Especially, it seemed, there must be a lack of gardeners; for, except on the terrace surrounded with a stone parapet in front of the house, where there was a parterre kept with some neatness, grass had spread itself over the gravel walks, and over all the low mounds once carefully cut as black beds for the shrubs and larger plants. Many of the windows had the shutters closed, and under the grand Scotch fir that stooped towards one corner, the brown fir-needles of many years lay in a small stone balcony in front of two such darkened windows. All round, both near and far, there were grand trees, motionless in the still sunshine, and, like all large motionless things, seeming to add to the stillness. Here and there a leaf fluttered down; petals fell in a silent shower; a heavy moth floated by, and, when it settled, seemed to fall wearily; the tiny birds alighted on the walks, and hopped about in perfect tranquillity; even a stray rabbit sat nibbling a leaf that was to its liking, in the middle of a grassy space, with an air that seemed quite impudent in so timid a creature. No sound was to be heard louder than a sleepy hum, and the soft monotony of running water hurrying on to the river that divided the park. Standing on the south or east side of the house, you would never have guessed that an arrival was expected.

But on the west side, where the carriage entrance was, the gates under the stone archway were thrown open; and so was the double door of the entrance-hall, letting in the warm light on the scagliola pillars, the marble statues, and the broad stone staircase, with its matting worn into large holes. And, stronger sign of expectation than all, from one of the doors which surrounded the entrance-hall, there came forth from time to time a lady, who walked lightly over the polished stone floor, and stood on the door-steps and watched and listened. She walked lightly, for her figure was slim and finely formed, though she was between fifty and sixty. She was a tall, proud-looking woman, with abundant grey hair, dark eyes and eyebrows, and a somewhat eagle-like yet not unfeminine face. Her tight-fitting black dress was much worn; the fine lace of her cuffs and collar, and of the small veil which fell backwards over her high comb, was visibly mended; but rare jewels flashed on her hands, which lay on her folded black-clad arms like finely-cut onyx cameos.[16]

The Scotch fir and the other trees are "grand", like Mrs Transome in her movements and flexibility. The combination of natural peace and neglect, the absence of gardeners and the presence of undisturbed wild life tell the story of Mrs Transome's life. Here uncultivated nature is the index to imposed economies.

The motto to Chapter III establishes the mixed nature of the Treby Magna location: it is the urban-rural scene of Marian Evans's years at Griff in Nuneaton and Foleshill in Coventry:

'Twas town, yet country too; you felt the warmth
Of clustering houses in the wintry time;
Supped with a friend, and went by lantern home.
Yet from your chamber window you could hear
The tiny bleat of new-yeaned lambs, or see
The children bend beside the hedgerow banks
To pluck the primroses.

Treby Magna, on which the Reform Bill had thrust the new honour of being a polling-place, had been, at the beginning of the century, quite a typical old market-town, lying in pleasant sleepiness among green pastures, with a rush-fringed river meandering through them. Its principal street had various handsome and tall-windowed brick houses with walled gardens behind them; and at the end, where it widened into the marketplace, there was the cheerful rough-stuccoed front of that excellent inn, the Marquis of Granby, where the farmers put up their gigs, not only on fair and market days, but on exceptional Sundays when they came to church.[17]

Such a mixture implies change, and *Felix Holt* is about political change and personal change. The motto is nostalgic for a personal past and an idealized innocence, appropriately for a story about moving away from the past.

Nature provides a foreground to the courtship of Esther by Harold Transome. Nature and nurture are in our our minds as Harold brings the conversation round to his need:

One fine February day, when already the gold and purple crocuses were out on the terrace – one of those flattering days which sometimes precede the north-east winds of March, and make believe that the coming spring will be enjoyable – a very striking group, of whom Esther and Harold made a part, came out at mid-day to walk upon the gravel at Transome Court. They did not, as usual, go towards the pleasure-grounds on the eastern side, because Mr Lingon, who was one of them, was going home, and his road lay through the stone gateway into the park.

Uncle Lingon, who disliked painful confidences, and preferred knowing "no mischief of anybody," had not objected to being let into the important secret about Esther, and was sure at once that the whole affair, instead of being a misfortune, was a piece of excellent luck. For himself, he did not profess to be a judge of women, but she seemed to have all the "points," and to carry herself as well as Arabella did, which was saying a good deal. Honest Jack Lingon's first impressions quickly became traditions, which no subsequent evidence could disturb. He was fond of his sister, and seemed never to be conscious of any change for the worse in her since their early time. He considered that man a beast who said anything unpleasant about the persons to whom he was attached. It was not that he winked; his wide-open eyes saw nothing but what his easy disposition inclined him to see. Harold was good fellow; a clever chap; and Esther's peculiar fitness for him, under all the circumstances, was extraordinary: it reminded him of something in the classics, though he couldn't think exactly what – in fact, a memory was a nasty uneasy thing. Esther was always glad when the old Rector came. With an odd contrariety to her former niceties she liked his rough attire and careless frank speech; they were something not point device that seemed to connect the life of Transome Court with that rougher, commoner world where her home had been.

She and Harold were walking a little in advance of the rest of the party, who were retarded by various causes. Old Mr Transome, wrapped in a cloth cloak trimmed with sable, and with a soft warm cap also trimmed with fur on his head, had a shuffling uncertain walk. Little Harry was dragging a toy-vehicle, on the seat of which he had insisted on tying Moro, with a piece of scarlet drapery round him, making him look like a barbaric prince in a chariot. Moro, having little imagination, objected to this, and barked with feeble snappishness as the tyrannous lad ran forward, then whirled the chariot round, and ran back to "Gappa," then came to a dead stop, which overset the chariot, that he might watch Uncle Lingon's water-spaniel run for the hurled stick and bring it in his mouth. Nimrod kept close to his old master's legs, glancing with much indifference at this youthful ardour about sticks – he had "gone through all that;" and Dominic walked by, looking on blandly, and taking care both of young and old. Mrs Transome was not there.

Looking back and seeing that they were a good deal in advance of the rest, Esther and Harold paused.

"What do you think about thinning the trees over there?" said Harold, pointing with his stick. "I have a bit of a notion that if they were divided into clumps so as to show the oaks beyond, it would be a great improvement. It would give an idea of extent that is lost now. And there might be some very pretty clumps got out of those mixed trees. What so you think?"

"I should think it would be an improvement. One likes a 'beyond' everywhere. But I never heard you express yourself so dubiously," said Esther, looking at him rather archly: "you generally see things so clearly, and are so convinced, that I shall begin to feel quite tottering if I find you in uncertainty. Pray don't begin to be doubtful; it is so infectious."

"You think me a great deal too sure – too confident?" said Harold.

"Not at all. It is an immense advantage to know your own will, when you always mean to have it."

"But suppose I couldn't get it, in spite of meaning?" said Harold, with a beaming inquiry in his eyes.[18]

The crocuses, the water-spaniel, and the trees, make us aware of the background to the conversation, the description, the plot revelations and, significantly and symbolically, the fact that "Mrs Transome was not there". Harold's approach to Esther is a tacit introduction of intent; and it also looks back to Jermyn's tree-felling and the deterioration of the estate, Esther's legal inheritance. Harold's concern for appearance – "so as to show the oaks beyond" – is an index to his character. It is admirably countered by Esther's different emphasis on the word "beyond". If we read this quickly, it is a background; if we read it slowly, we become aware of its symbolic and moral expansiveness. We are also aware of the difference in nurture between Harold and Esther.

In *Middlemarch* the town and its environs are a background to the narrative. The villages of Freshitt and Lowick are integral to the action, but *Middlemarch*, unlike the earlier works, is only occasionally close to the earth, that is, if we except the earthiness of public opinion.

Mrs Cadwallader's introduction is prefixed by a chapter motto which has clearly been written with the character in mind who sets off the narrative:

> "My lady's tongue is like the meadow blades,
> That cut you stroking them with idle hand.
> Nice cutting is her function: she divides
> With spiritual edge the millet-seed,
> And makes intangible savings."

As Mr Casaubon's carriage was passing out of the gateway, it arrested the entrance of a pony phaeton driven by a lady with a servant seated behind. It was doubtful whether the recognition had been mutual, for Mr Casaubon was looking absently before him; but the lady was quick-eyed, and threw a nod and a "how do you do?" in the nick of time. In spite of her shabby bonnet and very old Indian shawl, it was plain that the lodge-keeper regarded her as an important personage, from the low curtsy which was dropped on the entrance of the small phaeton.

"Well, Mrs Fitchett, how are your fowls laying now?" said the high-coloured, dark-eyed lady, with the clearest chiselled utterance.

"Pretty well for laying, madam, but they've ta'en to eating their eggs: I've no peace o' mind with 'em at all."

"Oh the cannibals! Better sell them cheap at once. What will you sell them a couple? One can't eat fowls of a bad character at a high price."

"Well, madam, half-a-crown: I couldn't let 'em go, not under."

"Half-a-crown, these times! Come now – for the Rector's chicken-broth on a Sunday. He has consumed all ours that I can spare. You are half paid with the

sermon, Mrs Fitchett, remember that. Take a pair of tumbler-pigeons for them –
little beauties. You must come and see them. You have no tumblers among your
pigeons."

"Well, madam, Master Fitchett shall go and see 'em after work. He's very hot on
new sorts: to oblige *you*."

"Oblige me! It will be the best bargain he ever made. A pair of church pigeons for
a couple of wicked Spanish fowls that eat their own eggs! Don't you and Fitchett
boast too much, that is all!"[19]

Here the nature and nurture theme is given an ironic underlining in economic
terms. Mrs Cadwallader has inherited breeding and married genteel poverty.
The dialogue with Mrs Fitchett is natural, fluent and articulate. The irony is
exactly expressive of differently nurtured women. But these nurtures prove to
be complementary, as they bargain and agree.

The uses of nature in *Middlemarch* are various. When Dorothea becomes
engaged to Casaubon she has to visit Lowick. It is November without, prologue
to winter within. The description here, as so often, has prophetic overtones
of sterility and imprisonment. A brilliant if passing entry into Celia's delightfully
irresponsible consciousness provides a contrast of character and destiny:

On a grey but dry November morning Dorothea drove to Lowick in company with
her uncle and Celia. Mr Casaubon's home was the manor-house. Close by, visible
from some parts of the garden, was the little church, with the old parsonage opposite.
In the beginning of his career, Mr Casaubon had only held the living, but the death
of his brother had put him in possession of the manor also. It had a small park, with
a fine old oak here and there, and an avenue of limes towards the south-west front,
with a sunk fence between park and pleasure-ground, so that from the drawing-room
windows the glance swept uninterruptedly along a slope of greensward till the limes
ended in a level of corn and pastures, which often seemed to melt into a lake under
the setting sun. This was the happy side of the house, for the south and east looked
rather melancholy even under the brightest morning. The grounds here were more
confined, the flower-beds showed no very careful tendance, and large clumps of trees,
chiefly of sombre yews, had risen high, not ten yards from the windows. The building,
of greenish stone, was in the old English style, not ugly, but small-windowed and
melancholy-looking: the sort of house that must have children, many flowers, open
windows, and little vistas of bright things, to make it seem a joyous home. In this
latter end of autumn, with a sparse remnant of yellow leaves falling slowly athwart
the dark evergreens in a stillness without sunshine, the house too had an air of autumnal
decline, and Mr Casaubon, when he presented himself, had no bloom that could be
thrown into relief by that background.

"Oh dear!" Celia said to herself, "I am sure Freshitt Hall would have been pleasanter
than this." She thought of the white freestone, the pillared portico, and the terrace
full of flowers, Sir James smiling above them like a prince issuing from his enchantment
in a rose-bush, with a handkerchief swiftly metamorphosed from the most delicately-
odorous petals – Sir James, who talked so agreeably, always about things which had
common-sense in them, and not about learning! Celia had those light young feminine

tastes which grave and weather-worn gentlemen sometimes prefer in a wife; but happily Mr Casaubon's bias had been different, for he would have had no chance with Celia.[20]

Irony signals the different perspectives of Celia and Dorothea. There is also a quietly insistent identification with the chosen area:

It was three o'clock in the beautiful breezy autumn day when Mr Casaubon drove off to his Rectory at Lowick, only five miles from Tipton; and Dorothea, who had on her bonnet and shawl, hurried along the shrubbery and across the park that she might wander through the bordering wood with no other visible companionship than that of Monk, the Great St Bernard dog, who always took care of the young ladies in their walks. There had risen before her the girl's vision of a possible future for herself to which she looked forward with trembling hope, and she wanted to wander on in that visionary future without interruption. She walked briskly in the brisk air, the colour rose in her cheeks ... there was nothing of an ascetic's expression in her bright full eyes, as she looked before her, not consciously seeing, but absorbing into the intensity of her mood, the solemn glory of the afternoon with its long swathes of light between the far-off rows of limes, whose shadows touched each other.[21]

(Interestingly, George Eliot deleted "alone, safe from Celia's companionship" in the manuscript, altering it to "with no other visible companionship" above).

But, above all, we have the focus on Dorothea's situation. It is seen here as so often against the natural background: her nurture involves a new appraisal and appreciation of life, through suffering, and through understanding Casaubon and her own illusion, through the recognition of her love for Will. She returns from her wedding journey in January, the limes in the avenue outside and the stag in the tapestry inside perhaps acting as a symbolic index to her depression and dreariness.

Bulstrode is also seen against a natural background when he buys Stone Court and acquires, passingly, a healthy attitude and occupation. The symbolic index is clear:

However, whether for sanction or for chastisement, Mr Bulstrode, hardly fifteen months after the death of Peter Featherstone, had become the proprietor of Stone Court, and what Peter would say "if he were worthy to know," had become an inexhaustible and consolatory subject of conversion to his disappointed relatives. The tables were now turned on that dear brother departed, and to contemplate the frustration of his cunning by the superior cunning of things in general was a cud of delight to Solomon. Mrs Waule had a melancholy triumph in the proof that it did not answer to make false Featherstones and cut off the genuine; and Sister Martha receiving the news in the Chalky Flats said, "Dear, dear! then the Almighty could have been none so pleased with the almshouses after all."

Affectionate Mrs Bulstrode was particularly glad of the advantage which her husband's health was likely to get from the purchase of Stone Court. Few days passed without his riding thither and looking over some part of the farm with the bailiff, and the evenings were delicious in that quiet spot, when the new hay-ricks lately set up were sending forth odours to mingle with the breath of the rich old garden. One evening, while the sun was still above the horizon and burning in golden lamps among the great walnut boughs, Mr Bulstrode was pausing on horseback outside the front gate waiting for Caleb Garth, who had met him by appointment to give an opinion on a question of stable drainage, and was now advising the bailiff in the rick-yard.

Mr Bulstrode was conscious of being in a good spiritual frame and more than usually serene, under the influence of his innocent recreation. He was doctrinally convinced that there was a total absence of merit in himself; but that doctrinal conviction may be held without pain when the sense of demerit does not take a distinct shape in memory and revive the tingling of shame or the pang of remorse. Nay, it may be held with intense satisfaction when the depth of our sinning is but a measure for the depth of forgiveness, and a clenching proof that we are peculiar instruments of the divine intention. The memory has as many moods as the temper, and shifts its scenery like a diorama. At this moment Mr Bulstrode felt as if the sunshine were all one with that of far-off evenings when he was a very young man and used to go out preaching beyond Highbury. And he would willingly have had that service of exhortation in prospect now. The texts were there still, and so was his own facility in expounding them. His brief reverie was interrupted by the return of Caleb Garth, who also was on horseback, and was just shaking his bridle before starting, when he exclaimed –

"Bless my heart! what's this fellow in black coming along the lane? He's like one of those men one sees about after the races."[22]

Unfortunately the health and serenity come too late to save him from the corrupting nature of the past, which reveals itself in the shape of his old associate Raffles.

If Bulstrode's response to nature is temporary and illusory, Dorothea's experience is different in quality and kind. After she has seen Will and Rosamond in what appears to be a compromising situation, she endures a night of anguish, then rises to contemplate men and women in the natural world. She is irradiated and elevated: the scene enlarges her vision and heals her suffering:

And what sort of crisis might not this be in three lives whose contact with hers laid an obligation on her as if they had been suppliants bearing the sacred branch? The objects of her rescue were not to be sought out by her fancy: they were chosen for her. She yearned towards the perfect Right, that it might make a throne within her, and rule her errant will. "What should I do – how should I act now, this very day, if I could clutch my own pain, and compel it to silence, and think of those three?"

It had taken long for her to come to that question, and there was light piercing into the room. She opened her curtains, and looked out towards the bit of road that lay in view, with fields beyond, outside the entrance-gates. On the road there was a man with a bundle on his back and a woman carrying her baby; in the field she could see figures moving – perhaps the shepherd with his dog. Far off in the bending sky was the pearly light; and she felt the largeness of the world and the manifold wakings of men to labour and endurance. She was a part of that involuntary, palpitating life, and could neither look out on it from her luxurious shelter as a mere spectator, nor hide her eyes in selfish complaining.

What she would resolve to do that day did not yet seem quite clear, but something that she could achieve stirred her as with an approaching murmur which would soon gather distinctness. She took off the clothes which seemed to have some of the weariness of a hard watching in them, and began to make her toilette. Presently she rang for Tantripp, who came in her dressing-gown.[23]

One of the great emotional sequences in *Middlemarch* is the final coming together of Will and Dorothea. George Eliot uses the storm to convey powerful emotion. The conflict and passion of the characters draws its strength, at least in part, from the elemental background, but that background is used subtly as notation of feeling:

He took her hand and raised it to his lips with something like a sob. But he stood with his hat and gloves in the other hand, and might have done for the portrait of a Royalist. Still it was difficult to loose the hand, and Dorothea, withdrawing it in a confusion that distressed her, looked and moved away.

"See how dark the clouds have become, and how the trees are tossed," she said, walking towards the window, yet speaking and moving with only a dim sense of what she was doing.

Will followed her at a little distance, and leaned against the tall back of a leather chair, on which he ventured now to lay his hat and gloves, and free himself from the intolerable durance of formality to which he had been for the first time condemned in Dorothea's presence. It must be confessed that he felt very happy at that moment leaning on the chair. He was not much afraid of anything that she might feel now.

They stood silent, not looking at each other, but looking at the evergreens which were being tossed, and were showing the pale underside of their leaves against the blackening sky. Will never enjoyed the prospect of a storm so much: it delivered him from the necessity of going away. Leaves and little branches were hurled about, and the thunder was getting nearer. The light was more and more sombre, but there came a flash of lightning which made them start and look at each other, and then smile. Dorothea began to say what she had been thinking of.

"That was a wrong thing for you to say, that you would have had nothing to try for. If we had lost our own chief good, other people's good would remain, and that is worth trying for. Some can be happy. I seemed to see that more clearly than ever, when I was the most wretched. I can hardly think how I could have borne the trouble, if that feeling had not come to me to make strength."

"You have never felt the sort of misery I felt," said Will; "the misery of knowing that you must despise me."

"But I have felt worse – it was worse to think ill –" Dorothea had begun impetuously, but broke off.

Will coloured. He had the sense that whatever she said was uttered in the vision of a fatality that kept them apart. He was silent a moment, and then said passionately –

"We may at least have the comfort of speaking to each other without disguise.

Since I must go away – since we must always be divided – you may think of me as one on the brink of the grave."

While he was speaking there came a vivid flash of lightning which lit each of them up for the other – and the light seemed to be the terror of a hopeless love. Dorothea darted instantaneously from the window; Will followed her, seizing her hand with a spasmodic movement; and so they stood, with their hands clasped, like two children, looking out on the storm, while the thunder gave a tremendous crack and roll above them, and the rain began to pour down. Then they turned their faces towards each other, with the memory of his last words in them, and they did not loose each other's hands.

"There is no hope for me," said Will. "Even if you loved me as well as I love you – even if I were everything to you – I shall most likely always be very poor: on a sober calculation, one can count on nothing but a creeping lot. It is impossible for us ever to belong to each other. It is perhaps base of me to have asked for a word from you. I meant to go away into silence, but I have not been able to do what I meant."

"Don't be sorry," said Dorothea, in her clear tender tones. "I would rather share all the trouble of our parting."

Her lips tembled, and so did his. It was never known which lips were the first to move towards the other lips; but they kissed tremblingly, and then they moved apart.

The rain was dashing against the window-panes as if an angry spirit were within it, and behind it was the great swoop of the wind; it was one of those moments in which both the busy and the idle pause with a certain awe.

Dorothea sat down on the seat nearest to her, a long low ottoman in the middle of the room, and with her hands folded over each other on her lap, looked at the drear outer world. Will stood an instant looking at her, then seated himself beside her, and laid his hand on hers, which turned itself upward to be clasped. They sat in that way without looking at each other, until the rain abated and began to fall in stillness. Each had been full of thoughts which neither of them could begin to utter.

But when the rain was quiet, Dorothea turned to look at Will. With passionate exclamation, as if some torture-screw were threatening him, he started up and said, "It is impossible?"[24]

In the early works nature is present as symbol and fact, but its function develops in imaginative and intellectual subtlety. The natural scene in *Felix Holt* and *Middlemarch* does not lack warmth: but what is apparent in these later novels is a growth of intellectual complexity in her conception of nature, as in much else. The heroines of the early works, for example, are closely identified with nature either directly or by analogy, but Esther and Dorothea are not close to the earth. In a sense their earlier nurture would lead one to expect this: the fine-ladyism of Esther and the finishing-school ladyism of Dorothea do not derive from close identification with nature, whereas Maggie's childhood, Dinah's affiliations with her faith and her aunt Poyser, even Hetty's in passing happiness or cruel adversity, are seen in a country setting.

The urban setting of "Amos" and "Janet's Repentance" anticipates in some degree the fuller and richer urbanization of *Middlemarch*, while "Mr Gilfil" looks forward to *Felix Holt*. Between 1857 and 1861 George Eliot inspiration-ally recalled the Midland village nature of her early nurture. It remained with her though it underwent change. While she was contemplating *Middlemarch* she wrote the "Brother and Sister" sonnets, and in their unequivocal recall, they show the importance of nature and early nurture in her life and art.

# 10. The Spoken Word

In the early 1860s George Eliot's supportive and sympathetic publisher, John Blackwood, wrote down some observations about his outstanding author for his wife. Of *Adam Bede*, he said: "The dialect of Lisbeth arose from her occasionally hearing her father when with his brothers revert to the dialect of his native district, Derbyshire. She could not tell how the feeling and knowledge came to her, but when Lisbeth was speaking she felt it was a real language which she heard."[1] In the following pages I will look closely at some examples of the "real language which she heard" in order to show how true was her ear, and how her manner of presenting what she heard developed from a localized register. I have made no attempt at technical or scholarly analysis of dialect; I have trusted the teller within the truth of her tale.

Just as nature and nurture complement each other in George Eliot's fiction, so dialect, fresh and vigorous in *Scenes* and *Adam Bede*, plays its part in the later works but without the deliberate local emphasis which characterizes the early fiction.

In the later novels the incidence of the received register is greater: this is because George Eliot is dealing with more urbanized groups, and often with people of a higher social class. I mentioned her remarks about dialect to Skeat (see pp. 4–5) and there are other instances in her Letters of her concern to be clearly understood and not to distort. A study of many of the footnotes in Thomas Noble's edition of *Scenes* shows George Eliot toning down the broader effects of dialect in the later editions published in her lifetime.

*Scenes* is rich in dialect. Mrs Hackit, precursor of Mrs Poyser, is individualized and authenticated through the quality of her caustic humour. She is kind-hearted, independent-minded, and domestically irreproachable. Here she is in defence of Amos:

"Ah," he answered, "the parson's boddered us into it at last, and we're to begin pulling down this spring. But we haven't got money enough yet. I was for waiting till we'd made up the sum, and, for my part, I think the congregation's fell off o' late; though Mr Barton says that's because there's been no room for the people when they've come. You see, the congregation got so large in Parry's time, the people stood in th' aisles; but there's never any crowd now, as I can see."

"Well," said Mrs Hackit, whose good-nature began to act now that it was a little in contradiction with the dominant tone of the conversation, "*I* like Mr Barton. I think he's a good sort o' man, for all he's not overburthen'd i' th' upper story; and his wife's as nice a lady-like woman as I'd wish to see. How nice she keeps her children! and little enough money to do't with; and a delicate creatur' – six children, and another a-coming. I don't know how they make both ends meet, I'm sure, now her aunt has left 'em. But I sent 'em a cheese and a sack o' potatoes last week; that's something towards filling the little mouths."[2]

and

"Well, I don't know about that," said Mrs Hackit, who had always the courage of her opinion, "but I know, some of our labourers and stockingers as used never to come to church, come to the cottage, and that's better than never hearing anything good from week's end to week's end. And there's that Track Society as Mr Barton has begun – I've seen more o' the poor people with going tracking, than all the time I've lived in the parish before. And there'd need be something done among 'em; for the drinking at them Benefit Clubs is shameful. There's hardly a steady man or steady woman either, but what's a dissenter."

During this speech of Mrs Hackit's, Mr Pilgrim had emitted a succession of little snorts, something like the treble grunts of a guinea-pig, which were always with him the sign of suppressed disapproval. But he never contradicted Mrs Hackit – a woman whose "pot luck" was always to be relied on, and who on her side had unlimited reliance on bleeding, blistering, and draughts.[3]

The dialect is discriminatingly ordered. Perhaps the moderation is owing to a combination of the common usage and occasional abusage which reflects Mrs Hackit's status in the community. Nanny, in the upstairs-downstairs interaction which moves the plot of "Amos", is freer and broader as she too engages in a defence of Amos:

Another mind that was being wrought up to a climax was Nanny's, the maid-of-all-work, who had a warm heart and a still warmer temper. Nanny adored her mistress: she had been heard to say, that she was "ready to kiss the ground as the missis trod on;" and Walter, she considered, was *her* baby, of whom she was as jealous as a lover. But she had from the first very slight admiration for the Countess Czerlaski. That lady, from Nanny's point of view, was a personage always "drawed out i' fine clothes," the chief result of whose existence was to cause additional bed-making, carrying of hot water, laying of table-cloths and cooking of dinners. It was a perpetually heightening "aggravation" to Nanny that she and her mistress had to "slave" more than ever, because there was this fine lady in the house.

"An' she pays nothin' for't neither," observed Nanny to Mr Jacob Tomms, a young gentleman in the tailoring line, who occasionally – simply out of taste for dialogue – looked into the vicarage kitchen of an evening. "I know the master's shorter o' money than iver, an' it meks no end o' difference i' th' housekeepin' – her bein' here, besides bein' obliged to have a charwoman constant."

"There's fine stories i' the village about her," said Mr Tomms. "They say as Muster Barton's great wi' her, or else she'd niver stop here."

"Then they say a passill o' lies an' you ought to be ashamed to goo an' tell 'em o'er again. Do *you* think as the master, as has got a wife like the missis, 'ud goo runnin' arter a stuck-up piece o' goods like that Countess, as isn't fit to black the missis's shoes? I'm none so fond o' the master, but I know better on him nor that."

"Well, I didn't b'lieve it," said Mr Tomms, humbly.

"B'lieve it? you'd ha' been a ninny if yer did. An' she's a nasty, stingy thing, that Countess. She's niver giv me a sixpence or an old rag neither, sin' here she's been. A-lyin' a bed an' a-comin' down to breakfast when other folks wants their dinner!"[4]

Here dialect is used to indicate social difference, but it is also social and moral commentary, effective and containing the spice of George Eliot's humour. Dialect is experienced by the ear and, like Hardy, she uses it without condescension. She heard and reproduced common utterance with a good ear and a sense of art. The humour, which is both conscious and unconscious, is enriched by the wit and wisdom of proverbial and traditional language.

The interaction of classes is found in "Mr Gilfil" too, and here it is a source of comfort to the oppressed Caterina:

She was roused from her absorption by a knock at the door. Mrs Bellamy was there. She had come by Mr Gilfil's request to see how Miss Sarti was, and to bring her some food and wine.

"You look sadly, my dear," said the old housekeeper, "an' you're all of a quake wi' cold. Get you to bed, now do. Martha shall come an' warm it, an' light your fire. See now, here's some nice arrowroot, wi' a drop o' wine in it. Tek that, an' it'll warm you. I must go down again, for I can't awhile to stay. There's so many things to see to; an' Miss Assher's in hysterics constant, an' her maid's ill i' bed – a poor creachy thing – an' Mrs Sharp's wanted every minute. But I'll send Martha up, an' do you get ready to go to bed, there's a dear child, an' tek care o' yourself."

"Thank you, dear mammy," said Tina, kissing the little old woman's wrinkled cheek; "I shall eat the arrowroot, and don't trouble about me any more to-night. I shall do very well when Martha has lighted my fire. Tell Mr Gilfil I'm better. I shall go to bed by-and-by, so don't you come up again, because you may only disturb me."

"Well, well, tek care o' yourself, there's a good child, an' God send you may sleep."[5]

The simple remedy may be curative, we feel, in the same way that this simple soul is. George Eliot also uses her rural characters, here again in "Mr Gilfil", as dramatic mouthpieces in narrative. When Caterina flees, she shelters with a former employee at Cheverel Manor, the coachman Knott and his wife Dorcas. Note the mixture of the self-delight in conveying information, the narrative rambling and conscious importance which make Knott's disclosure to Maynard Gilfil a complex register of action, character, and social class:

"For God's sake," said Maynard, "tell me what it is about Miss Sarti. Don't stay to tell me anything else now."

"Well, sir," said Knott, rather frightened by the parson's vehemence, "she come t'

our house i' the carrier's cart o' Wednesday, when it was welly nine o'clock at
night; and Dorkis run out, for she heared the cart stop, an' Miss Sarti throwed
her arms roun' Dorkis's neck an' says, 'Tek me in, Dorkis, tek me in,' an' went
off into a swoond, like. An' Dorkis calls out to me, – 'Dannel,' she calls – an' I
run out and carried the young miss in, an' she come roun' arter a bit, an'
opened her eyes, and Dorkis got her to drink a spoonful o' rum-an'-water – we've
got some capital rum as we brought from the Cross Keys, an' Dorkis won't let nobody
drink it. She says she keeps it for sickness; but for my part, I think it's a pity to drink
good rum when your mouth's out o' taste; you may just as well hev doctor's stuff.
Howiver, Dorkis got her to bed, an' there she's lay iver sin', stoopid like, an' niver
speaks, an' on'y teks little bits an' sups when Dorkis coaxes her. An' we begun to be
frightened, and couldn't think what had made her come away from the Manor, and
Dorkis was afeard there was summat wrong. So this mornin' she could hold no
longer, an' would hev no nay but I must come an' see; an' so I've rode twenty mile
upo' Blackbird, as thinks all the while he's a ploughin', an' turns sharp roun', ivery
thirty yards, as if he was at the end of a furrow. I've hed a sore time wi' him, I can
tell you, sir."[6]

"Janet's Repentance" is more urbanized, but a good example of George
Eliot's use of dialect to distinguish class and character is shown in Mr Jerome.
He sticks to his principles in supporting Tryan in opposition to Dempster,
and is physically frail: he anticipates in some ways the work ethic of Adam
Bede and Caleb Garth. This is an early stage in George Eliot's art:

"This way, Mr Tryan, this way," said the old gentleman; "I must take you to my
pastur fust, an' show you our cow – the best milker i' the country. An' see here at
these back-buildins, how convenent the dairy is; I planned it ivery bit myself. An' here
I've got my little carpenter's shop an' my blacksmith's shop; I do no end o' jobs here
myself. I niver could bear to be idle, Mr Tryan; I must al'ys be at somethin' or other.
It was time for me to ley by business and mek room for younger folks. I'd got money
enough, wi' only one daughter to leave it to, an' I says to myself, says I, it's time to
leave off moitherin' myself wi' this world so much, an' give more time to thinkin' of
another. But there's a many hours atween getting up an' lyin' down, an' thoughts are
no cumber; you can move about wi' a good many on 'em in your head. See here's
the pastur."
A very pretty pasture it was, where the large-spotted short-horned cow quietly
chewed the cud as she lay and looked sleepily at her admirers – a daintily-trimmed
hedge all round, dotted here and there with a mountain-ash or a cherry-tree.
"I've a good bit more land besides this, worth your while to look at, but mayhap
it's further nor you'd like to walk now. Bless you! I've welly an' acre o' potato-ground
yonters; I've a good big family to supply, you know." (Here Mr Jerome winked and
smiled significantly.) "An' that puts me i' mind, Mr Tryan, o' summat I wanted to
say to you. Clergymen like you, I know, see a deal more poverty an' that, than other
folks, an' hev a many claims on 'em more nor they can well meet; an' if you'll mek
use o' my purse any time, or let me know where I can be o' any help, I'll tek it very
kind on you."

"Thank you, Mr Jerome, I will do so, I promise you. I saw a sad case yesterday; a collier – a fine broad-chested fellow about thirty – was killed by the falling of a wall in the Paddiford colliery. I was in one of the cottages near when they brought him home on a door, and the shriek of the wife has been ringing in my ears ever since. There are three little children. Happily the woman has her loom, so she will be able to keep out of the workhouse; but she looks very delicate."

"Give me her name, Mr Tryan," said Mr Jerome, drawing out his pocket-book. "I'll call an' see her, I'll call an' see her."[7]

Of all George Eliot's fiction *Adam Bede* is the richest in dialect. The village community of Hayslope is brought positively alive through the speech of its inhabitants. In the narrative sequence, even before we get to the inventiveness of Mrs Poyser, there is the earthy idiom, rich in proverb and folk-language, of Lisbeth Bede. Though dialect is used for humour in *Adam Bede*, it is also eloquent of misery, adversity and conflict. The first scene in the workshop has the articulated interaction of Adam and Wiry Ben:

"Look there, now! I can't abide to see men throw away their tools i' that way, the minute the clock begins to strike, as if they took no pleasure i' their work, and was afraid o' doing a stroke too much."

Seth looked a little conscious, and began to be slower in his preparations for going, but Mum Taft broke silence, and said –

"Ay, ay, Adam, lad, ye talk like a young un. When y' are six-an'-forty like me, istid o' six-an'-twenty, ye wonna be so flush o' workin' for nought."

"Nonsense," said Adam, still wrathful; "what's age got to do with it, I wonder? Ye arena getting stiff yet, I reckon. I hate to see a man's arms drop down as if he was shot, before the clock's fairly struck, just as if he'd never a bit o' pride and delight in 's work. The very grindstone 'ull go on turning a bit after you loose it."

"Bodderation, Adam!" exclaimed Wiry Ben; "lave a chap aloon, will 'ee? Ye war a-finding faut wi' preachers a while agoo – y' are fond enough o' preachin' yoursen. Ye may like work better nor play, but I like play better nor work; that'll 'commodate ye – it laves ye th' more to do."

With this exit speech, which he considered effective, Wiry Ben shouldered his basket and left the workshop, quickly followed by Mum Taft and Sandy Jim. Seth lingered, and looked wistfully at Adam, as if he expected him to say something.

"Shalt go home before thee go'st to the preaching?" Adam asked, looking up.

"Nay; I've got my hat and things at Will Maskery's. I shan't be home before going for ten. I'll happen see Dinah Morris safe home, if she's willing. There's nobody comes with her from Poyser's, thee know'st."

"Then I'll tell mother not to look for thee," said Adam.

"Thee artna going to Poyser's thyself to-night?" said Seth, rather timidly, as he turned to leave the workshop.

"Nay, I'm going to th' school."[8]

Adam's more educated dialect is different from Wiry Ben's. At home he uses a relaxed and natural speech in the way that many of us do: it is convincing, an expression of impetuous emotion, for instance when he is frustrated by his father's failure:

"Ay, ay, Seth's at no harm, mother, thee mayst be sure. But where's father?" said Adam quickly, as he entered the house and glanced into the room on the left hand, which was used as a workshop. "Hasn't he done the coffin for Tholer? There's the stuff standing just as I left it this morning."

"Done the coffin?" said Lisbeth, following him, and knitting uninterruptedly, though she looked at her son very anxiously. "Eh, my lad, he went aff to Treddles'on this forenoon, an's niver come back. I doubt he's got to th' 'Waggin Overthrow' again."

A deep flush of anger passed rapidly over Adam's face. He said nothing, but threw off his jacket, and began to roll up his shirt-sleeves again.

"What art goin' to do, Adam?" said the mother, with a tone and look of alarm. "Thee wouldstna go to work again, wi'out ha'in thy bit o' supper?"

Adam, too angry to speak, walked into the workshop. But his mother threw down her knitting, and, hurrying after him, took hold of his arm, and said, in a tone of plaintive remonstrance –

"Nay, my lad, my lad, thee munna go wi'out thy supper; there's the taters wi' the gravy in 'em, just as thee lik'st 'em. I saved 'em o' purpose for thee. Come an' ha' thy supper, come."

"Let be!" said Adam impetuously, shaking her off, and seizing one of the planks that stood against the wall. "It's fine talking about having supper when here's a coffin promised to be ready at Brox'on by seven o'clock to-morrow morning, and ought to ha' been there now, and not a nail struck yet. My throat's too full to swallow victuals."

"Why, thee canstna get the coffin ready," said Lisbeth. "Thee't work thyself to death. It 'ud take thee all night to do't."

"What signifies how long it takes me? Isn't the coffin promised? Can they bury the man without a coffin? I'd work my right hand off sooner than deceive people with lies i' that way. It makes me mad to think on't. I shall overrun these doings before long. I've stood enough of 'em."[9]

With a somewhat different emphasis Dinah, from her working world, talks to Mr Irwine. George Eliot frees her from dialect, thus establishing community of feeling, even a form of equality, between them. In interaction with Lisbeth Dinah's difference is evident. Her language is that of the practised speaker, despite its warm, giving tone:

"Dinah," said Seth, "do come and sit down now and have your breakfast. We're all served now."

"Ay, come an' sit ye down – do," said Lisbeth, "an' ate a morsel; ye'd need, arter bein' upo' your legs this hour an' half a'ready. Come, then," she added, in a tone of complaining affection, as Dinah sat down by her side, "I'll be loath for ye t' go, but ye canna stay much longer, I doubt. I could put up wi' ye i' th' house better nor wi' most folks."

"I'll stay till to-night if you're willing," said Dinah. "I'd stay longer, only I'm going back to Snowfield on Saturday, and I must be with my aunt to-morrow."

"Eh, I'd ne'er go back to that country. My old man come from that Stonyshire side, but he left it when he war a young un, an' i' the right on't too; for he said as there war no wood there, an' it 'ud ha' been a bad country for a carpenter."[10]

Perhaps a greater emphasis on her dialect would have given Dinah a greater realism: however, the characters close to the earth in *Adam Bede* have their regional register enriched by the artistic imagination. Mrs Poyser's proverbial turns of phrase spring from her creative wit.

She is moved to inspirational utterance when she contemplates the shortcomings of others. As we might expect, Hetty is often on the receiving end of her wit:

"She's no better than a peacock, as 'ud strut about on the wall, and spread its tail when the sun shone if all the folks i' the parish was dying: there's nothing seems to give her a turn i' th' inside, not even when we thought Totty had tumbled into the pit. To think o' that dear cherub! And we found her wi' her little shoes stuck i' the mud an' crying fit to break her heart by the far horse-pit. But Hetty never minded it, I could see, though she's been at the nussin' o' the child ever since it was a babby. It's my belief her heart's as hard as a pebble."

"Nay, nay," said Mr Poyser, "thee mustn't judge Hetty too hard. Them young gells are like the unripe grain; they'll make good meal by-and-by, but they're squashy as yet. Thee't see Hetty'll be all right when she's got a good husband and children of her own."

"*I* don't want to be hard upo' the gell. She's got cliver fingers of her own, and can be useful enough when she likes, and I should miss her wi' the butter, for she's got a cool hand. An' let be what may, I'd strive to do my part by a niece o' yours, an' *that* I've done: for I've taught her everything as belongs to a house, an' I've told her her duty often enough, though, God knows, I've no breath to spare, an' that catchin' pain comes on dreadful by times. Wi' them three gells in the house I'd need have twice the strength, to keep 'em up to their work. It's like having roast meat at three fires: as soon as you've basted one, another's burnin'."[11]

Henry James felt that Mrs Poyser's proverbial fluency was too good to be true. In the following exchange with her husband George Eliot is certainly loading every rift with metaphor, simile, epigram:

"There's that short-horned Sally," she said, as they entered the Home Close, and she caught sight of the meek beast that lay chewing the cud, and looking at her with a sleepy eye. "I begin to hate the sight o' the cow; and I say now what I said three weeks ago, the sooner we get rid of her the better, for there's that little yellow cow as doesn't give half the milk, and yet I've twice as much butter from her."

"Why, thee't not like the women in general," said Mr Poyser; "they like the short-horns, as give such a lot o' milk. There's Chowne's wife wants him to buy no other sort."

"What's it sinnify what Chowne's wife likes? – a poor soft thing, wi' no more head-piece nor a sparrow. She'd take a big cullender to strain her lard wi', and then wonder as the scratchins run through. I've seen enough of her to know as I'll niver take a servant from her house again – all hugger-mugger – and you'd niver know, when you went in, whether it was Monday or Friday, the wash draggin' on to th' end o' the week; and as for her cheese, I know well enough it rose like a loaf in a tin last year. And then she talks o' the weather bein' i' fault, as there's folks 'ud stand on their heads and then say the fault was i' their boots."

"Well, Chowne's been wanting to buy Sally, so we can get rid of her if thee lik'st," said Mr Poyser, secretly proud of his wife's superior power of putting two and two together; indeed, on recent market-days he had more than once boasted of her discernment in this very matter of short-horns.

"Ay, them as choose a soft for a wife may's well buy up the short-horns, for if you get your head stuck in a bog your legs may's well go after it. Eh! talk o' legs, there's legs for you," Mrs Poyser continued, as Totty, who had been set down now the road was dry, toddled on in front of her father and mother. "There's shapes! An' she's got such a long foot, she'll be her father's own child."[12]

I give Mrs Poyser at length because she is the sublime example of George Eliot's use of dialect. If her rich, racy, inventive and often acid language is a shade too good to be true, it is also too true to be merely good. The great artist heightens effect by emphasis, and this is just what George Eliot has done with Mrs Poyser.

Although, as we have seen, Adam's register is a double one – witness his reportage to Mr Irwine of Hetty being tempted by Arthur – George Eliot is adept at keeping her dialect speakers in the mainstream of action. The disgrace which falls on the Poyser family is movingly conveyed in their natural register: Mrs Poyser, over-awed for once by the momentousness of the occasion, is almost put out of voice. The male Poysers combine – inadvertently but movingly – in a language rich in biblical phrase, stumbling and hesitant in its emotional power:

"I'm willing to pay any money as is wanted towards trying to bring her off," said Martin the younger when Mr Irwine was gone, while the old grandfather was crying in the opposite chair, "but I'll not go nigh her, nor ever see her again, by my own will. She's made our bread bitter to us for all our lives to come, an' we shall ne'er hold up our heads i' this parish nor i' any other. The parson talks o' folks pitying us: it's poor amends pity 'ull make us."

"Pity?" said the grandfather, sharply. "I ne'er wanted folks's pity i' *my* life afore . . . an' I mun begin to be looked down on now, an' me turned seventy-two last St Thomas's, an' all th' under-bearers and pall-bearers as I'n picked for my funeral are i' this parish and the next to 't. . . . It's o' no use now . . . I mun be ta'en to the grave by strangers."

"Don't fret so, father," said Mrs Poyser, who had spoken very little, being almost overawed by her husband's unusual hardness and decision. "You'll have your children wi' you; an' there's the lads and the little un 'ull grow up in a new parish as well as i' th' old un."

"Ah, there's no staying i' this country for us now," said Mr Poyser, and the hard tears trickled slowly down his round cheeks. "We thought it 'ud be bad luck if the old Squire gave us notice this Lady Day, but I must gi' notice myself now, an' see if there can anybody be got to come an' take to the crops as I'n put i' the ground; for I wonna stay upo' that man's land a day longer nor I'm forced to't. An' me, as thought him such a good upright young man, as I should be glad when he come to be our landlord. I'll ne'er lift my hat to him again, nor sit i' the same church wi' him . . . a man as has brought shame on respectable folks . . . an' pretended to be such a friend t' everybody. . . . Poor Adam there . . . a fine friend he's been t' Adam, making speeches an' talking so fine, an' all the while poisoning the lad's life, as it's much if he can stay i' this country any more nor we can."

"An' you t' ha' to go into court, and own you're akin t' her," said the old man. "Why, they'll cast it up to the little un, as isn't four 'ear old, some day – they'll cast it up t' her as she'd a cousin tried at the 'sizes for murder."

"It'll be their own wickedness, then," said Mrs Poyser, with a sob in her voice. "But there's One above 'ull take care o' the innicent child, else it's but little truth they tell us at church. It'll be harder nor ever to die an' leave the little uns, an' nobody to be a mother to 'em."[13]

The "great primitive passions" of anger, reproach and shame find an ancient, simple speech, and dialect is softened in order to facilitate the flow of feeling. They combine to produce direct utterance.

Comic dialect is part of the regional effect in *The Mill*. Mr and Mrs Tulliver use a dialogue which is more easily comprehended than Lisbeth Bede's, though they are a little above her on the social scale. The dialect is moderated in this first exchange, though perhaps there is a hint that in Tulliver's case excessive feeling might influence his utterance, as we see from his remarks about Wakem and the killing of the fowls:

"What I want, you know," said Mr Tulliver – "what I want is to give Tom a good eddication, an eddication as'll be a bread to him. That was what I was thinking of when I gave notice for him to leave the 'cademy at Ladyday. I mean to put him to a downright good school at Midsummer. The two years at the 'cademy ud ha' done well enough, if I'd meant to make a miller and farmer of him, for he's had a fine sight more schoolin' nor *I* ever got: all the learnin' *my* father ever paid for was a bit o' birch at one end and the alphabet at th' other. But I should like Tom to be a bit of a scholard, so as he might be up to the tricks o' these fellows as talk fine and write with a flourish. It 'ud be a help to me wi' these lawsuits, and arbitrations, and things. I wouldn't make a downright lawyer o' the lad – I should be sorry for him to be a raskill – but a sort o' engineer, or a surveyor, or an auctioneer and vallyer, like Riley, or one o' them smartish businesses as are all profits and no outlay, only for a big watch-chain and a high stool. They're pretty nigh all one, and they're not far off being even wi' the law, *I* believe; for Riley looks Lawyer Wakem i' the face as hard as one cat looks another. *He's* none frightened at him."

Mr Tulliver was speaking to his wife, a blond comely woman in a fan-shaped cap (I am afraid to think how long it is since fan-shaped caps were worn – they must be so near coming in again. At that time, when Mrs Tulliver was nearly forty, they were new at St Ogg's, and considered sweet things).

"Well, Mr Tulliver, you know best: *I've* no objections. But hadn't I better kill a couple o' fowl and have th' aunts and uncles to dinner next week, so as you may hear what sister Glegg and sister Pullet have got to say about it? There's a couple o' fowl *wants* killing!"

"You may kill every fowl i' the yard, if you like, Bessy; but I shall ask neither aunt nor uncle what I'm to do wi' my own lad," said Mr Tulliver, defiantly.

"Dear heart!" said Mrs Tulliver, shocked at this sanguinary rhetoric, "how can you talk so, Mr Tulliver? But it's your way to speak disrespectful o' my family; and sister Glegg throws all the blame upo' me, though I'm sure I'm as innocent as the babe unborn. For nobody's ever heard *me* say as it wasn't lucky for my children to have aunts and uncles as can live independent. Howiver, if Tom's to go to a new school, I should like him to go where I can wash him and mend him; else he might as well have calico as linen, for they'd be one as yallow as th' other before they'd been washed half-a-dozen times. And then, when the box is goin' backards and forrards, I could send the lad a cake, or a pork-pie, or an apple; for he can do with an extra bit, bless him, whether they stint him at the meals or no. My children can eat as much victuals as most, thank God."[14]

Tom and Maggie, the first because of his schooling, the second because of her reading, abjure dialect or have it abjured for them. But a low, humane and considerate character, Bob Jakin, uses words like coins in the practised manner of the survivor. Bob is *not* caricature, though he is type. His exchange with Mrs Glegg, already quoted (see pp. 66–7), reveals that the local words are the man when it comes to the opportunistic profit motive. There is a moving generosity about Bob, the spontaneous expressions reflecting the impulsiveness of his actions. He offers help to Tom by pressing nine sovereigns on him: he brings help to Maggie by buying her the books she loved, something outside the family range of understanding or sympathy. Here is the offer to Tom:

"Well, Bob," said Tom, feeling that the subject of the books was unseasonable, "I suppose you just came to see me because we're in trouble? That was very good-natured of you."

"I'll tell you how it is, Master Tom," said Bob, beginning to untwist his canvass bag. "You see, I'n been with a barge this two 'ear – that's how I'n been gettin' my livin' – if it wasn't when I was tentin' the furnace, between whiles, at Torry's mill. But a fortni't ago I'd a rare bit o' luck – I allays thought I was a lucky chap, for I niver set a trap but what I catched something, but this wasn't a trap, it was a fire i' Torry's mill, an' I doused it, else it 'ud ha' set th' oil alight, an' the genelman gen me ten suvreigns – he gen me 'em himself last week. An' he said first, I was a sperrited chap – but I knowed that afore – but then he outs wi' the ten suvreigns, an' that war summat new. Here they are – all but one!" Here Bob emptied the canvass bag on the table. "An' when I'd got 'em, my head was all of a boil like a kettle o' broth, thinkin' what sort o' life I should take to – for there war a many trades I'd thought on; for as for the barge, I'm clean tired out wi't, for it pulls the days out till they're as long as pigs' chitterlings. An' I thought first I'd ha' ferrets an' dogs, an' be a rat-catcher; an' then I thought as I should like a bigger way o' life, as I didn't know so well; for I'n seen to the bottom o' rat-catching; an' I thought, an' thought, till at last I settled I'd be a packman, for they're knowin' fellers, the packmen are – an' I'd carry the lightest things I could i' my pack – an' there'd be a use for a feller's tongue, as is no use neither wi' rats nor barges. An' I should go about the country far an' wide, an' come round the women wi' my tongue, an' get my dinner hot at the public – lors! it 'ud be a lovely life!"

Bob paused, and then said, with defiant decision, as if resolutely turning his back on that paradisiac picture –

"But I don't mind about it – not a chip! An' I'n changed one o' the suvreigns to buy my mother a goose for dinner, an' I'n bought a blue plush wescoat, an' a sealskin cap – for if I meant to be a packman, I'd do it respectable. But I don't mind about it – not a chip! My yead isn't a turnip, an' I shall p'r'aps have a chance o' dousing another fire afore long. I'm a lucky chap. So I'll thank you to take the nine suvreigns, Mr Tom, and set yoursen up with 'em somehow – if it's true as the master's broke. They mayn't go fur enough – but they'll help."

Tom was touched keenly enough to forget his pride and suspicion.

"You're a very kind fellow, Bob," he said, colouring, with that little diffident tremor in his voice, which gave a certain charm even to Tom's pride and severity, "and I shan't forget you again, though I didn't know you this evening. But I can't take the nine sovereigns: I should be taking your little fortune from you, and they wouldn't do me much good either."

"Wouldn't they, Mr Tom?" said Bob, regretfully. "Now don't say so 'cause you think I want 'em. I aren't a poor chap. My mother gets a good penn'orth wi' picking feathers an' things; an' if she eats nothin' but bread-an'-water, it runs to fat. An' I'm such a lucky chap: an' I doubt you aren't quite so lucky, Mr Tom – th' old master isn't, anyhow – an' so you might take a slice o' my luck, an' no harm done. Lors! I found a leg o' pork i' the river one day: it had tumbled out o' one o' them round-sterned Dutchmen, I'll be bound. Come, think better on it, Mr Tom, for old 'quinetence sake – else I shall think you bear me a grudge."

Bob pushed the sovereigns forward, but before Tom could speak, Maggie, clasping her hands, and looking penitently at Bob said –

"O, I'm so sorry, Bob – I never thought you were so good. Why, I think you're the kindest person in the world!"

Bob had not been aware of the injurious opinion for which Maggie was performing an inward act of penitence, but he smiled with pleaure at this handsome eulogy – especially from a young lass who, as he informed his mother that evening, had "such uncommon eyes, they looked somehow as they made him feel nohow."

"No indeed, Bob, I can't take them," said Tom; "But don't think I feel your kindness less because I say no. I don't want to take anything from anybody, but to work my own way. And those sovereigns wouldn't help me much – they wouldn't, really – if I were to take them. Let me shake hands with you instead."

Tom put out his pink palm, and Bob was not slow to place his hard, grimy hand within it.

"Let me put the sovereigns in the bag again," said Maggie; "and you'll come and see us when you've bought your pack, Bob."

"It's like as if I'd come out o' make-believe, o' purpose to show 'em you," said Bob, with an air of discontent, as Maggie gave him the bag again, "a-taking 'em back i' this way. I *am* a bit of a Do, you know; but it isn't that sort o' Do: it's on'y when a feller's a big rogue, or a big flat, I like to let him in a bit, that's all."

"Now, don't you be up to any tricks, Bob," said Tom, "else you'll get transported some day."

"No, no; not me, Mr Tom," said Bob, with an air of cheerful confidence. "There's no law again' fleabites. If I wasn't to take a fool in now and then, he'd niver get any wiser. But, lors! hev a suvreign to buy you and Miss summat, on'y for a token – just to match my pocket-knife."

While Bob was speaking he laid down the sovereign, and resolutely twisted up his bag again. Tom pushed back the gold, and said, "No, indeed, Bob; thank you heartily; but I can't take it." And Maggie, taking it between her fingers, held it up to Bob, and said, more persuasively –

"Not now – but perhaps another time. If ever Tom or my father wants help that you can give, we'll let you know – won't we, Tom? That's what you would like – to have us always depend on you as a friend that we can go to – isn't it, Bob?"

"Yes, Miss, and thank you," said Bob, reluctantly taking the money; "that's what I'd like – anything as you like. An' I wish you good-bye, Miss, and good-luck, Mr Tom, and thank you for shaking hands wi' me, *though* you wouldn't take the money."[15]

Again we notice that the quality of the dialect is preserved through the exercise of moderation, and what is present in the language is the warmth of the character *and* the moral identification of the author.

Silas has the speech habits of his own unnamed Northern background, but the locals of the Rainbow Inn and Dolly Winthrop are recognizably Warwickshire. Raveloe and its environs mark the extent of their world, and its speech habits the extent of their articulateness. Mr Macey is a good example of the easy, toned-down dialect which makes for humour: his complex rhetoric and the ready repetition of stories are part of an oral tradition:

"But *you* knew what was going on well enough, didn't you, Mr Macey? You were live enough, eh?" said the butcher.

"Lor bless you!" said Mr Macey, pausing, and smiling in pity at the impotence of his hearer's imagination – "why, I was all of a tremble: it was as if I'd been a coat pulled by the two tails, like; for I couldn't stop the parson, I couldn't take upon me to do that; and yet I said to myself, I says, 'Suppose they shouldn't be fast married, 'cause the words are contrairy?' and my head went working like a mill, for I was allays uncommon for turning things over and seeing all round 'em; and I says to myself, 'Is't the meanin' or the words as makes folks fast i' wedlock?' For the parson meant right, and the bride and bridegroom meant right. But then, when I come to think on it, meanin' goes but a little way i' most things, for you may mean to stick things together and your glue may be bad, and then where are you? And so I says to mysen, 'It isn't the meanin', it's the glue.' And I was worreted as if I'd got three bells to pull at once, when we went into the vestry, and they begun to sign their names. But where's the use o' talking? – you can't think what goes on in a 'cute man's inside."

"But you held in for all that, didn't you, Mr Macey?" said the landlord.

"Ay, I held in tight till I was by mysen wi' Mr Drumlow, and then I out wi' everything, but respectful, as I allays did. And he made light on it, and he says, 'Pooh, pooh, Macey, make yourself easy,' he says; 'it's neither the meaning nor the words – it's the re*ge*ster does it – that's the glue. So you see he settled it easy; for parsons and doctors know everything by heart, so as they aren't worreted wi' thinking what's the rights and wrongs o' things, as I'n been many and many's the time. And sure enough the wedding turned out all right, on'y poor Mrs Lammeter – that's Miss Osgood as was – died afore the lasses was growed up; but for prosperity and everything respectable, there's no family more looked on."

Every one of Mr Macey's audience had heard this story many times, but it was listened to as if it had been a favourite tune, and at certain points the puffing of the pipes was momentarily suspended, that the listeners might give their whole minds to the expected words. But there was more to come; and Mr Snell, the landlord, duly put the leading question.[16]

The Midland soul in Marian Evans is expressed in Mr Macey. Mr Macey is a teller of tales: she understands the motivation behind the telling and associates with it, for his structures are her structures, drawing on the cunning of the mind, the sense of an audience, the measured heartbeat of familiarity.

But in *Felix Holt* the texture of dialogue is somewhat different. That early verbal freshness has been written out. Admittedly, Tommy Trounsem is seen in contradistinction to the country-house family who bear his upmarketed name, the Jermyn-Johnson professionals and the 'working-class' Felix. Felix has no dialect, but instead the speech quality of the middle-class he despises. His mother, Mrs Holt, is recognizably in the great tradition of George Eliot's Midland eccentrics, but her humour is more laboured. Mrs Holt is a monologuist in the tradition we have noted, and here, in interaction with Rufus Lyon, we are in the company of two eccentrics whose language is the medium of their class and their individuality. But whereas Rufus Lyon is based on observation at least in part, Mrs Holt appears to be from invention. It is in *Felix Holt*, I believe, that George Eliot's ear for remembered dialect begins to let her down:

Mrs Holt paused, appearing to think that Mr Lyon had been successfully confuted, and should show himself convinced.

"Has any one been aspersing your husband's character?" said Mr Lyon, with a slight initiative towards that relief of groaning for which he had reproved Lyddy.

"Sir, they daredn't. For though he was a man of prayer, he didn't want skill and knowledge to find things out for himself; and that was what I used to say to *my* friends when they wondered at my marrying a man from Lancashire, with no trade, nor fortune but what he'd got in his head. But my husband's tongue 'ud have been a fortune to anybody, and there was many a one said it was as good as a dose of physic to hear him talk; not but what that got him into trouble in Lancashire, but he always said, if the worst came to the worst, he could go and preach to the blacks. But he did better than that, Mr Lyon, for he married me; and this I *will* say, that for age, and conduct, and managing –"

"Mistress Holt," interrupted the minister, "these are not the things whereby we may edify one another. Let me beg of you to be as brief as you can. My time is not my own."

"Well, Mr Lyon, I've a right to speak to my own character; and I'm one of your congregation, though I'm not a church member, for I was born in the General Baptist connexion: and as for being saved without works, there's a many, I dare say, can't do without that doctrine; but I thank the Lord I never needed to put *my*self on a level with the thief on the cross. I've done *my* duty, and more, if anybody comes to that; for I've gone without my bit of meat to make broth for a sick neighbour: and if there's any of the church members say they've done the same, I'd ask them if they had the sinking at the stomach as I have; for I've ever strove to do the right thing, and more, for good-natured I always was; and I little thought, after being respected by everybody, I should come to be reproached by my own son. And my husband said, when he was a-dying – 'Mary,' he said, 'the Elixir, and the Pills, and the Cure will support you, for they've a great name in all the country round, and you'll pray for a blessing on them.' And so I have done, Mr Lyon; and to say they're not good medicines, when they've been taken for fifty miles round by high and low, and rich and poor, and nobody speaking against 'em but Dr Lukyn, it seems to me it's a flying in the face of Heaven; for if it was wrong to take the medicines, couldn't the blessed Lord have stopped it?"

Mrs Holt was not given to tears; she was much sustained by conscious unimpeach-ableness, and by an argumentative tendency which usually checks the too great activity of the lachrymal gland; nevertheless her eyes had become moist, her fingers played on her knee in an agitated manner, and she finally plucked a bit of her gown and held it with great nicety between her thumb and finger. Mr Lyon, however, by listening attentively, had begun partly to divine the source of her trouble.

"Am I wrong in gathering from what you say, Mistress Holt, that your son has objected in some way to your sale of your late husband's medicines?"

"Mr Lyon, he's masterful beyond everything, and he talks more than his father did. I've got my reason, Mr Lyon, and if anybody talks sense I can follow him; but Felix talks so wild, and contradicts his mother. And what do you think he says, after giving up his 'prenticeship, and going off to study at Glasgow, and getting through all the bit of money his father saved for his bringing-up – what has all his learning come to? He says I'd better never open my Bible, for it's as bad poison to me as the pills are to half the people as swallow 'em. You'll not speak of this again, Mr Lyon – I don't think ill enough of you to believe *that*. For I suppose a Christian can understand the word o' God without going to Glasgow, and there's texts upon texts about ointment and medicine, and there's one as might have been made for a receipt of my husband's – it's just as if it was a riddle, and Holt's Elixir was the answer."

"Your son uses rash words, Mistress Holt," said the minister, "but it is quite true that we may err in giving a too private interpretation to the Scripture. The word of God has to satisfy the larger need of His people, like the rain and the sunshine – which no man must think to be meant for his own patch of seed-ground solely. Will it not be well that I should see your son, and talk with him on these matters? He was at chapel, I observed, and I suppose I am to be his pastor."[17]

We would not know that Mrs Holt was using dialect at all, but her realism is flawed: toning down has a different effect from aural omission.

In *Middlemarch* this movement away from dialect is confirmed. Dagley rings true, but his is a passing recall: Mrs Dollop rings true, but hers is an urbanized truth. Where in the early works a degree of dialect was felt to be integral, in *Middlemarch* unregional, interactive speech is employed, a record of communication between the different social classes. George Eliot's concern with her educated characters means that an emphasis on regional speech would be out of place. Lydgate and Ladislaw are outsiders with different though distinct cosmopolitan backgrounds, Dorothea and Celia went to a Swiss finishing school, and presumably Mrs Lemon polished Rosamond's speech as part of her prospectus. Mr Brooke, Casaubon, Sir James, Mrs Cadwallader, Bulstrode as another outsider and Fred as a university man, as well as the self-consciously educated Garths, all indicate that the class range precludes the need for dialect. What is present in *Middlemarch*, however, is a very marked development of idiosyncratic language, from Casaubon's reserved even frigid utterance, the repetitions of Mr Brooke, the wit and bite of Mrs Cadwallader, or the excessive auctioneering diction of Mr Borthrop Trumbull. These are examples only; by the time she writes *Middlemarch*, the personality of dialect has been largely replaced by the personality of dialogue. What is remarkable, a measure of George Eliot's achievement, is that there is no loss of character verisimilitude. Dialect is virtually absent from Peter Featherstone's speech, but that speech is fluent with the grasping power of a man who is determined to rule right up to death:

"It is very handsome of you, sir."
"I should think it is," said Mr Featherstone, locking his box and replacing it, then taking off his spectacles deliberately, and at length, as if his inward meditations had more deeply convinced him, repeating, "I should think it *is* handsome."
"I assure you, sir, I am very grateful," said Fred, who had had time to recover his cheerful air.
"So you ought to be. You want to cut a figure in the world, and I reckon Peter Featherstone is the only one you've got to trust to." Here the old man's eyes gleamed with a curiously-mingled satisfaction in the consciousness that this smart young fellow relied upon him, and that the smart young fellow was rather a fool for doing so.
"Yes, indeed: I was not born to very splendid chances. Few men have been more cramped than I have been," said Fred, with some sense of surprise at his own virtue, considering how hardly he was dealt with. "It really seems a little too bad to have to ride a broken-winded hunter, and see men, who are not half such good judges as yourself, able to throw away any amount of money on buying bad bargains."
"Well, you can buy yourself a fine hunter now. Eighty pound is enough for that,

I reckon – and you'll have twenty pound over to get yourself out of any little scrape," said Mr Featherstone, chuckling slightly.

"You are very good, sir," said Fred, with a fine sense of contrast between the words and his feeling.

"Ay, rather a better uncle than your fine uncle Bulstrode. You won't get much out of his spekilations, I think. He's got a pretty strong string round your father's leg, by what I hear, eh?"

"My father never tells me anything about his affairs, sir."

"Well, he shows some sense there. But other people find 'em out without his telling. *He'll* never have much to leave you: he'll most like die without a will – he's the sort of man to do it – let 'em make him mayor of Middlemarch as much as they like. But you won't get much by his dying without a will, though you *are* the eldest son."

Fred thought that Mr Featherstone had never been so disagreeable before. True, he had never before given him quite so much money at once.

"Shall I destroy this letter of Mr Bulstrode's, sir?" said Fred, rising with the letter as if he would put it in the fire.[18]

This is not specifically regional, but it is specifically varied, with the cut and thrust of conversation between two speakers of different education. In the early fiction dialect both moderated and in moderation plays an important though not the only part. But whether she uses dialect or not, we are conscious throughout George Eliot's writing of her easy control of dialogue. As her art develops, so that control increases: while she explores the old geographical area, she explores new areas of dialogue by increasing her social range of character. And although the dialogue of her characters has become much more standardized, their intonations, the movements of their minds and emotions seen in their speech, are recognizably of their time and place: what they say in interaction with others is quick with psychological truth.

# Conclusion

From those parts of her inner self and those parts of her outer life, the Marian Evans who became George Eliot began to create her fictions. As she wrote on, she looked back and recreated the areas she knew well as the foreground and background to her characters' lives. Throughout her London life she remained in contact with the Brays and Sara Hennell, and with her marriage to John Cross she renewed the broken ties with her brother Isaac. For twenty-three years she wrote with the one region she knew predominant in her imagination. She informed it with that imagination and with the insights derived from her life experience and knowledge. She gave to her regional particularities the much wider currency and culture of her time. But the wisdom and humanity of her fiction are rooted in her exploration of the heart and head in the heartlands she knew so well. She is not as determinedly or deterministically a regional novelist as Hardy, but she captures the spirit of place through the spirit of a small community or a larger more urbanized one. There may appear to be a growing away in her turning first to Florence in 1861 (*Romola* was published in 1862–3) and then in her final novel to the mixed locations of "Wessex", London and various parts of Europe; yet even after she had completed *Daniel Deronda* there are those few pages of a new novel set in the Midlands, and in *Impressions of Theophrastus Such* a looking back of personal, nostalgic tone. Her famous statement about her fictional creed and practice establishes the continuity of her work:

there has been no change in the point of view from which I regard our life since I wrote my first fiction – the 'Scenes of Clerical Life'. Any apparent change of spirit must be due to something of which I am unconscious. The principles which are at the root of my effort to paint Dinah Morris are equally at the root of my effort to paint Mordecai.[1]

The words "spirit", "principles", "paint" and, above all, "root", here significantly repeated, show the consistency, the constancy of her concerns. The returning to the past is the dominant factor in her fictional achievement.

# References

## KEY

Most references below are given with author, title, and date, but the following abbreviations are used for works, editions etc. which are frequently cited:

Cabinet: *The Works of George Eliot. Cabinet Edition*, 1878–80 (William Blackwood and Sons)
Clarendon: *The Clarendon Edition of the Novels of George Eliot*, 1980–  (Clarendon Press, Oxford)
Haight: *George Eliot: A Biography*. By Gordon S. Haight, 1968 (Oxford University Press)
Letters: *The George Eliot Letters*, ed. Gordon S. Haight, 9 vols, 1954–78 (Yale University Press)
"Amos": "The Sad Fortunes of the Reverend Amos Barton"
"Gilfil": "Mr Gilfil's Love Story"

## INTRODUCTION

1. *Letters I*, 284, GE to Mr and Mrs Charles Bray, 30th May 1849.
2. Quoted in *Haight*, 272, GHL Journal 28th Jan. 1859.
3. *Letters II*, 166, GE to Mr and Mrs Charles Bray and Sara Sophia Hennell, [19th July 1854].
4. "Brother and Sister", sonnet xi, 13–14.
5. "A Minor Prophet", 192, and quoted as a motto by her husband, J. W. Cross, in his *George Eliot's Life: As related in her Letters and Journals* (1885).
6. "Brother and Sister", sonnet vi, 14.
7. *Letters II*, 407, GE Journal 6th Dec. 1857.
8. *Haight*, 212.
9. *Letters III*, 83, John Gwyther to the Editor of *Blackwood's*, 13th June 1859.
10. "Amos", ch i.
11. *Haight*, 212.
12. *Local Habitations: Regionalism in the Early Novels of George Eliot* (1970), 103.
13. *Letters IX*, 39, GE to Walter W. Skeat, [1872?].
14. *Letters III*, 371, GE to John Blackwood, 12th Jan. 1861.
15. *Letters IX*, 39, GE to Walter W. Skeat, [1872?].
16. William Wordsworth, "Michael", 146–8.
17. John Prest, *The Industrial Revolution in Coventry* (1960), 144.
18. *Felix Holt*, Introduction, 5–7 (Clarendon).
19. Michael Drayton, *Polyolbion, The Thirteenth Song*, 1–2, 8–12. As Fred C. Thomson points out, Drayton wrote "That shire", "country then", "vertue", "thou breathd'st".

20. Frederick Napier Broome in *The Times*, 7th March 1873.
21. *Letters V*, 441, GE to John Blackwood, 19th Sept. 1873.
22. *Coventry Herald*, 16th March 1849.
23. *Middlemarch*, I, iv, 39 (Clarendon).
24. *Letters I*, 165, GE to Mrs Charles Bray, 20th Nov. 1843.
25. *Impressions of Theophrastus Such*, "Looking Inward", 6 (Cabinet).
26. Ibid., "Looking Backward", 24 (Cabinet).
27. Ibid., 42–3 (Cabinet).
28. *Letters II*, 97, GE to Mrs Charles Bray [16th Apr. 1853].
29. *Letters III*, 196, GHL to his sons, 10th Nov. 1859.
30. *Local Habitations*, viii.
31. *Letters III*, 90, fn. 4.
32. *Letters IV*, 201, GE to Sara Sophia Hennell, 14th Sept. 1865.
33. *Letters III*, 128–9, GE to Mme Eugène Bodichon, 11th Aug. 1859.

## 1. FACTS AND FICTIONS: LIFE AND SELF

1. George Eliot, "Self and Life", 1–24.
2. Edward Dowden, *Contemporary Review*, Aug. 1872.
3. *The Mill on the Floss*, Book VI, ch iv, 345 (Clarendon).
4. See Cynthia Secor, *The Poems of George Eliot: A Critical Edition with Introduction and Notes* (University Microfilms, 1969), 223–4.
5. *Letters V*, 60, GE Journal 19th Oct. 1869.
6. *Letters II*, 346, Vincent Holbeche to GE 9th June 1857.
7. "Brother and Sister", sonnet i.
8. Secor, p. 61.
9. "Brother and Sister", sonnet ix.
10. *The Mill on the Floss*, Book I, ch v, 31–2 (Clarendon).
11. "Brother and Sister", sonnet viii, 1–10.
12. *The Mill on the Floss*, Book I, ch v, 35–6 (Clarendon).
13. S. Parkinson, *Scenes from the George Eliot Country* (1888), 14.
14. *Letters II*, 331–2, GE to Isaac Pearson Evans, 26th May 1857.
15. Ibid., 332.
16. *Letters II*, 346, Vincent Holbeche to GE 9th June 1857.
17. *Letters II*, 349, GE to Vincent Holbeche, 13th June 1857.
18. *The Mill on the Floss*, Book VII, ch i, 426–7 (Clarendon).
19. *Letters II*, 213–14, GE to Mrs Charles Bray, 4th Sept. [1855].
20. *The Mill on the Floss*, Book VI, ch xiv, 412–13 (Clarendon).
21. Ibid., Book VII, ch v, 458–9 (Clarendon).
22. *Letters VII*, 280, Isaac Pearson Evans to GE 17th May 1880.
23. *Letters VII*, 287, GE to Isaac Pearson Evans, 26th May 1880.
24. *Silas Marner*, ch xviii, 244–6 (Cabinet).
25. *Felix Holt*, Book III, ch xlix, 389–91 (Clarendon).
26. Ibid., Book III, ch l, 392–3.
27. See, for example, *Letters VII*, 273–5, 296–9, 336–7.
28. *Middlemarch*, Book VIII, ch lxxiv, 739–41 (Clarendon).

29. Ibid., Book VIII, ch. lxxiv, 731–2.
30. Ibid., Book VIII, ch lxxxi, 784–7.
31. Ibid., Finale, 821.
32. Ibid., Finale, 822.
33. Ibid., Finale, 818.

## 2. FACTS AND FICTIONS: FAMILY AND OTHERS

1. *Letters III*, 158, GHL to Charles Holte Bracebridge, 19th Sept. 1859.
2. *Letters III*, 155, GE to Charles Bray, [19th Sept. 1859].
3. *Letters III*, 168, GE to Charles Bray, 30th Sept. [1859].
4. *Adam Bede*, ch xix, 316–17 (Cabinet).
5. *Middlemarch*, Book VI, ch lvi, 544–5 (Clarendon).
6. *Haight*, 2–3.
7. *The Mill on the Floss*, Book I, ch vii, 62–4 (Clarendon).
8. *Letters III*, 159, GHL to Charles Holte Bracebridge, 19th Sept. 1859.
9. Quoted by William Mottram, *The True Story of George Eliot* (1905), p. 240.
10. *Letters III*, 99, GE to Mr and Mrs Charles Bray and Sara Hennell, 27th June 1859.
11. *Letters II*, 502–3, GE Journal 30th Nov. 1858.
12. *Adam Bede*, Book I, ch ii, 29–31 (Cabinet).
13. *Letters II*, 503, GE Journal 30th Nov. 1858.
14. "Amos", ch ii, 22–3 (Clarendon).
15. *Letters III*, 86, GE to John Gwyther, 15th June 1859.
16. Lady Newdigate-Newdegate, *The Cheverels of Cheverel Manor* (1898), 131.
17. "Gilfil", ch iv, 111 (Clarendon).
18. Ibid., ch xx, 183 (Clarendon).
19. *Letters II*, 347, GE to John Blackwood, 11th June 1857.
20. *Letters II*, 375, GE to John Blackwood, 18th Aug. 1857.
21. "Janet's Repentance", ch i, 191 (Clarendon).
22. Ibid., v, 224–5 (Clarendon).
23. Kathleen Adams, *George Eliot Country* (1988), 27.
24. "Janet's Repentance", ch ix, 248–51 (Clarendon).
25. *Letters II*, 347, GE to John Blackwood, 11th June 1857.
26. *Letters I*, 165, GE to Mrs Charles Bray, 20th Nov. [1843].
27. *Haight*, 3.
28. *Adam Bede*, Book I, ch vii, 122–3 (Cabinet).
29. Ibid., Book IV, ch xxxv, 113–14 (Cabinet).
30. Ibid., Book IV, ch xxxii, 85–87 (Cabinet).
31. *Letters IV*, 97, GE to R. H. Hutton, 8th Aug. 1863.
32. *Adam Bede*, Book II, ch xxi, 360 (Cabinet).
33. *The Mill on the Floss*, Book III, ch iv, 194–5 (Clarendon).
34. *Silas Marner*, ch xiv, 186–7 (Cabinet).
35. *The Mill on the Floss*, Book V, ch iii, 284 (Clarendon).

## 3. A SENSE OF PLACE

1. "Amos", ch i, 7–8 (Clarendon).
2. "Gilfil", ch ii, 87–9 (Clarendon).
3. *The Mill on the Floss*, Book VI, ch ix, 377–8 (Clarendon).
4. Ibid., Appendix A, 464–5 (Clarendon).
5. Ibid., Book I, ch xii, 101–3 (Clarendon).
6. *Letters VI*, 45–6, GE to Mrs William Griffiths, 9th May 1874.
7. *The Mill on the Floss*, Book I, ch iv, 24–5 (Clarendon).
8. Ibid., Book I, ch v, 35 (Clarendon).
9. Ibid., Book V, ch i, 262–3 (Clarendon).
10. "Brother and Sister", sonnet iv.
11. "Janet's Repentance", ch ii, 196–7 (Clarendon).
12. *Silas Marner*, ch i, 6–7, and ch ii, 21–2 (Cabinet).
13. Ibid., ch iii, 34, 36 (Cabinet).
14. *Felix Holt*, Book I, ch viii, 96–7 (Clarendon).
15. *Middlemarch*, Book IV, ch xxxvii, 348–9 (Clarendon).
16. Ibid., Book I, ch vi, 52–3.
17. Ibid., Book I, ch x, 86–7.
18. Ibid., Book I, ch x, 88.
19. Ibid., Book I, ch xi, 94.
20. Ibid., Book I, ch xi, 95.
21. Ibid., Book I, ch xi, 99.
22. Ibid., Book I, ch xii, 103.
23. Ibid., Book I, ch xii, 114.
24. Ibid., Book II, ch xiii, 124.
25. Ibid., Book II, ch xv, 139.
26. Ibid., Book II, ch xv, 144, 146.
27. Ibid., Book II, ch xv, 146.
28. Ibid., Book II, ch xv, 152.
29. Ibid., Book II, ch xvi, 152.
30. Ibid., Book I, ch xi, 93–4.
31. Ibid., Book I, ch xi, 93.
32. Ibid., Book I, ch xi, 94.
33. Ibid., Book I, ch xii, 101–2.
34. "Brother Jacob", afterword by Beryl Gray (1989), 18–21.
35. *Felix Holt*, Book I, ch iii, 40–44 (Clarendon).
36. "Janet's Repentance", ch xv, 278–9 (Clarendon).
37. *Adam Bede*, Book V, ch xliii, 215 (Cabinet).
38. *The True Story of George Eliot*, 39.
39. *Felix Holt*, Book III, ch xlvi, 366 (Clarendon).
40. *Adam Bede*, Book V, ch xlv, 239–40 (Cabinet).
41. *Felix Holt*, Book III, ch xlv, 362 (Clarendon).
42. *Haight*, 381–2.
43. *Felix Holt*, Book II, ch xxxiii, 268–71 (Clarendon).
44. *Adam Bede*, Book I, ch xii, 192 (Cabinet).
45. Ibid., Book I, ch xii, 192–3 (Cabinet).

46. Ibid., Book I, ch xiii, 204–5 (Cabinet).
47. "Gilfil", ch ii, 97–8 (Clarendon).
48. Ibid., ch ii, 99 (Clarendon).

## 4. RELIGION AND CLERICS

1. *Felix Holt*, Book I, ch iii, 44 (Clarendon).
2. Ibid., Book II, ch xix, 173 (Clarendon).
3. *Letters I*, 12–13, GE to Maria Lewis, 6–8th Nov. 1838.
4. See *Letters I*, 120–1, GE to Maria Lewis, 13th Nov. 1841, fn. 9.
5. See *Letters I*, 66, GE to Maria Lewis, 17th Sept. 1840.
6. *Letters I*, 27–8, GE to Maria Lewis, 17th July 1839.
7. *Letters I*, 58–9, GE to Maria Lewis, 20th July 1840.
8. Ibid., fn. 8.
9. *Letters II*, 273, GHL to John Blackwood, 15th Nov. 1856.
10. *Letters II*, 275, John Blackwood to GHL, 18th Nov.1856.
11. *Letters II*, 277, GHL to John Blackwood, 22nd Nov. 1856.
12. "Amos", ch vi, 52–5 (Clarendon).
13. Ibid., ch i, 9–10 (Clarendon).
14. "Gilfil", ch i, 77, 80–1 (Clarendon).
15. "Janet's Repentance", ch viii, 244, 245–6 (Clarendon).
16. *Letters I*, 171, Sara Sophia Hennell to Mrs Charles Christian Hennell, Jan. 1844.
17. *Letters I*, 206, Mrs Charles Bray to Sara Sophia Hennell, 14th Feb. 1846.
18. *Adam Bede*, Book I, ch iii, 52–3 (Cabinet).
19. Ibid., ch v, 97–9 (Cabinet).
20. *The Mill on the Floss*, Book II, ch i, 118–19 (Clarendon).
21. Ibid., Book VII, ch ii, 436–7 (Clarendon).
22. *Letters I*, 278, GE to Sara Sophia Hennell, 9th Feb. 1849.
23. *Letters III*, 205 [GE Journal 18th Nov. 1859].
24. *The Mill on the Floss*, Book IV, ch iii, 252–3 (Clarendon).
25. *Letters III*, 382, GE to John Blackwood, 24th Feb. 1861.
26. *Silas Marner*, ch x, 126–9 (Cabinet).
27. *Felix Holt*, Book I, ch iv, 47–8 (Clarendon).
28. Ibid., Book II, ch xv, 150 (Clarendon).
29. Ibid., ch xxiii, 200–2 (Clarendon).
30. Ibid., ch xxiv, 210 (Clarendon).
31. Ibid., ch xxiv, 209 (Clarendon).
32. *Middlemarch*, Book I, ch ix, 70 (Clarendon).
33. Ibid., Book II, xviii, 174–5 (Clarendon).
34. Ibid., Book V, lii, 504–8 (Clarendon).
35. Valentine Cunningham, *Everywhere Spoken Against* (1975), 189.
36. *Impressions of Theophrastus Such*, 29, 30, 31–2 (Cabinet).

# 5. POLITICS

1. See A. T. Kitchel, *Quarry for Middlemarch* (1950), and Fred C. Thomson's Clarendon edition of *Felix Holt*, Appendix A, in which he prints selections from the "Quarry" for this novel, 400–6.
2. *Letters IV*, 248, GE to John Blackwood, 27th Apr. 1866.
3. *Felix Holt*, Introduction, xvii–xx (Clarendon).
4. Ibid., Book I, ch ii, 30–31 (Clarendon).
5. Ibid., Book II, ch xxxiii, 264–5 (Clarendon).
6. Coventry Lent Assizes, Saturday 24th Mar. 1832, 8.
7. Ibid., 9.
8. Whitley, T. W., *The Parliamentary Representation of the City of Coventry (From the Earliest Times to the Present Date* (1894), 297.
9. *Felix Holt*, Book I, ch xi, 122–3 (Clarendon).
10. *Middlemarch*, Book IV, ch xxxix, 386–8 (Clarendon).
11. Ibid., Book V, ch li, 492–7 (Clarendon).
12. Coventry Lent Assizes, 10.
13. Reprinted in Bert G. Hornback's edition of *Middlemarch* (1977), 701–2.

# 6. EDUCATION IN MANY FORMS

1. *Adam Bede*, Book II, ch xxi, 350–1 (Cabinet).
2. *The True Story of George Eliot*, 25.
3. J. W. Cross, *George Eliot's Life* . . ., Vol 1, 19 (1885).
4. *The Mill on the Floss*, Book I, ch iii, 16–17 (Clarendon).
5. Ibid., Book II, ch i, 119 (Clarendon).
6. Ibid., 121.
7. Ibid., 128–9.
8. *Haight*, 35.
9. Robert Liddell, *The Novels of George Eliot* (1977), 111.
10. *Felix Holt*, Book I, ch v, 61–2 (Clarendon).
11. *Letters* I, 51–2, GE to Maria Lewis, 2[8]th May 1840.
12. *Middlemarch*, "Finale", 820 (Clarendon).
13. Ibid., 819 (Clarendon).

# 7. CLASS AND LEISURE

1. *Silas Marner*, ch vi, 68–73 (Cabinet).
2. Ibid., ch xi, 154–8 (Cabinet).
3. *Adam Bede*, Book III, ch xxii, 380–3 (Cabinet).
4. Ibid., Book III, ch xxv, 414–17 (Cabinet).
5. Ibid., Book VI, ch liii, 344–6 (Cabinet).
6. *Felix Holt*, Book I, ch xii, 125–6 (Clarendon).
7. *Middlemarch*, Book I, ch x, 86–8 (Clarendon).

8. *The Mill on the Floss*, Book I, ch vi, 42–3 (Clarendon).
9. *Silas Marner*, ch iv, 50–3 (Cabinet).
10. *The Mill on the Floss*, Book V, ch i, 268–9 (Clarendon).
11. *Letters I*, 62, GE to Maria Lewis, 12th Aug. 1840 and I, 23, to Maria Lewis, 16th Mar. 1839.
12. *Haight*, 7.
13. *Middlemarch*, Book VII, ch lvii, 556 (Clarendon).
14. *Letters I*, 247, GE to John Sibree Jnr, 11th Feb. 1848.
15. *The Mill on the Floss*, Book VI, ch vii, 366–7 (Clarendon).

## 8. WORKING LIFE

1. *Letters I*, 77, GE to Maria Lewis, 27th Jan. [1841].
2. "Amos", ch ii, 25–7 (Clarendon).
3. *Haight*, 1–2.
4. *Adam Bede*, Book I, ch iv, 68–9 (Cabinet).
5. Ibid., Book VI, ch liii, 346–8 (Cabinet).
6. Ibid., Book I, ch vi, 104–8 (Cabinet).
7. Ibid., Book I, ch vii, 120–1, 123 (Cabinet).
8. *The Mill on the Floss*, Book III, ch i, 171–3 (Clarendon).
9. Ibid., Book III, ch v, 201–3 (Clarendon).
10. Ibid., Book V, ch ii, 282–5 (Clarendon).
11. *Silas Marner*, ch i, 3–5 (Cabinet).
12. Ibid., ch v, 64–5 (Cabinet).
13. *Middlemarch*, Book III, ch xxxiii, 309–11 (Clarendon).
14. Ibid., Book III, ch xxiv, 239–41 (Clarendon).
15. Ibid., Book IV, ch xl, 390–2 (Clarendon).
16. Ibid., Book I, ch x, 89–91 (Clarendon).
17. Ibid., Book V, ch xlv, 444–7 (Clarendon).
18. *Felix Holt*, Book I, ch iv, 56–7 (Clarendon).

## 9. NATURE AND NURTURE

1. Blanche Colton Williams, *George Eliot: A Biography* (1936), 290.
2. *George Eliot: Centenary Essays and an unpublished fragment*, ed. Anne Smith (1980), 10–11.
3. *Essays of George Eliot* (1963), ed. Thomas Pinney, 268–9.
4. *Letters I*, 85–6. GE to Martha Jackson, Mar. 1841.
5. *Letters I*, 111. GE to Maria Lewis, 1st Oct. 1841.
6. "Gilfil", ch iv, 110 (Clarendon).
7. Ibid., ch v, 115–16 (Clarendon).
8. *Adam Bede*, Book I, ch iv, 70–1 (Cabinet).
9. *Letters III*, 60. GE to John Blackwood, 29th Apr. 1859.
10. *The Mill on the Floss*, Book V, ch i, 263 (Clarendon).
11. Ibid., Book VII, ch iv, 459 (Clarendon).
12. *Silas Marner*, ch xiv, 192–4 (Cabinet).

13. Ibid., 196–7 (Cabinet).
14. Ibid., 200–1 (Cabinet).
15. Ibid., Conclusion 270 (Cabinet).
16. *Felix Holt*, Book I, ch i, 13–14 (Clarendon).
17. Ibid., Book I, ch iii, 40 (Clarendon).
18. Ibid., Book III, ch xliii, 342–3 (Clarendon).
19. *Middlemarch*, Book I, ch vi, 51–2 (Clarendon).
20. Ibid., Book I, ch ix, 71–2 (Clarendon).
21. Ibid., Book I, ch iii, 26–7 (Clarendon).
22. Ibid., Book V, ch liii, 511–12 (Clarendon).
23. Ibid., Book VIII, ch lxxx, 776–7 (Clarendon).
24. Ibid., Book VIII, ch lxxxiii, 798–800 (Clarendon).

# 10. THE SPOKEN WORD

1. *Letters III*, 427, John Blackwood to Mrs John Blackwood 15th [June] 1861.
2. "Amos", ch i, 14 (Clarendon).
3. Ibid., ch i, 15–16 (Clarendon).
4. Ibid., ch vii, 59 (Clarendon).
5. "Gilfil", ch xvi, 162 (Clarendon).
6. "Gilfil", ch xix, 173 (Clarendon).
7. "Janet's Repentance", ch viii, 246–7 (Clarendon).
8. *Adam Bede*, Book I, ch i, 12–13 (Cabinet).
9. Ibid., Book I, ch iv, 56–7 (Cabinet).
10. Ibid., Book I, ch xi, 177 (Cabinet).
11. Ibid., Book I, ch xv, 232–3 (Cabinet).
12. Ibid., Book II, ch xviii, 284–5 (Cabinet).
13. Ibid., Book V, ch xl, 190–1 (Cabinet).
14. *The Mill on the Floss*, Book I, ch ii, 8–9 (Clarendon).
15. Ibid., Book III, ch vi, 209–11 (Clarendon).
16. *Silas Marner*, ch vi, 76–7 (Cabinet).
17. *Felix Holt*, Book I, ch iv, 50–1 (Clarendon).
18. *Middlemarch*, Book II, ch xiv, 132–3 (Clarendon).

# CONCLUSION

1. *Letters VI*, 318, GE to Elizabeth Stuart Phelps, 16th Dec. 1876.

# Select Bibliography

## WORKS BY GEORGE ELIOT:

*Scenes of Clerical Life* (Blackwood's Magazine, Jan.–Nov. 1857)
*Adam Bede*, 3 vols (William Blackwood and Sons, 1859)
*The Mill on the Floss*, 3 vols (William Blackwood and Sons, 1860)
*Silas Marner: The Weaver of Raveloe* (William Blackwood and Sons, 1861)
"Brother Jacob" (*Cornhill Magazine*, July 1864)
*Felix Holt: The Radical*, 3 vols (William Blackwood and Sons, 1866)
*Middlemarch: A Study of Provincial Life* (William Blackwood and Sons, Dec. 1871–Dec. 1872)
   [issued in eight parts]
*The Legend of Jubal and Other Poems* (William Blackwood and Sons, 1874)
*Daniel Deronda* (William Blackwood and Sons, Feb.–Sept. 1876) [issued in eight parts]
*Impressions of Theophrastus Such* (William Blackwood and Sons, 1879)


*Essays and Leaves from a Notebook* (William Blackwood and Sons, 1884)
*The Essays of George Eliot*, ed. T. Pinney (Routledge and Kegan Paul, 1963)
*George Eliot: Selected Essays, Poems and Other Writings*, ed. A. S. Byatt and Nicholas Warren (Penguin, 1990)
*Annotated Editions of the Novels and 'Scenes of Clerical Life'* (The Penguin English Library, 1965–80)
*The Clarendon Edition of the Novels of George Eliot* (Oxford, 1980–   )


## BIOGRAPHIES, CRITICAL STUDIES, ARTICLES

Adams, Kathleen, *Those of Us Who Loved Her* (George Eliot Fellowship, 1980)
Ashton, Rosemary, *George Eliot* (Oxford University Press, 1983)
Auster, Henry, *Local Habitations: Regionalism in the Early Novels of George Eliot* (Harvard University Press, 1970)
Beaty, Jerome, "History by Indirection: The Era of Reform in *Middlemarch*", *Victorian Studies* I (1958), 173–9.
——'*Middlemarch' From Notebook to Novel: A Study of George Eliot's Creative Method* (University of Illinois Press, 1960)
Beer, Gillian, *George Eliot* (Harvester Press, 1986)
Bennett, Joan, *George Eliot: Her Mind and Her Art* (Cambridge University Press, 1948)
Blind, Mathilde, *George Eliot* (W. H. Allen, 1883)

Carroll, David (ed.), *George Eliot: The Critical Heritage* (Routledge & Kegan Paul, 1971)

Cross, J. W., *George Eliot's Life as Related in her Letters and Journals*, 3 vols (William Blackwood & Sons, 1885)

Cunningham, Valentine, *Everywhere Spoken Against: Dissent in the Victorian Novel* (Clarendon Press, 1975)

Deakin, Mary, *The Early Life of George Eliot* (Manchester University Press, 1913)

Haight, Gordon, S. (ed.), *The George Eliot Letters*, 9 vols (Yale University Press, 1954–78)

—— (ed.), *A Century of George Eliot Criticism* (Methuen, 1966)

—— *George Eliot: A Biography* (Oxford University Press, 1968)

Hanson, L. & E., *Marian Evans and George Eliot* (Oxford University Press, 1952)

Haldane, Elizabeth, *George Eliot and her Times: A Victorian Study* (Hodder & Stoughton, 1927)

Hardy, Barbara, *The Novels of George Eliot: A Study in Form* (Athlone Press, 1959)

—— (ed.), *Middlemarch: Critical Approaches to the Novel* (Athlone Press, 1967)

Harvey, W. J., *The Art of George Eliot* (Chatto & Windus, 1961)

Holmstrom, J. and Lerner, L. (eds), *George Eliot and her Readers: A Selection of Contemporary Reviews* (The Bodley Head, 1966)

Knoepflmacher, U. C., *George Eliot's Early Novels: The Limits of Realism* (University of California Press, 1968)

Laski, Marghanita, *George Eliot and Her World* (Thames & Hudson, 1973)

Leavis, F. R., *The Great Tradition* (Chatto & Windus, 1948)

Mottram, William, *The True Story of George Eliot in Relation to 'Adam Bede' Giving the Real Life History of the More Prominent Characters* (Francis Griffiths, 1905)

Noble, Thomas A., *George Eliot's 'Scenes of Clerical Life'* (Yale University Press, 1965)

Pinney, Thomas, "The Authority of the Past in George Eliot's Novels", *Nineteenth-Century Fiction* 21 (1966), 131–47.

Redinger, Ruby, *George Eliot: The Emergent Self* (The Bodley Head, 1975)

Smith, Anne (ed.), *George Eliot: Centenary Essays and an Unpublished Fragment* (Vision Press, 1980)

Stephen, Sir Leslie, *George Eliot* (Macmillan, 1902)

Stump, Reva, *Movement and Vision in George Eliot's Novels* (University of Washington Press, 1959)

Uglow, Jennifer, *George Eliot* (Virago, 1987)

Williams, Blanche Colton, *George Eliot: A Biography* (Macmillan, 1936)

Woolf, Virginia, "George Eliot", in *The Common Reader* (Hogarth Press, 1932), 166–76

# Index

Since there is a full list of references on pp. 239–46, this index has been kept short and simple. Concentration is on George Eliot's works, with main character and place references, together with a selective general index. There are no specific entries under Marian Evans/George Eliot; she is present on every page of the book.

# INDEX

*Also available from Allison & Busby*

# HARDY'S PEOPLE: FIGURES IN A WESSEX LANDSCAPE

by Joanna Cullen Brown

In this fascinating book, illustrated with contemporary photographs, Joanna Cullen Brown has collected and linked passages from Thomas Hardy's extensive writings to provide a full but accessible picture of life in the British countryside in the late Georgian and Victorian era. These extracts are arranged according to theme: there are sections on folklore, medicine and disease, music, dialect, the law, power and poverty, farming, poaching and rural skills, religion and education, entertainments, eating and drinking and love. The result is a brilliantly written and lovingly assembled picture of Dorset life – the country year, the people and their activities and attitudes – in 'the true voice of humane feeling' (*Times Literary Supplement*).

ISBN 0 7490 0079 1     paperback     £11.95

# A JOURNEY INTO THOMAS HARDY'S POETRY

by Joanna Cullen Brown

This journey of exploration into Hardy's poetry has all the delights of discovery. Though Hardy's feelings were deep and intense, he was a private and complex man who prized understatement and reticence. Reading beneath the surface of his poems reveals not only his honesty, as he constantly explored and faced up to reality, but also his compassion for the disadvantaged, his joy in living and in beauty, his wit, irony and sense of the absurd – and a surprisingly modern approach to life that confronts many of the dilemmas of twentieth-century men and women.

Setting the theme for each poem discussed, Joanna Cullen Brown quotes the text in full as she unravels its meanings and connections. This is a journey that leads to a growing sense of excitement and involement: we are caught by what we find as Hardy's world – and our own – unfolds. This book will open windows for everyone who reads it.

Joanna Cullen Brown's 'careful analyses are particularly recommended to those coming to [Hardy's] verse for the first time, but are also rich in insights and allusions valuable to those coming back to it on a basis of long acquaintance' (Martin Fagg, in the *Times Educational Supplement*).

ISBN 0 85031 865 3     paperback     £6.99

# LET ME ENJOY THE EARTH: THOMAS HARDY AND NATURE

by Joanna Cullen Brown

Photographs by Simon McBride

Thomas Hardy wrote of what he knew, the rural and market-town life of the West Country, peopling a small shire with the full spectrum of humanity, and through imagination creating an entire world. In this full, detailed and beautifully illustrated survey of the Nature of that world, Joanna Cullen Brown begins in the places them-selves: the heaths and hills and valleys of Hardy's childhood, the views and landscapes that are named in the poetry and only thinly disguised in the novels. She then turns to his writing on all the specific features of Nature – the seasons, animals, insects, birds – following up with an examination of how Hardy's language is infused with the imagery of Nature, more so, perhaps, than that of any great writer before him. She has chosen many of the finest passages from the greatest of Hardy's works to illustrate the relationship between individuals and the vast landscape, its aspect sometimes reflecting, sometimes enhancing their inner lives, its dread power and beauty affirming their joy but indifferent to their misery.

Finally, she analyses Hardy's philosophy, his 'seemings', his belief in a cruel and random Nature, and beyond it the inexplicable 'First Cause'. We learn of an old man's final, stoic conclusions, but see their origins in a young country-man watching land and heavens, water and weather, with a novelist's eye and the searing sensitivity of a true poet.

Writing in *The Tablet*, Ronald Blythe said of *Let Me Enjoy the Earth* that Joanna Cullen Brown 'has the gift of showing the reader the source of things while never breaking down the wholeness of either the poetry or the novels in the process.'

ISBN 0 7490 0083 X  paperback  £9.99
ISBN 0 85031 875 0  hardback  £14.99

# TURGENEV

## by Henri Troyat

### translated from the French by Nancy Amphoux

Turgenev grew up in an environment of wealth, land and privilege, but his childhood was scarred – and his later life haunted – by the misery of the serfs, which developed in him a deep compassion, and by the violence and cruelty of his mother, from which arose his obsession with powerful, domineering women.

While still a young man, he fell under the spell of the celebrated opera singer, Pauline Viardot, 'the Incomparable', his 'beloved angel', and decided to devote his life to her, though she would neither leave her husband nor become his mistress. As this peculiar ménage travelled about Europe, Turgenev discovered an affinity for self-exile and an international vantage-point, finding that he could write most vividly about his native land when he was far from it.

Troyat paints a compelling portrait of this ambiguous genius, this perpetual wanderer caught between an outgoing and a conservative nature, throughout his life adoring the unattainable, and, like many a great son of Russia, loving the Motherland but ever fascinated and drawn by the life and art of the West.

In her *Spectator* review, Tessa Waugh commented that 'So full of sympathy and understanding is Troyat's portrait of Turgenev that the reader is immediately tempted to rush back to the novels of the man himself who was a misfit in every aspect of his life.'

ISBN 0 7490 0076 7      paperback      £6.99

# GORKY

by Henri Troyat

translated from the French by Lowell Bair

Maxim Gorky, the author of *Mother* and *The Lower Depths*, whose novels, plays and memoirs depict working-class life in both the old and new Russia, was born in 1868. He was a friend and colleague of the great Russian writers of this century, including Tolstoy, and, politically sensitive to events around him, he witnessed the extraordinary and sudden transition from the tsarist to the communist regimes. His harsh life, first in Russia, then in exile and finally in the newly formed Soviet Union, where he became the first president of the Soviet Writers' Union, until his mysterious death in 1936, is portrayed in a dramatic and powerful manner.

It was a turbulent and dangerous era when, as under Stalin, writers disappeared, were eliminated, or, as in Gorky's case, were manipulated by the government; an era which Troyat evokes with frightening clarity. In its review of the French edition, *Le Monde* wrote that 'Troyat depicts a man whose path was haunted by injustice and despotism', while *L'Express* commented that 'Like an elegant lawyer, Henri Troyat requests the reader's indulgence for his client in a biographical novel filled with moving and harsh pages.' Ann Pasternak Slater writing in the *Sunday Telegraph* commented that 'the biography is gripping, the enigma of its subject haunting' and *The Tribune* reviewer stated that 'Henri Troyat is a real master of the art of biography and a full picture of Maxim Gorky's life emerges.'

ISBN 0 85031 926 9       hardback       £16.99